INTO THE QUAGMIRE

INTO THE QUAGMIRE

Lyndon Johnson and the Escalation of the Vietnam War

Brian VanDeMark

New York   Oxford
OXFORD UNIVERSITY PRESS
1991

Oxford University Press

Oxford   New York   Toronto
Delhi   Bombay   Calcutta   Madras   Karachi
Petaling Jaya   Singapore   Hong Kong   Tokyo
Nairobi   Dar es Salaam   Cape Town
Melbourne   Auckland

and associated companies in
Berlin   Ibadan

Published by Oxford University Press, Inc.,
200 Madison Avenue, New York, New York 10016

Oxford is a registered trademark of Oxford University Press

Library of Congress Cataloging-in-Publication Data
VanDeMark, Brian
Into the quagmire : Lyndon Johnson and the escalation
of the Vietnam War / Brian VanDeMark.
p.   cm.   Includes bibliographical references.
ISBN 0–19–506506–9
1. Vietnamese Conflict, 1961–1975—United States
2. United States—Politics and government—1963–1969.
3. Johnson, Lyndon B. (Lyndon Baines), 1908–1973.
I. Title.   DS558.V36   1991
959.704′3373—dc20   90–6829

2 4 6 8 10 9 7 5 3 1

Printed in the United States of America
on acid-free paper

To my parents and Dian

Preface

SOME YEARS AFTER leaving the presidency, Lyndon Johnson reflected
on the Vietnam War's significance to both his historical reputation and the
American experience. "The struggle in Vietnam," LBJ rightly observed in his
memoirs, "inspired one of the most passionate and deeply felt debates in
our nation's life." "That debate will go on," he correctly added, for as
Johnson himself realized, succeeding generations of historians "will make
[their] judgments on the decisions made and the actions taken."[1]

LBJ had voiced similar thoughts as President. As early as 1965, Johnson
sensed that the Vietnam War would determine his ultimate place in history,
overshadowing all else, including his extraordinary domestic reform program, the Great Society. LBJ, one associate vividly remembered, talked
"about this all the time."[2]

How, then, should historians interpret this epochal event of Johnson's
presidency and 1960s American life? Vietnam's very importance demands a
thorough, critical, but sensitive understanding of the people and forces
which together shaped the struggle. The privilege of hindsight, if not humil-
ity, calls for nothing less. For, as Carl von Clausewitz, the pre-eminent
student of war, once wrote, "we see . . . things in the light of their result,
and to some extent come to know and appreciate them fully only because
of it."[3]

I have tried to heed this advice in analyzing LBJ's Vietnam decisions from
November 1964 through July 1965—the pivotal months when Johnson
launched the bombing of North Vietnam and dispatched major U.S. ground
combat forces to South Vietnam, thus fixing America on a course of massive
military intervention in the region. I have sought to reconstruct those events

in their widest possible light, stressing the tangle of international and domestic pressures confronting LBJ and his advisers during this watershed period.

I feel this approach best recaptures the contemporary context in which decisionmakers acted, while also illuminating the immense complexities and tensions surrounding the war. I believe these insights, in turn, offer readers a clearer, deeper understanding of LBJ's—and America's—Vietnam ordeal.

I make no claim, though, to exhausting study of this important subject—only broadening and, hopefully, enriching perceptions of it. Such goals, however modest, remain the historian's proper task. Richard Hofstadter, a wise and gifted practitioner of this craft, put it best, I think: "The closer the historian comes . . . to the full texture of historical reality, the more deeply is he engulfed in a complex web of relationships which he can hope to understand only in a limited and partial way."[4]

With that thought in mind, I hope the following account casts added light on Lyndon Johnson and the escalation of the Vietnam War, while moving the reader to reflect further on this fateful chapter in modern American history.

Although writing is a solitary labor, all historians rely on others for help along the way. I am no exception. I have several people to thank for advice and assistance in preparing this book.

First is the archival staff at the Lyndon Baines Johnson Library in Austin, Texas—particularly its chief Vietnam curator, Dr. David C. Humphrey. LBJ Library archivists extended a rare blend of skillful help and warm courtesy during my many visits to Austin. Thanks also are due to the library's LBJ Foundation, for a Moody grant-in-aid to defray travel and research expenses.

This book began as a dissertation in history at the University of California, Los Angeles. Throughout much of the project, UCLA's Department of History provided a stimulating and collegial environment in which to teach and write. It also bestowed generous and welcome fellowship support. UCLA's University Research Library furnished a rich storehouse of books and, at times, a quiet haven for reflection.

Two fine historians deserve particular thanks for their guidance and support over many years. Professor Robert A. Divine of the University of Texas at Austin first stimulated my interest in diplomatic history, and inspired me to do my best. My doctoral mentor, Professor Robert Dallek of UCLA, proved a model scholar and teacher, from whom I learned much indeed. His example and encouragement, quite simply, made this a better book.

I have also benefited from the rare privilege of assisting Mr. Clark M. Clifford in preparing his memoirs. Working with Mr. Clifford and his distinguished coauthor, Richard C. Holbrooke, deepened my appreciation for

both the complexities and the burdens of governance. Mr. Clifford, moreover, graciously allowed me to quote from his forthcoming autobiography.
I have, however, neither sought nor received Mr. Clifford's endorsement of
the views expressed in this book.

A word of thanks must also go to my publisher, Sheldon Meyer, editors
David Bain and Stephanie Sakson-Ford, and all the other talented and
friendly people at Oxford University Press, who helped make the manuscript a book.

Finally, I wish to acknowledge a very special and heavy debt to my wife,
Dian Owen VanDeMark. Her encouragement, understanding, and, above
all, her extraordinary forbearance sustained me from beginning to end.

Washington, D.C.   B. V.
January 1990

Contents

Introduction

VIETNAM DIVIDED AMERICA more deeply and painfully than any event since the Civil War. It split political leaders and ordinary people alike in profound and lasting ways. Whatever the conflicting judgments about this controversial war—and there are many—Vietnam undeniably stands as the greatest tragedy of twentieth-century U.S. foreign relations.

America's involvement in Vietnam has, as a result, attracted much critical scrutiny, frequently addressed to the question, "Who was guilty?"—"Who led the United States into this tragedy?" A more enlightening question, it seems, is "How and why did this tragedy occur?" The study of Vietnam should be a search for explanation and understanding, rather than for scapegoats.

Focusing on one important period in this long and complicated story—the brief but critical months from November 1964 to July 1965, when America crossed the threshold from limited to large-scale war in Vietnam—helps to answer that question. For the crucial decisions of this period resulted from the interplay of longstanding ideological attitudes, diplomatic assumptions, and political pressures with decisive contemporaneous events in America and Vietnam.

Victory in World War II produced a sea change in America's perception of its role in world affairs. Political leaders of both parties embraced a sweepingly new vision of the United States as the defender against the perceived threat of monolithic communist expansion everywhere in the world. This vision of American power and purpose, shaped at the start of the Cold War, grew increasingly rigid over the years. By 1964–1965, it had become an ironbound and unshakable dogma, a received faith which policymakers unquestioningly accepted—even though the circumstances which had fostered its creation had changed dramatically amid diffused authority and power among communist states and nationalist upheaval in the colonial world.

Policymakers' blind devotion to this static Cold War vision led America into misfortune in Vietnam. Lacking the critical perspective and sensibility to reappraise basic tenets of U.S. foreign policy in the light of changed events and local circumstances, policymakers failed to perceive Vietnamese realities accurately and thus to gauge American interests in the area prudently. Policymakers, as a consequence, misread an indigenous, communist-led nationalist movement as part of a larger, centrally directed challenge to world order and stability; tied American fortunes to a non-communist regime of slim popular legitimacy and effectiveness; and intervened militarily in the region far out of proportion to U.S. security requirements.

An arrogant and stubborn faith in America's power to shape the course of foreign events compounded the dangers sown by ideological rigidity. Policymakers in 1964–1965 shared a common postwar conviction that the United States not only should, but could, control political conditions in South Vietnam, as elsewhere throughout much of the world. This conviction had led Washington to intervene progressively deeper in South Vietnamese affairs over the years. And when—despite Washington's increasing exertions—Saigon's political situation declined precipitously during 1964–1965, this conviction prompted policymakers to escalate the war against Hanoi, in the belief that America could stimulate political order in South Vietnam through the application of military force against North Vietnam.

Domestic political pressures exerted an equally powerful, if less obvious, influence over the course of U.S. involvement in Vietnam. The fall of China in 1949 and the ugly McCarthyism it aroused embittered American foreign policy for a generation. By crippling President Truman's political fortunes, it taught his Democratic successors, John Kennedy and Lyndon Johnson, a strong and sobering lesson: that another "loss" to communism in East Asia risked renewed and devastating attacks from the right. This fear of reawakened McCarthyism remained a paramount concern as policymakers pondered what course to follow as conditions in South Vietnam deteriorated rapidly in 1964–1965.

Enduring traditions of ideological rigidity, diplomatic arrogance, and political vulnerability heavily influenced the way policymakers approached decisions on Vietnam in 1964–1965. Understanding the decisions of this period fully, however, also requires close attention to contemporary developments in America and South Vietnam. These years marked a tumultuous time in both countries, which affected the course of events in subtle but significant ways.

Policymakers of 1964–1965 lived in a period of extraordinary domestic political upheaval sparked by the civil rights movement. It is difficult to overstate the impact of this upheaval on American politics in the mid-1960s. During 1964–1965, the United States—particularly the American South—experienced profound and long overdue change in the economic, political, and social rights of blacks. This change, consciously embraced by the liberal administration of Lyndon Johnson, engendered sharp political hostility among conservative southern whites and their deputies in Congress—hostility which the politically astute Johnson sensed could spill over into the realm of foreign affairs, where angry civil rights opponents could exact their revenge should LBJ stumble and "lose" a crumbling South Vietnam. This danger, reinforced by the memory of McCarthyism, stirred deep political fears in Johnson, together with an abiding aversion to failure in Vietnam.

LBJ feared defeat in South Vietnam, but he craved success and glory at home. A forceful, driving President of boundless ambition, Johnson sought to harness the political momentum created by the civil rights movement to enact a far-reaching domestic reform agenda under the rubric of the Great Society. LBJ would achieve the greatness he sought by leading America toward justice and opportunity for all its citizens, through his historic legislative program.

Johnson's domestic aspirations fundamentally conflicted with his uneasy involvement in Vietnam. An experienced and perceptive politician, LBJ knew his domestic reforms required the sustained focus and cooperation of Congress. He also knew a larger war in Vietnam jeopardized these reforms by drawing away political attention and economic resources. America's increasing military intervention in 1964–1965 cast this tension between Vietnam and the Great Society into sharp relief.

Johnson saw his predicament clearly. But he failed to resolve it for fear that acknowledging the growing extent and cost of the war would thwart his domestic reforms, while pursuing a course of withdrawal risked political ruin. LBJ, instead, chose to obscure the magnitude of his dilemma by obscuring America's deepening involvement as South Vietnam began to fail. That grave compromise of candor opened the way to Johnson's eventual downfall.

Events in South Vietnam during 1964–1965 proved equally fateful. A historically weak and divided land, South Vietnam's deeply rooted ethnic, political, and religious turmoil intensified sharply in the winter of 1964–1965. This mounting turmoil, combined with increased communist military attacks, pushed Saigon to the brink of political collapse.

South Vietnam's accelerating crisis alarmed American policymakers, driving them to deepen U.S. involvement considerably in an effort to arrest Saigon's political failure. Abandoning the concept of stability in the South *before* escalation against the North, policymakers now embraced the concept of stability *through* escalation, in the desperate hope that military action against Hanoi would prompt a stubbornly elusive political order in Saigon.

This shift triggered swift and ominous consequences scarcely anticipated by its architects. Policymakers soon confronted intense military, political, and bureaucratic pressures to widen the war. Unsettled by these largely unforeseen pressures, policymakers reacted confusedly and defensively. Rational men, they struggled to control increasingly irrational forces. But their reaction only clouded their attention to basic assumptions and ultimate costs as the war rapidly spun out of control in the spring and summer of 1965. In their desperation to make Vietnam policy work amid this rising tide of war pressures, they thus failed ever to question whether it could work—or at what ultimate price. Their failure recalls the warning of a prescient political scientist, who years before had cautioned against those policymakers with "an infinite capacity for making ends of [their] means."[1]

The decisions of 1964–1965 bespeak a larger and deeper failure as well. Throughout this period—as, indeed, throughout the course of America's Vietnam involvement—U.S. policymakers strove principally to create a viable non-communist regime in South Vietnam. For many years and at great effort and cost, Washington had endeavored to achieve political stability and competence in Saigon. Despite these efforts, South Vietnam's political disarray persisted and deepened, until, in 1965, America intervened with massive military force to avert its total collapse.

Few policymakers in 1964–1965 paused to mull this telling fact, to ponder its implications about Saigon's viability as a political entity. The failure to re-examine this and other fundamental premises of U.S. policy—chief among them Vietnam's importance to American national interests and Washington's ability to forge political order through military power—proved a costly and tragic lapse of statesmanship.

INTO THE
QUAGMIRE

In front a precipice, behind a wolf.

Latin proverb

1

To the Crossroads in Vietnam

A COOL DRIZZLE shrouded Austin, Texas, the night of November 3, 1964, but that could not dampen the excitement of the crowd gathered at Municipal Auditorium along Town Lake restlessly awaiting the President's arrival. Throughout the day, commentators had been predicting a big victory for Lyndon Johnson over Barry Goldwater and early returns amply confirmed their judgment. LBJ appeared headed toward the greatest landslide in American presidential history.[1]

After voting that morning, the President had returned to his ranch outside Johnson City. In the early evening, he had helicoptered to Austin, motoring downtown to the Driskill Hotel. There, Johnson watched television returns for several hours, before attending a reception in his honor at the governor's mansion. Finally, shortly after 1:00 a.m., LBJ headed for Municipal Auditorium. Slipping in quietly, the President burst on stage to the wild cheers of his fellow Texans.

Johnson savored the moment. After more than thirty years in government, LBJ had scored the supreme political triumph. Assuming the presidency on Kennedy's assassination the year before, Johnson had now been elected in his own right. He had won a resounding mandate to pursue his own course—both at home, in his cherished vision of a "Great Society," and abroad, where Vietnam remained a critical issue.

Heretofore, LBJ had consciously continued his predecessor's Vietnam policy. This reflected Johnson's sense of institutional duty, loyalty to established commitments, and political caution in an election year. Henceforward, the options would be his to define, the direction his to choose, the consequences his to bear.

To say Vietnam had become LBJ's responsibility is not, however, to deny

3

the weight of previous decisions. In coming months, Johnson would face new and fateful choices in Vietnam, but his answers to those choices would be conditioned by the cumulative legacy of three administrations spanning nearly twenty years.

America's involvement in Vietnam derived from its international position at the end of World War II. In 1945, the wartime coalition between the Soviet Union and the United States began to weaken once its sole aim—the defeat of Nazi Germany—seemed secure. Hitler's collapse soon threw America's and Russia's political and strategic differences into sharp relief across Europe and Asia. By 1947, those differences had hardened; World War II had given way to the Cold War.

In its competition with Russia, the United States accepted new and extensive responsibilities, including leadership of a western alliance whose junior partners, Britain and France, lacked the ability to defend their accumulated global commitments. America assumed that task against perceived Soviet expansion. President Truman articulated this role in his special message to Congress of March 1947, pledging the United States "to support free peoples who are resisting attempted subjugation by armed minorities or by outside pressures." This principle—the doctrine of global containment—extended the range of American interests dramatically, linking national security to the defense of freedom throughout the world.[2]

Subsequent events reinforced this widened conception of U.S. security. In September 1949, Russia detonated its first atomic bomb; a few weeks later, China fell to Mao's communists. These shocks spawned a more threatening perception of the Cold War among American leaders, who sensed a heightened communist challenge demanding a heightened U.S. response. This new thinking emerged in a national security directive submitted to President Truman in April 1950. It became known as NSC-68. The Cold War, according to NSC-68, had entered a critical and fateful period requiring a "rapid and sustained build-up" of American political commitments and military strength.[3]

Washington soon implemented its new strategy in the complicated realm of Asia, where Cold War dynamics interacted with post-colonial nationalism. When communist North Korean forces crossed the thirty-eighth parallel on June 25, 1950, President Truman responded by sending troops to South Korea and increasing military assistance to allied governments in the region, including French Vietnam.

Since the end of World War II, France had struggled to reassert control over its former colony amid a nationalist revolt led by the communist Vietminh under Ho Chi Minh. Washington, fearful of alienating French cooperation in postwar European defense, had indirectly aided France's neocolonial effort through financial credits and military equipment beginning in the fall of 1945. Conditioned initially by strategic concerns in Europe and now by fears of monolithic communist expansion in Asia, the United States committed itself to the preservation of French rule in Indochina.

Truman's successor, Dwight Eisenhower, sustained this commitment even as France's hold over Vietnam gradually weakened. In early 1954, Vietminh forces launched their final offensive against French colonialism. By April, the Vietminh had isolated several thousand elite French troops at the outpost of Dienbienphu, threatening an end to France's presence in Vietnam.

Although rejecting U.S. intervention to rescue the beleaguered French garrison, Eisenhower reiterated his intention to contain communist influence in Indochina. Invoking the "falling domino" principle, Ike predicted dire consequences flowing from Vietminh victory in Vietnam. "[If] [y]ou have a row of dominos set up," the President explained at a news conference, and "you knock over the first one, . . . what will happen to the last one is the certainty that it will go over very quickly." This, in turn, would spark a "disintegration" having "the most profound influences" on western interests. Eisenhower thus publicly bound American security to a non-communist Vietnam.[4]

The transition from French to American involvement in Vietnam followed the 1954 Geneva Conference. That July, France and the Vietminh signed an armistice ending French colonialism in Southeast Asia and creating the separate states of Cambodia, Laos, and Vietnam. Among their major provisions, the Geneva Agreements established a temporary partition of Vietnam at the seventeenth parallel, dividing a Vietminh-controlled North from a western-aligned South; stipulated the eventual reunification of Vietnam through countrywide elections scheduled for July 1956, for which the Vietminh, in return, agreed to regroup its forces above the seventeenth parallel, thus relinquishing control over much territory south of that line; prohibited the introduction of additional troops and military supplies into either northern or southern Vietnam, as well as the establishment of foreign military bases and alliances; and formed an International Commission for Supervision and Control (ICSC) to enforce its terms. The United States, though it declined to endorse the Geneva Accords, promised to "refrain from the threat or the use of force to disturb them. . . ."[5]

Unhappy with the conference results, which had ratified Vietminh control over northern Vietnam, Eisenhower's administration resolved to preserve a non-communist southern Vietnam. The Southeast Asia Treaty Organization (SEATO) Pact, signed at Manila in September 1954, marked an important step in this direction. A protocol to the SEATO treaty pledged Washington to the defense of southern Vietnam, thus deepening America's commitment to the regime.[6]

As Eisenhower broadened U.S. support of southern Vietnam, its new leader, Ngo Dinh Diem, consolidated his control over the region throughout 1954 and 1955. Bolstered by massive infusions of American economic and military aid, Diem systematically quelled internal dissent through repression of civil liberties and detention of political and religious opponents.

Diem displayed similar imperiousness toward the Geneva Agreements, which he never acknowledged as binding. In 1956, he thwarted the proposed election leading to reunification, citing the absence of free, unfettered voting in the North. Yet Diem himself had rigged a plebiscite ousting French-installed Emperor Bao Dai the year before, with more than 99 percent of the vote.

Demographic disparities between North and South cemented Diem's aversion to countrywide balloting. In 1956, southern Vietnam's population stood at fewer than twelve million, while northern Vietnam's exceeded fifteen million. This difference represented a powerful disincentive to Diem's participation in all-Vietnam elections.

President Eisenhower readily supported Diem's decision, suspecting Ho Chi Minh's popularity as much as his devotion to fair and democratic voting. As Ike candidly remarked in his memoirs, "I . . . never talked or corresponded with a person knowledgeable in Indochinese affairs who did not agree that had elections been held as of the time of the fighting, possibly 80 per cent of the population would have voted for the Communist Ho Chi Minh as their leader. . . ." By acquiescing in this action, however, Eisenhower's administration sealed the political division of Vietnam.[7]

Through Diem, Washington hoped to build a viable, non-communist government in South Vietnam. But Diem's arbitrary rule and authoritarian manner provoked mounting domestic reaction. By 1958, popular unrest among non-communists and former Vietminh alike had given way to open rebellion against the regime. Shortly thereafter, in 1959, Ho Chi Minh manifested his own imperiousness toward the Geneva Accords by initiating support of the southern, communist-led insurgency.[8]

Hanoi's decision resulted from several factors. By 1959, Ho Chi Minh had lost hope of achieving reunification through diplomacy because of Saigon's and Washington's steadfast intransigence toward countrywide elections. At the same time, having recovered from its war with France and consolidated its internal position, North Vietnam had developed sufficient strength to pursue militarily what it had been denied politically. Finally, Diem's tightening repression had generated an enticing degree of political disaffection within South Vietnam, which Hanoi could exploit through its small, but dedicated, cadre of underground southern Vietminh.[9]

During this same period, Eisenhower increased U.S. military support to Diem. Assuming responsibility for training and equipping the South Vietnamese Army (ARVN) from the departing French, Washington bolstered its Military Assistance and Advisory Group (MAAG) forces, first sent to Vietnam in 1950 to organize and strengthen the army. From 1954 to 1959, the number of American advisers climbed along with Vietcong opposition to Diem's regime. By the close of Ike's tenure in 1961, Washington's commitment to South Vietnam had deepened considerably.

John F. Kennedy, the new President, affirmed this commitment during a period of rising Cold War tensions which compelled him, however reluctantly, to expand it significantly. Kennedy entered the White House at a crucial juncture in postwar affairs, punctuated by nationalist upheaval and intense Sino-Soviet competition. As the states of Africa and Asia emerged from European rule, China and Russia curried their favor by championing "wars of liberation" from colonial oppression. Interpreting these developments as a challenge to America's leadership, JFK responded vigorously, pledging the United States to activism in the third world.

A series of international crises during his first year intensified Kennedy's concern for maintaining a non-communist South Vietnam. In 1961, JFK challenged Castro's Cuba at the Bay of Pigs with disastrous results; engaged Khrushchev at the stormy Vienna summit; witnessed the construction of the Berlin Wall; and began sensitive negotiations on the neutralization of Laos. Seeing himself on the defensive, Kennedy determined to demonstrate his resolve by standing firm in South Vietnam.

Diem's position, meanwhile, had declined markedly by the fall of 1961. Facing heavier Vietcong attacks, he petitioned the United States for additional economic and military aid. Before answering Diem's appeal, Kennedy dispatched his personal military adviser, Maxwell Taylor, and National Security Council (NSC) staff member Walt Rostow to Saigon to assess conditions and recommend appropriate action.

Taylor's and Rostow's report, submitted to the President in November, urged a substantial increase in American support to South Vietnam, including more U.S. advisers, equipment, and even limited numbers of combat troops. These recommendations, Taylor and Rostow noted, meant a fundamental "transition from advice to partnership" in the war by boldly expanding American participation in counterinsurgency operations.[10]

Though rejecting the introduction of combat troops, Kennedy accepted the recommendation for more advisers, in keeping with his administration's strategy of "flexible response." This doctrine, which emerged as a reaction to Eisenhower's strategy of "massive retaliation"—a strict reliance on atomic weapons as a deterrent to aggression—postulated the strengthening of conventional forces, thereby enabling the United States to confront what it perceived as communist-inspired "wars of liberation" without resort to nuclear weapons or a superpower confrontation. Under this strategy, the number of

American military advisers in South Vietnam multiplied dramatically, reaching over 16,000 by the end of 1963. This action marked a crucial escalation in U.S. involvement, clearly perceived by contemporary policymakers. As Secretary of State Dean Rusk later observed, Kennedy's decision carried America "beyond the levels of troops that were in effect permitted by the 1954 agreements. . . ."[11]

As the United States assumed a much deeper role in the war, Diem's hold over the South continued to weaken. Despite America's growing military presence, the Vietcong expanded its control throughout many parts of the country. Feeling increasingly besieged, Diem intensified his repression.

As a Catholic mandarin, Diem had always suspected the motives and power of South Vietnam's Buddhist bonzes, who had never acquiesced to his rule. When political unrest encouraged by the bonzes erupted in the summer of 1963, Diem and his brother, Ngo Dinh Nhu, raided the pagodas, arresting and detaining thousands of Buddhists. Angered by Saigon's harsh response, Washington began distancing itself from Diem and preparing for a coup. After several false starts, that coup occurred on November 1, 1963. With the Kennedy administration's tacit consent, a military cabal deposed the regime, abruptly killing both Diem and Nhu.

JFK's own assassination followed three weeks later. But before his death, America's commitment to South Vietnam had entered a new and troublesome period. For Diem's overthrow—however predictable given his peremptory rule—unleashed powerful and unpredictable forces of fateful significance to U.S.-Vietnamese relations. The responsibility for this development rested with John Kennedy; its consequences confronted his successor, Lyndon Johnson.

LBJ assumed office at this critical moment as a seasoned politician but inexperienced diplomat. During his formative years, Johnson received little exposure to foreign affairs. "When I was a boy," he later recalled, "we never had these issues of our relations with other nations so much. We didn't wake up with Vietnam and have Santo Domingo for lunch and the Congo for dinner."[12]

LBJ focused his attention, quite naturally, on Texas politics, which seemed far removed from international concerns. Johnson utilized his mastery of state affairs to launch a political career, first as assistant to south Texas Congressman Richard Kleberg, then as state National Youth Administration director, and finally as U.S. representative from central Texas.

LBJ arrived in Washington as a new congressman just as Hitler's armies prepared their march across Europe. The western democracies' belated response to fascist aggression created a lasting impression on the young Johnson. Like many of his generation, LBJ interpreted appeasement as a dangerous seed yielding bitter fruit—a lesson Johnson carried throughout his legislative career and into the White House. "[E]verything I knew about history," LBJ subsequently remarked, "told me that if I got out of Vietnam . . . then I'd be doing exactly what Chamberlain did [before] World War II. I'd be giving a big fat reward to aggression."[13]

Johnson's experiences before the Second World War influenced his perception of the Cold War that followed. The West had failed to check fascist aggression in the late 1930s; it must not compound this error by failing to halt communist expansion in the late 1940s.

LBJ stressed this view during House debate over Truman's request for aid to Greece and Turkey in the spring of 1947. "[W]hether Communist or Fascist," Johnson told his colleagues, "the one thing a bully understands is force, and the one thing he fears is courage." "[H]uman experience," he added, "teaches me that if I let a bully of my community make me travel back streets to avoid a fight, I merely postpone the evil day. Soon he will try to chase me out of my house." LBJ felt America had hesitated to confront its bullies in the past: "We have fought two world wars because of our failure to take a position in time. When the first war began Germany did not believe we would fight. . . . Thus the Kaiser was led to believe that we were complacent and lacked courage. Unrestricted submarine warfare began, and so we went to war." The same, Johnson argued, applied to those days before World War II, when "the siren songs of appeasers convinced us it was none of our business what happened in Europe or the world, and thus France was sacrificed to Fascist ambitions, and England's destiny was fought out in the skies over London." But America had learned its lesson; today, "[w]henever security of this country is involved, we are willing to draw the quarantine line—and we would rather have it on the shores of the Mediterranean than on the shores of the Chesapeake Bay or the Gulf of Mexico," LBJ concluded.[14]

Johnson's foreign policy record as senator and, later, majority leader in the 1950s mirrored the bipartisan commitment to containment characteristic of the decade. Although LBJ opposed American intervention at Dienbienphu in 1954, he generally supported Eisenhower's diplomatic initiatives, guiding many of the President's foreign policy measures through the Senate. This cooperation reflected Johnson's devotion to executive leadership on international issues dating back to Franklin Roosevelt and his caution born of a limited background in world affairs. "If you're in an airplane, and you're flying somewhere," LBJ once observed to his fellow senators, "you don't run up to the cockpit and attack the pilot. Mr. Eisenhower is the only President we've got." Johnson deferred to the pilot's position and his experience.[15]

As Vice President under Kennedy, Johnson broadened his exposure to

international affairs and first encountered Vietnam as a policy issue. During
May 1961, he traveled to Southeast Asia at the President's request, meeting
with Diem and other leaders.

In his report of that trip to Kennedy, LBJ plainly endorsed America's
containment policy in Indochina. "The battle against Communism must be
joined in Southeast Asia with strength and determination," Johnson wrote;
otherwise, he added, we might as well "throw in the towel in the area and
pull back our defenses to San Francisco and a 'Fortress America' concept."
Invoking an expansive view of U.S. security, LBJ predicted apocalyptic
consequences stemming from American withdrawal from the region. "Without [Washington's] inhibitory influence," he warned, "the vast Pacific becomes a Red Sea." To avoid this result, Johnson urged "a major effort to
help these countries defend themselves."

LBJ alerted Kennedy to the implications of his recommendation. "This
decision," he reminded the President, "must be made in a full realization of
the very heavy and continuing costs involved in terms of money, of effort
and of United States prestige. It must be made with the knowledge that at
some point we may be faced with the further decision of whether we commit major United States forces to the area or cut our losses and withdraw
should our other efforts fail."

Johnson did not, however, endorse a military solution in Vietnam. In
fact, LBJ downplayed the relevance of American combat troops, whose
involvement was "not only not required" but "not desirable." In his opinion, "hunger, ignorance, poverty and disease"—not "the momentary threat
of Communism itself"—posed the "greatest danger" to Southeast Asian stability. "We must—whatever strategies we evolve—keep these enemies the
point of our attack," Johnson stressed. Only then could Washington retain
the discretion LBJ deemed essential.[16]

With Kennedy's death, that discretion fell to Johnson. Yet initially he exer-
cised it sparingly. Elevated to the presidency by extraordinary circumstances, LBJ felt a special duty to maintain Kennedy's policies and advisers.
In the months following the assassination, Johnson later said, "I constantly
had before me the picture that Kennedy had selected me as executor of his
will, it was my duty to carry on and this meant his people as well as his
programs. They were part of his legacy."[17]

If the senior advisers remained the same, their relationship with the new
President did not. LBJ kept Dean Rusk as Secretary of State, Robert Mc-
Namara as Secretary of Defense, and McGeorge Bundy as Special Assistant
for National Security Affairs, but their relative influence shifted along with
the change in administration.

Dean Rusk's stock rose on the White House exchange. Although Kennedy had respected Rusk and trusted his counsel, JFK had often acted as his own Secretary of State. Johnson, by contrast, delegated significant authority to Rusk over foreign policy and relied more heavily on his personal judgment. LBJ liked and trusted his Secretary of State; "Rusk," he proudly boasted on one occasion, "has the compassion of a preacher and the courage of a Georgia cracker. When you're going in with the Marines, he's the kind you want on your side."[18]

Johnson and Rusk, as this comment suggested, shared a natural rapport reflecting their similar backgrounds and world views. Rusk, also a native rural Southerner, had traveled a long road to national prominence. Born in Cherokee County, Georgia, he had been encouraged by his mother—like LBJ's mother, a former schoolteacher—to pursue lofty ambitions. But where Johnson followed a political path to power, Rusk pursued education as his route to success. After graduating from college in 1931, he attended Oxford University as a Rhodes scholar, studying international relations. Rusk pursued this interest during a semester at the University of Berlin in 1933, where he witnessed Hitler's ascent to power.

The rise of Nazi Germany created a profound impression on Rusk, as it did on the young Texas congressman. Appalled by the West's timidity toward Hitler, Rusk developed a staunch devotion to collective security against fascist aggression which he subsequently applied, with equal force, against the specter of monolithic communist aggression. The underlying conflict in world affairs, Rusk later observed, "is between a U.N. kind of world and those trying to build a world revolution." The communists' "declared doctrine of world revolution," he quickly added, "ought to be as credible as *Mein Kampf*."[19]

A strong military heritage reinforced Rusk's firm demeanor. Both of his grandfathers had served in the Confederate Army. Rusk followed this tradition as an ROTC member throughout high school and college, serving as cadet commander and, later during World War II, as military adjutant to General Joseph Stillwell in the China-Burma-India theater.

After the war, Rusk left the Army for the State Department, working under the soldier-statesman George Marshall, whose dual qualities he so admired. The Korean War gave Rusk the opportunity to apply those qualities in his position as Assistant Secretary of State for Far Eastern Affairs. Rusk entered his new post at a turbulent moment for the State Department, as conservatives pilloried its role in the recent "loss" of China. Although Rusk did not participate directly in China policy—being preoccupied with U.N. affairs—the virulent domestic reaction it provoked reinforced his inclination toward a tough response when communist forces invaded South Korea that June. Rusk carried the lessons of China and Korea into his years as Secretary of State and applied them to Vietnam.

Rusk's colleague, Defense Secretary Robert McNamara, maintained the respect and confidence Johnson had accorded him as Vice President. At Kennedy's first Cabinet meeting in 1961, it was "the fellow from Ford [Motor Company] with Stacomb on his hair" who had impressed LBJ most. Johnson valued McNamara's dedication and intelligence as much as he did Rusk's judgment. He also admired McNamara's ceaseless energy, which rivaled his own. McNamara, LBJ once noted approvingly, "is the first one to work and the last one to leave. When I wake up, the first one I call is McNamara. He is there at seven every morning, including Saturday. The only difference is that Saturday he wears a sport coat."[20]

The key to McNamara's success was his efficiency. Trained as an economist and statistician at the Harvard Business School, he approached problems—whether in industry or government—in a rigorously analytical manner, utilizing an evaluative process to produce the desired result with minimum expense and waste. During World War II, McNamara devoted his skill at systems analysis to the Army Air Corps, devising a statistical control system governing its flow of material and personnel.

After the war, McNamara and several Air Force colleagues joined the ailing Ford Motor Company. There the "Whiz Kids" applied their analytical expertise to the automaker's financial and administrative troubles. McNamara's fortunes rose along with Ford's profits throughout the 1950s. By 1960, he became president of the company, the first non-family member to hold that position.

Shortly thereafter, Kennedy appointed the Ford executive his Secretary of Defense, seeking to harness McNamara's abilities to a Pentagon whose administrative structure and strategic doctrine JFK considered outdated. McNamara enthusiastically embraced the challenge. Using principles of cost accounting, he reorganized the Defense Department, establishing firm civilian control over military spending. McNamara also supervised the expansion of conventional forces as part of the Kennedy administration's new concept of "flexible response."

McNamara's devotion to "flexible response" fostered attention to its application—as in Vietnam, where America's advisory presence steadily increased in the early 1960s. During this period, he developed a particular, almost proprietary, interest in a region fast becoming the testing ground for Washington's current theories of limited war against guerrilla insurgency. Primed with a natural assurance in the service of the latest military techniques, McNamara confidently assumed major responsibility for this issue.

Unlike McNamara and Rusk, McGeorge Bundy's comfortable association with John Kennedy did not carry over to his successor. Kennedy and Bundy had enjoyed a common New England heritage, urbane sophistication, and interest in diplomacy which facilitated easy communication. Spontaneity and candor had governed relations between them.

JFK's White House had represented a familiar environment to Bundy; LBJ's White House seemed considerably less so. Bundy later admitted that his first days under the new President were "a stressful three months." Under Kennedy, Bundy had enjoyed free access to the Oval Office; when he called unannounced on Johnson shortly after the assassination, LBJ delivered a sharp rebuke. "Goddammit, Bundy," Johnson snapped, "I've told you that when I want you I'll call you."[21]

Johnson's and Bundy's distant partnership reflected their many contrasts. LBJ's ancestors comprised the rural gentry of central Texas; Bundy's, the core of Boston's elite. Johnson's formal education had been modest and undistinguished. At Groton, Yale, and Harvard, where he had been a Junior Fellow and later dean of the faculty of arts and sciences, Bundy had demonstrated exceptional intellectual ability. LBJ concentrated his attention on domestic affairs. Bundy's expertise, instead, lay in foreign affairs. Johnson remained staunchly Democratic throughout his political career, while Bundy embraced a bipartisan commitment to public service like his mentor, Henry Stimson.[22]

Bundy approached his work as national security adviser with the moral certitude of his heritage. "Mother's sense of righteousness," Bundy's sister remembered, "was very deep and so was Mac's. Mother always conveyed to us her profound belief in the clear difference between right and wrong. . . . For her, things were black and white." "It's an outlook," his sister added, "that descends directly from the Puritans and we all have it. But Mac has it more than the rest of us."[23]

A confidence born of distinguished custom reinforced this attitude. Bundy viewed himself as the heir of a foreign policy tradition, symbolized by the admired Stimson, which stressed American leadership in world affairs, guided by a knowledgeable and enlightened elite committed to national, rather than narrow political, interests. He represented the embodiment of Establishment power and, some thought, of Establishment arrogance. John Mason Brown, who shared a cabin with Army Lieutenant McGeorge Bundy, military aide to Admiral Alan Kirk, aboard Kirk's flagship *Augusta* during the D-Day landings, later recalled:

On D-plus-one, I was summoned to the admiral's quarters and all the brass were having breakfast, including General [Omar] Bradley. Mac was there too—the lowly lieutenant. Bradley was explaining some invasion move, and at one point he said, "And then we go in here." Mac said—in effect—"No we don't." And Bradley accepted it.[24]

Johnson felt painfully removed from the Establishment tradition which Bundy represented. Never as comfortable in the international realm as in the domestic one, LBJ remained sensitive to Bundy's experience in this area. Many people, Johnson once noted plaintively, "say that I am not qualified in foreign affairs like Jack Kennedy and those other experts. I guess I was just born in the wrong part of the country." Such feelings kept the two men's relationship a distant one.[25]

In November 1963, the new President and his advisers confronted a South Vietnam in flux. The recent coup against Diem had unleashed a panoply of conflicting forces jeopardizing Saigon's fragile stability. This kaleidoscopic turmoil would soon trigger a series of political crises undermining military efforts against the insurgency and drawing the United States deeper into the war.

The source of South Vietnam's turbulence lay in its social and political structure, which had been fashioned under French colonialism and perpetuated under Diem's regime. France had ruled Vietnamese society indirectly, through a primarily Catholic and French-educated elite deriving influence and prestige from its connection with the French and faithfully supporting their rule. This neo-mandarin class had substituted for the independent Vietnamese polity which France never permitted. Elective institutions for the channeling of political conflict had been forbidden. Denied a competitive, pluralistic process, Vietnam had never developed a tradition of responsible political opposition; dissent had expressed itself, instead, in conspiracies of small, clandestine groups distrustful of one another and the government. Later observers, such as American Ambassador Maxwell Taylor, would note a similar tendency in South Vietnamese politics:

> As the past history of this country shows, there seems to be a national attribute which makes for factionalism and limits the development of a truly national spirit. Whether this tendency is innate or a development growing out of the conditions of political suppression under which successive generations have lived is hard to determine. But it is an inescapable fact that there is no national tendency toward team play or mutual loyalty to be found among many of the leaders and political groups within South Vietnam.[26]

Diem had preserved this legacy of the French and, with it, Vietnam's peculiar political tradition, which flowered in the months after his death. Freed from its restraints, South Vietnam's deep-rooted volatility exploded in a confusing array of suspicious and antagonistic political forces. Buddhists, religious sects such as the Cao Dai and Hoa Hao, students, and ambitious young generals of the armed forces all began struggling to control South Vietnam's political direction independently of their rivals.

American policymakers had scarcely expected this unsettling development when they had acquiesced in the coup against Diem. Troubled by Diem's mounting repression and its effect on civil order and the anti-insurgency campaign, Washington had failed to anticipate the explosive political tension which Diem himself had nurtured. "Until the fall of Diem and the experience gained from the events of the following months," an American official later remarked, "I doubt that anyone appreciated the magnitude of the centrifugal political forces which had been kept under control by his iron rule."[27]

The destabilizing impact of those centrifugal forces soon became apparent. On January 30, 1964, General Nguyen Khanh and several confederates overthrew the Military Revolutionary Council (MRC), the junta established by General Duong Van Minh following Diem's assassination just three months before.

Nguyen Khanh, the coup's leader, was a shrewd and intriguing figure. Short, stocky, and taciturn, he compensated for his natural reticence with a physical flair, often sporting a goatee and paratrooper's red beret. Barely thirty-six when he assumed power, Khanh already possessed a keen political sensibility. The son of a wealthy planter, he had received education and military training from the French before joining the Vietminh in 1947. A few months later, disillusioned by communist domination of the nationalist movement, Khanh rejoined the French, becoming an army officer in 1949. Following the Geneva Accords of 1954, he embraced Diem's government, rising to become deputy Army Chief of Staff in 1960.

Khanh's devotion to Diem, however, proved superficial. When Diem encountered growing domestic unrest in 1963, Khanh first encouraged the president to declare martial law; then, as Diem's fortunes declined, he began plotting with other young generals against the regime. The junta rewarded Khanh's participation in the coup by appointing him I Corps Commander in the north, where he laid plans for his own seizure of power in January, with the knowledge, if not consent, of American military officers.

Washington recognized the new Khanh regime, but with few illusions. Most American observers considered Khanh an able general who always kept personal interests uppermost in his mind. The Central Intelligence Agency considered him an "ambitious and ruthless man." Deputy Ambassador Alexis Johnson, who came to know Khanh well, judged him "bright and beguiling," but also "mercurial . . . and utterly devoid of character." Johnson's superior, Maxwell Taylor, depicted him even more vividly. To Taylor, Khanh seemed "a skillful if unscrupulous croupier in the political roulette as played in Saigon, one who knew how to give the wheel a new spin whenever the ball seemed about to settle on the wrong number." But perhaps Khanh's fellow countrymen understood and characterized him best. As one

South Vietnamese acquaintance later remarked, "Khanh was little more than a clown whose only claim to rule lay in his capacity for scheming."[28]

As Khanh settled into power, the United States moved toward deeper involvement in Vietnam. Diem's ouster had not dampened the insurgency as Washington had hoped, and Johnson's administration reacted by increasing military pressure against Hanoi, which continued to support the insurgency. On February 1, 1964, LBJ authorized an intensification of covert operations against North Vietnam, code-named PLAN 34A, first begun by Kennedy in 1961. Supplementing guerrilla raids against the communist "Ho Chi Minh" infiltration trail into the South, Johnson approved reconnaissance flights over Laos, commando raids along the North Vietnamese coast, and naval shelling of military installations in the Tonkin Gulf.

Saigon's political situation, meanwhile, remained in a state of precarious equilibrium over the next six months, as Khanh battled rival factions for control of the government, inaugurated a national mobilization campaign to bolster the armed forces, and struggled to reinvigorate the languishing rural pacification program.

Military conditions also remained shaky. The Vietcong readily perceived the chaos swept in by Diem's assassination and moved to exploit it. Aiming to topple Khanh's fragile regime, the VC renewed the offensive, gradually expanding their control of the countryside.

Yet South Vietnam's fortunes failed to improve, despite LBJ's February decisions. Washington responded by replacing General Paul Harkins as Commander of the United States Military Assistance Command, Vietnam (COMUSMACV), whose persistent optimism increasingly contradicted events. President Johnson named General William Westmoreland as Harkins' successor in late June.

Westmoreland seemed, by tradition and training, a natural choice; he unmistakably possessed "the habit of command." Born in South Carolina, where the Confederacy's martial ethic endured long after the Civil War, Westmoreland early settled on a military career. After high school, he studied at the Citadel in Charleston, before securing appointment to West Point through his former Sunday school teacher, Congressman James F. Byrnes. At the Military Academy, Westmoreland displayed a remarkable instinct for leadership, graduating as the class of 1936's first captain of cadets.

During World War II, Westmoreland commanded an infantry battalion through the North Africa, Sicily, and Normandy campaigns. Following the war, Westmoreland became a paratrooper, leading an airborne combat team in Korea.

In addition to the time-honored virtue of battlefield courage, Westmoreland also demonstrated talent in the contemporary art of administration, highly valued in the postwar Army. Like McNamara, Westmoreland attended the Harvard Business School, developing management skills employed at the Pentagon during the mid-1950s and at West Point, as superintendent from 1960 to 1963. Westmoreland symbolized the modern soldier-administrator, combining personal bravery and professional ability.

Soon after Westmoreland arrived, Washington's ambassador to Saigon, Henry Cabot Lodge, Jr., returned to the United States to pursue the Republican Party's presidential nomination. Johnson chose Maxwell Taylor as Lodge's successor.

Taylor shared Westmoreland's military background. As a young boy growing up in Missouri, he had listened avidly to his grandfather—a Confederate cavalry officer—recount tales of the Civil War. Stirred by these memories, Taylor entered the Military Academy, graduating fourth in his class in 1922. Over the following years, he compiled a distinguished record spanning several continents and several wars: officer of the 82nd and 101st Airborne divisions during World War II; superintendent of West Point; military governor of Berlin; commander of ground forces in Japan and Korea; Army chief of staff; chairman of the Joint Chiefs of Staff (JCS).

Taylor did not, however, lack preparation for his new assignment in South Vietnam. Although a professional Army officer, he occupied several posts throughout his career reflecting America's political involvement in East Asia. In the late 1930s, Taylor served as a military attaché in Tokyo and Peking, acquiring knowledge of Asian languages and cultures. He returned to the Far East at the end of the Korean War, commanding the Eighth Army in the months before the armistice. During this time, Taylor followed the Korean negotiations closely, broadening his understanding of the intimate link between force and diplomacy.

Taylor's identification with Asia deepened during the Kennedy years when, as JFK's special military representative, he urged a substantial increase in U.S. military assistance to South Vietnam. Taylor subsequently supervised this effort as JCS chairman from 1962 through 1964. He arrived in Saigon a general-turned-diplomat firmly devoted to Washington's commitment to South Vietnam.

Less than a month after Taylor's arrival, events in the Tonkin Gulf collided with electoral politics in the United States to produce a volatile mixture spelling further American escalation in Vietnam. On August 2, North Vietnamese gunboats attacked the U.S. destroyer *Maddox* on an electronic intelligence-gathering mission in the Tonkin Gulf. Two days later, *Maddox* and another destroyer, *C. Turner Joy,* reported a second attack in heavy seas which, though never definitively confirmed, prompted a swift reaction by the administration. Having swallowed the first assault without retaliation,

Johnson and his advisers seized on fragmentary evidence of a second to launch reprisal air strikes against North Vietnamese torpedo-boat bases and oil-storage depots near the seventeenth parallel.

LBJ used the sense of urgency created by this incident to seek a congressional resolution authorizing him "to take all necessary measures to repel any armed attack against the forces of the United States and to prevent further aggression" in Southeast Asia. Congress willingly obliged, following its custom in moments of perceived crisis. The House adopted the resolution unanimously on August 6; the Senate followed suit the next day, approving the measure by an overwhelming vote of 88-2.[29]

Johnson's actions reflected short-term expedience rather than long-term calculation. The President did not secretly embrace escalation and then turn to Congress to endorse it; his objective was more immediate and less sinister. By ordering air strikes against North Vietnam and securing passage of the "Tonkin Gulf" Resolution, LBJ sought to answer his military foe and his political opponents with one stroke.

Three weeks earlier in San Francisco, Republicans had nominated right-winger Barry Goldwater on a platform demanding tougher military action in Vietnam. The August measures allowed Johnson to blunt this conservative criticism of his policy while demonstrating resolve against North Vietnam. They served as an international signal which also promised domestic political dividends.

LBJ walked a narrow path on Vietnam during the fall election campaign—seeking to deflect Goldwater's charge of weakness while capitalizing on Goldwater's hawkishness, which the public feared. Johnson balanced these conflicting goals by proclaiming continued support for a non-communist South Vietnam in moderate terms designed to contrast with the belligerence of his opponent.

LBJ first voiced this delicate political strategy in a speech to American lawyers shortly before the Democratic convention. Johnson reminded his audience of America's firm but limited commitment to South Vietnam. For ten years the United States had followed a "consistent pattern" in Southeast Asia, according to LBJ: first, the U.S. acknowledged "that the South Vietnamese have the basic responsibility for the defense of their own freedom"; second, the United States would engage its strength and resources "to whatever extent needed to help others repel aggression." Johnson pledged to follow this pattern without risking escalation. In a thinly veiled reference to Goldwater, he warned that "others are eager to enlarge the conflict" by supplying "American boys to do the job that Asian boys should do." LBJ rejected this course, stressing that "such action would offer no solution at all to the real problem of Vietnam." He promised a responsible but prudent policy preserving Washington's commitment while avoiding the dangers of an expanded war.[30]

Johnson echoed this general theme in the following weeks. Eager to avoid charges of both extremism and weakness, the President steered a middle course, pledging neither to escalate nor to withdraw from Vietnam.

In his first appearance after receiving the nomination, LBJ projected an image of restraint in Vietnam. "I have had advice," he told his fellow Texans, "to load our planes with bombs and drop them on certain areas that I think would enlarge the war and . . . result in our committing a good many American boys to fighting a war that . . . ought to be fought by the boys of Asia to help protect their own land." "[F]or that reason," Johnson said, "I haven't chosen to enlarge the war. Nor have I chosen to retreat and turn it over to the Communists."[31]

At a campaign stop in Oklahoma four weeks later, the President again stressed the moderation of his Vietnam policy. LBJ dismissed those who would "go north and drop bombs" as well as those who would "go south and get out"; "we are not," he said, "about to start another war and we're not about to run away from where we are."[32]

Gradually, however, Johnson shifted his emphasis away from the need to maintain a steady course in Vietnam toward the hazards of a wider war. During a meeting with newspaper editors in New Hampshire on September 28, LBJ underscored his reluctance to bomb North Vietnam as Goldwater advocated. "I want to be very cautious and careful," Johnson told his audience, before "I start dropping bombs around that are likely to involve American boys in a war in Asia with 700 million Chinese." "[L]osing 190 lives in the period that we have been out there is bad," he added, "[b]ut it is not like the 190,000 that we might lose the first month if we escalated that war." LBJ would preserve peace and stability by getting "the boys in Vietnam to do their own fighting." Sensing popular fear of Goldwater's extremism, Johnson answered those fears in language designed to reflect his caution.[33]

As election day neared, LBJ's rhetoric grew even less ambiguous. Scenting a strong political advantage, the President moved toward an outright rejection of American combat involvement. That assertion came in a speech at Akron, Ohio, on October 21. Though dismissing retreat from South Vietnam, Johnson assured his audience that he was "not about to send American boys 9 or 10,000 miles away from home to do what Asian boys ought to be doing for themselves."[34]

Absorbed in a sensitive election fight, LBJ had pledged not to expand the war. He had articulated a safe and steady policy on Vietnam—without the surprises which could upset his chances for victory. This reflected Johnson's desire, as expressed to an aide during this period, to "keep the lid on." "I don't want to have headlines about some accident in Vietnam," the President admonished him.[35]

But events did not accommodate Johnson. Developments in South Vietnam throughout the summer and fall of 1964 slowly undermined his repeated promises not to escalate the conflict. Saigon's increasing inability to fight its own war weakened the President's assurance that U.S. forces would not have to.

South Vietnam's mounting military paralysis during this period mirrored the political turmoil continuing to plague the country. Less than two weeks after the Tonkin Gulf reprisals, General Khanh, emboldened by America's show of support, brazenly issued his "Vungtau Charter," a constitution granting him sweeping presidential powers. Khanh's charter also conveniently abolished the position of Chief of State, thereby removing his strongest rival, General Minh, from the government.

If this new arrangement pleased Nguyen Khanh, it did not please the South Vietnamese people, who had emerged from another dictatorship only nine months before. Students, political opponents, and Buddhist monks took to the streets, protesting the general's new dispensation. The demonstrations climaxed on August 25, when a crowd of youths forced Khanh from his home, compelling him to self-denunciation. "Down with military power," the ambitious general cried to his angry audience, "down with dictatorships, down with the army!" Hours after this humiliating performance, Khanh withdrew his fledgling constitution and resigned.[36]

Events over the next two days exposed the muddled state of South Vietnamese affairs. No sooner did Khanh quit his post than a group of ambitious young officers within the MRC—known as the "Young Turks"—voted to reinstate him as part of a temporary ruling triumvirate. The troika's members included Khanh, whom the public had recently repudiated; Minh, who distrusted Khanh as much as Khanh distrusted him; and General Tran Thien Khiem, who had conspired with Khanh to overthrow Minh's junta the previous January. The prospects for stability did not seem encouraging.

Not all ARVN officers welcomed this new arrangement, however. Many Catholics within the army, who had supported Diem's rule, resented the rising Buddhist influence in South Vietnam, which they associated with Khanh. Two of them—General Lam Van Phat, former Interior Minister under Khanh, and General Duong Van Duc, commander of ARVN's IV Corps in the Mekong delta south of Saigon—vented their anger through a maneuver familiar to Khanh—the military coup.

On September 13, Phat and Duc marched troops into the capital, seizing important government installations. The revolt, however, met resistance from forces led by Air Vice-Marshal Nguyen Cao Ky and General Nguyen

Chanh Thi, both younger officers loyal to the government. Ky and Thi managed to suppress the attempted coup. Their action preserved Khanh's regime, while strengthening the Young Turks' voice within South Vietnam. Khanh retained his power, but at further cost to his political independence.

Not surprisingly, as Khanh's authority diminished, his attention to the issue of civilian government—which he had long promised to establish—suddenly increased. Two weeks after the failed coup, Khanh made an apparent move in this direction. On September 26, he inaugurated the High National Council (HNC), a cabinet of elders charged with drafting a provisional constitution and convening a national convention to serve as an interim legislature.

Despite its imposing commission, most South Vietnamese dismissed the HNC as a political tool contrived by Khanh to legitimate his continued rule. The council, whose members were as old as they were ineffectual, soon became known throughout Saigon as the "High National Museum."

At the end of October, the seventeen-member HNC submitted a draft constitution to General Khanh. He approved the plan and, on November 1, named a civilian government with former Saigon mayor Tran Van Huong as premier and the HNC's chairman, Phan Khac Suu, as chief of state.

The new ministry posed little threat to Khanh's control. Huong was a schoolteacher—not a politician—who accepted the premiership reluctantly. "I'm not sure whether I should be congratulated or offered condolences," he remarked when informed of his appointment. Huong's colleague, Suu, was an aging technocrat who, because of imprisonment and torture under Diem, could barely focus his attention on matters of detail. To Ambassador Taylor, the chief of state appeared "old beyond his years and clearly lacking in physical stamina." Despite his frail constitution, Suu still harbored a healthy personal ambition.[37]

Americans in Saigon reacted to South Vietnam's first civilian government since the fall of Diem with hopes about its effectiveness tempered by doubts about its ability. They looked to Huong's administration for democratic reforms which would invigorate the flagging war effort, but questioned whether it could achieve this objective. In a cable to the State Department on November 3, Taylor offered a guarded view of the new cabinet which, he noted, "will be composed largely of men without governmental experience who will have to learn their trade on the job." Even "under favorable conditions," Taylor observed, it would take "three to four months" for Huong and Suu to get it "functioning well." Khanh and his military cohorts, meanwhile, would anxiously await the first sign of trouble. Once Huong's government "appears to falter," the ambassador predicted, "the generals may be expected to make a new grasp for political power."[38]

* * *

This, then, marked the state of South Vietnamese affairs as Johnson embarked on his own administration in November 1964. In the year since Diem's death, Saigon had yet to establish a viable, responsive government capable of ruling the country or forcefully confronting the insurgency. The ceaseless intrigue among South Vietnam's politicians and generals—so inimical to political stability and military success—persisted.

The communists had skillfully exploited Saigon's divisions. The Vietcong had strengthened their presence in rural areas, whose inhabitants remained isolated from the central government, and in urban centers, where factional disputes encouraged ready manipulation. North Vietnam had also turned Saigon's tumult to good advantage, using ARVN's intrusive attention to politics to boost its infiltration of men and supplies into the south.

As the South Vietnamese army continued to fight largely among itself rather than against the rebels, the war effort deteriorated markedly. VC military successes increasingly threatened the fragile regime. This development, in turn, put growing pressure on President Johnson and his advisers to expand U.S. involvement in the conflict. South Vietnam's instability had fostered conditions which would soon test the limits—and strength—of America's containment strategy in Southeast Asia.

2

"The Day of Reckoning
Is Coming"

LYNDON JOHNSON's main concern in the fall of 1964 had been his election contest with Barry Goldwater, not the war in Vietnam. For a President engaged in an exhilarating and undeniably successful campaign, Vietnam seemed a distant and unwanted problem.

But the din of American electoral politics could not obscure South Vietnam's accelerating decline. However much LBJ wished to avoid the issue, Saigon's mounting troubles posed new and inescapable choices for his administration.

To prepare himself for these choices, Johnson established an interagency task force shortly before the election. This board—formally designated the "NSC Working Group on South Vietnam/Southeast Asia"—had been charged with reviewing America's commitment in the region and recommending appropriate courses of action to the President through a "Principals Group" composed of LBJ's top advisers. It represented, as one participant noted, "the most comprehensive" Vietnam policy review "of any in the Kennedy and Johnson Administrations."[1]

The Working Group first met on the morning of November 3, 1964, about the time Johnson cast his election ballot in Texas. Although its members focused their attention on Vietnam, their deliberations occurred in an atmosphere punctuated by a trio of recent international events which generated new pressures on the administration to stand fast in Southeast Asia.

Less than three weeks before, on October 15, Nikita Khrushchev had been abruptly ousted as head of the Soviet Union and replaced by a pair of new leaders: Leonid Brezhnev as First Secretary and Alexei Kosygin as Premier. Khrushchev's sudden overthrow created considerable apprehension in Wash-

ington as to the course of Soviet policy under the new regime. This apprehension stemmed in part from America's limited understanding of Soviet
leadership changes. Power had changed hands in Russia only twice before
since the Bolshevik Revolution, both times prompting chaotic disruption
in Soviet affairs. What, U.S. analysts wondered, would be the consequences
of this latest shift? Abandonment of Khrushchev's emerging "peaceful co-
existence" with the United States? Narrowing of the Sino-Soviet split, as
Kremlin contenders vied for control by courting Peking? Lacking clear
answers to these questions, many experts believed America had to reaffirm
its international commitments—including support of South Vietnam—in
order to deter renewed Soviet adventurism.

The day after the Kremlin's purge, China had exploded its first atomic
device over Lop Nor, a salt-encrusted lake bed in the barren Taklamakan
Desert. Although U.S. intelligence had anticipated this event for some
weeks, it nevertheless intensified a principal fear of contemporary Washington—the image of an aggressive China threatening the security of Southeast
Asia.

This fear, however exaggerated, reflected deeply rooted perceptions. Johnson and his advisers viewed China in 1964 much like Truman and his advisers had viewed Russia after World War II—as a militantly expansive
force to be contained until mellowed by internal forces or external pressures.
LBJ had stressed this theme in a public address on Peking's atomic test on
October 18. "No American should treat this matter lightly," Johnson had
warned. "Until this week only four powers [America, Britain, Russia, and
France] had entered the dangerous world of nuclear explosions." "Whatever
their differences," the President had said, "all four are sober and serious
states, with long experience as major powers in the modern world." "Communist China," he had added after a long pause, "has no such experience."[2]

Washington's image of a belligerent China drew much of its color from
Peking's own rhetoric. For years, Mao and his followers had persistently
denounced U.S. "imperialism," while ridiculing America as a "paper tiger."
By pulling Uncle Sam's beard, China served its competition with Russia
for leadership of the communist bloc. But Americans interpreted these propaganda attacks far differently. Peking's bellicose rhetoric seemed to confirm
Washington's perception of a hostile power determined to impose its hegemony over Asia.

Many Americans shared their government's view of an aggressive China.
Time, one of the nation's most popular and influential magazines, depicted
Peking's leaders during this period as "Marxists with Manchu ambitions."
"In the vast sweep of country from Angkor Wat to the Great Wall, from
the Yellow Sea to the Pamirs," went a *Time* cover story, "Red China seeks
hegemony." Opinion surveys revealed equally pervasive fears among the

public. A Gallup poll conducted that November showed that Americans considered China a "greater threat to world peace" than Russia by a nearly three-to-one margin.[3]

A nuclear China intensified these fears, while raising new strategic concerns. Pentagon officials, who vividly recalled China's punishing intervention in the Korean War, now faced an army of two and a half million, equipped with atomic weapons. The combination appeared a potent threat, no longer checked by an American nuclear advantage.

More important than any military gain, however, was the psychological leverage which Washington attached to Peking's nuclear capability. By becoming the first Asian nation to master the atom, U.S. officials believed China had dramatically strengthened its influence in a region—Southeast Asia—which many considered a crucial ideological battleground between Peking and Washington.

Domestic political factors greatly intensified these anxieties. For Democratic leaders of the 1960s, the issue of China prompted haunting memories of the recent past. All remembered the "loss" of China and its McCarthyist reaction, so devastating to the Democratic party. They also remembered the Korean agony, which had bled Truman of his congressional and public support. For Johnson, these remained darkly instructive lessons. As he later recalled:

> I knew Harry Truman and Dean Acheson had lost their effectiveness from the day that the Communists took over in China. I believed that the loss of China had played a large role in the rise of Joe McCarthy. And I knew that all these problems, taken together, were chickenshit compared with what might happen if we lost Vietnam.[4]

LBJ seemed determined, even obsessed, with avoiding Truman's ordeal. This dread of a conservative backlash—much more than personal pride or fear of another "Munich"—conditioned Johnson's basic attitude toward Vietnam. As he had remarked in private shortly after assuming the presidency: "I am not going to lose Vietnam. I am not going to be the President who saw Southeast Asia go the way China went."[5]

Renewed fears about China had been followed by a third and final shock in Vietnam. On November 1, Vietcong guerrillas, using captured U.S. ordnance, had shelled the large American airbase at Bienhoa, twelve miles north of Saigon, killing five Americans and destroying five B-57 jet bombers. Unlike the previous August, LBJ had ordered no reprisals, wanting nothing to disrupt the impending election.

The Bienhoa attack, despite Johnson's decision not to retaliate, had marked an important turning point in the war. Previously, the Vietcong had concentrated their strikes on South Vietnamese targets; now, U.S. forces had come under direct attack. This brazen assault on American forces seemed an ominous challenge to the administration, one testing Washington's military commitment in the region.

Into this atmosphere of increased pressures stepped the Working Group on Vietnam. Its members, operating in a climate of heightened international tensions, would shape the direction of Vietnam policy far into the future. How that direction came to be defined reflected accommodation among conflicting viewpoints within the administration.

The White House had selected William Bundy, older brother of Johnson's national security adviser, McGeorge Bundy, to head the Working Group. Bundy was already heavily involved in Vietnam planning. For nearly four years, he had been at or near the center of Vietnam decision-making—first as director of the Pentagon's military assistance program to Saigon from 1961 to 1964, then as Assistant Secretary of State for Far Eastern Affairs, his current post.

From the beginning, Bundy had harbored a strong commitment to American policy in South Vietnam. In 1961, that policy had included support for Ngo Dinh Diem. But as Diem's popularity and effectiveness had declined, Bundy had lost faith in his ability to rally the South Vietnamese people against the communist insurgency.

Like many in Washington, Bundy had welcomed the 1963 coup against Diem, believing it offered new opportunities to create a stable and democratic government in Saigon. But those opportunities had never materialized. Instead of ushering in political stability, Diem's ouster had unleashed furious social and political turmoil exacerbated by military interference in government affairs. Bundy now confronted, in the fall of 1964, a weak South Vietnamese government whose future he scarcely trusted, but whose complexion had been defined in the aftermath of a coup sanctioned by himself and other American officials.

This tension between Bundy's sense of responsibility for Saigon's present and his skepticism about Saigon's future manifested itself in his first report to the Working Group. Although Bundy feared the loss of South Vietnam, suggesting that it "would be a major blow to our basic policies," he questioned whether South Vietnam could, in fact, be saved, given its endemic political problems. "The basic point," Bundy observed, "is that we have never thought we could defend a government or a people that had ceased to care strongly about defending themselves, or that were unable to maintain the fundamentals of government."

Bundy blamed this inability on South Vietnam's troubled history. Political burdens from Saigon's past pressed heavily against its future. South Vietnam had much to overcome, he said, including:

A bad colonial heritage of long standing, totally inadequate preparation for self-government by the colonial power, a colonialist war fought in half-baked fashion and lost, [and] a nationalist movement taken over by Communists ruling in the other half of an ethnically and historically united country, the Communist side inheriting much the better military force and far more than its share of the talent. . . .

"[T]hese are the facts that dog us to this day," Bundy confessed. He could not escape them, whatever his fears about the loss of South Vietnam. Caught between these conflicting realities, Bundy seemed hesitant—unsure what course to follow.[6]

The Joint Chiefs' representative on the Working Group, Vice Admiral Lloyd Mustin, was more certain. He expressed the military's belief that action against North Vietnam was the answer to problems within South Vietnam.

Mustin's and the Joint Chiefs' recommendation stemmed from their radically different perception of South Vietnam's troubles. They identified external aggression, not internal instability, as the primary problem. For this reason, improving Saigon's effectiveness seemed, to them, an incidental goal at best. Mustin and the Joint Chiefs sought little from a South Vietnamese government; they simply wanted a government which would "afford [a] platform upon which the . . . armed forces, with US assistance, prosecute the war."[7]

With Bundy and Mustin stressing such different problems, the Working Group seemed incapable of agreeing on options for the President. But there was a third member of the group whose thinking bridged their division: John McNaughton.

McNaughton had joined the Working Group as Robert McNamara's personal representative. It was his close association with the Defense Secretary that had first drawn McNaughton into Vietnam planning. As McNamara had assumed greater day-to-day responsibility for Vietnam, he had turned to McNaughton, the Department's general counsel and then Assistant Secretary for International Security Affairs, for advice and assistance on this difficult issue.

McNamara had enlisted a man of similar intellectual temperament, who shared his boss's penchant for translating the facets of a problem into statistical probabilities in order to facilitate precise, objective decisions. McNaughton's legal background, particularly his expertise in the field of evidence, encouraged him to view issues with the cold logic so valued by his profession. He was a brilliant lawyer and able bureaucrat whose rigorous analytical manner had earned McNamara's respect.

McNaughton's standing in the Working Group benefited from this fact. It also benefited from McNaughton's position in relation to Bundy and

Mustin. He reconciled their divergent viewpoints. Because of this, Mc-Naughton would greatly influence the Working Group's final recommendations to the President.

McNaughton's thinking reflected a precarious compromise between competing perspectives on Vietnam. He shared Bundy's misgivings about Saigon's political future, understanding that "[p]rogress inside SVN [was] important" but suspecting that it was "unlikely despite our best ideas and efforts. . . ."

This realization, paradoxically, led McNaughton to support Mustin's call for increased military pressure against Hanoi. If the South Vietnamese government could not be made more stable and effective, then the only solution, he thought, lay in weakening the Vietcong's ability to challenge that government, by reducing its reliance on North Vietnamese support.

McNaughton knew such action would not address the fundamental issue. "Action against North Vietnam," he admitted, "is to some extent a substitute for strengthening the government of South Vietnam." But because McNaughton saw little hope of solving the root problem of Saigon's political disorder, he chose to focus on a secondary one—Hanoi's support of the insurgency—which seemed more amenable to American action. As McNaughton reasoned, "a less active VC (on orders from DRV [Hanoi] can be matched by a less efficient GVN [Saigon]. We therefore should consider squeezing North Vietnam."

McNaughton included action against North Vietnam in the options he proposed to the Working Group. They were: continuing along present lines, which he labeled Option A; escalating immediately and heavily against North Vietnam, which he labeled Option B; and escalating gradually—first against infiltration routes in Laos, then against North Vietnam itself—which he labeled Option C.

McNaughton's options seemed to lack any attention to the propriety of withdrawal. This was not the case. He considered withdrawal an inevitable result of Option A. McNaughton deliberately rejected this course in favor of Option C. "If Option C is tried and fails," he argued, it "would still leave behind a better odor than Option A: It would demonstrate that [the] US was a 'good doctor' willing to keep promises, be tough, take risks, get bloodied, and hurt the enemy badly."[8]

McNaughton wanted the United States to continue playing the "good doctor"—ministering to a patient he considered beyond resuscitation—in order to dramatize America's anti-communist resolve. By this logic, a hopeless case actually required more intensive treatment—deepening America's commitment in the face of South Vietnam's deepening failure—if only to prove Washington's determination—its toughness—to the rest of the world.

McNaughton's logic prevailed. The Working Group's chairman soon embraced Option C. Bundy believed it offered more hope than the deteriorating status quo inherent in Option A, and appeared "more controllable and less risky" than the major escalation contemplated under Option B.

Although Bundy endorsed Option C, he feared the domestic political repercussions of military action that failed to produce quick, decisive results. Bundy sensed Option C was "inherently likely to stretch out and to be subject to major pressures both within the US and internationally." This could force the administration into a vice between conservatives clamoring for heavier bombing and liberals demanding an end to it.

Such a scenario reminded him of America's experience during the Korean War. Bundy hastened to note its painful lessons:

> As we saw in Korea, an "in-between" course of action will always arouse a school of thought that believes things should be tackled quickly and conclusively. On the other side, the continuation of military action . . . will arouse sharp criticism in other political quarters.

He had not forgotten the MacArthur affair, nor domestic disillusionment with the war. For these reasons, Bundy retained an uneasiness toward McNaughton's recommendation, even as he endorsed it.[9]

With the Working Group's planning almost finished, Secretary of State Rusk reported the emerging consensus on Option C to Ambassador Taylor, scheduled to return shortly to Washington for meetings with the President. Cabling Taylor on November 8, Rusk signaled Washington's growing sentiment for tougher measures against North Vietnam. Those measures initially involved reprisals "against any repetition . . . along the lines of the Bien Hoa attack." Should this fail to deter Hanoi, the Secretary added, "we would propose . . . to initiate in January a program of slowly graduated military actions against the North. . . ." While contemplating substantial escalation against Hanoi, Rusk stressed that planners believed "no course of action can succeed unless we are able to stiffen the GVN to set its house in order. . . ."[10]

As Washington readied for major decisions on Vietnam, President Johnson pondered the possibilities and limits of his election victory. The voters had given LBJ an enormous mandate, and comfortable margins to his party in both houses of Congress. Democrats now controlled the Senate 68 to 32, having added another seat to their already heavy majority, first acquired in 1958. It was in the House, however, where Goldwater's rout had cost the Republicans most dearly. Johnson and his party had gained 37 seats, giving them a stunning 295 to 140 advantage.

Armed with these awesome congressional majorities, the President seemed destined to achieve his cherished domestic program. Nothing, it now appeared, stood between LBJ and the fulfillment of his Great Society.

But Johnson, the seasoned politician, knew better. He realized this blessing was also a potential curse—that his mandate was a fragile and ephemeral commodity in the world of political rivalry and jealousy. LBJ reflected on this irony to friends at the time. "When you win big, you can have anything you want for a time," he said. "You come home with that big landslide and there isn't a one of them who'll stand in your way." "No," he sneered, "they'll be glad to be aboard and to have their photograph taken with you and be part of all that victory. They'll come along and they'll give you almost everything you want for a while, and then"—LBJ paused for a moment—"they'll turn on you. They always do." He could almost see it. "They'll lay in waiting, waiting for you to make a slip and you will. They'll give you almost everything and then they'll make you pay for it. They'll get tired of all those columnists writing how smart you are and how weak they are and then the pendulum will swing back."[11]

Johnson seemed haunted by the prospect of a confrontation with Congress, strangely obsessed with political constraints in this, the afterglow of his greatest political triumph. These fears sprang from an experience in LBJ's early political career. Johnson had first entered Congress in May 1937, just three months after Franklin Roosevelt had introduced his notorious Supreme Court reorganization bill. LBJ never forgot how Congress had seized on FDR's court-packing plan, attacking the President and crippling his political effectiveness just months after his landslide victory in the 1936 election.

Now, after the 1964 election, Johnson feared a repetition of Roosevelt's ordeal. He had no illusions about the present Congress's ability to humble him in the same way that a past one had humbled FDR. LBJ fretted about this to *New York Times* Managing Editor Turner Catledge shortly after his November victory. "Franklin Roosevelt came back here in 1937 after the biggest landslide in history," he reminded Catledge, a reporter in New Deal Washington, "[b]ut by April he couldn't get Congress to pass the time of day." Johnson paused heavily, then whispered, "You're not going to catch me getting into a mess like that."[12]

LBJ intended to avoid this fate by steering clear of any issue, such as Vietnam, which might provoke his opponents on the Hill. Johnson explained his concern to staff aides in early 1965. "I was just elected President by the biggest popular margin in the history of the country, fifteen million votes," he told them. But that margin had begun to slip. "Just by the natural way people think," LBJ said, "I have already lost about two of these fifteen." "If I get in any fight with Congress," he hastened to add, "I will lose another couple of million, and if I have to send more of our boys into Vietnam, I may be down to eight million by the end of the summer." In Johnson's mind, Vietnam seemed as big a threat to his Great Society as the Supreme Court bill had been to Roosevelt's New Deal.[13]

These were the pressures bearing on the President when William Bundy arrived at the White House on the afternoon of November 19 to brief him about the Working Group's efforts. Three members of the Principals Group— Rusk, McNamara, and McGeorge Bundy—also attended this meeting.

Rusk opened the discussion by reminding LBJ that important decisions on Vietnam lay ahead. He told Johnson the Working Group had begun preparing specific options to assist that process, and they would be ready for the President's decision by December 1.

LBJ then asked William Bundy to summarize the Working Group's proposals. Bundy outlined three choices: Option A, which he characterized as a continuation of present policies; Option B, which he termed a "hard/fast squeeze" against North Vietnam; and Option C, which he described as a slower, more controlled squeeze against Hanoi.

Utilizing what bureaucrats called the "Goldilocks Principle," Bundy had presented a list of options heavily structured toward Option C. Option A, given Saigon's rapid deterioration, seemed "too soft"; Option B, carrying substantial hazards of a wider war, seemed "too hard"; but Option C, which fell between these two, seemed "just right" and, therefore, most attractive and most acceptable. It appeared to avoid the pitfalls of A and B—preserving South Vietnam's future at least risk. To underscore his preference for Option C, Bundy described it to Johnson as the most sophisticated alternative— one which required a high degree of control Bundy felt sure Washington could manage.

LBJ listened to the Working Group's chairman without comment. At this point, McGeorge Bundy interjected. He noted the Working Group had begun focusing on Option C and would continue doing so, unless the President instructed otherwise. Johnson did not.

McGeorge Bundy then commented that work had not advanced on the "devil's advocate" exercise—the case for a negotiated withdrawal from South Vietnam. Rusk and William Bundy responded that Undersecretary of State George Ball had assumed the "devil's advocate" exercise but, because of other responsibilities, had made only limited progress.[14]

LBJ voiced no objection to the absence of a withdrawal option. He knew momentum mounted daily within the government for Option C and would only intensify if he remained silent. But Johnson expressed no desire to broaden the Working Group's deliberations, to extend his range of choices. He let the focus on Option C continue, increasing the likelihood it would be the one he ultimately adopted. LBJ may have dreaded the choices before him,

but not enough to consider withdrawal. That idea seemed too dangerous—
too politically explosive—to merit serious attention.[15]

Similar thoughts guided the Principals when they met, five days later, to
review the Working Group's progress.[16] The Principals first tackled Option
A. Continuing along present lines meant further deterioration, they felt,
eventually leading to a U.S. withdrawal. They conceded, however, that
South Vietnam might come apart under any option. Despite this admission,
Rusk, in particular, remained adamantly opposed to Option A. He believed
the consequences of a South Vietnamese collapse would be catastrophic to
U.S. interests, seriously undermining America's position in Southeast Asia.
For these reasons, Rusk considered withdrawal unthinkable.

With Rusk so vigorously opposed, Option A appeared doomed. Yet no
one present forcibly advocated heavy escalation under Option B. They all
gravitated to Option C.

Here is where the Principals focused their attention. But rather than
analyzing the merits of Option C, they simply concentrated on its execution.
The decision, itself, seemed a foregone conclusion.

The Principals suspected Option C might provoke increased North Vietnamese infiltration into the South—so strongly, in fact, that Rusk and Bundy
suggested introducing American ground troops near the DMZ to deter such
a reaction. Ball expressed serious doubts about committing U.S. combat
forces, citing France's experience during the Indochina War. He considered
an air campaign "better," because it would avoid "the French dilemma."
Though opposed to American ground intervention, Ball seemed amenable
to American bombing.

The Principals finally addressed the issue of negotiations, proposed by the
Working Group as an adjunct to escalation. They displayed little interest
in this side of the equation. Bundy saw "no hurry," he said, in pursuing
early talks. Like the others, he wished to strengthen Washington's bargaining leverage before approaching the negotiating table.[17]

As the Principals in Washington moved toward endorsement of Option C,
President Johnson restlessly pondered his Vietnam predicament at the LBJ
Ranch in Texas. Johnson knew important decisions awaited his return to
the White House after Thanksgiving. Seeking advice about which path to
follow, LBJ summoned his old Senate mentor, Richard Russell, to the ranch.

Russell visited Johnson on November 24. The senator conveyed a sense of
his meeting with LBJ to reporters when he returned to Washington the
following day. "We either have to get out or take some action to help the
Vietnamese," Russell said, remembering his conversation with the President,
because "[t]hey won't help themselves." "We made a big mistake going [in]

there," he added, "but I can't figure . . . any way to get out without scaring the rest of the world."[18]

Johnson's own frustration erupted during a news conference on November 28. Standing on the front lawn of LBJ's ranch, correspondents asked the President whether he contemplated expansion of the war into North Vietnam. Johnson, glancing wistfully toward the Pedernales River streaming past before him, offered a frank but bitter reply. "I don't want to give you any particular guideposts," he said, "[b]ut when you crawl out on a limb, you always have to find another one to crawl back on."[19]

The Working Group, which had been seeking that limb for the President, submitted its final report to the Principals on Thanksgiving Day, November 26. Bundy and McNaughton endorsed gradual escalation against North Vietnam, even as they raised doubts about its effectiveness. They expected bombing to weaken the Vietcong, but not to vanquish it, because the VC's "primary" strength remained "indigenous." They expected bombing to inhibit North Vietnam's infiltration of men and supplies, but not to stop it, because Hanoi, "[e]ven if severely damaged . . . could still direct and support the Viet Cong . . . at a reduced level."

Why did Bundy and McNaughton recommend a course promising such meager results? The answer lay in Bundy's assessment of the American interests at stake. Bundy depicted Washington's commitment to Saigon as a crucial symbol of its global credibility. Losing South Vietnam meant "a major blow" to that credibility, he asserted, undermining others' faith in America's resolve. Because of this, Bundy deemed the preservation of a non-communist South Vietnam essential, whatever the limits of escalation against North Vietnam.

With Bundy's political considerations in mind, McNaughton evaluated the proposed options. Although he favored Option C, McNaughton astutely analyzed the other two. Option A promised further deterioration, perhaps leading to American withdrawal. Yet it also meant, in McNaughton's words, that "defeat would be clearly due to GVN failure, and we ourselves would be less implicated than if we tried Option B or Option C, *and failed*. . . ." Besides, he added, "the most likely result would be . . . an eventually unified Communist Vietnam [which] would reassert its traditional hostility to Communist China and limit its own ambitions to Laos and Cambodia."

Option B, on the other hand, offered greater military results, tempered by the danger of a wider war. Hanoi and the Vietcong might be bombarded into a settlement, McNaughton wrote, but only at "considerably higher risks of major military conflict . . . with Communist China"—a prospect few wished to invite.

That left Option C, which McNaughton considered "more controllable
and less risky" than Option B and more likely than Option A "to achieve
at least part of our objectives, . . . even if it ended in the loss of South
Vietnam. . . ."

McNaughton's assessment of the various options, though persuasive,
masked deep contradictions. He had dismissed Option A because it meant
eventual American defeat, yet he suspected a similar outcome even under
Option C. He had discounted Option B out of fear of a wider war, but
could not anticipate with certainty how the enemy would respond to "controlled" escalation under Option C. McNaughton had embraced Option C
because it provided room for both his fear of losing South Vietnam and his
doubts about saving it.[20]

The same day Bundy and McNaughton tendered their final report to the
Principals, Ambassador Taylor arrived in Washington for the upcoming
White House meeting on December 1. Taylor brought with him a long and
gloomy report on the South Vietnamese situation, which one administration
official later characterized as "the bluntest high-level appraisal in the whole
story of American policy in Vietnam."[21]

Taylor reported that the Vietcong had made dramatic gains in recent
months, increasing in number as their control over the countryside expanded. Saigon's pacification program, meanwhile, had slipped so badly that
it now required "heroic treatment to assure revival." He blamed this deterioration on the current South Vietnamese government, whose "continued
ineffectiveness" stifled military progress. The Ambassador doubted this—or
any other—government could master Saigon's political divisions. "Indeed,"
he wrote, "in view of the factionalism existing in Saigon and elsewhere
throughout the country, it is impossible to foresee a stable and effective
government under any name in anything like the near future."

Since South Vietnam seemed unable to halt its decline, Taylor believed
the United States had to perform this task for it, by pressing attacks against
North Vietnam. The Ambassador expressed some anxiety about this approach. "[T]hese actions may not be sufficient to hold the present government upright," he confessed. But he saw no alternative to escalation, given
Saigon's desperate condition. Washington, Taylor concluded, must "be prepared for emergency military action against the North if only to shore up a
collapsing situation."[22]

Taylor repeated this suggestion, and General Westmoreland's reservation
to it, during a meeting with the Principals the next morning. He told them
Westmoreland favored postponing military action against North Vietnam
until political conditions in South Vietnam improved—perhaps six months.[23]

Taylor doubted Saigon could hold together for six months; he believed

Washington had to act sooner. The Ambassador conceded air strikes against Hanoi might not improve Saigon's political health. The others acknowledged this possibility, but endorsed Option C nonetheless.[24]

William Bundy, who also attended this meeting, put the Principals' recommendation into an "action paper" designed to serve as the focus of discussion at the December 1 White House meeting.

In his paper, Bundy outlined the proposed scenario: "first phase" "armed reconnaisance strikes" against infiltration routes in Laos, followed by "second phase" "graduated military pressures," or bombing, against North Vietnam. The "first phase" of Option C would start immediately. The "second phase" would be implemented later—if Saigon improved its effectiveness "to an acceptable degree" and Hanoi failed to yield "on acceptable terms." But Bundy qualified this requirement and, in doing so, revealed the planners' deepest concern. "[I]f the GVN can only be kept going by stronger action," he wrote, then "the US is prepared . . . to enter into a second phase program. . . ." Here lay the fundamental reason for Option C. Bundy and his colleagues viewed escalation primarily as a desperate remedy for South Vietnam's political decline.[25]

Tuesday, December 1, dawned sunny and cold in Washington, D.C. The previous day's snow, the first of the season, had covered the capital in a thin blanket of white. This wintry scene contrasted vividly with the humid, sweltering atmosphere of Saigon, whose troubles would occupy center stage at the White House that morning.

Johnson had returned to the White House over the weekend from his Thanksgiving vacation at the LBJ Ranch. His principal advisers, now assembled in the Cabinet Room, awaited the President's arrival.[26]

LBJ strode through the doorway shortly before noon. Pulling his high-backed black leather chair up to the Cabinet table, Johnson began by asking Taylor about South Vietnam's political situation.

The Ambassador sketched a dismal picture. "Weak government and Vietcong strength" continued to plague Saigon, he reported. Huong's month-old regime "won't collapse immediately," Taylor figured, but it already appeared a "losing game."

The President grudgingly agreed. It "looks like Huong is on a newspaper out in [the] middle of [the] Atlantic," LBJ muttered—whichever way he "moves, [he will] get wet and sink."

Johnson knew this spelled trouble. The "most essential [thing] is a stable government," LBJ stressed, indispensable to any progress. *"What's there we can do to hold it together?"* he lamented. "You can't use LeMay's bombers and McNamara's missiles."

Johnson knew political problems demanded political remedies. Huong needed "to pull all [of South Vietnam's] groups together," just as he had pulled Americans together following Kennedy's assassination.

"How [to] bring these people together," LBJ repeated—this represented the greatest problem. However difficult, Johnson wanted it done, even "if it takes all fifty [states] and [the] Rockefeller[s'] money." "They do it *or else*," he said, glowering at Ambassador Taylor.

Until South Vietnam achieved political stability, LBJ hesitated to expand American military action. Johnson saw "no point hitting the North," he explained, "if [the] South [is] not together."

The longer LBJ spoke, the madder he got. Suddenly, his frustration erupted. "Why not say 'This is it!'" the President shouted, and vow "not [to] send Johnson City boy[s] out to die if they [continue] acting as they are."

After this outburst, Johnson's anger subsided. He turned his attention to the military situation, quizzing Taylor about Vietcong and ARVN force levels.

The Ambassador cited "80-100,000 VC," which included "34,000 hard core; 60-80,000 regular and part-time" troops. South Vietnam's army, he noted by comparison, comprised "550,000 [soldiers]; 200,000 regulars."

The figures astounded Johnson: "How [can] 34,000 lick 200,000?"

General Wheeler, sensing the President's discontent with military progress, interjected praise for MACV's "excellent" counterinsurgency program.

An excellent program that had "failed," LBJ retorted.

This comment reflected Johnson's irritation at the growing pressure for dramatic new steps. The "day of reckoning [is] coming," he said, and "[I] want to be sure we've done everything we can." "[There have] got to be some things still to do," LBJ pleaded, but "what?"

To Taylor, the answer seemed clear. "We must get Hanoi out of the [infiltration] business," he told the President.

"But hadn't we better shape up *before* we do anything" against the North? Johnson responded. Otherwise, it would be like "send[ing] [a] widow woman to slap Jack Dempsey."

LBJ returned to this theme several minutes later. America's first objective in South Vietnam, the President emphasized, must be "to *pull [a] stable government together*." Turning to Taylor, he admonished the Ambassador: "Before Wheeler saddles up, try everything."

To emphasize his point, Johnson likened Saigon to a sickly patient. He hesitated "to sock" South Vietnam's "neighbor" with Saigon's "fever" running at "104 degrees." LBJ wanted South Vietnam "to get well first," so that when he told "Wheeler to slap, we can take [North Vietnam's] slap back."

"[I] doubt that Hanoi will slap back," Taylor answered.

"Didn't MacArthur say the same?" Johnson shot back.

Taylor, bridling at the President's reluctance, pressed LBJ to act. The "measures mentioned [are] needed," he said, "[b]ut not enough." The Ambassador felt he could "keep [Huong's] government going, fumbling" for "two or three months"—"not much time" to turn things around. Eventually, a move North would be necessary—along the lines of Option C. Taylor had finally brought the President to a verdict on escalation.

Johnson, having stubbornly resisted a decision, now accepted the Working Group's recommendations. "[The] plans you've got now," he said, "[are] all right." But LBJ then repeated his demand that Taylor "do [his] damndest in South Vietnam" before Washington moved into the second phase of Option C.

Yet Johnson remained wary, uncertain about the escalation he had just approved. Turning to McNamara, the President asked if he, too, believed "it's downhill in South Vietnam no matter what we do *in* country."

"Yes," McNamara replied.

LBJ had the reassurance he needed. "I agree" to go ahead, he said, but "[I] want conditions as favorable as we can get them." That meant giving Taylor "one last chance" to improve political conditions in Saigon. "If more of the same," the President declared, looking toward Wheeler, "then I'll be talking to you, General."[27]

Johnson had made a crucial decision which fundamentally altered America's involvement in Vietnam. The United States, heretofore assisting South Vietnam, now stood to become a direct participant in the war by bombing North Vietnam. LBJ had, to be sure, only conditionally approved this critical transition. But few expected Saigon's government to be strengthened through renewed political efforts—not William Bundy, not McNaughton, not Taylor, not McNamara, probably not the President himself. And if South Vietnam's political situation failed to improve, Johnson had now consented to go North.

LBJ's decision entailed deep and troubling contradictions. Again and again, Johnson had preached the need for stable, effective government in Saigon, convinced that action against the North demanded unity in the South. And yet, having stressed this requirement, he had authorized plans to bomb Hanoi should unity in Saigon prove elusive.

What is more, LBJ had assigned eleventh-hour persuasion to a man who seriously questioned its effectiveness. The President looked to Taylor to forestall implementation of Option C's "second phase." But the Ambassador had vigorously promoted bombing. Johnson had entrusted the political solution to a man who, more than most, favored the military solution.

Taylor, himself, knew from personal experience how elusive LBJ's demand for political stability and effectiveness in South Vietnam remained. He intended to see through the President's request, but with little expectation of success.

3

"Stable Government
or No Stable Government"

HAVING CONDITIONALLY approved the bombing of North Vietnam, President Johnson hesitated to implement this step while South Vietnam remained mired in political turmoil. LBJ still hoped that strengthening Saigon's government—and therefore its ability to combat the Vietcong—might lessen the urgency of striking Hanoi, which continued to support the insurgency.

While any hope remained, Johnson refused to reveal his alternate course. He chose, instead, to conceal it—from the public, the Congress, and much of the bureaucracy. Writing to Rusk, McNamara, and McCone on December 7, LBJ warned them to keep his December 1 decision quiet. "I consider it a matter of the highest importance," Johnson wrote his top advisers, "that the substance of this position should not become public except as I specifically direct." To ensure their compliance, the President held Rusk, McNamara, and McCone directly acountable, ordering them "to take personal responsibility . . . for insuring that knowledge of all parts of it"—the immediate strikes against Laos as well as the contemplated strikes against North Vietnam—"is confined as narrowly as possible to those who have an immediate working need to know."[1]

LBJ had pledged his subordinates to secrecy, but not himself. Troubled by the worsening situation in South Vietnam and the growing pressure for escalation, Johnson turned to an old Senate friend for advice on his dilemma.

Mike Mansfield's relationship with Lyndon Johnson dated back many years. The two had first met during the 1940s, as young congressmen in the House of Representatives. Their friendship had deepened when Mansfield joined the Senate in 1953. LBJ and his southern Democratic colleagues, who

39

wielded enormous influence there, had welcomed the soft-spoken Montanan into their inner circle.

Mansfield had moved easily within this group, his partisan loyalty and modest manner earning the Senate Majority Leader's respect without challenging his position. By 1957, Johnson had elevated Mansfield to Majority Whip. Three years later, Mansfield had returned the favor, supporting LBJ in his contest with JFK for the 1960 Democratic presidential nomination.

As Vice President, Johnson had maintained close ties with his successor as Senate Majority Leader, counseling Mansfield on the handling of Kennedy's legislative initiatives. LBJ had grown to trust Mansfield as an important and effective political ally. When Johnson himself sought election as President in 1964, he had offered Mansfield the second spot on his ticket. Mansfield, having witnessed LBJ's own unhappiness as Vice President, had declined Johnson's offer.

More than personal friendship and party loyalty, however, bound these two men together. Mansfield was also a perceptive student of Asian history, whose knowledge of Vietnam the President deeply respected.

Mansfield's interest in Asia had begun when he was a young Marine stationed in the Philippines, China, and Siberia during the 1920s. Mansfield had pursued this interest in college, at the University of Montana, where he became a professor of Far Eastern history in the 1930s. Later, as a member of the House Foreign Affairs and Senate Foreign Relations committees, Mansfield had witnessed the collapse of U.S.-Chinese relations and America's assumption of France's position in Southeast Asia.

Unlike many in Cold War Washington who had perceived these events through the stark prism of anti-communism, Mansfield had grasped a more complex reality. He had endorsed America's commitment to a non-communist South Vietnam, but also the need for stable, effective government in Saigon. Throughout the late 1950s and early 1960s, Mansfield had cautioned first Eisenhower and then Kennedy to secure a viable South Vietnamese regime—one which ably governed its people. U.S. success in Southeast Asia, he had warned, turned on this central issue.

The senator did not hesitate to offer similar warnings to Johnson. An independent man, secure in his convictions, Mansfield spoke frankly with a President whose domineering manner intimidated many others. LBJ respected Mansfield's candor and listened to his advice, particularly because the senator tendered it discreetly, as demonstrated by his private letter to Johnson on December 9. After learning from LBJ about the recent White House meeting, Mansfield wrote to warn his friend that Option C would take the United States "further and further out on a sagging limb." He saw little wisdom in expanding the war northward while political conditions in the south remained shaky. "[T]he government in Saigon is not adequate . . .

for negotiating a bonafide settlement," Mansfield wrote Johnson, "let alone for going ahead into North Viet Nam."

The senator then recounted Saigon's growing dependence on Washington, which he considered an ominous development:

> When Ngo Dinh Diem was in power there was at least a government with some claim to legitimacy and some tangible roots in its own people. Even when [Duong Van] "Big Minh" was momentarily in charge there might have been something to work with since he came fresh from a revolution with some claim to popular support. But we are now in the process of putting together make-shift regimes in much the same way that the French were compelled to operate in 1952–54.

Mansfield judged this to be precarious ground on which to build a military campaign against Hanoi. He believed the consequences of escalating the conflict, given Saigon's political weakness, would be "appalling." "Even short of nuclear war," Mansfield told LBJ, "an extension of the war may well saddle us with enormous burdens and costs in Cambodia, Laos and elsewhere in Asia, along with those in Viet Nam."

The senator cautioned Johnson against bombing aimed "to demonstrate the firmness of our will or our capacity to inflict damage." "We have amply demonstrated both," he reminded the President, "time and again." Instead, Mansfield urged LBJ "to think and act in a political sense in South Viet Nam"—to foster a government which could speak "with some native validity and authority" when the time for negotiations came, as he believed it should, given America's dangerous "over-commitment."

Should the President reject negotiations, Mansfield warned him to expect "years and years of involvement and a vast increase in the commitment" which, he hastened to add, "should be spelled out in no uncertain terms to the . . . nation."

Mansfield had spoken bluntly. He feared the course Johnson contemplated and had warned him of its dangers. He had admonished LBJ not to escalate, while advising candor whatever the decision. If the President considered the preservation of a non-communist South Vietnam truly vital to American interests, then Mansfield beseeched Johnson to express, fully and publicly, the costs of that commitment.[2]

Mansfield's letter captured LBJ's attention, echoing his own concerns about Saigon's political future. It reawakened doubts in the President's mind—enough that Johnson pressed his national security adviser, McGeorge Bundy, to answer them. Wasn't Mansfield right, after all, about South Vietnam's crippled condition? Hadn't LBJ, himself, raised similar points at the December 1 meeting?

Bundy submitted his rebuttal to the President several days later. While acknowledging the need for "a more effective and better supported government in Saigon," Bundy dismissed Mansfield's warning against escalation. "[I]t would be a mistake to make a commitment against any U.S. action . . . beyond the borders of South Vietnam," he wrote. To do so, Bundy argued, meant ignoring Hanoi's support of the Vietcong. He urged Johnson to stay the course. That entailed "years of involvement in South Vietnam," Bundy admitted, "though not necessarily 'a vast increase in the commitment,'" as Mansfield had predicted.[3]

Whatever his lingering doubts, LBJ sustained his earlier decision. On December 14, 1964, American bombers launched their first attacks against communist infiltration routes in Laos. The "first phase" of escalation, code-named BARREL ROLL, had begun.

Ambassador Taylor, meanwhile, had returned to Saigon armed with new instructions from the President. These instructions reflected Johnson's mounting frustration with Saigon and his desire for political improvement. LBJ cited two "primary causes" of trouble in South Vietnam: Saigon's instability and Hanoi's support of the Vietcong insurgency. Johnson did not, however, consider these problems "of equal importance"; he believed there must be "a stable, effective government to conduct a successful campaign against the Viet Cong even if the aid of North Vietnam for the VC should end." "While the elimination of North Vietnamese intervention will raise morale on our side and make it easier for the government to function," LBJ continued, "it will not in itself end the war against the Viet Cong." That required the political wherewithal Saigon had yet to muster. Until it did, Johnson hesitated to "incur the risks which are inherent in such an expansion of hostilities. . . ."

LBJ first wanted Saigon to meet certain "minimum criteria." They were hardly ambitious: an ability "to speak for and to its people"; the maintenance of "law and order in its principal centers of population"; and the effective execution of operations "by military and police forces completely responsive to its authority." So far, Johnson had seen little progress in any of these areas. Instead, he saw repeated evidence of "heedless self-interest and shortsightedness among nearly all major groups in South Vietnam."

Despite his lack of faith in the Saigon regime, LBJ authorized Taylor to initiate joint planning for the bombing of North Vietnam. Johnson instructed the ambassador, however, to emphasize the contingency of such planning—to make clear that air strikes against Hanoi would commence only "after the GVN has shown itself firmly in control."[4]

Taylor delivered the President's message to South Vietnamese leaders on December 7. The ambassador told Huong and Khanh to shape up their government; Washington would not initiate strikes against Hanoi, he said, until Saigon put its own house in order. That meant greater cooperation among South Vietnam's political factions.

It also meant military loyalty to civilian rule. For although Khanh had relinquished control to Huong, Taylor remained suspicious of the general's motives, expecting him to mount a coup the moment Huong faltered. The ambassador therefore urged Khanh "to express public confidence in the government and the firm intention to uphold it." The general, describing himself as happy to be "outside" politics, heartily accepted Taylor's proposal.[5]

Whatever Taylor's exhortations, Tran Van Huong's five-week-old government remained perilously fragile. A quiet, unassuming man with gentle instincts, Huong seemed ill-suited to hold the reins over South Vietnam's fiercely antagonistic rivalries.

In early December, Huong faced growing pressure from the Buddhists, who had tasted power in their confrontation with Diem the year before and now wanted more. Weeks earlier, Buddhists had launched street demonstrations against the government, assailing its appointment of Catholics to high ministerial positions. Hesitating at first, Huong had instituted martial law on November 25. The Buddhists had countered with more demonstrations, threatening to topple the government.

By early December, Buddhist leaders had begun organizing Huong's downfall. Two bonzes guided this strategy: Thich Tam Chau and Thich Tri Quang.

Thich Tam Chau seemed an unlikely agitator. A slight, soft-spoken man, Chau had evinced little interest in politics earlier in his career as head of the Institute for Execution of the Dharma, the intellectual center of South Vietnamese Buddhism. Chau had eschewed secular affairs, preferring Buddhist theology to partisan debate.

But Diem's mounting repression had shattered Chau's isolation. As Diem had tightened religious restrictions in the early 1960s, Chau had moved into the political arena, joining other Buddhists in protests against the president.

After Diem's ouster, Chau had remained politically active, relishing his newfound influence. By 1964, he had assumed direction of the Buddhist Institute for Secular Affairs as well, using this pulpit to denounce Catholic influence in first Khanh's and then Huong's cabinet. No government seemed acceptable to Chau anymore. As the bonze told newspapermen in early December, "It is better to have a political vacuum than have Huong in power."[6]

Chau's cohort, Thich Tri Quang, shared this sentiment. Well-educated, ambitious, and clever, Quang possessed a political acumen far exceeding his sense of political responsibility. He pressed Buddhist demands militantly and incessantly, whatever their effect on South Vietnam's fragile equilibrium. The only government the Buddhists wanted, Tri Quang frankly admitted, was any "government that agrees with our policy."[7]

Quang had first gained notoriety in May 1963, when, as the leader of Buddhists in Hué, he had organized the first massive protests against Diem, including the self-immolation of bonzes so shocking to Washington and the rest of the world. But Diem's downfall had not ended Quang's activism. As the newly appointed chief of the High Clerical Council, Quang had accused both Khanh and Huong of perpetuating discrimination against Buddhists and conspiring to reimpose dictatorial controls over political and religious expression.[8]

Quang's behavior reflected an arrogant sense of Buddhism's righteousness and power, itself a product of the bonzes' unexpectedly rapid success at helping ARVN to topple Diem in the fall of 1963. This success had fostered heady feelings among Quang and others, who perceived South Vietnam on the threshold of a "Buddhist Renaissance." This perception heightened Quang's expectations, while reducing his willingness to compromise. It also encouraged his disposition to scheme in order to hasten that Renaissance's arrival.

By December 1964, Quang sought to assert Buddhism's primacy in South Vietnam, with himself as its leader. He faced competition from Chau for this position. As both men struggled to control the movement, each pressed his verbal attacks against the government. Quang increased his pressure by demanding Khanh's resignation from the army and a reorganization of the cabinet. Chau followed suit. He abandoned his more moderate criticism of Huong and declared that, he, too, now opposed the prime minister. On December 10, the Buddhist "Struggle Committee," under Chau's and Quang's joint control, issued a communique denouncing the government and refusing any cooperation with Huong.

As the crisis mounted, Huong turned to Khanh for support, testing the general's commitment made in Taylor's presence on December 7. Khanh publicly endorsed Huong's government, promising to defend it against the Buddhists.

But General Khanh had his own agenda, despite assurances to Huong. Since yielding authority to the prime minister, Khanh had awaited his opportunity to reassert control. The Buddhist challenge offered that opportunity. Early in the morning of December 20, Khanh secretly approached Tri Quang, seeking his cooperation in a coup against Huong.[9]

Later that morning, Khanh's "Young Turks," led by Air Vice-Marshal Ky and General Thi, arrested several members of the High National Council, citing its refusal to sign legislation removing Khanh's old enemy, General Minh, and several of his allies, from the army. The Young Turks seized this occasion as a pretext to dissolve the HNC, creating an Armed Forces Council (AFC), under Khanh's control, as its replacement.

The action, predictably, infuriated Taylor, who immediately summoned the plotters to his embassy office. Rather than confront Taylor personally, Khanh sent Ky, Thi, and two other members of the new AFC—Rear Admiral Chung Tan Cang, chief of the South Vietnamese Navy, and Brigadier General Nguyen Van Thieu, the bright and ambitious new commander of ARVN's IV Corps—to face the ambassador.

The showdown began shortly after noon. Like a principle confronting wayward students, Taylor curtly greeted his visitors, many of whom had attended a dinner at Westmoreland's residence on December 8, where the ambassador had stressed the need for stable government.

"Do all of you understand English?" Taylor opened.

Yes, the Young Turks answered.

Taylor then launched his rebuke. "I told you all clearly," he said, that "we Americans were tired of coups." "I made it clear that all the military plans which I know you would like to carry out are dependent on governmental stability." "Now," he snorted, "you have made a real mess." His voice rising, Taylor added a warning: "We cannot carry you forever if you do things like this."

Perhaps the Young Turks knew better. Ky certainly did. Stung by Taylor's suggestion that he had thwarted the objective agreed on over dinner at Westmoreland's just days earlier, Ky sarcastically challenged the ambassador. "[Y]ou didn't waste your dinner," he said to Taylor, "because I can tell you, Mr. Ambassador, that I never had such a good piece of steak. As a poor man in a poor country I have never had the chance to eat such a good steak as you gave to us." "No," Ky went on, "I really appreciated your dinner."

Satisfied that his irony had registered, Ky suddenly switched gears, professing to Taylor his solemn loyalty to civilian rule. "We trust and support Huong," he declared; "We have no political ambitions." Having purged the government of its "bad members," Ky and his fellow officers were "now ready to go back to our units."

At this, Taylor finally exploded. "You cannot go back to your units, General Ky. You are up to your necks in politics!"

Ky insisted the Young Turks had no intention "to grab power."

Whatever the intention, retorted Taylor, "it is the consequence of what you have done."

The ambassador then turned to Khanh's role in the morning's events. Had Khanh directed the HNC's dissolution? Taylor asked.

"Yes," the Young Turks admitted.

Taylor, exasperated and bitter, looked toward the Young Turks leaving his office and said: "You people have broken a lot of dishes and now we have to see how we can straighten out this mess."[10]

One sure way, Taylor thought, lay in confronting Khanh—giving "shock treatment," as he explained to Washington, "to restore a sense of responsibility to the leadership of this unhappy land." So, the following morning, Taylor called on the general. The real showdown had come.[11]

Who ordered the HNC abolished? Taylor demanded.

The "army," Khanh replied.

Taylor had heard enough. He told Khanh that he had lost the ambassador's confidence; it would be best for Khanh to step down.

Taylor had forced the issue—laying out, in unambiguous terms, his displeasure at the general's scheming. He knew this might provoke more trouble from Khanh. But, as Taylor cabled Washington about their encounter, "If the military get away with this irresponsible intervention in the government and with flaunting proclaimed U.S. policy, there will be no living with them in the future."[12]

During his bout with Taylor, Khanh had intimated a willingness to step down, as the ambassador had requested. But the general sounded a different note to journalists the next day. Excoriating Taylor for activities "beyond imagination," Khanh defended the AFC's exploit. The military's decision "to again assume their responsibility before history is proof of their good faith," he proclaimed. Their action, Khanh suggested in an accompanying release, "speaks up for the political maturity of the Vietnamese armed forces."[13]

With these remarks, General Khanh had seized the offensive. Soon he launched a public campaign to oust Ambassador Taylor. But with Washington's backing, including a threatened cutoff of military aid to ARVN, and behind-the-scenes discussions between American embassy officials and South Vietnamese officers, the crisis gradually subsided, with Taylor and Khanh reaching an uneasy standoff.

Saigon's latest political skirmish exasperated President Johnson. LBJ wanted South Vietnamese bickering to stop; instead, he got news of the military's coup against the HNC and Khanh's vendetta against Taylor. The turmoil Johnson hoped to end, in order to avoid taking action against North Vietnam, had only worsened.

Discouraged and anxious about these developments, LBJ called Walter Lippmann to the White House shortly before Christmas to discuss the war. Johnson knew the journalist's position on Vietnam—negotiated U.S. withdrawal leading to a neutralized Southeast Asia. Though not administration policy, LBJ respected Lippmann's knowledge of foreign affairs and valued his advice.

During their conversation in the Oval Office that afternoon, the President openly mourned his situation. "This is a commitment I inherited," he complained to Lippmann. "I don't like it," Johnson grumbled, "but how can I pull out?"[14]

LBJ's uneasiness also reflected his sensitivity to popular opinion. Recent polls indicated deep division over the wisdom of American involvement in the war, with less than half the public—47 percent—believing "we did the right thing in getting into the fighting." Surveys also revealed growing discontent over Johnson's handling of Vietnam policy, with 50 percent saying that LBJ was "handling affairs there badly." This latter figure particularly concerned the President. Johnson knew his detractors included many conservatives who wished to prosecute the war more vigorously, to discard political pressure on Saigon in favor of military pressure against Hanoi.[15]

This thought dogged the President, at that moment preparing his upcoming Great Society agenda. For LBJ's agenda included a dramatic, and politically sensitive, shift in budgetary priorities: a 49 percent ($3.6 billion) increase in social spending, to be offset, in part, by a 2 percent ($1 billion) reduction in defense expenditures.[16]

Johnson expected strong opposition to this shift from proponents of military spending, including many powerful conservatives chairing key congressional committees. He feared these conservatives might vent their opposition indirectly, by championing escalation, in public, as a remedy to South Vietnam's decline and, in private, as a check on the President's social reforms. LBJ explained his fear privately to close friends at the time:

> If we get into this war I know what's going to happen. Those damn conservatives . . . in Congress . . . [are] going to use this war as a way of opposing my Great Society legislation. . . . They hate this stuff, they don't want to help the poor and the Negroes. . . . But the war, oh, they'll like the war. They'll take the war as their weapon. They'll be against my programs because of the war. I know what they'll say, they'll say they're not against it, not against the poor, but we have this job to do, beating the Communists. We beat the Communists first, then we can look around and maybe give something to the poor.[17]

Johnson anticipated rising conservative pressure in Congress; he encountered immediate conservative pressure in the media. Journalistic critics, impatient with the President's watchful posture, began pushing for stronger action in Vietnam.

They included, first and foremost, Joseph Alsop, a veteran Washington insider and confirmed Cold Warrior. Through his close contacts with high government officials, Alsop had quickly learned of LBJ's December 1 Vietnam conference. Johnson's marked reluctance at this meeting infuriated the hawkish Alsop, who started privately lobbying for tougher measures. In secret talks with Ambassador Taylor in Saigon later that month, Alsop assailed LBJ's hesitation, warning, in Taylor's words, that South Vietnam's situation was "deteriorating at such [a] rate [that] it is folly to withhold drastic military action"—even though Alsop perceived "no chance for Huong['s] government or any other government to achieve any degree of real stability." Alsop pressed his case relentlessly; as Taylor reported to the State Department through back channels, the columnist had urged the ambassador to "use [a] pistol on Washington to highjack the required decisions from timorous chiefs of [the] seventh floor and elsewhere."[18]

Alsop soon carried his escalatory crusade into print. On December 23, in his widely syndicated column, Alsop brusquely attacked Johnson's military reluctance in Vietnam. When urged to adopt tougher measures at a recent White House meeting, he wrote, "the President dodged the choice by saying that he first wanted to see what could be done about the political situation." Alsop chided LBJ's caution, suggesting that "if sterner measures are not taken pretty soon . . . the United States is almost certainly doomed to suffer the greatest defeat in American history."

Using this image, Alsop tried to goad Johnson to action. "There are plenty of discouraged Americans in Saigon who think the President . . . cannot bring himself to take the measures needed to avert defeat," he taunted. "But since the President has the means to avert defeat, he cannot disclaim responsibility." Alsop knew LBJ's political vulnerabilities and seized on them mercilessly: "It does not seem credible that Lyndon B. Johnson intends to accept and preside over such a defeat."[19]

Alsop renewed his pressure campaign in an editorial on December 30. This time, Alsop invoked JFK's action during the Cuban Missile Crisis to illustrate the political courage LBJ supposedly lacked. "For Lyndon B. Johnson," Alsop solemnly declared, "Viet-Nam is what the second Cuban crisis was for John F. Kennedy." Seeking again to provoke the proud Texan, he wrote, "If Mr. Johnson ducks the challenge, we shall learn by experience about what [it] would have been like if Kennedy had ducked the challenge in October, 1962." Alsop understood Johnson's insecurity in the realm of foreign affairs as well as his sensitivity to comparisons with Kennedy, and did not hesitate to exploit these weaknesses against him.[20]

Johnson suffered Alsop's attacks quietly. He spent the Christmas holidays in Texas pondering ways to reverse South Vietnam's decline without resort to the bombing of North Vietnam, which could jeopardize congressional attention to his domestic reforms.

LBJ hungered for solutions to Saigon's troubles that did not involve the risks of escalation against Hanoi. One possible solution arrived in a letter from E. Palmer "Ep" Hoyt, publisher of the *Denver Post* and a longtime Johnson confidant. Hoyt's associate editor, Bill Hosokawa, had just returned from South Vietnam with thoughts on the political and military situation, which Hoyt forwarded to his close friend, the President.

LBJ rarely read unsolicited mail, but he read this letter closely. Hosokawa's memo teemed with unvarnished observations seldom expressed to the President by his advisers. "The solution to Vietnam's problems lie *within* the country," Hosokawa wrote, "because they rise from *within* the country." As evidence, Hosokawa cited these items:

> This is a civil war, an insurrection, rather than an invasion. The largest percentage of the rebel Viet Cong forces are made up of South Vietnamese who have joined the Communist cause.

> The Viet Cong guerrillas are largely self-sufficient. They get 90 per cent of their military supplies in raids on government outposts, i.e., they are waging their war with U.S. weapons. When they run short of guns or ammunition they don't have to depend on supply lines from the north; they simply stage another raid.

> . . . [T]here are few vulnerable supply lines as we know them—only a few rail lines, highways and bridges in North Vietnam, and none in the border areas. What comes down from the north comes over jungle trails, on the backs of coolies, and most of these trails are invisible from the air. The threat to bomb cities and supply dumps in the north in retaliation for attacks in the south is a dangerous game of blackmail that could quickly escalate.

> . . . [T]he war in South Vietnam would continue for a long, long time even if we sealed that country off from the North. The guerrillas in South Vietnam have able, self-sufficient leadership. This leadership is encouraged and directed in a general way from the North, but none of this could be stopped simply by sealing off the borders.

Given these realities, Hosokawa believed the solution in South Vietnam lay in creating "a strong government that will unite the nation's war effort." Washington should "make clear in no uncertain terms that the first order of business is to establish a stable government so that the war can be won," the journalist concluded.[21]

Hosokawa's reasoning appealed to Johnson, evoking his own deepest concerns about Vietnam. LBJ forwarded this letter to McGeorge Bundy at the White House, along with a short personal note. "I very much agree with Hosokawa," Johnson wrote his adviser. "Put your good mind to work along this line and let's get something else moving on this front."[22]

South Vietnam's political climate, however, remained stubbornly volatile, with continuing Buddhist agitation weakening Huong's government and narrowing the likelihood of achieving the stability LBJ deemed essential.

As Johnson's hopes for political order in Saigon diminished, Vietcong terrorism intensified, creating new pressures to bomb North Vietnam, which LBJ wished to avoid. On December 24, a car bomb destroyed the U.S. officers' billet in Saigon—the Brink Hotel—killing two Americans and wounding thirty-eight others. Ambassador Taylor promptly urged Johnson to retaliate against Hanoi, both "to dampen [the] wave of terrorism which we can expect if [the] Brink affair goes unpunished" and, as Taylor particularly stressed, because "[w]e are nearing [the] point where drastic remedies must be found if we are to keep our [South] Vietnamese patient alive."[23]

LBJ resisted Taylor's overture. As he had following the November Bien-hoa attack, Johnson ordered no reprisals.

The President explained his thinking in a personal cable to Taylor on December 31. LBJ's greatest concern remained Saigon's persistent instability. Although most observers blamed the Vietcong for the Brink's explosion, rumors pointing to Khanh persisted. No one really knew who planted the bomb. Johnson considered this reason enough to refrain from hitting Hanoi. "This uncertainty," he wrote the ambassador, "is just one sign of the general confusion in South Vietnam which makes me feel strongly that we are not now in a position which justifies a policy of immediate reprisal."

LBJ had grown tired of repeated pleas for striking North Vietnam. "Every time I get a military recommendation," he pointedly reminded Taylor, "it seems to me that it calls for large-scale bombing." "I have never felt that this war will be won from the air," Johnson emphasized. The President had continually resisted such demands, convinced the war could be won only in the South.

But LBJ sensed a growing need to adopt tougher measures, if only to answer the chorus of critics clamoring for tougher action. Since Johnson doubted bombing was the answer, he turned his attention to another option—the introduction of U.S. ground troops. LBJ wrote Taylor:

> I am ready to look with great favor on that kind of increased American effort, directed at the guerrillas and aimed to stiffen the aggressiveness of Vietnamese military units up and down the line. Any recommendation that you or General Westmoreland make in this sense will have immediate attention from me, although I know that it may involve the acceptance of larger American sacrifices. We have been building our strength to fight this kind of war ever since 1961, and I myself am ready to substantially increase the number of Americans in Vietnam if it is necessary to provide this kind of fighting force against the Viet Cong.

Johnson stressed, however, that he had reached no firm decision; "I am not giving any order at all in this message," he hastened to note. "But in this tough situation in which the final responsibility is mine and the stakes are very high indeed, I have wanted you to have this full and frank statement of the way I see it."[24]

Although Taylor had failed to win LBJ's approval for air reprisals, he did not welcome Johnson's contemplated alternative. The ambassador explained his reservations to the introduction of American ground forces in a telegram to the President on January 6, 1965.

Taylor's thinking was simple. "[T]heir military value," he argued, "would be more than offset by their political liability." An old soldier himself, Taylor understood ARVN's weaknesses—its political interference, its low morale, its lassitude in the field. Introducing U.S. troops would not solve these problems; indeed, it might exacerbate them. As Taylor told LBJ:

> The Vietnamese have the manpower and the basic skills to win this war. What they lack is motivation. The entire advisory effort has been devoted to giving them both skill and motivation. If that effort has not succeeded there is less reason to think that U.S. combat forces would have the desired effect. In fact, there is good reason to believe that they would have the opposite effect by causing some Vietnamese to let the U.S. carry the burden while others, probably the majority, would turn actively against us. Thus intervention with ground combat forces would at best buy time and would lead to ever increasing commitments until, like the French, we would be occupying an essentially hostile foreign country.

Taylor harbored few illusions about South Vietnam's army. He had watched, at close hand, as Washington lavished financial resources and military equipment on ARVN, and still its operational effectiveness continued to deteriorate. If the United States assumed a greater share of the fighting, Taylor expected even worse results, with ARVN shifting more and more responsibility to American forces, until the U.S. found itself struggling against guerrillas in a distant land, unsupported by the army and resented by the people.[25]

Having counseled the President against American ground troops, Taylor still faced a rapidly worsening situation. The Vietcong had pressed their attacks in the countryside, wresting additional territory from an army whose "senior generals," in the ambassador's words, remained "closeted . . . plotting against the Huong government." Taylor, fearing for South Vietnam's future, considered new U.S. action imperative.[26]

But what action? Certainly not more political exhortation, in Taylor's judgment. His faith in this approach had been destroyed by Khanh and the Young Turks. Their move against the HNC had convinced Taylor that President Johnson's objective—stability in the South before strikes against the North—could never be met. The ambassador looked, therefore, to the bombing option, trusting military escalation to accomplish what political persuasion had not: order in South Vietnam.

Taylor made his case in a separate cable on January 6. He painted a dark picture for the President. "We are faced with a seriously deteriorating situation," Taylor told Johnson. Despite South Vietnam's military jeopardy, he perceived no end to the reckless squabbling among its leaders. "We cannot expect anything better than marginal government and marginal pacification progress," Taylor bluntly confessed, "unless something new is added to make up for those things we cannot control."

Here was the nub of America's dilemma. The things Washington could least influence or control lay at the heart of Saigon's troubles. Taylor identified them clearly: "chronic factionalism, civilian-military suspicion and distrust, absence of national spirit and motivation, lack of cohesion in the social structure, lack of experience in the conduct of government." These attributes reflected traditions deeply rooted in South Vietnam's political past. They were not easily susceptible to change, nor to U.S. pressure, as the ambassador had painfully learned.

Taylor recognized the imperative of political order in Saigon, but having lost hope of achieving that order through solemn appeals to the South Vietnamese, he turned, once again, to military action against the North Vietnamese.

The ambassador acknowledged LBJ's reluctance on this score. "I know that this is an old recipe with little attractiveness," he admitted. But Taylor perceived no alternative. "We are presently on a losing track and must risk a change," warning that "to take no positive action now is to accept defeat in the fairly near future."

Should Johnson approve his plan, Taylor saw few problems in implementing it. Washington could simply "look for an occasion to begin air operations" against Hanoi. "When decided to act," he suggested, "we can justify that decision on the basis of infiltration, of VC terrorism, of attacks on DESOTO patrols or any combination of the three." Having urged bombing as therapy for the South's political malaise, Taylor seemed ready to explain it in very different terms—as a response to aggression from the North.[27]

Ambassador Taylor's January 6 cables precipitated a feeling of crisis in Washington. His dark analysis, expressed in blunt and alarming tones, jolted policymakers who hoped current efforts might somehow stabilize Saigon's rapidly worsening situation. As soon as Taylor's telegrams reached the White House, LBJ immediately summond McNamara, Rusk, Ball, and McGeorge Bundy for a crucial conference in the Cabinet Room.

Twilight had begun to settle over Washington as the meeting began shortly after 5 p.m. The President and his advisers quickly focused on Taylor's grave prognosis and recommendations. Secretary of State Rusk, speaking first, stressed the seriousness of the moment. "We can't fail to make every effort to change the situation on the scene," he told the others, "because the alternatives are so grim."

McNamara agreed that "we should do all we can" in South Vietnam, but he feared "it won't be enough unless we do more." The ceaseless bickering among Saigon's various factions had crushed his faith in South Vietnam's political future. McNamara read from Taylor's December 20 conversation with the Young Turks, which Bundy had sent Johnson the previous night, to underscore his pessimism about further exhortation.

George Ball voiced even gloomier doubts about Saigon's political fortunes. "[This is] not a country—[but] a piece of one," he quipped, and one that had grown "damned tired after twenty years" of war. Ball then delivered a grim diagnosis: "[This] regime has got [the] smell of death. You can't pin 'em together."

Ball saw an ominous road ahead. Conceding that "[our] options are all bad," he felt that "risks of escalation [are] too great, if [the South Vietnamese] regime remains slippery." "We should make [a] heroic effort—but not delude ourselves," Ball advised the President, flatly adding, "We should be looking at diplomatic tracks to a bad end."

McNamara resisted Ball's assessment, arguing that stepped-up pacification efforts promised some improvement. Ball strongly disagreed: "We can do all manner of [these] things, but this doesn't get to [the] root of it"—the interminable political squabbling in Saigon, which Ball considered beyond Washington's power to mend.

Still, Ball offered no clear solution. "[D]o we take [the] diplomatic initiative?" he mused. "[D]o we risk escalation?" or "[Do we] keep on till we get asked out?"

Rusk judged the latter option unthinkable and unnecessary. "[I]n Asia, [we] have made bricks without mortar for twenty-five years," he asserted.

"You haven't" in South Vietnam, LBJ shot back, evidently frustrated.

McGeorge Bundy chimed in with his own assessment. He believed circumstances warranted instituting the long-postponed "Phase II" air strikes against North Vietnam, thus paving a "strong road to negotiations."

Ball questioned Bundy's logic. "[B]e aware of assumptions," he cautioned—particularly the notion that "[i]f we escalate the war it will strengthen [Saigon's] base."

President Johnson expressed similar doubts. "[I am] skeptical of [the] view that escalation can help us in [building] morale," he said.

"[E]scalation can bring two-way activity," Ball continued, therefore, "we must be ready to talk." After all, "large responses are possible."

"We all agree" on that, Bundy said, but something must be done to avert Saigon's imminent collapse.

Rusk shared Bundy's frustration, but not his enthusiasm for systematic strikes against North Vietnam. "Reprisal specifics are one thing," the Secretary of State remarked, "but 'Phase II' is quite another."

LBJ fully agreed. He let Rusk finish, then wondered aloud: "How can we go down the reprisal road without being ready? [I] have never thought reprisals would help stabilize the [South Vietnamese] government. They're not sufficiently effective to bring you to the conference table." But the President felt ensnared, "because escalation is dangerous and pulling out is dangerous."

Johnson resolved this desperate dilemma by approving reluctantly what he had questioned just moments before. "We are going to have reprisals," he said, hoping they "may help to give [Saigon] more stability." Again, the pressure of events had led LBJ to embrace what he instinctively mistrusted—escalation against North Vietnam.[28]

That evening, the President cabled his decision to Ambassador Taylor in Saigon. At last, Johnson expressed his intention "to adopt a policy of prompt and clear reprisal," but "without present commitment as to the timing and scale" of regular attacks against the North. LBJ, reluctant as ever, wanted to proceed slowly, testing the effectiveness of separate reprisals before launching a regular bombing campaign.[29]

He also wanted to proceed quietly, without revealing his step to the public. Rejecting McGeorge Bundy's advice to announce the new measure, Johnson instructed Taylor to reveal the decision through "inconspicuous background briefings rather than [a] formal public statement."[30]

This maneuver reflected LBJ's continued reluctance to confront publicly the problems of Vietnam. Johnson sensed the ominous trend of events—the interminable disorder in Saigon crippling the war effort and increasing the pressure in Washington to take stronger action—and feared its consequences: an Americanized war diverting national attention and resources from his legislative program. LBJ intended to minimize these political dangers by minimizing public awareness and debate.

It must be remembered, after all, that the Great Society, not Vietnam, represented Johnson's top concern at the beginning of 1965. Just three days before notifying Taylor of his acceptance of reprisal bombings, LBJ had delivered his State of the Union address. In that speech, Johnson had sketched his priorities during the coming year. Vietnam had received scant attention. In little more than 130 words, LBJ had briefly reaffirmed America's commitment to Saigon. The bulk of Johnson's address—more than 2,600 words—had been devoted to his expansive reform agenda: aid to education, health care for the elderly and the poor, urban planning, beautification, voting rights, support for the arts.[31]

LBJ elaborated these themes in his inaugural address on January 20. Standing on the Capitol steps in the brisk early afternoon sunshine, the President described, in moving language, his deepest desires for the country. "For every generation there is a destiny," he said. "For some, history decides." But, "[f]or this generation"—the America of 1965—"the choice must be our own."

Johnson had made those choices. "In a land of great wealth, families must not live in hopeless poverty. In a land rich in harvest, children just must not go hungry. In a land of healing miracles, neighbors must not suffer and die untended. In a great land of learning and scholars, young people must be taught to read and write." "For [the] more than 30 years that I have served this Nation," LBJ proclaimed, "I have believed that this injustice to our people, this waste of our resources, was our real enemy."[32]

Johnson's soaring rhetoric reflected his soaring hopes for the Eighty-ninth Congress. Graced with large Democratic majorities in both houses, LBJ anticipated a historic legislative session. In these circumstances, to quote William Bundy, "a major foreign crisis—let alone a war—was the last thing he wanted."[33]

Yet Vietnam would not go away; it kept looming closer, occupying more of the President's time and demanding tougher choices. The political crosscurrents Johnson was now piloting demanded extraordinary navigational skill.

To smooth his administration's passage, LBJ convened a meeting with Senate and House leaders on January 22, to discuss foreign developments, particularly Vietnam. Having recently authorized reprisal strikes against Hanoi, Johnson wanted Congress aboard, in order to forestall legislative debate jeopardizing his domestic reforms.[34]

LBJ opened by recounting his Vietnam troubles. He wrestled with the problem "all the time, day and night," he declared. The President said he now wanted to put the issue "on the table" for those present.

LBJ then mentioned his administration's "increased military activity" in Southeast Asia. But rather than discuss specifics, Johnson shifted to the importance of bipartisanship in foreign policy. He laid great stress on a "nonpolitical" approach to world affairs, citing Vandenberg's relationship with Truman and his own with Eisenhower. By the same token, the President felt Republicans should be in on his "foreign policy take-offs" as well as "crash landings." Slowly and carefully, LBJ prepared the political ground for escalation—seeking to disarm potential critics by involving them, if only implicitly, in his decision.

Johnson then asked Secretary Rusk to review South Vietnam's current situation. Rusk stressed Saigon's political instability, labeling it "our greatest problem in South Vietnam." He analyzed its consequences with devastating clarity. Until Saigon achieved political unity, Rusk perceived no end to Hanoi's interference. North Vietnam looked at the mounting disorder and took encouragement, convinced South Vietnam would eventually fall into its lap.

Rusk had addressed Hanoi's involvement in the conflict, without emphasizing its military support and political influence over the Vietcong—themes
commonly stressed in his public statements on the war. The Secretary, in
this private moment, had revealed his deepest concern, which centered on
Saigon's governmental turmoil.

This remained the President's deepest concern, too. LBJ told the congressional leaders that South Vietnamese, not American, forces must ultimately carry the struggle. "We cannot control everything that they do,"
Johnson said, but "we have to count on their fighting their [own] war."[35]

For Saigon to fight its own war, it first needed to mend its ruinous political
divisions. And this it still failed to do, thanks to General Khanh. His liqui-
dation of the HNC had seriously weakened Huong's government. Now
Khanh, having maneuvered himself back into partial power, intended to
complete the process by forcing Huong from office. Huong, the target of
Khanh's ambition, explained his situation well: "a thousand gold coins
won't buy a day of tranquility for a man in my position." Most observers
simply awaited Khanh's next move. As one Saigon official had remarked at
the time of the HNC's dissolution, "This is just the first act. Everyone is in
suspense to see how the coup finally ends."[36]

Before the final curtain, however, Khanh staged a conciliatory intermis-
sion. In feigned response to Taylor's pressure, Khanh signed, along with
Huong and Suu, a joint communique, reaffirming the military's unqualified
commitment to civilian rule. The agreement, released on January 9, 1965,
also mandated a new interim legislature—the "Constituent Assembly"—to
replace the toppled HNC.

Khanh had made his peace, however temporary, with Huong. That left
the Buddhists as the major element outside the coalition. Thich Tam Chau
and especially Thich Tri Quang now held the balance of political power
between Huong and Khanh; their allegiance would determine the final
victor.

Khanh understood that in order to regain power, he would have to parley
with the Buddhists. The general therefore approached Chau and Quang
once more, seeking their help in bringing down Huong.[37]

The bonzes readily obliged, resuming their anti-government agitation. On
January 12, Quang's followers launched a general strike in Hué. The same
afternoon, in Saigon, Chau denounced Huong's alleged persecution of religious dissenters.

As opposition to the government mounted, the American embassy received word of Khanh's latest plotting. Ambassador Taylor, whose personal
relationship with Khanh was in tatters, sent his deputy, Alexis Johnson, to
confront the general.

During their meeting, Johnson questioned Khanh about his latest political interference. The general, dressed in paratrooper's uniform and red beret, vehemently denied any intention of "returning to power." He laughingly dismissed rumors of a coup.[38]

Huong took them seriously. In a desperate attempt to neutralize military opposition to his civilian government, Prime Minister Huong appointed several Young Turks to the cabinet on January 18, including General Thieu and Air Vice-Marshal Ky. Through this reshuffle, Huong hoped to co-opt Khanh, by luring his supporters into the government and associating them with its policies. Instead, Huong's action gave the military an even larger voice in the government, while magnifying perceptions of his own weakness.

Emboldened by Huong's appeasement, the Buddhists intensified their agitation. Quang and Chau launched hunger strikes on January 20 aimed to hasten the Prime Minister's ouster. The two bonzes also dispatched a delegation to Taylor, urging him to force Huong's resignation, which the ambassador refused to do.

When these efforts failed to produce the desired result, the Buddhist leadership ordered their followers back into the streets. On January 23, mobs demonstrated before the American embassy in Saigon and sacked the United States Information Service Library in Hué.[39]

This triggered Khanh's final maneuver. Within hours, the Young Turks appointed by Huong began murmuring doubts about the Prime Minister's ability to govern. Khanh soon chimed in with his own public criticism, censuring Huong's response to the Buddhist revolts and hinting that "a more definite settlement is needed."[40]

The AFC imposed that settlement. On January 27, the Young Turks deposed Tran Van Huong's government, citing its inability "to cope with the present critical situation," and immediately petitioned Khanh to solve the crisis.[41]

General Khanh stood to reclaim the power he had relinquished but never stopped coveting. Yet his past pledges of loyalty to civilian rule now prevented Khanh, ironically, from assuming direct control. He therefore engineered the appointment of a figurehead premier, Nguyen Xuan Oanh, to serve both as his personal instrument in the government and as a buffer between himself and Ambassador Taylor.

Khanh's latest escapade, however predictable, threw U.S. policymakers into turmoil. One of the policymakers, John McNaughton, rushed to the Pentagon the morning after Khanh's coup to assess its implications with his boss, Secretary of Defense McNamara.

McNaughton arrived shortly before eight. He found McNamara already at his desk. Voicing a common frustration throughout Washington, Mc-

Naughton blurted that yesterday's events offered good reason to "dump" South Vietnam. After all, he told McNamara, Khanh's scheming had sabotaged the political stability on which America had staked its hopes. Yet McNaughton sensed a dilemma. Even if Khanh had betrayed Washington's desire to "help [a] friend," it still faced the need to contain China.

McNamara agreed, fearing U.S. withdrawal from South Vietnam would only shift the conflict with Peking to Malaysia and Thailand. And those countries would undoubtedly "go fast," he figured.

McNaughton then suggested three alternatives: striking North Vietnam, pulling back to a stronger position elsewhere in Southeast Asia, or simply plugging away along present lines. McNamara immediately dismissed the third option; to keep plugging, he commented, was to keep "drifting." Negotiation, given their assumptions about China, appeared equally untenable.

That left air strikes against Hanoi, which McNaughton seriously questioned. Bombing North Vietnam "might, but probably won't" help South Vietnam, he asserted. McNamara disagreed. He believed bombing would bolster political conditions in Saigon.

McNamara worried, however, about the projected scope of bombing. As outlined by the Working Group in November, air strikes would proceed slowly—first isolated reprisals, then systematic bombing. McNamara feared this "gradual squeeze" risked alienating American public support unless it produced quick and decisive results. He therefore rejected reprisals as "[t]oo narrow," favoring sustained air operations against North Vietnam instead.[42]

McNamara discussed his thoughts with McGeorge Bundy later that morning. Khanh's latest coup had disillusioned both men, destroying their hope that Saigon would ever achieve the stability Washington deemed essential. But rather than interpreting this as compelling cause for American disengagement, McNamara and Bundy interpreted it as requiring even deeper American involvement. If Saigon could not put its own house in order, they reasoned, then Washington would have to do so for it, through stepped-up military action against Hanoi.

Bundy conveyed his and McNamara's thinking to the President in a memo the same morning. "[B]oth of us," Bundy wrote Johnson, "are now pretty well convinced that our current policy can lead only to disastrous defeat." He then summarized that policy. "What we are doing," Bundy said, "is to wait and hope for a stable government." "Our December directives," he added, "make it very plain that wider action against the Communists will not take place unless we can get such a government."

Clearly, that effort had failed. Political conditions had not improved; they had worsened considerably. But rather than provoking doubts about the wisdom of escalation, this trend prompted Bundy and McNamara toward even bolder action. For these men were determined to do something—anything—to arrest South Vietnam's failure, including abandoning the objective of stability before escalation. They therefore urged LBJ to change "policy and priorities"—to seek stability *through* escalation.

Theirs was a fateful departure, and Bundy knew it. "Both of us understand the very grave questions presented by any decision of this sort," he wrote the President. "We both recognize," he added, "that the ultimate responsibility is not ours." But convinced the present course spelled certain defeat, he and McNamara felt "the time has come for harder choices."

Bundy admitted Rusk did not share their judgment. Rusk did not deny "that things are going very badly [or] that the situation is unraveling." "What he does say," Bundy told Johnson, "is that the consequences of both escalation and withdrawal are so bad that we must simply find a way of making our present policy work." "This would be good if it was possible," Bundy said. "Bob and I do not think it is."[43]

This memo marked Bundy's and McNamara's desperate response to desperate circumstances. Their colleague, George Ball, spelled out well the two men's thinking. "There had been a whole sordid series of coups, a feeling that the whole political fabric of South Vietnam was beginning to disintegrate, and that we had to do something . . . if we were going to keep this damned thing from falling apart," Ball later said, explaining Bundy's and McNamara's logic. "It [would be] a great bucker-upper for South Vietnam."[44]

Their logic prevailed. During a meeting with Bundy and McNamara that afternoon, Johnson agreed to prepare for action. "Stable government or no stable government," LBJ conceded, "we'll do what we have to do—we will move strongly. I'm prepared to do that," he at last declared.[45]

At this same meeting, the President decided to send McGeorge Bundy to South Vietnam to discuss planning for bombing operations with Ambassador Taylor and General Westmoreland. Before leaving for Saigon, Bundy cabled Taylor about the purpose of his upcoming visit. He wrote:

> The . . . central aspect of [the] current situation is the present and future prospect for "stable government." Present directives make such a government an essential prerequisite for important additional U.S. . . . action, but we now wonder whether this requirement is either realistic or necessary. If not, then we need to consider what actions are possible both within SVN and against the North while [the] GVN lacks [this] desired stability.[46]

Washington had clearly lost hope of achieving political cohesion in Saigon. Now it would seek that cohesion through escalation, in the belief that bombing the North would somehow resuscitate the South.

Bundy's mission to South Vietnam symbolized Johnson's long-postponed acceptance of the bombing he had embraced, in principle, nearly two months before. After weeks of agonizing and delay, LBJ had finally set in motion a policy fundamentally transforming America's role in the Vietnam War.

Johnson knew this, but took no comfort in that knowledge. Events on the evening of Bundy's departure for Saigon help explain why.

A military transport plane carrying Bundy and his party left Andrews Air Force Base late on February 2. That same night, in Selma, Alabama, Martin Luther King, Jr., sat in jail, reading the Bible. King and nearly 800 others had been arrested the day before on the steps of the Dallas County courthouse, protesting Alabama's discriminatory voting requirements. Armed with the recently passed Civil Rights Act, King and his followers had begun their final crusade against black disfranchisement in the South.

President Johnson intended to support King's crusade. His call for voting rights legislation in the State of the Union address testified to that. But LBJ realized this support entailed political dangers. Johnson's backing of King risked provoking southern conservatives in Congress who, if unwilling to challenge the President publicly on this issue, would exact their political revenge should LBJ stumble and lose Vietnam.

Bombing, with all its limitations, appeared more palatable to Johnson because it offered an important measure of insurance against this threat. As LBJ confided to friends at the time, "If I don't go in now and they show later that I should have, then they'll be all over me in Congress. They won't be talking about my civil rights bill, or education or beautification." "No sir," Johnson added with certainty, "they'll push Vietnam up my ass every time. Vietnam. Vietnam. Vietnam. Right up my ass."[47]

With this image haunting his mind, LBJ approached the threshold of escalation in Vietnam. That threshold was crossed during Bundy's trip to Saigon. In the course of that trip, the administration confronted a spectacular incident which propelled it headlong into a dramatic expansion of the war.

4

"*A Bear by the Tail*"

MCGEORGE BUNDY and his party landed at Tansonhut airport outside Saigon on the morning of February 4. Ambassador Taylor and General Westmoreland greeted the delegation, then drove them to the American embassy in the city. There, Bundy questioned local U.S. officials about Saigon's political troubles and whether those troubles could be solved without moving against Hanoi. The officials were doubtful. They knew a stable and effective government was essential, but conceded, as Bundy reported to Washington, that "[g]etting it is something else again."[1]

Bundy reached the same conclusion during his meetings with South Vietnamese leaders later that day. The parade of ambitious generals, ineffectual politicians, and dissident Buddhists—openly distrustful and hostile toward one another—confirmed Bundy's lack of faith in Saigon's political future. "The current situation among non-communist forces," Bundy cabled President Johnson that evening, "gives all the appearances of a civil war within a civil war."[2]

The South Vietnamese seemed utterly incapable of putting their own house in order. The bombing of North Vietnam which Bundy had urged, back in Washington, as a way to avert South Vietnam's political collapse appeared, on the scene, more necessary than ever.

Over the next two days—February 5 and 6—Bundy discussed various bombing proposals with embassy and MACV officials. He then asked John McNaughton, a member of his traveling party, to draft a specific program of air attacks. McNaughton outlined a plan of graduated strikes against North Vietnam tied, initially, to a "specific atrocity" and, thereafter, to a more general "catalogue of VC outrages." McNaughton completed his plan on the afternoon of February 6.[3]

* * *

As McNaughton finished drafting his bombing plan at the American embassy in Saigon, Vietcong guerrillas 240 miles north in Pleiku prepared for attacks which seemed almost tailored to McNaughton's scenario.

Pleiku, a traditional marketing center for Montagnard tribesmen, lay in a key area near the Laotian and Cambodian borders, where communist infiltration trails fanned out into South Vietnam's central highlands. These densely forested jungle paths, though barely forty miles from Pleiku, contrasted vividly with the gently rolling hills, dotted with trees, that marked the site of ARVN's II Corps headquarters and Camp Holloway, an American airbase two miles away.

At two o'clock on the morning of February 7, the Vietcong launched simultaneous attacks against both targets. Loaded down with explosive packets, VC guerrillas cut through ARVN headquarter's barbed-wire perimeter and silently crawled up a low hill toward the U.S. advisers' single-story barracks. Within moments, the compound exploded in a hail of dynamite charges.

At almost the same instance, mortar shells rained down on nearby Camp Holloway. Under cover of the shelling, guerrillas crossed a large clearing and bombarded the airfield with grenade launchers and demolition satchels. The twin assaults killed eight American soldiers, wounded over a hundred others, and destroyed ten U.S. aircraft.

The probable motives behind these attacks were as complex as the circumstances in which they occurred. Three days before, as the Bundy Mission had arrived in Saigon, a Soviet delegation headed by Premier Kosygin had left Moscow for Hanoi. The likely purpose of Kosygin's visit was to rebuild the Soviet Union's influence in North Vietnam, which had withered under Khrushchev. The Kremlin could thus bolster its position in Hanoi vis-à-vis the Chinese, while discouraging the United States from broadening the war. The Soviets probably also wished to forestall North Vietnamese actions which would provoke American reprisals, thereby raising the stakes in a war Russia wished to keep limited.

Hanoi, for its part, may have wished to offset its uneasy reliance on Peking by involving Moscow more deeply. By staging an attack likely to prompt a U.S. response, as at Pleiku, North Vietnam could put its Russian guest on the spot, making it difficult, if not impossible, for Kosygin to deny additional military assistance, including jet fighters and advanced surface-to-air missiles.

The Vietcong, on the other hand, may have feared that Hanoi, at Kosygin's urging, would negotiate a settlement with Washington at their expense. The VC could discourage such a settlement by launching an assault against an American installation, apt to provoke U.S. retaliation against North Vietnam.

Perhaps the most likely explanation for the Pleiku incident, however, lay in the established pattern of Vietcong attacks and American responses to them. Since its inception, the Vietcong had aimed to exploit South Vietnam's political instability and dissipate its already weak morale. Attacks on U.S. facilities and personnel were one way of achieving these goals; they underscored South Vietnam's reliance on American military support, while also exposing the vulnerability of that support. More important, the VC had staged dramatic assaults against U.S. targets in recent months—Bienhoa in November and the Brink Hotel in December—which had not prompted American reprisals. The Vietcong may well have believed that Pleiku offered another opportunity to strike without risk of retaliation.

Whatever the motive behind the Pleiku attack, it afforded Bundy an occasion—however sudden and unexpected—to recommend the air strikes he had been planning for several days. Bundy hinted as much to a reporter some weeks later. "Mac, what was the difference between Pleiku and the other incidents [i.e. Bienhoa and the Brink Hotel]?" the reporter asked. Bundy hesitated a moment and said, "Pleikus are like streetcars"—that is, one is sure to come along sooner or later, and you can hop aboard. Pleiku seemed a propitious moment to begin the bombing of North Vietnam which Bundy and others had already embraced as a remedy to South Vietnam's political failure.[4]

When news of the Pleiku attack reached Saigon later that morning, General Westmoreland rushed to MACV headquarters. Ambassador Taylor and Bundy arrived just minutes later.

Bundy telephoned the White House, where it was still Saturday evening, February 6. Cyrus Vance, McNamara's deputy at the Pentagon, took the call at the secretary's desk between the Oval Office and the Cabinet Room. Though troubled by Kosygin's presence in Hanoi, Bundy recommended, with Taylor's and Westmoreland's concurrence, an immediate reprisal against North Vietnam. Vance relayed Bundy's message to the President.

Johnson, who had prepared himself for this decision before Bundy's departure, now moved quickly. He hastily convened an NSC meeting in the Cabinet Room.[5]

LBJ started by asking General Wheeler to outline the timing of a reprisal strike. Wheeler said that planes could be over their targets within hours of a presidential decision. Then Johnson himself presented a list of four targets in southern North Vietnam, together with the estimates of military and civilian casualties. LBJ had taken command. He seemed ready to act.

Most of the others seemed ready too. Even George Ball, who harbored doubts about the wisdom of escalation, agreed that "action must be taken." Sitting before the President, Ball's personal skepticism weakened. Rather than express his private reservations about air strikes, Ball concentrated instead on how to "handle" them "publicly." "We must make clear that the North Vietnamese and the Viet Cong are the same," he said. "We retaliate against North Vietnam," Ball suggested, "because Hanoi directs the Viet Cong, supplies arms, and infiltrates men."

If Ball's comments sounded out of tune with what he had argued privately with Rusk, McNamara, and Bundy, they harmonized perfectly with Johnson's current thinking. The President's mind seemed settled, and Ball hesitated to challenge it.[6]

Ball read Johnson correctly. The President had, indeed, said Ball, "decided to make the air strikes." "We have kept our gun over the mantel and our shells in the cupboard for a long time now," LBJ snorted, angrily recalling his restraint following the Bienhoa and Brink attacks. "And what was the result?" he fumed. "They are killing our boys while they sleep in the night." Johnson had had enough; he was prepared to move.

The President spoke with a forcefulness that silenced most of those present. But not Mike Mansfield. Unlike Ball, who hesitated to confront this domineering man, Mansfield challenged him directly. Looking straight at Johnson across the Cabinet table, Mansfield cautioned him to re-examine his decision. Even if the North Vietnamese directed the attack, he said, it should have "opened many eyes." "[T]he local populous in South Vietnam is not behind us," Mansfield labored to note, or "else the Viet Cong could not have carried out their surprise attack." He urged the President to weigh this fact carefully, because a reprisal strike meant that America would no longer be "in a penny ante game."

Johnson was not in a reflective mood. He heard Mansfield out, and then brusquely ordered a reprisal strike.[7]

Four hours later, U.S. bombers roared off Navy carriers steaming in the Tonkin Gulf and struck military barracks and storage facilities at Donghoi, fifty miles north of the DMZ. This operation, code-named FLAMING DART, marked the first American air strike against North Vietnam since the previous August.

Several hours after the reprisal attack—it was now Sunday morning, Washington time—President Johnson summoned his advisers and congressional leaders to assess its results.[8]

Mike Mansfield had left the previous day's session feeling uneasy. He had watched LBJ, who felt personally challenged by the communist attack, react angrily, abruptly ordering a U.S. reprisal with little thought about its consequences. Mansfield wanted to temper Johnson's anger before he plunged

America irrevocably into war. The senator therefore urged LBJ to pursue a diplomatic solution to the crisis. "I would negotiate. I would not hit back. I would get into negotiations," the senator cautioned Johnson.

"I just don't think you can stand still and take this kind of thing," LBJ snapped, still smarting from the Pleiku attack, "you just can't do it."

The U.S. reprisal for the Pleiku attack had been only partly successful. All but one of the four planned targets had been weathered in. Should planes return to bomb the other three, as Ambassador Taylor now recommended?

McNamara said no, as did Ball, who spoke up with a boldness he lacked the evening before. Ball had been willing to go along quietly with a single reprisal, but the idea of a second strike, which might signal the beginning of a sustained offensive, prompted his objection. "Secretary McNamara is right in recommending that we should not hit today the three targets not hit yesterday," Ball observed, "If we do so, the Communists will get a wrong signal and think that we are launching an offensive . . . rather than merely retaliatory strikes to attacks by the North Vietnamese and the Viet Cong."

Ambassador Thompson also opposed a second strike. "We have completed our reprisal action for the North Vietnamese surprise attack," he said. "Another attack cannot be called reprisal." Unless Johnson intended to embark on a radically new course, Thompson believed, "[n]o additional air strikes should be made now."

House Minority Leader Gerald Ford failed to perceive Ball's and Thompson's distinction. "Why should we only hit one out of four targets?" he asked. "If the plan to strike four was good, why should we not complete it?"

The President's answer to Ford reflected his continued reluctance to take the big step. A single reprisal was one thing, he told Ford; systematic bombing was quite another. Johnson said he would give "consideration to Taylor's recommendation," but for the time being, he ordered no further strikes. LBJ still hesitated to commit himself.[9]

About eleven o'clock that night, McGeorge Bundy arrived back in Washington with a report aimed to hasten LBJ's decision. The report, which Bundy had outlined before the Pleiku attack and finished during his long flight back to the United States, urged the immediate and systematic bombing of North Vietnam.

Bundy took his report to the White House, where he delivered it personally to Johnson. LBJ stayed up late that night studying Bundy's report. What he read must have troubled him deeply. "The situation in Vietnam is deteriorating," Bundy opened, "and without new U.S. action defeat appears inevitable. . . ." South Vietnam seemed on the verge of collapse. The Vietcong had extended their control over the countryside, while the government's pacification program continued to flounder. Bundy believed this trend, if not checked, would surely lead to "Communist domination."

Although the South Vietnamese did not find the prospect of communist domination "attractive," Bundy sensed little determination on their part to prevent it. Instead, he described a "worrisome lassitude" and "distressing absence of positive commitment to any serious social or political purpose" among the Vietnamese people.

South Vietnam's problems were especially grave, Bundy argued, because of the American interests intertwined with them. He defined those interests to Johnson in graphic and expansive terms:

> The stakes in Vietnam are extremely high. The American investment is very large, and American responsibility is a fact of life which is palpable in the atmosphere of Asia, and even elsewhere. The international prestige of the United States, and a substantial part of our influence, are directly at risk in Vietnam.

Given this view of the stakes, it was not surprising that Bundy dismissed the idea of a negotiated withdrawal, which he derided as "surrender on the installment plan."

Bundy wanted Johnson to halt South Vietnam's decline, not to extricate the United States from it. A policy of "graduated and continuing reprisal" against North Vietnam seemed "the most promising" way to do this, he suggested.

Bundy explained his objective. "Action against the North," he noted, "is usually urged as a means of affecting the will of Hanoi to direct and support the VC." That was not Bundy's purpose. "[O]ur primary target," he stressed, "is the improvement of the situation in *South* Vietnam."

Bundy argued that bombing Hanoi would stiffen Saigon politically. Sustained attacks against the North would produce "a sharp immediate increase in optimism in the South," thereby increasing "the readiness of Vietnamese factions . . . to join together in forming a more effective government."

Bundy considered this urgent because the present government, in his words, had been reduced to "caretaker" status. His description of the current Saigon regime was shocking. It "can execute military decisions and . . . give formal political support to joint US/GVN policy," Bundy wrote Johnson. "That is about all it can do," he added.

South Vietnam's political situation demanded quick treatment, and the Pleiku attacks offered a good occasion to begin that treatment. "These attacks and our reaction to them," suggested Bundy, "have created an ideal opportunity for the prompt . . . execution of sustained reprisals."

Bundy then outlined the proposed transition—how LBJ could stretch the day's single strike against Donghoi into a systematic bombing campaign against North Vietnam. Initially, he proposed relating "our reprisals to those acts of relatively high visibility such as the Pleiku incident." Later—after reprisals were "under way"—Bundy felt it would "not be necessary to con-nect each specific act against North Vietnam to a particular outrage in the South." Having established a "generalized pattern of reprisal" in response to "specific atrocities," Johnson could move quietly into sustained bombing.

Bundy hoped this plan would produce results in South Vietnam; he knew it involved costs to the United States. A bombing program, he wrote the President,

> implies significant U.S. air losses even if no full air war is joined, and it seems likely that it would eventually require an extensive and costly effort against the whole air defense system of North Vietnam. U.S. casualties would be higher—and more visible to American feelings—than those sustained in the struggle in South Vietnam.

Bundy counseled Johnson to accept these costs, even if he could not assure him that bombing would change the course of the war. Why? Because Bundy considered bombing an essential defense against potential conserva-tive criticism. Even if the bombing "fails," Bundy told the President, "the policy will be worth it." "At a minimum," he reminded Johnson, "it will damp down the charge that we did not do all that we could have done, and this charge will be important in many countries, including our own." Here, in different language, was the President's own concern. Bombing, despite all its limitations, would offer protection against conservative attacks in the wake of a South Vietnamese collapse—which seemed frighteningly possible at that moment.

Bundy had argued his position skillfully. He sensed that Johnson's reluc-tance to deepen America's involvement in Vietnam related to Vietnam's potential impact on the Great Society. Therefore, Bundy reduced the case for sustained bombing to its political essentials, which he knew would resonate in LBJ's mind.

If Bundy understood Johnson's reluctance and how to exploit it, he also recognized Johnson's furtiveness and wished to dispel it. For this reason, Bundy ended his report with a delicate plea for Presidential frankness. "At its very best the struggle in Vietnam will be long," he wrote. Therefore, "[i]t seems . . . important," he concluded, "that this fundamental fact . . . and our understanding of it be made clear to our own people. . . ." Bundy had urged Johnson to escalate, but had also urged him to admit, publicly and forthrightly, the costs of escalation.[10]

Bundy's plea, especially his political calculations, struck home with LBJ.

As he said later of the report, "I was impressed by its logic and persuaded strongly by its arguments." Johnson's fears about the international and particularly the domestic repercussions of losing South Vietnam had overcome his reservations about the wisdom of escalation against North Vietnam.[11]

Having accepted, at last, the idea of sustained bombing which he had resisted for months, LBJ convened a meeting with his top advisers and congressional leaders at 10:30 the next morning.[12]

Johnson opened the meeting by summarizing his current thinking. LBJ said he had approved a "program" of "further pressure" against North Vietnam last December, but had delayed implementing it in the hope that Ambassador Taylor could secure a stable government in South Vietnam. Taylor had failed; the political situation in Saigon had not improved.

The President said he was now ready to adopt the December "program." But rather than describe the bombing as Bundy's report had explained it—an "extensive and costly" expansion of the war entailing "higher" and "more visible" American casualties—Johnson characterized it as an effort to defeat North Vietnamese aggression *"without escalating the war"* (emphasis added). LBJ had revealed his bombing decision, while carefully concealing its dimensions.

LBJ then asked McGeorge Bundy to outline the report which had prompted his decision. Taking his lead from the President, Bundy summarized his report in vague and general terms—so vague, in fact, that Representative Ford was uncertain what Bundy had recommended. Was it the December program? he asked Bundy. Johnson quickly interrupted. Sidestepping Ford's question about the nature of Bundy's recommendation, the President emphasized the support for it within the administration. All members of the country team, as well as his top advisers, backed the recommendation, Johnson declared, again without revealing its full dimensions.

The Minority Leader kept pressing, however. Did this "program" require "additional U.S. personnel and . . . financial assistance?" Ford asked. Here was the kind of question LBJ dreaded—a question about more guns for Vietnam, which meant less butter for his Great Society. Johnson swiftly assured the House Republican Leader that his "program" required no additional expenditures. If he needed more resources in the future, the President added, he would request them from Congress.

Johnson's comments still baffled Ford. What did the President intend to do, he again asked, just react to future Vietcong provocations? LBJ responded vaguely. All VC attacks did call for a "response," the President replied, but he did not intend to limit his actions to retaliating against VC attacks. Artfully, Johnson had implied a policy of sustained bombing without explicitly stating it.

Senator Dirksen then asked what would happen if the United States pulled out of South Vietnam—if Washington reduced its commitment now rather than deepening it. McGeorge Bundy, as he had in his report to Johnson, ascribed fateful consequences to an American withdrawal. Bundy said that a U.S. pullout would weaken the confidence of other nations in America's resolve, from East Asia to West Berlin.

Dirksen then raised the issue of another congressional resolution. Johnson vigorously denied this need, whatever "the views of a few Senators"—referring to Ernest Gruening and Wayne Morse; the Tonkin Gulf Resolution, together with the constitutional powers of the presidency, enabled him to carry out his decision. The assertion, forcefully made here, hid that much older resolve on Johnson's part to avoid renewed congressional debate over Vietnam at the expense of his reform agenda.

Quieted by LBJ's show of authority, Dirksen turned to the issue of public disclosure. What could he tell the press? Dirksen asked. Johnson urged him not to say that Washington was "broaden[ing] the war." Clearly, then, despite his decision to adopt a new and far-reaching policy, Johnson intended to project the image of continuity—to suggest this great departure represented no departure at all.[13]

LBJ was considerably more candid in his cable to Ambassador Taylor that evening reporting his bombing decision. Johnson recalled the conditions he had set, back in December, for undertaking air strikes against North Vietnam. "We then felt it important to establish as strong a government as possible," the President wrote, "and you have been doing your level best to that end." But Taylor's efforts—thanks to Khanh, the Young Turks, and the Buddhists—had failed. The Saigon government was in shambles, with little likelihood that South Vietnam's competing factions would ever make peace.

Johnson had resigned himself to this fact. "I am now prepared to go forward with the best government we can get," he said, "and accordingly . . . I have today decided that we will carry out our . . . plan for continuing action against North Vietnam. . . ." LBJ stressed that his primary objective was to bolster morale in Saigon, not to punish Hanoi for its aggression. The President hoped, as he wrote Taylor, "that the building of a minimum government will benefit by . . . assurances from us to the highest levels [of the South Vietnamese government] that we . . . intend to take continuing action." Johnson now intended to seek through force against North Vietnam what Taylor had failed to achieve through persuasion in South Vietnam.

LBJ had approved the bombing offensive, but he wanted to postpone launching it until Soviet Premier Kosygin, still in North Vietnam, had left the country. Thus, Johnson instructed Taylor to delay informing Oanh's government of his decision "until we have determined precise opening moves, and until Kosygin is safely out of Hanoi." This would allow Washington time to plan its strikes, while also avoiding any affront to the Soviet leader.[14]

But the Vietcong did not give Johnson the time he wanted. On the evening of February 10, VC guerrillas bombed a U.S. army billet at Quinhon, eighty miles east of Pleiku along the central South Vietnamese coast, killing twenty-three Americans and wounding twenty-one others.

When LBJ received word of the Quinhon attack, he called the NSC into session once more.[15]

McNamara, speaking for himself and the Joint Chiefs, urged the President to begin sustained bombing immediately. The Pentagon had already prepared a target list, he noted, and the VC attack justified implementing it right away.

Quinhon had increased the pressure on Johnson to launch the bombing he had wished to postpone for several days. It had not, however, lessened LBJ's determination to conceal his basic decision. Johnson warned those seated around the Cabinet table to keep quiet about any change in policy. LBJ wanted no disclosures to the press, he cautioned. Johnson would hold department heads responsible for any leaks from their subordinates, he pointedly added.

LBJ then probed his advisers about the bombing. Should we proceed? he asked, still leery about making the fateful commitment. Vice President Humphrey suggested postponing the bombing until Kosygin, soon heading for North Korea, had left the Far East. Ambassador Thompson, the Soviet expert at the meeting, also urged delay, warning Moscow might interpret the bombing as a deliberate effort to humiliate Russia. Thompson, like Humphrey, had criticized the timing of the bombing, not the bombing itself. Johnson had apparently decided that issue, and neither seemed eager to challenge it.

Discussion then shifted to public disclosure. LBJ claimed the White House had gone into "great detail" about the Donghoi raid, but he did not think it "necessary" following another one. Press statements should be limited to a "generalized description" of U.S. action, Johnson insisted. LBJ remained determined to obscure the escalation.

Finally, at the end of the meeting, Johnson approved the recommended strike plan.[16]

Less than twelve hours later, American and South Vietnamese bombers struck military barracks and storage facilities near Chaple and Chanhhoa, North Vietnam. This attack—the second in four days—marked the end of reprisals and the beginning of a systematic bombing campaign.

LBJ had crossed the divide, committing American forces directly to the war. Yet Johnson's White House barely hinted at this fundamental shift in its statement to the press. On February 7, the administration had explained the Donghoi raid as a "retaliatory attack" launched in specific reprisal for the Pleiku incident. "As in the case of . . . the Gulf of Tonkin last August," the release had carefully noted, "the response is appropriate and fitting." A one-shot affair. Now, on February 11, the White House characterized its latest attack as a response to "further . . . provocations" designed to halt a "continuation of aggressions and outrages." President Johnson had masked the transition to sustained bombing in language which suggested almost no transition at all.[17]

LBJ obscured this momentous transition in private conversations as well. Chatting with visitors to the Oval Office during this period, Johnson ridiculed talk of "crisis" as exaggerated and unnecessary. "They woke us up in the middle of the night, and we woke them up in the middle of the night," LBJ said in describing the first air attack. "Then they did it again, and we did it again," he breezily remarked of the second. No dramatic change, no new commitment—just a predictable response to provocation.[18]

Perhaps the clearest evidence of Johnson's intention to conceal his bombing decision lay in McGeorge Bundy's remark to his brother, the Assistant Secretary of State, charged with notifying other governments of the administration's military action. "Look, get this straight," McGeorge warned his brother, William, "the President does not want this depicted as a change of policy."[19]

Why had Johnson insisted on cloaking this fateful step in the muffled tones of apparent continuity? Clearly, LBJ wished to forestall domestic and international pressure for negotiations until the bombing had strengthened America's bargaining leverage with North Vietnam. But, more important, perhaps, Johnson feared the bombing's impact on the Great Society. LBJ, in February 1965, wanted nothing to divert congressional attention from his legislative initiatives, now arriving almost daily on the Hill; he knew nothing would divert it quicker than talk of escalating into major war. Therefore, Johnson deliberately concealed his bombing decision, hoping to save South Vietnam without jeopardizing his Great Society.

Although LBJ had committed himself to the bombing, its scope and objectives remained largely undefined. How many strikes? Of what intensity? Seeking what particular results? As Johnson considered these questions, George Ball prepared a memorandum offering answers far different from those of most of his colleagues.

McGeorge Bundy and Robert McNamara had urged bombing as a way to prevent Saigon's collapse, as a way to preserve America's commitment to South Vietnam. Though Ball had opposed their recommendation, LBJ had accepted it. Ball, therefore, shifted tactics. He now urged bombing as a means to "increase United States bargaining power . . . to the point where a satisfactory political solution" became possible. If Ball could not block the bombing, he hoped to divert it, toward achieving a negotiated withdrawal from South Vietnam.

Ball also challenged McNamara and Bundy by stressing bombing's potential dangers. He emphasized several risks, particularly the likelihood of North Vietnamese retaliation. Ball believed bombing might prompt Hanoi to send as many as 125,000 troops down the Ho Chi Minh Trail and across the DMZ into South Vietnam. Such action "would clearly require substantial increases of US ground, air and naval forces," he warned.

More ominous was the threat of Chinese intervention. Mounting air attacks, Ball noted, might trigger "direct engagement of Chinese planes operating from the sanctuary of Chinese territory." This, in turn, would generate enormous pressure to "knock out" the Chinese air bases. Peking might up the ante even further, moving "massive ground forces" into Southeast Asia. Washington would then face an agonizing prospect: committing "five to eight divisions with a total troop strength . . . of 300,000 men" or even resorting to atomic weapons, thus raising "the most profound political problems."

Ball emphasized these risks because he believed bombing's effectiveness had been exaggerated. Ball doubted North Vietnam would submit easily:

[S]hort of a crushing military defeat . . . Hanoi would never abandon the aggressive course it has pursued at great cost for ten years and give up all the progress it has made in the Communization of South Viet-Nam. For North Viet-Nam to call off the insurgency in South Viet-Nam, close the border, and withdraw the elements it has infiltrated into that country would mean that it had accepted unconditional surrender.

Vanquishing Hanoi would require a massive bombing effort—one that entailed substantial risk of nuclear war with China. Ball did not believe Johnson wished to accept such a risk.

Ball had urged LBJ to limit his risks but not to avoid them entirely. He had stressed the hazards of bombing, without opposing the policy itself. Ball still hesitated to challenge Johnson's decision directly.[20]

Ball met with LBJ on February 13 to discuss his memorandum. Johnson took the memo, skimmed it quickly, and then asked Ball to summarize it. Ball reviewed each point. The President listened impatiently. He had his own concerns about escalation. He, too, harbored doubts about the bombing. But he had made his decision, and nothing Ball said had changed it.

Later that afternoon, Johnson approved a program of continuing air strikes against various targets in southern North Vietnam. It fell to Acting Secretary of State Ball, ironically, to report LBJ's decision to Ambassador Taylor in Saigon. Ball cabled Taylor that the attacks, scheduled to begin "as early as possible," would occur "about once or twice a week and involve two or three targets on each day of operation."

Although this plan represented a fundamental shift in American involvement—from advisory assistance to direct participation in the war—Johnson remained determined to obscure the transition. The President would not go to Congress. He would not address the people. Instead, Ball informed Taylor, Johnson planned to reveal the bombing, "in general terms," through a press statement. LBJ was tiptoeing to war in Vietnam.[21]

Johnson seemed ready, at last, to move against Hanoi. He had approved a program of continuing air strikes, and a time frame within which they would begin. After much hesitation, LBJ had finally committed himself to the bombing. But just as Johnson prepared to act, he received a memo from Vice President Humphrey which shook his resolve. Humphrey's memo, analyzing the domestic repercussions of escalation, upset the determination of a President concerned, above all else, with Vietnam's impact on the Great Society.

Hubert Humphrey occupied a difficult position in Lyndon Johnson's administration. The Vice President was an experienced politician of independent convictions, who owed his present office to one man: LBJ. He was an ardent liberal, committed to domestic reform, in an administration increasingly absorbed with the problem of Vietnam.

Johnson viewed Humphrey much as Kennedy had viewed him—a valuable asset in dealing with Congress on domestic issues, not a trusted adviser on foreign policy. Humphrey knew the Hill well and could help guide the President's Great Society measures through its chambers. He knew little, however, about decision-making on Vietnam.

The NSC meeting on February 10 had changed that. Humphrey had listened as Johnson, McNamara, and Bundy discussed bombing in familiar terms—debating not its merits, only its implementation. Humphrey had raised doubts which LBJ had brushed aside. Whatever his qualms about escalation, Johnson seemed unconcerned with Humphrey's opinion; after all, he was no expert on foreign affairs.

But the Vice President was an expert on American politics and shared LBJ's devotion to the Great Society. Therefore, when Humphrey sent Johnson a memo on February 15 warning him about the bombing's dangers to the Great Society, LBJ took notice.

Humphrey realized that Johnson was on the threshold of major escalation, and wanted to prevent it. He reminded LBJ of the recent presidential campaign. Goldwater, he wrote, had "stressed the Vietnam issue, advocated escalation, and stood for a military 'solution.' " "By contrast we stressed steadiness, staying the course, not enlarging the war. . . ." The voters had voiced their preference—overwhelmingly against Goldwater's "trigger-happy" image.

But now Johnson seemed to be adopting the very position the voters had rejected. Humphrey considered this not just politically dangerous but strategically foolish. "We have never stood for military solutions alone, or for victory through air power," he said. "We have always stressed the political, economic and social dimensions" of world problems.

Vietnam was a perplexing war, Humphrey added—one that the American people found hard to fathom. He cautioned LBJ to remember this, as he pondered escalation:

> American wars have to be politically understandable by the American public. There has to be a cogent, convincing case if we are to enjoy sustained public support. In World Wars I and II we had this. In Korea we were moving under United Nations auspices to defend South Korea against dramatic, across-the-border, conventional aggression.

In Vietnam, the United States had no such advantage:

> The public is worried and confused. Our rationale for action has shifted away now even from the notion that we are there as advisers on request of a free government, to the simple and politically barren argument of our "national interest." We have not succeeded in making this national interest interesting enough at home or abroad to generate support. The arguments in fact are probably too complicated (or too weak) to be politically useful or effective.

Americans, bewildered by the complexities of Vietnam, failed to perceive what America's stakes in Vietnam were. Saigon's chaos only increased the public's confusion, while undermining "political support for our policy." As Humphrey remarked, people simply "can't understand why we would run grave risks to support a country which is totally unable to put its own house in order."

Selling the commitment was hard enough; selling escalation would be even harder. If the public did not understand recent events in South Vietnam, Humphrey argued, the administration would find it still more difficult "to justify dramatic 150 plane U.S. air bombardments" against North Vietnam.

Rather than deepen a commitment that few Americans grasped, Humphrey urged Johnson to reduce it. He knew this would not be easy. "It is always hard to cut losses," he admitted. But if there ever was a time to withdraw, now was it. Goldwaterism had just been slain:

> 1965 is the year of minimum political risk for the Johnson Administration. Indeed it is the first year when we can face the Vietnam problem without being preoccupied with the political repercussions from the Republican right.

Here was a rare moment, in which a Democratic President, armed with political muscle, could liquidate a flawed commitment at low political cost.

The American people had not elected Johnson for his military zeal. Goldwater had offered that. Humphrey emphasized LBJ's very different qualities—his "political ingenuity," his ability to fashion "political solutions"—and appealed to them. "People will be counting" on Johnson, Humphrey said, "to use on the world scene his unrivaled talents as a politician."

If LBJ failed to exploit his particular strength and embraced escalation instead, Humphrey predicted political opposition "from new and different sources" would "steadily mount." Liberals, independents, and labor—not right-wing successors of McCarthy—would abandon the President and sunder the Democratic coalition essential to passage of his Great Society.[22]

Humphrey's warnings shook Johnson, challenging his most basic political assumptions. LBJ had always discounted liberal pressures, fearing conservative ones far more deeply. "If he had a problem," a White House official remembered him saying, "it was the hawks, not the doves, whom he dismissed as a band of 'rattlebrains.' " "I am far more afraid of the right wing than I am of the left wing," Johnson had said to another. Yet Humphrey had suggested a new and frightening possibility: escalation in Vietnam risked alienating the very core of LBJ's political strength and therefore his political effectiveness.[23]

Haunted by this prospect, Johnson began wavering on his bombing decision. In a meeting with McNamara and Bundy later on February 15, LBJ suggested the idea of launching strict reprisals in response to attacks on U.S. installations rather than a systematic bombing campaign. The President seemed to be pulling back, fearing the political consequences of escalation.

McGeorge Bundy, lacking Johnson's unique political concerns, perceived LBJ's vacillation quite differently. To him, it seemed a troublesome retreat from a previously approved policy. Bundy endeavored to stiffen his boss's resolve.

The following day, Tuesday, February 16, Bundy sent Johnson a memo urging LBJ to confirm his bombing decision. He carefully prodded the President, citing a "deep-seated need" within the bureaucracy "for assurance that the decision has in fact been taken."[24]

Bundy acknowledged the weight of Johnson's move, noting its implications:

[T]hose of us who favor continuing military action against the North do see it as a major watershed decision. However much it is based on continuing aggression in the South (as it should be), it amounts to a U.S. decision to mount continuing pressure against Hanoi by use of our air and naval superiority. This is not the same, in operational terms, as what we did last August. And it is not the same as a policy of episodic retaliation for particular attacks against large numbers of Americans. It is very different indeed. . . .

Bombing was a major decision that Bundy implored Johnson to ratify as "the one possible means of turning around a desperate situation which has been heading toward a disastrous U.S. defeat."[25]

LBJ met with Bundy, McNamara, and several others that afternoon to discuss his advisers' concerns. Bundy, anxious to get the bombing in motion, asked McNamara, "How much more do you need to carry out our decision?"

"Nothing," McNamara answered—like Bundy, impatient to get the bombing under way. He needed only the President's approval "before [the] end of Wednesday [February 17] for [air strikes beginning] Friday [February 19]."

"I don't object to Friday," Johnson said, sullenly adding, "[it is] probably as good a day as any." LBJ felt driven by frustration and desperation to send American bombers against Hanoi. As he told his audience, "I'm just hoping out of hope they'll draw people in Saigon together."

Although the President had once again agreed to follow Bundy's and McNamara's course, he steadfastly resisted their advice to disclose the course forthrightly. When Bundy suggested releasing a public statement, Johnson flatly refused, declaring, "I'm not going to announce a new policy."[26]

Whatever doubts LBJ still harbored about the bombing diminished considerably in light of other information he received that evening. After tentatively approving air strikes on February 8, Johnson had quietly commissioned polls to gauge public reaction to the new course. A keen politician, LBJ remained extraordinarily sensitive to popular feeling. He hungered for indications about how Americans would respond to the bombing.

The polls which Bill Moyers, a trusted confidant, brought Johnson that night revealed overwhelming support for the post-Pleiku air strikes, nearly 83 percent. A substantial majority—69 percent—also favored bombing Hanoi in order to prevent political collapse in Saigon, even though 58 percent believed this might well provoke Chinese intervention.

The public's vigorous support for military action reflected the importance it attached to the U.S. commitment to South Vietnam, which a majority of respondents agreed was necessary "to win victory over aggression" (56 percent); "to defend the security of the United States" (63 percent); "to keep the Communists from taking over all of Southeast Asia" (79 percent).

Against these results, LBJ seemed far more reluctant than most of his countrymen to deepen America's involvement in the Vietnam War. Johnson's hesitancy, in fact, explained much of the public's earlier dissatisfaction with his policy. Before Pleiku, LBJ's approval rating on Vietnam had hovered at 41 percent; after the post-Pleiku air strikes, the figure had jumped to 60 percent.[27]

For a President sensitive to Vietnam's domestic impact, these figures represented a spur to action. Sustained bombing appeared politically safe—even advantageous—to a man who always proceeded cautiously. "Never move up your artillery until you move up your ammunition," he liked to say. Now, Johnson seemed to have the ammunition he needed.[28]

If LBJ still had any qualms about the bombing, his meeting with former President Eisenhower the next morning finally laid them to rest. Ike, living in retirement in Gettysburg, had come to Washington for a few days, and Johnson invited him to the White House for a private talk.

LBJ had great respect for Eisenhower's judgment, both as a soldier and as a statesman. Johnson considered him not only "the best general that I've ever known anything about" but also a "wise and experienced man who knew so well the problems and the burdens of the Presidency." LBJ wanted Ike's views on his bombing decision.[29]

Johnson began by asking Eisenhower for his thoughts on South Vietnam. The former President, seated along with McNamara, Wheeler, and Mc-George Bundy at the Cabinet table, told LBJ that his first duty was to contain communism in Southeast Asia. Ike warned, however, that South Vietnam could never be secured from communist attacks through U.S. efforts alone; even a "Roman Wall" of American soldiers could not defeat the Vietcong and stop North Vietnamese infiltration. Ultimate responsibility for that, he said, rested with Saigon.

Yet Eisenhower believed Washington could help by weakening Hanoi's will to continue the war. Bombing would not end the infiltration, but it would discourage the North, he asserted, while making it pay a cost for continuing its aggression.

Ike urged Johnson to abandon his policy of strict retaliation. He said retaliatory strikes had helped raise South Vietnamese morale, but the time had come for LBJ to shift to a "campaign of pressure" against North Vietnamese targets.

Johnson asked Eisenhower about the possibility of escalation, notably Chinese or Russian intervention. LBJ, who remembered Korea vividly, remained sensitive to that experience as he contemplated the bombing of North Vietnam. Eisenhower suggested that if they threatened to intervene, the President should pass word "to take care lest dire results occur to them." Ike then recounted how he had achieved an armistice in Korea. After the early months of the war under Truman, there had been a "gentlemen's agreement" that the United States would not cross the Yalu or use nuclear weapons. Once he became President, Eisenhower said, he let the Chinese know that the "gentlemen's agreement" was off, and that if the war continued, he would not feel bound by its constraints.

Eisenhower also addressed the issue of negotiations, which he advised

Johnson to avoid for the moment. Once LBJ initiated bombing, Ike believed America's position would be strengthened. Only then, he felt, should Johnson start to bargain.

LBJ then mentioned the Tonkin Gulf Resolution. Johnson asked Eisenhower if he considered the resolution sufficient to cover the impending action. Ike compared it favorably to the Formosa Resolution of 1955, which had granted him wide discretion in defending Taiwan against attack from mainland China. LBJ said he had used the Formosa Resolution as his model.

Eisenhower ended his discussion with Johnson by emphasizing the importance of Washington's commitment to South Vietnam. The United States had "put its prestige onto the proposition of keeping Southeast Asia free," Ike said, referring to his own 1954 pledge to Diem. "We cannot let the Indochinese peninsula go," he cautioned. Someone at the table, probably General Wheeler, suggested it might take six to eight American divisions to prevent that. Ike hoped they would not be needed. But if they were, then "so be it," he said.

Eisenhower's message was clear: save South Vietnam, whatever the costs. Gone was the hesitation that Ike had displayed at the time of Dienbienphu. No longer on the hot seat himself, Eisenhower had dispensed hawkish advice freely to Johnson. He had roundly endorsed the bombing, suggested brinkmanship with China, if necessary, and recommended ground escalation as a last resort. Eisenhower's strong judgments overpowered LBJ's lingering doubts.[30]

At an NSC meeting the next day, President Johnson formally set February 20 as the launching date for regular bombing strikes against North Vietnam. After weeks of doubt and delay, LBJ seemed resigned to act. As he told those gathered around him in the Cabinet Room, "I don't want to bomb those places, I really don't, but I don't see any other way."

Still, Johnson hesitated to reveal this escalatory step. During the meeting, Johnson rejected McGeorge Bundy's advice to announce his bombing decision to the American public and the U.N. Security Council. Instead, as a State Department telegram to Far Eastern embassies that night reported, the President wanted the "focus of public attention [to] be kept as far as possible on DRV aggression; not on joint GVN/US military operations." "There will be no comment of any sort on future actions," the cable stressed.[31]

LBJ was ready to go North, even if he was not ready to admit it publicly. After nearly two weeks of agonizing indecision—first authorizing the bombing, then stepping back from it—Johnson had approved a specific date for beginning air attacks. But just as Washington prepared to implement the President's long-awaited decision, Saigon's political situation erupted once again, forcing a postponement. The instability in South Vietnam which had sparked the calls for bombing now worked, ironically, to delay it.

* * *

Nguyen Khanh's time was running out. The general's hold over the difficult reins of South Vietnamese power, which he had controlled—either directly or indirectly—for more than a year, had steadily weakened. Throughout the fall of 1964 and into 1965, Khanh had relied increasingly on the Young Turks within the military to preserve his position. They had squelched Phat's and Duc's coup against him in September, supported his dissolution of the High National Council in December, and backed his ouster of Huong in January. But at each stage, Khanh's dependence on the Young Turks had deepened. The source of his strength had gradually become the source of his greatest potential opposition. The Young Turks readily acknowledged their opportunistic arrangement with Khanh. "Each side is using the other," one Young Turk admitted to reporters in January. "Later we shall see who wins."[32]

Khanh's troubles with Taylor increased the Young Turks' likelihood of success. The more Khanh undermined government stability, the more he angered Ambassador Taylor and diminished his support among Americans. This allowed the Young Turks of the Armed Forces Council—who rivaled Khanh in ambition—to position themselves as an alternative.

By early February, the Young Turks had resolved to prevent Khanh from recapturing direct authority. After forcing Huong's removal, Khanh had selected Oanh as Huong's temporary successor, whom the general intended to use as his personal instrument until he himself could reclaim power. But the Young Turks foiled this scheme. On February 16, the Armed Forces Council secured Phan Huy Quat's appointment as Prime Minister.

Phan Huy Quat was no puppet of Khanh. A native North Vietnamese Buddhist, Quat had built a record of personal integrity and independence while serving a succession of Vietnamese regimes. He was an anomaly in the bare-knuckled politics of Saigon. Combining "long experience in government with intelligence, determination, and decency," in the accurate words of his chief of staff, Bui Diem, Quat "was as stable and competent as Nguyen Khanh had been mercurial and deficient."[33]

Though trained as a physician, the quiet and unassuming Quat had devoted most of his energies to politics. As a founder and leading theorist of the nationalist Dai Viet party, he had opposed Japanese occupation, reimposition of French colonialism, and Ho Chi Minh's communism. At Bao Dai's urging, Quat had accepted the post of Education and then Defense Minister in the early 1950s, attempting to strengthen the government's separation from France and its support among the people. His relations with Diem, however, had been strained. In April 1960, Quat had signed the Caravelle Manifesto—petitioning Diem for reforms—which had soon landed him in jail. Shortly after Diem's assassination, Khanh had appointed him

Foreign Minister, a post he held until Huong's installation in November 1964.[34]

Although Quat had worked in Khanh's cabinet, he had frequently expressed criticism of the general's rule. Quat considered Khanh an imperious ruler who habitually placed personal above national interests. Therefore, Quat's appointment as Premier dramatically symbolized Khanh's decline and the rise of the Young Turks. To amplify their new political strength, the Young Turks of the AFC had made clear that they—not Nguyen Khanh—would "act as a mediator until the government is popularly elected."[35]

As perceptions of Khanh's vulnerability mounted, several Catholic officers in the South Vietnamese Army who resented Khanh's growing intimacy with the Buddhist Tri Quang began organizing their own scheme to remove him from power, once and for all. Three figures guided this plot: Tran Thien Khiem, an old competitor of Khanh, who had helped him topple the Minh regime in January 1964, only to be banished to Washington as South Vietnam's Ambassador; Lam Van Phat, the neo-Diemist general who had led the unsuccessful coup against Khanh the previous September; and Pham Ngoc Thao, a shadowy figure and inveterate intriguer who, as Khiem's press attaché in Washington, helped plan the coup before returning to Saigon in late December to set it in motion.

Thao's efforts—in cooperation with Khiem and Phat—to topple Khanh masked a deeper allegiance: Thao was a clandestine Vietcong agent who used his Catholic allies' antipathy toward Khanh to intensify South Vietnam's political instability. With schemers like Khiem and Phat at hand, the communists did not have to look far—or work hard—to exploit Saigon's divisions; the South Vietnamese Army provided ready, if unwitting, resources.[36]

Pham Ngoc Thao's career offered a striking example of Vietnam's byzantine political culture. A French-educated Catholic, Thao had joined the Vietminh resistance during the Japanese occupation, rising to become chief of its Saigon espionage apparatus in 1947. That same year, he had guided the training of an erstwhile Vietminh cadet named Nguyen Khanh.

Thao had ostensibly split with the communists after the Geneva Accords. During the ensuing years, he had developed close ties with another French-trained Catholic, Archbishop Ngo Dinh Thuc, brother of Ngo Dinh Diem. Thao's friendship with Thuc had brought him into contact with Diem, whom he had served as chief of Kienhoa province and, later, director of the strategic hamlet program.

But like many other army officers, Thao's allegiance to Diem had evaporated as the president tightened his dictatorial rule in the early 1960s. In the fall of 1963, Thao had joined the coup against Diem, leading the tank assault against the presidential palace on November 2. The coup plotters had distrusted this slippery figure always at the center of the latest political intrigue—even if they did not suspect his association with the Vietcong; shortly after Diem's assassination, the junta had shipped off Thao to the United States for military training at Fort Leavenworth. By 1964, Thao was in Washington working for Ambassador Khiem, who had lost his power struggle with Khanh.

At the end of December, Khanh had ordered Thao back to Saigon. He had gotten word of Thao's and Khiem's intrigue, and intended to quash it by arresting Thao upon his return. Thao had slipped back into South Vietnam but had eluded Khanh and begun preparing the coup against him.

In mid-February, as Thao readied to strike against Khanh, he contacted Air Vice-Marshal Ky. Thao sensed the growing division between the general and his Young Turks, and decided to probe their reaction to his impending coup. From a phone booth in Saigon, Thao called Ky.

"Ky, listen to me," Thao said. "Khanh is screwing things up royally." "I'm going to get rid of the son of a bitch," he snapped, and "I want to know what your position is on it."

Ky, already hatching his own plans, promised nothing. "Khanh's treated me well," he replied. "Between you and him I'm neutral," Ky added, with an air of seeming detachment. If Thao did not have the Young Turks' support, he also did not face their active opposition—or so Ky had led him to believe.[37]

With the Armed Forces Council apparently neutralized, Thao moved against Khanh. On the afternoon of February 19, Thao and his confederate, General Lam Van Phat, marched forces into Saigon, capturing the government radio station and ARVN headquarters. Khanh narrowly escaped capture, first by quietly slipping out an unarmed side gate at military headquarters, then hastily departing Tansonhut airport just as Phat's tanks rolled on to the runway.

Meanwhile, Air Vice-Marshal Ky, who had pledged his neutrality to Thao, began rallying forces against the rebels. From Bienhoa airbase north of Saigon, Ky dispatched several planes to bomb Phat's dissident troops at Tansonhut and elsewhere throughout the city. General Westmoreland stopped Ky at the last moment by reminding him that Tansonhut also housed over six thousand U.S. military forces.

At this point, Westmoreland and Ambassador Taylor intervened to engineer a compromise. Fearing Thao planned to remove not just Khanh but also Quat's civilian government, Taylor and Westmoreland sought a solution ending both the coup and Khanh's interference in politics.

Working through Ky's U.S. liaison officer, Brigadier General Robert Rowland, Taylor and Westmoreland arranged a meeting between Ky and the coup leaders at Bienhoa that evening. Thao and Phat arrived under

Rowland's protection. Later that night, Ky and other Young Turks of the Armed Forces Council agreed to remove Khanh, if Thao and Phat withdrew their forces. The coup plotters agreed. Early on the morning of February 20, government troops entered Saigon, and Thao's and Phat's forces disbanded.

The Armed Forces Council now moved to oust Khanh, apparently fulfilling its bargain with Thao and Phat. In fact, this "bargain" allowed the Young Turks to implement their own, well-prepared scheme against Khanh. Saigon had indeed become, as one observer noted, "the capital of the double cross."[38]

Ky and the other Young Turks had learned the art of intrigue well; they had studied under a master. They had supported Khanh's return to de facto power in late January, hoping to place him in an exposed position from which he could be toppled when an opportune moment arose.

But Khanh, sensing the Young Turks' growing restiveness, added his own Machiavellian twist to this intricate drama of betrayal: he opened contact with the National Liberation Front (NLF), the political arm of the Vietcong. With his support among army officers waning, Khanh began looking toward an accommodation with the NLF—with himself, of course, as the head of a new South Vietnamese government.

Khanh prepared the way by releasing the wife of Huynh Tan Phat, a prominent communist member of the NLF, from jail in mid-January 1965. Shortly thereafter, Khanh sent Phat a letter offering to cut a deal. Phat expressed great interest in the general's proposal, replying that he and the NLF eagerly wished to extend Khanh their "friendly cooperation."[39]

Khanh's cleverness had finally outrun his ambition. By approaching the NLF, Khanh gave the Young Turks the excuse they needed to secure U.S. assent to his removal. In light of Khanh's past schemes, the Young Turks' warning of a more reckless one in the future convinced Taylor that Khanh must go.[40]

With the Americans' hearty blessing, the Young Turks voted out Khanh as chairman of the Armed Forces Council on the morning of February 20. The secretary of the AFC telephoned Khanh, who was now at his Vungtau retreat southeast of Saigon, busily counterplotting a last-ditch coup against his former protégés. When informed of the Council's decision, the general exploded, refusing to step down.

The AFC turned to the Americans to provide the necessary persuasion. Westmoreland sent Colonel Jasper Wilson, Khanh's old U.S. Army adviser, to Vungtau the following night. Wilson explained the situation. Khanh had lost the support of the army, the government, and the United States—he was through. To hasten Khanh's cooperation, Wilson promised him a face-saving exit from South Vietnam. After soliciting assurances from Prime Minister

Quat that his travel "expenses" would be amply covered, the general relinquished. Khanh's scheming had finally ended.

On February 25, Vietnamese and American dignitaries gathered at Tansonhut to see Khanh off as Saigon's "roving ambassador." Among those lining the tarmac was Maxwell Taylor. As Khanh approached the airplane ramp, Taylor offered him a frosty farewell, which barely disguised the Ambassador's relief at his nemesis's departure. Privately describing the scene soon after, Taylor wrote, " 'Stinker No. 1' . . . was finally put into orbit. . . ."[41]

The political crisis which led to the exit of General Khanh also led to the postponement of President Johnson's bombing decision. Ambassador Taylor had been notified of LBJ's decision just four hours before Thao and Phat launched their abortive coup on February 19; later that same day, he cabled the State Department urging a postponement of the air strikes slated to begin on February 20. Washington immediately accepted Taylor's recommendation.[42]

Frustrated by Saigon's latest squabble, and its delaying effect on the bombing, Taylor waited impatiently as the Young Turks checked first Thao and Phat, and then Khanh. Within hours of the Young Turks' final triumph in the early morning of February 21, the Ambassador telegraphed Washington, urging a commencement of air strikes the following day.

Secretary Rusk rejected Taylor's proposal. He agreed the bombing should begin as soon as possible, but only after the situation in Saigon had stabilized. Rusk hoped that would not take long—perhaps just a day or two—but until then, Taylor would have to wait.[43]

Satisfying Taylor meant reconvincing the President. The struggle among Thao and Phat and the Young Turks and Khanh had reawakened Johnson's abiding frustration with South Vietnam, and with it, his suspicions about escalation. "We've got a bear by the tail," LBJ moaned to friends after hearing news of Saigon's latest shenanigans, and he wasn't sure how to handle the bear.[44]

Johnson seemed racked, once again, by indecision. He had approved the air strikes after much hesitation, only to be confronted by more political upheaval in South Vietnam. Would LBJ reschedule the bombing?

At this crucial moment, Dean Rusk sent Johnson an important memo. Rusk rarely wrote the President, preferring to speak privately with him. But knowing Johnson faced renewed—and momentous—choices, Rusk felt it "desireable and timely . . . to put down an outline of my own thinking about . . . South Viet Nam."

Rusk's thinking was certain: LBJ had to do whatever was necessary to avert South Vietnam's collapse. "I am convinced," he wrote the President, "that it would be disastrous for the United States and the free world to permit Southeast Asia to be overrun by the Communist North." "I am also convinced," he added, "that everything possible should be done to throw back the Hanoi-Viet Cong aggression"—even at "the risk of major escalation. . . ."

Rusk's faith in America's commitment did not mean faith in South Vietnam's political future. In fact, Saigon's endless turmoil troubled him just as deeply as it troubled Johnson. Without the "elementary platform" of stable government, Rusk sensed that "other efforts in the military and political field are likely to prove fruitless." He explained in painful detail the consequences of South Vietnam's political instability:

> Political confusion in Saigon (a) diverts military leaders away from their main job of fighting the Viet Cong, (b) undermines the capacity of administration throughout the country to take effective action in pacification and the non-military measures required to organize the countryside, (c) undermines the morale and sense of purpose of the American people, (d) frustrates our effort to obtain increasing help from other free world countries to South Viet Nam, (e) most important of all, convinces Hanoi and its communist allies that if they persist in their present course of action, they have every prospect of victory, and, (f) finally, . . . makes it almost impossible to activate political processes which have the prospect of resulting in the security of South Viet Nam.

Rusk had analyzed Saigon's deficiencies with exceptional insight. But his fear of the consequences to the United States should South Vietnam fall blinded him to those insights. No matter how grave Saigon's shortcomings, Rusk seemed unable to translate those shortcomings into compelling cause for American disengagement. "Negotiation as a cover for the abandonment of Southeast Asia to the Communist North cannot be accepted," he flatly stated. The President had to maintain course; the bombing must proceed.[45]

Bolstered by Rusk's fervent defense of America's commitment, LBJ authorized a rescheduling of the bombing, to begin on February 26. The following day, Rusk cabled Taylor the news he had awaited.[46]

Throughout the month, Johnson had wavered back and forth on the bombing—approving Bundy's recommendation of February 7; stepping back from it after reading Humphrey's warnings on February 15; reconfirming it on February 18 after Bundy's and Eisenhower's cajoling; demurring, yet again, following the Thao-Phat-Khanh eruption of February 19-20. And now, on February 24, LBJ committed himself once more. His continuing fears about the repercussions of failure in South Vietnam had brought him back to acceptance of bombing. These fears overrode whatever hesitation Johnson still harbored about South Vietnam's instability. Nothing, it seemed, could banish those fears—not even a long and impassioned plea against escalation which George Ball sent LBJ that afternoon.

* * *

George Ball was a maverick on Vietnam. He perceived limitations in bomb-ing among those who stressed its advantages, saw danger in continued in-volvement among those who feared withdrawal, and, most important, asked *why* among those who largely asked *how*.

Ball's skepticism toward bombing derived from his experience as a direc-tor of the Strategic Bombing Survey at the end of World War II. Charged with assessing the impact of Allied bombing on the German war effort, Ball had been struck by its limited effect on civilian morale and industrial production. If Germany—a modern, industrialized nation with numerous strategic targets—had endured heavy bombing and continued its military production, how could the United States compel North Vietnam—an under-developed, agrarian country with few strategic targets—to cease its support of the Vietcong through human transport down hundreds of miles of jungle trails?

Ball's earlier career had also sensitized him to the political frustrations of Western involvement in Vietnam. Throughout the late 1940s and early 1950s, Ball had worked closely with the French government during its pro-tracted ordeal in Indochina. He had witnessed the terrible disruptions un-leashed by France's colonial adventure, dividing its people and poisoning its politics for nearly a decade. Ball shuddered to see America incur similar frustrations by going to war in Vietnam.

But he had watched Kennedy move in that direction, by increasing Amer-ica's advisory presence. Ball was largely removed from these 1961–1963 deci-sions, concentrating his attention as Undersecretary of State on economic and European affairs, where his interests and affections centered. Because of his separation from Vietnam policymaking during the Kennedy years, Ball could view the consequences of JFK's decisions with a detachment which Rusk, McNamara, and Bundy, who had been more deeply involved, could not.

Ball's detachment encouraged him to question the basic assumptions gov-erning America's commitment to South Vietnam as that country's deteriora-tion quickened and the option of escalation gained currency in the new LBJ administration. At the end of September 1964, he had begun work on a memorandum challenging the conventional verities on Vietnam and the wisdom of American military intervention. Recognizing the sensitivity of this endeavor, Ball had proceeded cautiously. He had worked on his memo away from the State Department, dictating most of it into a tape recorder at home. For two weeks, Ball later recalled, "I'd get up at three or four in the morning . . . go into [my] library . . . and dictate through the night."

Ball had completed his lengthy study in early October. Convinced he "should never treat with the President on an *ex parte* basis," Ball had sent copies to Rusk, McNamara, and McGeorge Bundy. The four had spent two Saturday afternoons the following month discussing Ball's memorandum.

His conclusions had rankled Rusk and Bundy; they had "absolutely horrified" McNamara. "He treated it like a poisonous snake," Ball remembered, regarding it "as next to treason that this had been put down on paper."[47]

Chilled by his colleagues' reaction, Ball had hesitated to pass his memo to President Johnson. Instead, he had chosen to wait. Ball explained this decision in his memoirs:

> [T]he President was then engaged in his election campaign and was troubled with a thousand problems. It did not seem a propitious time for a confrontation, so I decided to wait until I could get his full attention.[48]

Once the campaign ended, Ball had delayed another three and a half months before sending his memo to Johnson. During this interval, LBJ had made several critical decisions: he had approved the principle of bombing in December; prepared for action in January; and decided to strike North in early February. Ball knew, at least, of the latter two decisions—he had attended the Cabinet Room conference on January 6 and cabled Taylor about Johnson's bombing policy on February 13. And yet he had continued to withhold his memo.

Why had Ball hesitated so long before passing his lengthy dissent to LBJ? Not out of personal fear of Johnson; Ball enjoyed a comfortable relationship with the President. Johnson knew Ball opposed deeper American involvement in Vietnam. But he also knew Ball would never publicize his opposition. "George," LBJ once said to him, "you're like the school teacher looking for a job with a small school district in Texas. When asked by the school board whether he believed that the world was flat or round, he replied: 'Oh, I can teach it either way.' " "That's you," laughed Johnson, "you can argue like hell with me against a position. but I know outside this room you're going to support me. You can teach it flat or round." LBJ respected Ball's independent views; he tolerated them because this "teacher" answered to "school board chairman" Johnson.[49]

Policy, not personality, explained Ball's delay. Ball had never opposed the idea of bombing per se. He sensed its dangers and limitations, as he had warned the President earlier in January and February, but considered those dangers and limitations tolerable—hoping, as he did, that bombing would produce negotiations leading to a politically acceptable American withdrawal. As long as LBJ contemplated only bombing, Ball therefore kept the memo to himself. But by late February, Ball had begun hearing rumblings within the State Department and Pentagon about the need for U.S. combat forces to protect the launching sites of air strikes against the North.

Such rumblings touched the deepest fear in Ball—the specter of an American land war in Vietnam. This prospect unnerved him, evoking haunting memories of France's nightmare a decade before. Unalterably opposed to

U.S. combat involvement, Ball now saw the force of events pushing Johnson toward that very abyss.

As a result, Ball finally decided to act. He gave his memo to Bill Moyers at lunch on February 24, who passed it to the President that afternoon.

Ball's memo swam against the rushing tide of current thinking on Vietnam. Ball dismissed the thesis that bombing Hanoi could somehow rectify Saigon's grave political problems. "Even if [South Vietnam's] deterioration is checked," he wrote, "there seems little likelihood of establishing a government that can (a) provide a solid center around which the broad support of the Vietnamese people can coalesce or (b) conduct military operations with sufficient effectiveness to clean up the insurgency."

Why had America committed itself to such a weak entity? The "primary motive," Ball concluded, was "unquestionably political." The United States was in South Vietnam to demonstrate its anti-communist resolve—its commitment to global containment.

Since political calculations precipitated Washington's involvement, Ball felt the costs of that involvement should be measured in political terms. America's commitment to South Vietnam should be judged by its impact on "U.S. prestige," "the credibility of our commitments elsewhere," and its "effect on our alliances." If judged by these criteria, Ball believed the U.S. effort in South Vietnam would fail.

To begin with, South Vietnam suffered unusual—if not unique—problems which undermined its symbolic importance to the free world. South Vietnam, in Ball's words, was simply "not Korea"; America's commitment to Saigon lacked the significance of its earlier commitment to Seoul. He explained why:

a. We were in South Korea under a clear UN mandate. Our presence in South Viet-Nam depends upon the continuing request of the GVN plus the SEATO protocol.

b. At their peak, UN forces in South Korea (other than ours and those of the ROK) included 53,000 infantrymen . . . provided by fifty-three nations. In Viet-Nam we are going it alone with no substantial help from any other country.

c. In 1950 the Korean government under Syngman Rhee was stable. It had the general support of the principal elements in the country. There was little factional fighting and jockeying for power. In South Viet-Nam we face governmental chaos.

d. The Korean War started only two years after Korean independence. The Korean people were still excited by their newfound freedom; they were fresh for the war. In contrast, the people of Indochina have been fighting for almost twenty years—first against the French, then for the last ten years against the NVN. All evidence points to the fact that they are tired of conflict.

e. Finally, the Korean War started with a massive land invasion by 100,000 troops. This was a classical type of invasion across an established border . . . It gave us an unassailable political and legal base for counteraction. In South Viet-Nam there has been no invasion—only a slow infiltration. Insurgency is by its nature ambiguous. The Viet Cong insurgency does have substantial indigenous support. . . . As a result, many nations remain unpersuaded that Hanoi is the principal source of the revolt. And, as the weakness of the Saigon Government becomes more and more evident, an increasing number of governments will be inclined to believe that the Viet Cong insurgency is, in fact, an internal rebellion.

South Vietnam was a chaotic and dispirited regime plagued by a tangled web of internal and external subversion, not a vibrant polity threatened by direct aggression. Its peculiar problems diminished America's political objective of defending democracies against communist expansion.

South Vietnam's precarious situation also undermined the purpose of U.S. military escalation. What benefit, asked Ball, were air attacks against Hanoi if Saigon's political turmoil continued? Reducing North Vietnamese support for the Vietcong on behalf of "a disorganized South Vietnamese Government . . . unable to eliminate the insurgency" would "at best bring a Pyrrhic victory," he wrote.

Even this scenario, which assumed some success against North Vietnam, seemed overly optimistic to Ball. Hanoi had committed itself to the reunification of Vietnam long ago. And now, with South Vietnam in the throes of political confusion, that goal appeared close to fruition. American military pressure would not change Hanoi's perception. As long as North Vietnam "believes victory is near," Ball wrote, "it will probably be willing to accept very substantial costs from United States air action."

And inflict substantial costs in return. Air power constituted Washington's greatest military advantage. Hanoi understood this, and would react to American bombing by assuming that each party was now free "to fight the kind of war best adapted to its resources." Land troops comprised North Vietnam's particular advantage. If the United States unleashed its massive air power, Ball felt the North Vietnamese "would be clearly tempted to retaliate by using ground forces, which they possess in overwhelming numbers."

Such an outcome foreshadowed what Ball considered the gravest misperception of all: that Washington could somehow anticipate, much less control, the consequences of escalation. Ball mocked the notion, popular among men like Taylor, McNamara, and McGeorge Bundy, that military force, carefully applied and gradually increased, could be managed and contained:

It is in the nature of escalation that each move passes the option to the other side, while at the same time the party which seems to be losing will be tempted to keep raising the ante. To the extent that the response to a move can be controlled, that move is probably ineffective. If the move is effective, it may not be possible to control—or accurately anticipate—the response.

War was an unpredictable and unruly tiger, and once "on the tiger's back," said Ball, "we cannot be sure of picking the place to dismount."

Instead, he feared the tiger would carry America deeper and deeper into the morass of Vietnam. Bombing would lead to increased infiltration; increased infiltration would lead to attacks on the bases launching air strikes; these attacks would lead to U.S. ground forces to protect the bases; U.S. ground forces would lead to a revolutionary change in the management of the war; an Americanized war would lead to domestic frustration and bitterness more serious than Korea a decade before.

The logic of events frightened Ball, prompting him to weigh the political costs of escalation against the political benefits of continued involvement. He summarized the prevailing assumption:

. . . the United States must successfully stop the extension of Communist power into South Viet-Nam if its promises are to have credence. . . . [F]ailing such an effort our Allies around the world would be inclined to doubt our promises and to feel that they could no longer safely rely upon American power against Communist aggressive ambitions.

Here was the driving force of American action, the principle on which so much planning hinged. It had guided U.S. policy in Southeast Asia for years and, in the process, had approached the status of dogma. Ball was willing to play the heretic, to ask whether America's allies viewed its effort in Vietnam as Americans assumed they did.

This was no easy task. Having devoted great effort to South Vietnam's cause, Americans wanted to believe its allies considered that effort worthwhile. But Ball thought not. He acknowledged the painful reality of Allied thinking on Vietnam:

They fear that as we become too deeply involved in a war on the land mass of Asia, we will tend to lose interest in their problems. They believe that we would be foolish to risk bogging ourselves down in the Indochina jungle. They fear a general loss of confidence in American judgment that could result if we pursued a course which many regarded as neither prudent nor necessary.

From this picture emerged a radically different perception of America's political stakes in Vietnam. "What we might gain by establishing the steadfastness of our commitments," Ball wrote, "we could lose by an erosion of confidence in our judgment."

Ball had brought the argument back to his main contention—that the costs of Washington's political commitment should be measured in the broadest political terms. If viewed in this light, policymakers might see that escalation "would create enormous risks for the United States and impose costs incommensurate with the possible benefits." He beseeched this re-examination be undertaken "before we commit military forces to a line of action that could put events in the saddle and destroy our freedom to choose policies that are at once the most effective and the most prudent."[50]

Ball had spoken forcefully and passionately against escalation. But he had also spoken belatedly. Ball had withheld his memo from Johnson during the pivotal months when LBJ moved ever closer to bombing. He had hesitated to step forward and, in doing so, had done little to check the escalatory momentum. Ball had failed to assert his convictions as the pressure for intervention had grown.

But it was still not too late. The bombing of North Vietnam had yet to begin. The President now had Ball's memo, and the continuing freedom to choose his policy.

Johnson studied Ball's memorandum during the evening of February 24. The next morning, Bill Moyers called Ball to say the President had read and reread his memo. Johnson had "found it fascinating," Moyers remarked, "and wanted to know why he had not read it before."[51]

Late on the afternoon of February 26, Ball, McNamara, and Rusk met with the President in the Oval Office to discuss Ball's long and critical memorandum. Johnson had examined the document carefully. He questioned several of Ball's contentions, even recalling the specific pages where they appeared. LBJ seemed concerned, if not convinced, by his arguments.

McNamara was less impressed. As he had in several previous meetings, McNamara discounted the hazards of bombing. "George here," he said, "is exaggerating the dangers." "It is not a final act," he added. Bombing was controllable. Its risks were manageable, McNamara contended, and far less serious than those of withdrawal.[52]

Rusk did not share McNamara's confidence. He understood Saigon's troubles too well to expect much from bombing. But Rusk feared the loss of South Vietnam more than he doubted the efficacy of bombing. The President had to go forward, he said, despite the risks of escalation.

Ball failed to convert Johnson. LBJ would proceed with the bombing. The President had already decided; his thinking had gone too far toward major escalation.

Whatever his hopes, Ball had privately feared just this. "I had a . . . sense of fatality that I wasn't going to keep it from happening," he later admitted. "It would indeed happen. Once you get one of those things going, it's just like a little alcohol; you're going to get a taste for more. It's a compelling thing."[53]

* * *

The systematic bombing of North Vietnam had been scheduled to begin on February 26, the same day as Ball's conference with Johnson. But poor weather over target areas forced a postponement. For three succeeding days, cloud cover over southern North Vietnam delayed the air strikes.[54]

Finally, on March 2, 1965, over one hundred U.S. war planes launched from carriers in the South China Sea and airbases in South Vietnam struck the North Vietnamese ammunition depot at Xombang. The long-awaited air offensive against Hanoi, code-named ROLLING THUNDER, had begun.

The bombers which roared across the DMZ that day symbolized a deeper crossing for the United States. Johnson had committed America to direct participation in the war. LBJ had reached this decision only after much agonizing and delay. But from it would flow, almost immediately, a host of sweeping consequences both for his presidency and his country's involvement in the Vietnam War.

5

"Where Are We Going?"

LIKE THE OPENING of a floodgate, Johnson's bombing decision unleashed a torrent of new and fateful military pressures. Even before ROLLING THUNDER began, General Westmoreland cabled Washington, seeking ground forces to protect the airfield at Danang, launching site of bombing strikes against the North.

Westmoreland's call represented a striking departure from past requests. Although over 23,000 U.S. advisers had reached South Vietnam by 1965, their mission remained unchanged from the first arrivals in 1950: to assist and train ARVN to fight its own war against the Vietcong. Westmoreland now sought to inject American ground forces directly into the conflict.

Westmoreland's request alarmed Ambassador Taylor, who, although a former Army general, had failed to anticipate the need for troops to protect the airfields when he recommended air strikes early on. What is more, Taylor had urged a similar deployment to President Kennedy back in November 1961. But his thinking had changed drastically since then. Taylor's experience as ambassador had sensitized him to Saigon's deep political divisions and how seriously those divisions undermined both governmental stability and military effectiveness. The incessant squabbling among Buddhists, generals, and politicians had sapped his faith in South Vietnam's war effort, while stirring grave doubts about the wisdom of direct American intervention. Taylor now firmly opposed committing U.S. ground troops to Vietnam.

Yet Westmoreland's request seemed the first step in this very direction. When Taylor learned of the plan, he recalled fearing "[t]his would be the nose of the camel coming into the tent." "Once you put that first soldier ashore," he added privately at the time, "you never know how many others are going to follow him." Taylor resolved to check Westmoreland's request before that first soldier stepped ashore.[1]

The ambassador immediately cabled Washington, forcefully warning against Westmoreland's plan. Taylor's telegram bristled with "grave reservations" about the "wisdom and necessity" of sending Marines to Danang. "Such action," he cautioned the President, "would be [a] step in reversing [the] long standing policy of avoiding commitment of ground combat forces in SVN."

Taylor recounted why Washington had carefully avoided this step in the past. Conventional forces lacked effectiveness in this most unconventional war. The American G.I., "armed, equipped, and trained as he is," the ambassador wrote, "is not [a] suitable guerrilla fighter for Asian forests and jungles." France had "tried to adapt their forces to this mission and failed," Taylor reminded Johnson; "I doubt that U.S. forces could do much better," he said.

Taylor also tackled the argument, promoted by Westmoreland and the JCS, that a Marine deployment would free large numbers of ARVN troops to conduct offensive operations against the Vietcong. Only one battalion would be released, Taylor noted. He considered this insufficient to offset the risks incurred by committing American troops. Better to improve South Vietnamese security around the airbase, Taylor concluded, than to send in Marines to perform a task which "has not been done adequately in [the] past."

The ambassador's comments reflected his growing disillusionment with Saigon's prosecution of the war. Taylor had seen too many generals fighting one another for political control rather than the Vietcong on the battlefield. He feared American ground forces would only accelerate this trend by reducing ARVN's immediate burdens. "Once it becomes evident that we are willing [to] assume such new responsibilities," Taylor explained, "one may be sure that [the] GVN will seek to unload other ground force tasks upon us." And Washington could not then easily refuse its ally. "Once this policy is breached," he concluded, "it will be very difficult to hold [the] line."[2]

However compelling Taylor's warning, it lacked the weight of Westmoreland's appeal. Westmoreland was the commander in the field, with authority over American forces and responsibility for their safety. This fact also conditioned Johnson's response to his request. Westmoreland had tied the security of U.S. personnel and installations to approval of his request. How could LBJ jeopardize the lives of American boys? Had he not approved the bombing, whose planes and pilots Westmoreland now sought to protect? The President faced a crucial decision constrained by the political pressures of his role as commander in chief and his prior approval of the bombing.

Not surprisingly, Johnson granted Westmoreland's request. But he strictly limited the Marines' mission. Westmoreland had initially proposed using the Marines in patrol sweeps around the airbase. LBJ rejected this strategy, restricting the Marines to the airfield itself and prohibiting any offensive operations against the Vietcong.

Secretary Rusk relayed Johnson's decision to Saigon on February 26. Rusk instructed Taylor to leave the South Vietnamese "in no doubt" that the Marine deployment was "for a limited purpose and that [the] GVN must continue [to] have full responsibility in [the] pacification program." LBJ had accepted Westmoreland's plan without forgetting Taylor's warnings.[3]

Nine days later, on the morning of March 8, a flotilla of naval transports slowly chugged toward Nam O Beach on the western rim of Danang Bay. The landing craft, struggling against stiff winds and rough seas, carried the first American ground troops to the Asian mainland since the end of the Korean War. The Marines, dressed in full battle gear, splashed ashore, according to an eyewitness, "as if re-enacting Iwo Jima."[4]

Instead of hostile enemy troops, the Marines encountered a cordial welcoming committee. Local South Vietnamese officials hailed their arrival. Danang's mayor had also mobilized a bevy of pretty young Vietnamese women, draped in close-fitting *ao dai* tunics, who showered the first Marines wading ashore with garlands of yellow dahlias and red gladiolas. It seemed so pleasant and so easy. Further back on the beach, however, stood a group of veteran U.S. Army advisers, silently watching the spectacle beneath darkening skies.

The Marine landing at Danang only intensified Johnson's anxiety about the bombing. Never comfortable with his decision, LBJ became increasingly nervous about its consequences. Already he had authorized American ground forces to South Vietnam—something he scarcely contemplated just weeks before.

The bombing seemed dangerous, uncertain, full of hazards. And not central to victory, the President believed. Johnson still felt the war would be won or lost in the South, in the struggle between the government and the guerrillas for the allegiance of the people.

LBJ wanted renewed effort in South Vietnam, now that he had agreed, at last, to strike against North Vietnam. Johnson had authorized the air war and, in return, expected results in the ground war.

The President assigned this task to Army Chief of Staff General Harold K. Johnson. He ordered General Johnson to South Vietnam to canvass the military situation and find ways to improve it.

Shortly before General Johnson left for Saigon, LBJ summoned him to the White House. ROLLING THUNDER had begun the day before. The President appeared nervous and apprehensive about this latest step. "Bomb, bomb, bomb. That's all you know," he complained to the general. "Well,"

LBJ demanded, "I want to know why there's nothing else. You generals have all been educated at the taxpayers' expense, and you're not giving me any ideas and any solutions for this damn little pissant country." "Now, I don't need ten generals to come in here ten times and tell me to bomb," he growled. "I want some solutions. I want some answers." As the two men descended the White House elevator after their breakfast meeting in the family quarters, LBJ turned to the Army Chief of Staff, stared him closely in the face with a finger pointed at his chest, and in a low voice said, "You get things bubbling, General."[5]

Johnson seemed particularly anxious about Vietnam in early March. Each day, events forced new and unpleasant choices, while further constricting the President's options. This growing sense of foreboding also affected LBJ's three principal advisers—McNamara, Rusk, and McGeorge Bundy—who met to discuss Vietnam the evening of March 5.

Bundy reported their feelings in a long memo to Johnson the next morning. "Dean Rusk, Bob McNamara, and I spent 2½ hours together last night on Vietnam," Bundy informed the President. He was blunt about the outcome: "Two of the three of us think that the chances of a turn-around in South Vietnam remain less than even." Bundy rested this startling conclusion on a grim but abiding fact: "[T]here is no evidence yet that the new government has the necessary will, skill and human resources which a turn-around will require."

As a result, all three sensed more and deeper trouble ahead. This likelihood so disconcerted McNamara, in fact, that he now pressed for the opening of "real talks" in the belief, wrote Bundy, "that we will need a conference table if things go worse, as he expects."

The mounting sense of gloom gripping these men had become palpable, driving them to contemplate grave eventualities. Where before each had talked of eventual success, they now stressed the need for "contingency planning" for "either escalation by the enemy or continued sharp deterioration in South Vietnam." That Johnson's closest advisers favored such planning, even if "very, very privately," intensified LBJ's anxiety enormously.[6]

Lady Bird noticed her husband's growing anxiety during a dinner conversation with friends the next evening. Surrounded by old colleagues and trusted aides, the President vented his fears and frustrations. "I can't get out," he sighed, and "I can't finish it with what I've got." "So what the Hell can I do?" he moaned.[7]

Johnson voiced similar trepidation to Rusk, McNamara, and McGeorge Bundy on March 9. That afternoon, LBJ reactivated the "Tuesday Lunch"— his privy council on foreign and defense affairs—for the first time since September 1964.

John McNaughton, McNamara's Vietnam assistant, joined the Principals for lunch in the Mansion to report on his recent fact-finding trip to Saigon. McNaughton delivered unsettling news. The "thing is much worse" than Washington imagined, he said, describing the general mood throughout South Vietnam as "troubled."

McNaughton then sketched three equally unpleasant remedies: (1) increased "pressure on [the] North"—which McNaughton labeled a "squeeze"; (2) "[n]o squeeze but [a] sustained reply" including "lots of U.S. and, if possible, allied troops"; or (3) recognizing "it's a loser" and determining "how to get out with limited humiliation."

The President followed McNaughton uneasily. "What good have [our] strikes done?" he wanted to know.

They have provided "a bargaining [chip]," Rusk answered.

Johnson, persistently skeptical, again raised the issue of political stability. Did McNaughton anticipate further coups, despite the bombing?

"Yes[,] there will be another coup" was McNaughton's unhappy prediction.

"I'd much prefer to stay in South Vietnam," LBJ drearily said, "But after fifteen months[,] we all agree we have to do more."[8]

Johnson felt snared by the bombing. Having taken the big step, he sensed the difficulty—the impossibility—of reversing it. LBJ felt locked on a perilous course, studded with unknown hazards, with little confidence that he could navigate the journey successfully.

An event in the American South two days earlier compounded Johnson's worries. On the morning of March 7, over 500 blacks had marched out of Selma, Alabama, toward Montgomery, fifty-three miles to the east, to protest Negro disfranchisement at the Alabama State Capitol.

The marchers did not get far. After crossing the Edmund Pettus bridge on the outskirts of town, they met state troopers camped 300 yards down the Jefferson Davis Highway. The armed troopers, clad in navy jackets and sky-blue helmets, stood shoulder-to-shoulder across both sides of the four-lane highway. "You will not be allowed to march any further!" a trooper bellowed through his bullhorn. "You've got two minutes to disperse!"

Less than a minute later, the troopers stormed the procession, pummeling the marchers with nightsticks and tear gas. Local white vigilantes entered the fray. "O.K., nigger," snarled a posseman, whipping a black woman with barbed wire-laced rubber tubing, "You wanted to march—now march!" Slowly, painfully, the bloodied and choking marchers retreated back across the bridge.

The Selma confrontation shocked the nation, riveting new attention on the administration's proposed voting rights bill—the cornerstone of LBJ's Great Society. Johnson was determined to pass this bill, despite resistance from southern conservatives. Yet he knew guiding it through congressional committees chaired by powerful southerners would be difficult, if not impossible. They might seize on the widening conflict in Vietnam to bury his dream of voting reform.

This prospect plagued Johnson, who felt torn between standing firm in Vietnam and avoiding a massive escalation inimical to the voting rights bill and his other domestic initiatives. LBJ mediated these conflicting pressures by purposefully concealing his bombing decision.

At a press conference on March 13 dominated by the Selma crisis and the voting rights issue, Johnson also confronted questions about recent air strikes against North Vietnam. He deliberately downplayed their significance, stressing the "continuity" of his latest Vietnam action:

> [O]ur policy there is the policy that was established by President Eisenhower, as I have stated, since I have been President, 46 different times, the policy carried on by President Kennedy, and the policy that we are now carrying on.

In rambling and evasive terms, Johnson had suggested no military departure, avoiding any mention of the bombing offensive he had approved barely two weeks before.[9]

If LBJ hoped to keep the issue of Vietnam dormant in coming weeks, he was quickly disappointed. The day after his news conference, Army Chief of Staff Johnson returned from South Vietnam with recommendations to increase the American military effort there substantially. Among other things, General Johnson urged intensifying the air offensive against North Vietnam, creating a multinational anti-infiltration force along the DMZ, and deploying a U.S. Army division, approximately 16,000 soldiers, near Saigon or in the central highlands.[10]

The Johnson Report reflected the Pentagon's growing demands for tougher action in Vietnam. ROLLING THUNDER was not yet two weeks old, and already the military told LBJ more was needed.

McGeorge Bundy had begun to think so too. Bundy had initially pushed bombing as a means to bolster South Vietnam politically, and, secondarily, to inhibit North Vietnam militarily. But ROLLING THUNDER had neither alleviated Saigon's governmental chaos nor substantially impaired Hanoi's support of the Vietcong. Bombing was failing, in short, to meet his objectives. But rather than leading Bundy to question the wisdom of escalation, these shortcomings compelled him to contemplate even greater escalation —a substantial ground force deployment—in the hope that troops would somehow accomplish what bombs had not.

Bundy distilled his thinking in a memo to the President, McNamara, and Rusk on March 16. He conceded bombing was not working and probably wouldn't in the future. "[T]here appear to be three things that Hanoi can do," Bundy wrote: "it can stop its infiltration; it can withdraw forces and supplies under its control in the South; it can order its people not to use force against the government in the South." But "[n]one of these is likely," he predicted, "and it is questionable whether any of them will be ordered under the pressure of our air operations alone."

Precisely because bombing was not working, Bundy felt driven to urge an even bolder step—the introduction of large numbers of American combat soldiers. "This U.S. ground presence," he argued, "is likely to reinforce both pacification efforts and Southern morale, while discouraging the VC from their current expectation of early victory"—the same stubbornly elusive goals Bundy had sought through bombing.[11]

As Bundy gravitated toward larger ground forces, Westmoreland submitted a formal request for them. On March 17, barely a week after the Marines' arrival at Danang, the general cabled Washington asking for more. Westmoreland wanted another Marine Battalion Landing Team (BLT) to protect the helicopter base at Phubai, on the northern coast near Hué.

Westmoreland's request startled Ambassador Taylor. It seemed to confirm what he had cautioned President Johnson against the month before: that the prohibition on ground troops, once breeched, would generate irresistible pressures to escalate the war.

Again, Taylor cabled Washington, reiterating his previous warnings. "This proposal for introducing the BLT," he advised Johnson, "is a reminder of the strong likelihood of additional requests for increases in U.S. ground combat forces in SVN." Taylor had no doubt where such increases would lead. They would encourage the South Vietnamese "to an attitude of 'let the United States do it,'" leaving America to shoulder an ever-greater share of the war-fighting burden.

The ambassador knew the character of Saigon's ambitious generals. He had watched them conspire first against Huong and then against their own leader, Khanh. With American troops on hand, these generals could pursue their political infighting with increased vigor, leaving military operations to their hapless ally. Taylor feared—and expected—just this. Indeed, the ambassador suggested, "it remains to be proved" that ARVN "would perform better by the stimulation of the U.S. presence rather than worse in a mood of relaxation at passing the Viet Cong burden to the U.S."

Aside from its dulling effect on ARVN determination, Taylor worried that direct American intervention also posed serious political risks by reawakening Vietnamese fears of western imperialism. The Vietminh had challenged the French legionnaires a decade before, and in the process had scored a major political triumph. U.S. troops could prove a similar target, the ambassador reasoned, increasing "our vulnerability to Communist propaganda . . . as we appear to assume the old French role of alien colonizer and conqueror." ARVN's listlessness meant an Americanized war, and an Americanized war meant political trouble. Potent reasons, Taylor concluded, to resist further U.S. ground deployments.[12]

Taylor's gloomy forecast compounded Johnson's anxiety. The military pressures continued to mount and, with them, his fears about deeper American involvement in Vietnam.

As LBJ pondered the Johnson Report and Westmoreland's request, he turned to his old Senate colleague, Mike Mansfield, once more. Johnson told Mansfield about these latest demands, seeking the majority leader's advice about how to answer them.

Mansfield responded in a letter to LBJ on March 18. He reminded the President, who had rejected his advice against bombing, that these latest pressures stemmed directly from it—"that if United States air attacks were continued it would be necessary . . . to safeguard American forces already in Viet Nam by the addition of American combat forces on the ground. . . ."

Now those forces had been requested. Mansfield urged Johnson to meet these requests with the fewest possible troops. For the troops themselves, he warned, carried the seeds of even greater escalation. The Vietcong would not react to the bombing by pitting "their weakness against our strength"—air power—"but their strength against our weakness"—land forces. And with American soldiers the target of increasing VC attacks, Mansfield feared LBJ would be drawn "into deploying progressively larger numbers of United States ground troops throughout the country."

This, in turn, would provoke North Vietnamese escalation. As Mansfield observed,

> Under present conditions Hanoi . . . has no effective way of retaliating against the air-attacks. But if we have large numbers of our troops in Viet Nam, the Communists would have meaningful United States targets against which to launch their principal strength. Hanoi could strike back at us by sending main forces into the South.

It was a sobering scenario, which Mansfield admonished Johnson to avert by strictly limiting any deployment.[13]

Mansfield's comments underscored what the President himself increasingly recognized. LBJ knew any decision on further troop commitments involved serious potential consequences. Yet he chose to conceal this fact, to deflect public attention from the crucial choices at hand.

During a press conference in Texas on March 20, Johnson announced Taylor's return to Washington the following week, while dismissing speculation that the ambassador's visit coincided with important pending decisions. "There are no immediate issues which make the meeting urgent," LBJ told reporters gathered on the front porch of his ranch. "It is a regu-

lar—repeat—regular periodic visit, part of our continuous consultations. . . ."
Anticipating questions about the recent escalation in Vietnam, Johnson pre-
empted the troublesome queries. "Our policy in Viet-Nam is the same as it
was 1 year ago," LBJ insisted, "and to those of you who have inquiries on
the subject, it is the same as it was 10 years ago."[14]

Why had the President, with General Johnson's report and General Westmoreland's request before him, suggested business as usual in Vietnam?
LBJ's decision related, once again, to domestic political pressures. For as he
privately wrestled with the troop question, the Selma crisis neared its climax.
Three days before, on March 17, black protesters had won a federal court
order granting them the right to march, unobstructed and unmolested,
from Selma to Montgomery. Almost immediately, Alabama Governor George
Wallace had refused state protection for the marchers, pleading fiscal constraints. President Johnson had foiled Wallace's challenge, however, by fed-
eralizing the Alabama National Guard and dispatching U.S. marshals along
the proposed route.

This, then, marked the climate of events on the morning of LBJ's March
20 news conference, held just one day before the planned Selma-to-Mont-
gomery march. The voting rights struggle had reached a critical juncture,
whose outcome would sharply affect—perhaps determine—the fate of Johnson's voting rights bill. LBJ wanted nothing to jeopardize this bill, by diverting congressional or public attention from the voting rights issue. That
included, most especially, Vietnam.

The President achieved his goal, at least temporarily. Martin Luther
King, Jr., and his fellow marchers set out from Selma on March 21, under
the watchful eye of federal troops and the entire nation. Over the next three
days, the marchers trekked across rural Alabama, playing out a drama with
implications far beyond the cotton fields and towns they passed along the
way. Finally, on March 24, the 25,000 marchers arrived, triumphantly, in
Montgomery. A large and symbolic step toward the voting rights bill had
been taken.

As Johnson reflected on the success of the Selma march, his national security
adviser, McGeorge Bundy, reflected on the choices ahead in Vietnam. Bundy
realized the administration had reached a turning point in its policy, that
General Johnson's and General Westmoreland's requests, if approved, meant
a dramatic increase in American military involvement. For this reason,
Bundy felt a need to clarify his own thinking about U.S. interests and objectives in light of these momentous choices.

On March 21, Bundy sat down and put his ideas in writing. In these
notes, Bundy expressed his private thoughts about Vietnam with astonishing

candor, arguing out the premises and goals of a policy he had helped, in so many ways, to fashion.

America's "cardinal" objective in Vietnam, Bundy reasoned, was *"not* to be a Paper Tiger"—"not to have it thought," in his words, "that when we commit ourselves we really mean no high risks." The allusion to Mao's aspersion against the United States reflected Bundy's palpable fear of communist China. Like so many in contemporary Washington, Bundy harbored a deep suspicion of Chinese expansion. It was Peking, he and others believed, which lay behind Hanoi's involvement in South Vietnam. And it was Peking, they believed, which must be convinced of U.S. resolve—even at the risk of war with China.

The importance which Bundy attached to containing perceived Chinese expansion related as much to American politics as to American security interests. For Bundy lived in an age fresh with the memory of Chiang's fall and the rise of McCarthy. He understood only too well the political repercussions for a Democratic administration which failed to hold the line against Asian communism. Though he questioned—perhaps even doubted—ultimate American success in South Vietnam, Bundy judged it politically imperative to continue the effort. This reasoning was strikingly apparent in his following proposition: "[I]n terms of domestic US politics, which is better: to 'lose' now or to 'lose' after committing 100,000 men?" "[T]he latter," Bundy figured, "[f]or if we visibly do enough in the South, any failure will be, in that moment, beyond our control." And beyond political reproach from the right.

Whatever his view of the political stakes—international and domestic—in Vietnam, Bundy considered the military stakes quite limited. Should South Vietnam fall to the communists, he anticipated the results would be "marginal," "for on a straight military account, the balance [of world power] remains as it was. . . ." Bundy clearly rejected the "domino" principle and a communist Vietnam's threat to American security.

This admission was important. It forced Bundy to reassess the wisdom of Washington's deepening commitment. If, in the final analysis, a communist Vietnam posed little danger to U.S. security, was escalation to prevent or postpone this outcome essential? Were the costs, in American lives and treasure, warranted?

Even Bundy, in this guarded moment, seemed to waver—to express doubt on this crucial question. "[T]he whole game," he privately confessed, "is less than it today appears, both *in status and in consequences* . . . because the result elsewhere would not be earthshattering—*win or lose.*" What is more, he continued, Washington could "claim special circumstances whenever [it] want[ed]." Saigon's political debilities were so severe. so profound, and there for all the world to see.

And yet Bundy could not bring himself to change his basic judgment, to act on the insights he had so forcefully articulated. As if to reconvince himself, Bundy concluded his thoughts with a personal peroration. The "battle in the South must go on!" he finished.[15]

Bundy's soliloquy had centered on U.S. troops in South Vietnam, but it was the U.S. bombing of North Vietnam which preoccupied President Johnson and his top advisers at their "Tuesday Lunch" two days later.

McNamara, Rusk, and Bundy joined LBJ in the second-floor dining room of the Mansion at 2:45 that afternoon. The intimate, well-appointed room, walled by murals depicting famous Revolutionary War battles, provided a fitting setting for this high-level deliberation on war strategy.

Johnson, seated in a large leather chair at one end of the oblong mahogany table, dominated the session with his physical presence and searching questions. "Where are we going?" he demanded to know. ROLLING THUNDER had entered its fourth week without tangible results, and the pressure for further steps increased daily.

McNamara tried to reassure LBJ, telling him that "our message *may* be getting through" to "Hanoi" and "China," but his uncertainty scarcely comforted the President.

Rusk seemed hardly more encouraging. He detected "some signs" of communist reaction, but as yet, no diplomatic "doors" had been opened.

"Do[n't] they know we're willin' to talk?" Johnson shot back in evident frustration.

LBJ was baffled. North Vietnam continued to spurn negotiations, to resist the mounting air attacks. How could this small, underdeveloped country possibly resist America's overwhelming might?

Frustrated by Hanoi's diplomatic intransigence, Johnson turned to military measures. Leaning over a map of Vietnam spread atop the table, LBJ slowly ran his fingers down the ROLLING THUNDER target list. "You can revisit targets," he said, glancing up at McNamara. "I don't wanna run out of targets and I don't wanna go to Hanoi." Johnson intended to keep pressuring North Vietnam, without resorting to all-out air attacks which might provoke war with China or Russia.[16]

As LBJ struggled over the future course of bombing, military chiefs drafted plans for further troop deployments. On March 19, Admiral Sharp, commander of American forces in the Pacific, cabled his support for Westmoreland's Phubai proposal, along with a request for another Marine battalion to Danang. The following day, March 20, the Joint Chiefs submitted their own plan to McNamara. It recommended a much bigger deployment— two U.S. divisions to South Vietnam's northern and central provinces.[17]

When McNamara received these requests, he ordered his assistant, John

McNaughton, to prepare a study of options for the Principals. McNaughton submitted his study to McNamara, Rusk, and McGeorge Bundy on March 24. In it, he described a South Vietnam racing toward collapse:

> The situation . . . is bad and deteriorating. The VC have the initiative. Defeatism is gaining among the rural population, . . . in the cities, and even among the soldiers. . . . The Hop Tac [pacification] area around Saigon is making little progress; the Delta stays bad; the country has been severed in the north. GVN control is shrinking to enclaves, some burdened with refugees.

South Vietnam had entered a steep decline, which McNaughton feared would not " 'bottom out' unless major actions are taken." He perceived three choices, each entailing special risks: "(a) Will-breaking strikes on [the] DRV; (b) large troop deployments; (c) exit by negotiations." McNaughton quickly dismissed the first option. Massive bombing of North Vietnam threatened major escalation, perhaps leading to nuclear war with China and Russia. Besides, he doubted Hanoi would "cave" in to such attacks or that the Vietcong would even "obey a caving DRV."

McNaughton also considered negotiated withdrawal highly problematic. He believed Washington could limit political damage caused by withdrawal by emphasizing the "uniqueness and congenital impossibility of [the] SVN case (e.g. Viet Minh held much of SVN in 1954, long sieve-like borders, unfavorable terrain, no national tradition, few administrators, mess left by French, competing factions, . . . etc.)." But even these realities, McNaughton felt, could not offset the "overwhelming" risk of "humiliation" to the United States.

That left larger troop deployments. Here, McNaughton recommended the two battalions favored by Westmoreland and Sharp, together with one of the JCS's two requested divisions—approximately 20,000 soldiers.

Although McNaughton had endorsed a major increase in America's ground presence, he worried over its consequences. "Once US troops are in," McNaughton wrote the Principals, "it will be difficult to withdraw them . . . without admitting defeat." Moreover, he expected these requests would be only the first of many; 20,000 American soldiers could not possibly reverse South Vietnam's declining situation. "It will take massive deployments (many divisions)," McNaughton expressly warned the Principals, dismissing any notion of limited troop commitments.

McNaughton clearly perceived the trend toward ever-mounting involvement. Once sizable U.S. troops had been committed, more and more would be requested. Eventually, perhaps hundreds of thousands of American soldiers would be fighting a war of unlimited duration.

It was a sobering scenario, but one McNaughton considered tolerable, because he judged it "essential—however badly [Southeast Asia] may go over the next 1-3 years—that [the] US emerge as a 'good doctor.' " "We must have kept promises, been tough, taken risks, gotten bloodied, and hurt the enemy very badly," he reasoned.

McNaughton's thinking reflected a belief, shared by many contemporaries, in the indivisibility of global containment. Even if South Vietnam could not be saved (and McNaughton doubted this seriously), he felt the United States had to persist, if only to prove its anti-communist resolve. America had to spend its strength on a losing cause, paradoxically, to prove its credibility elsewhere.[18]

Such reasoning demanded greater U.S. involvement, now that South Vietnam verged on failure. But if most observers agreed Washington had reached a crossroads, not everyone believed, like John McNaughton, that an Americanized war should be the next turn.

Certainly not Mike Mansfield, whom President Johnson telephoned again on the morning of March 24. Troubled by the growing pressure for a major troop commitment, LBJ spilled his concerns to Mansfield. Mansfield sensed the anxiety in Johnson's voice—the pull on him toward deeper involvement—and cautioned LBJ against it. The Majority Leader elaborated his thoughts in a long letter to Johnson that evening, pleading against further U.S. intervention.

"I have written frankly and at length," Mansfield told his longtime friend, "out of deep concern over the present trend of events in Viet Nam." "We are in very deep already and in most unfavorable circumstances," he warned, urging Johnson to avoid getting in deeper.

What had brought the administration to this ominous juncture? Mansfield cited, as his reader doubtless lamented, the commitments LBJ had inherited. "In my judgment we were in too deep long before you assumed office," he wrote. But that was little consolation; Johnson was now the President. It was his responsibility to decide what course to follow.

Mansfield considered the present one—a continued escalation of U.S. involvement—most dangerous. "In the end," he wrote, "I fear that this course . . . will play havoc with the domestic program of the Administration . . . and with our interests and constructive influence elsewhere in the world." Escalation threatened to damage not only LBJ's Great Society but the very sources of American power.

It was an extravagant perception of American power, ironically, which now threatened to harm its substance, according to Mansfield. Heretofore, he noted, Washington had assumed it could "make whatever expenditure of American lives and resources, on an ascending scale, is necessary in order for us to exercise . . . primacy over what transpires in South Viet Nam"—

"[t]hat in the absence of unconditional capitulation of the Viet Cong, our military involvement must continue and be increased as necessary. . . ."

Mansfield emphatically rejected this assumption. American power was not unlimited, nor, more important, were American interests in South Vietnam. "[W]e are there not to take primary responsibility," he reasoned, "but to provide whatever assistance is wanted and can be used effectively by the Vietnamese themselves." An Americanized war would undermine both of these principles, by raising the cost in U.S. lives and resources as it weakened South Vietnamese independence.[19]

While Johnson pondered Mansfield's warning against committing more American troops, he confronted new pressure to do precisely this at an NSC meeting on March 26.[20]

CIA Director McCone opened the meeting with a sobering report on ROLLING THUNDER. Bombing had not inhibited North Vietnam's infiltration, he told the President, nor forced it to the bargaining table. "Hanoi remains unconvinced that they cannot win out militarily," McCone said, summarizing current intelligence assessments. "They are not yet ready to negotiate."

How, then, to shore up South Vietnam's declining fortunes, if not more American troops? McNamara addressed the generals' plans in this area. "We now have 28,000 U.S. troops in Vietnam," he said, and "Ambassador Taylor and General Westmoreland are asking for 10,000 more." McNamara had linked Taylor—who actually opposed Westmoreland—to the general's two-battalion request, while avoiding any mention of the Joint Chiefs' two-division proposal.

McNamara's omission doubtlessly reflected Johnson's wishes. LBJ, uneasy and uncertain about the larger troop proposal, aimed to conceal its dimensions from the bureaucracy, Congress, and public, hoping to limit political pressure for escalation and therefore danger to his domestic agenda.

General Wheeler went along with Johnson, for the time being at least. Rather than press LBJ for the two divisions, Wheeler alluded to a "proposal" for U.S. combat troops to "be looked at when . . . Taylor arrives here next week." "A second action program is being drawn up," he added of the JCS request submitted six days earlier.[21]

Ambassador Taylor arrived back in Washington on the morning of March 28 to a minimum of press speculation, just as President Johnson had intended. Stepping off his military transport jet, Taylor held a brief plane-side news conference. The Ambassador proclaimed improvement in South Vietnam, adding that his visit entailed normal and periodic discussions.[22]

The following day, however, Taylor went to the Pentagon to discuss the Joint Chiefs' two-division proposal. Under their plan, one Marine division would go to the northern provinces and one Army division to the central highlands—a total of more than 32,000 new U.S. forces engaged in active combat.

As he had in cables to President Johnson, Taylor challenged these additional deployments. He particularly questioned their political wisdom. Anti-American sentiment lay just beneath the surface in South Vietnam, Taylor warned the Joint Chiefs, and committing large numbers of U.S. troops risked igniting it, stirring dangerous perceptions of neo-colonialism among the people.

The ambassador's comments impressed McNamara, reinforcing his own anxieties about larger ground forces. McNamara told the Chiefs their proposal would have to be studied further in light of Taylor's reservations.[23]

That study came the next afternoon, during the President's Tuesday Lunch with McNamara, Rusk, and McGeorge Bundy. McNamara, in this private setting, reviewed the cumulative troop requests with much greater candor than he had at the NSC meeting four days earlier. Sensitive to Johnson's concerns about the domestic repercussions of larger deployments, he tried to estimate the minimum level necessary to meet military needs. McNamara figured an "additional 20,000 conventional [i.e. combat] reinforcement," plus "two more Marine battalions"—to Phubai and Danang.[24]

All this talk about troops disconcerted Johnson. He wanted to address other issues—of an economic and political nature—which he understood better and which he felt played an equally important role in overcoming the insurgency. What about regional development—creating an Inter-Asian Bank along the lines of the Inter-American bank? LBJ wondered. How about "land reform"? he asked. Like the captain seeking harbor from a gathering storm, Johnson sought shelter in the familiar instrument of social reform, hoping this, somehow, would lessen his military burdens.[25]

And lessen his domestic political concerns as well, which had become acute by late March 1965. For the President confronted demands for more troops and thus a wider war just as many of his Great Society initiatives approached crucial junctures in their legislative journeys. The Elementary and Secondary Education bill neared a final congressional vote; the Medicare/Medicaid bill awaited floor action in the House; hearings on the Voting Rights bill had begun in both chambers. LBJ faced a wrenching dilemma: a deepening Vietnam commitment jeopardizing his emerging Great Society.

Johnson chose to brook this dilemma by denying, publicly, that it existed. Late on the afternoon of April 1, LBJ called a surprise news conference. Standing before the hastily assembled reporters in the White House Theater, Johnson waxed cheerfully on the Great Society's progress through Congress. Seventy days into his term, LBJ had the legislature playing his tune. His bills were moving. Johnson could not resist favorable comparison with FDR's New Deal. Congress has "passed more measures already than were passed the first 100 days of the Roosevelt administration," LBJ proudly noted.

When the issue of Vietnam arose, however, Johnson's sunny disposition evaporated. A correspondent who had learned about an important White House meeting on Vietnam later that evening asked whether "dramatic" proposals would be discussed. LBJ's eyes, which had glimmered with talk of the Great Society, narrowed perceptibly. "I know of no far-reaching strategy that is being suggested or promulgated," he answered. Struggling to quell rumors about troop increases he feared might scuttle his domestic reforms, Johnson added cryptically:

> I hear the commentators . . . talk about the dramatics of this situation, the great struggle that was coming about between various men and the top level conferences that were in the offing, where revolutionary decisions were being made, and I turned off one of my favorite networks and walked out of the room. Mrs. Johnson said, "What did you say?" And I said, "I didn't say anything but if you are asking me what I think, I would say God forgive them for they know not what they do."

In an oblique but poignant way, LBJ seemed to implore the press not to dramatize the troop issue, for that would raise political dangers he wished to avoid.[26]

From his press conference in the White House Theater, Johnson crossed the portico to the Cabinet Room, where his very closest Vietnam advisers awaited him.[27]

LBJ opened this crucial session by discussing his surprise meeting with reporters. By calling it at the last minute, Johnson had hoped to dodge troublesome rumors about troop increases in Vietnam. But the press had confronted him with these rumors, and shaken him with their unexpected diligence. LBJ admitted, rather sheepishly, that he had assured reporters "no great decisions [were] to be discussed" at this gathering.

Rusk broke the awkward silence by reviewing American objectives in Vietnam. He identified four goals—all tied to Hanoi's support of the southern insurgency: an end to the infiltration of native southerners regrouped north following the 1954 Geneva Accords; an end to the infiltration of military and logistical supplies; an end to the direction of many Vietcong operations; and a withdrawal of recently introduced North Vietnamese regulars.

ROLLING THUNDER had failed to curtail any of these in a meaningful way. Johnson and his advisers wondered whether it ever would—short of a massive bombardment which might trigger Chinese and Russian intervention. Rusk summarized the administration's predicament vividly: *"How to make pressure* without reaching [the] flash point," he wondered.

This fear of crossing the "flash point"—of sparking, through stepped-up pressure in Vietnam, a direct confrontation between the nuclear super-powers—troubled LBJ constantly. For Johnson remembered the Korean War and the Cuban Missile Crisis as vividly as he remembered the Munich Conference. The images of Chinese armies surging across the Yalu and of nuclear brinkmanship in the Caribbean haunted him as fully as Chamberlain's protestation of "peace in our time"—perhaps more so, because of their immediacy. LBJ later recalled:

> In the dark at night, I would lay awake picturing my boys flying around North Vietnam, asking myself an endless series of questions. What if one of those targets you picked today triggers off Russia or China? What happens then?[28]

Plagued by the specter of nuclear conflagration, Johnson hesitated to unleash unlimited bombing.

But if LBJ eschewed all-out air attacks for understandable reasons, he had to find other ways to pressure North Vietnam. Negotiations appeared one option. Johnson saw "no harm" in asking for talks through the ICSC, he said, but feared "great harm if they tell anyone they are asking for us." Harm not only to Washington's bargaining leverage with Hanoi but also to the President's domestic political standing. For LBJ deeply feared the right wing—the "great beast" he called it—which, as George Ball remembered him saying, "would come in and insist that we really blow the whole place apart."[29]

Whatever the objections from the right, Johnson looked to negotiations as a way to end North Vietnam's support of the Vietcong and thus arrest the insurgency. Securing the former meant ending the latter, LBJ and his advisers had repeatedly insisted to the public.

Actual circumstances, however, revealed a more complex and disturbing picture. The Vietcong resistance, though receiving supplies, training, operational assistance, and even small numbers of troops from North Vietnam, rested on a bedrock of discontented South Vietnamese, which no amount of U.S. military or diplomatic pressure on Hanoi could erase.

Rusk indirectly acknowledged this sobering reality. The Secretary confessed, quite candidly, that he was "not sure Hanoi can deliver on cessation" of the southern insurgency, even if it could be coerced into trying. CIA Director McCone also doubted North Vietnam's ability to turn the Vietcong off like a faucet, though he considered a "substantial reduction . . . possible."[30]

Rusk's and McCone's appraisals unsettled the President. How could the VC guerrillas be subdued, if not by pressure against Hanoi?

Johnson was frustrated and bewildered. "If we can just get our feet on their neck," he muttered, referring to the stubbornly elusive insurgency. Exasperated by the complexities of the situation, LBJ alternated between expressions of uncertainty and anger. Would pledges of economic assistance, such as "rural electrification" and "brotherhood operation[s]," coax the Vietcong to abandon their struggle? he asked. A moment later, Johnson seemed full of uncompromising determination. "We have set our hand to [the] wheel," he declared, and America had to persevere. "Get plenty more targets," the President barked at McNamara and Wheeler, as "damn many planes" as necessary "to find 'em and kill 'em." Then back again to the idea of inducements: "hold out [the] promised land," he said. LBJ intended to punish and reward the VC into submission—to awe the insurgency with America's destructive power, while seducing it with dispensations of America's economic largesse.

Whatever Johnson's long-range theorizing about the Vietcong problem, he faced a more immediate decision: whether to commit more U.S. troops to save South Vietnam. General Wheeler stressed the urgency of the situation. "We are losing the war out there," he said, pressing LBJ to approve the Joint Chiefs' two-division proposal.

Johnson hesitated to grant the big request. "Have we exhausted all the possibilities with foreign forces?" he asked, seeking to strengthen America's political position while diffusing its military burdens.

Wheeler summarized the extent of allied assistance to South Vietnam: South Korea might muster, at Washington's urging, one combat division; Australia, one battalion; the Philippines, perhaps one regimental combat team. No help from Great Britain, France, New Zealand, or even Japan, which lay much closer to Indochina than the United States.

After reviewing America's lonesome commitment, Wheeler again pressed LBJ for a decision on the two divisions. Johnson deferred the JCS proposal. But he agreed to Westmoreland's two-battalion request and, much more important, to change the Marines' mission from base security to active combat.

In parrying the larger force proposal, LBJ had yielded a crucial concession. The troop numbers had been moderated, but their function had been broadened significantly. U.S. ground forces would now directly enter the war.[31]

Johnson's reluctant decision to commit additional soldiers and to change their mission only deepened his anxiety about Vietnam's domestic repercussions. With American troops involved in the fighting, U.S. casualties and costs would surely rise, straining the political consensus and economic resources sustaining the Great Society. Fearing these effects on his domestic program, LBJ elected to veil his latest decision—even before the full National Security Council, which he convened the following afternoon.[32]

At this meeting, Johnson skirted the previous day's decisions by focusing on political issues. He asked Ambassador Taylor, who had briefed House and Senate leaders earlier that morning, to report on the mood of Congress. House members seemed satisfied with the administration's Vietnam efforts. But Taylor sensed trouble in the Senate. Fulbright, he said, had voiced concern over rumors the President might send three or four new divisions to South Vietnam. The senator had also questioned whether the Tonkin Gulf Resolution covered such deployments, Taylor added.

If Fulbright's comments troubled LBJ, he did not show it. Johnson could simply see no reason, he professed, why additional forces required another congressional resolution. LBJ's glib deflection of Fulbright's criticism masked deep fear of renewed legislative debate over Vietnam at this critical juncture in his Great Society agenda.

Johnson knew his approval of additional deployments also threatened that agenda. To lessen the threat, he decided to limit knowledge of those deployments and their new combat mission to his very closest advisers. Using Wheeler, Taylor, and McGeorge Bundy—each privy to the previous day's decisions—LBJ cleverly concealed those decisions from the larger NSC group.

Like a director guiding his players, Johnson asked General Wheeler what specific measures would be instituted. Taking his cue from LBJ, Wheeler noted the two-battalion deployment, but not the new combat mission. Taylor also played his assigned role, reviewing what he would tell the media: "No dramatic change in strategy; we will try to do better what we are doing now."

Lest any of those present suspected something more, McGeorge Bundy cautioned everyone to use the President's April 1 press comments as a guide in their public statements. "Under no circumstances," he said under Johnson's watchful eye, "should there be any reference to the movement of U.S. forces or other future courses of action."

Not everyone yielded to LBJ's orchestration, however. John McCone, who had attended the previous day's "off-the-record" meeting, recognized what President Johnson was doing and disliked it.

A soft-spoken man with silvery-white hair and rimless glasses, McCone's professorial bearing concealed a strong-willed and decisive temperament. Chosen by Kennedy to succeed Allen Dulles as CIA Director after the Bay of Pigs debacle, McCone had guided the agency with the confidence and determination of a successful industrialist turned government servant.

McCone had begun his career in the late 1930s, when he had helped launch the giant Bechtel Corporation. During World War II, he had devoted his energies to directing California's massive shipbuilding program. After several years in the private sector, McCone had returned to public service, as Truman's Undersecretary of the Air Force in the early 1950s, and, later, chairman of Eisenhower's Atomic Energy Commission. In these positions, McCone had developed a reputation as a driving administrator, whose exacting methods punctuated his independent nature.

Forceful in ideology as in temperament, McCone affirmed a resolute anticommunism. He was a veteran Cold Warrior, who viewed the complexities of Asian nationalism amid East-West geopolitical competition through the stark lens of a tightly controlled and monolithic communism.

These assumptions conditioned McCone's perception of the Vietnam struggle. He believed the trouble lay solely in Hanoi—that the North Vietnamese held an iron hand over the Vietcong and thus were the key to forcing their submission.

LBJ's agreement to commit more ground forces and to change their mission therefore troubled McCone. Unless Washington intensified its air strikes against the North, inflicting enough damage to threaten Hanoi's vital interests, McCone felt sending more U.S. troops into the South would prove futile.

McCone hinted as much at the NSC meeting. The current level of bombing had not reduced North Vietnam's support of the insurgency, he told those gathered around the Cabinet table; if anything, Hanoi's position had hardened. With each successive week of bombing, McCone continued, Washington would face increasing international and domestic pressure to stop it— just as the administration sent additional ground forces to South Vietnam. The prospects were sobering: a larger number of American soldiers fighting a guerrilla war of peripheral significance.[33]

President Johnson, startled by McCone's bluntness, quickly ended the meeting.[34]

LBJ had concealed the change in strategy from the bureaucracy in Washington because he feared its effect on his legislative drive in Congress. But Johnson could not conceal the new combat strategy in South Vietnam. He could only muffle its implementation, which LBJ instructed Rusk to do in reporting his decision to the American mission in Saigon.

On April 3, Secretary Rusk cabled Alexis Johnson, Taylor's second in command, that the President had approved two additional Marine battalions, along with a change in their mission, which now included "counterinsurgency combat operations." The course of American involvement had shifted dramatically. Yet Rusk instructed the embassy to convey a very different impression—that Washington was "continuing on [the] course previously set." "In keeping [to] this policy," Rusk added, the "deployments . . .

will be spaced over [a] period [of] time with publicity re all deployments kept at [the] lowest key possible."[35]

Johnson's effort to cloak the Marines' new mission related to the Army units scheduled to arrive with them: a logistics command and an engineering construction group sent to lay the foundation for expanded military operations. These units reflected the compromise struck between LBJ and the Joint Chiefs on April 1. Although Johnson had deflected the Chiefs' two-division proposal, he had agreed to pave the way for future deployments. Fearful of antagonizing the Pentagon brass and their conservative allies in Congress, LBJ had left the door open to larger commitments.

This concession illustrated the growing military pressures on Johnson, themselves a product of his earlier bombing decision. At the end of February, LBJ had approved the Marine deployment to Danang, specifically prohibiting their use in combat. At the beginning of April, he had repealed that prohibition, added two battalions, and authorized the groundwork for two divisions more. In less than five weeks, Johnson had reversed himself dramatically. ROLLING THUNDER had altered the flow of policy toward the military, and LBJ was finding their requests increasingly difficult to resist.

Indeed, on April 5, Johnson finally consented to preparations for the two-division deployment. That afternoon, McNamara informed General Wheeler of the President's decision, instructing him to begin arranging for their dispatch to South Vietnam.[36]

The Joint Chiefs, anticipating LBJ's consent, had already begun planning for the larger deployments. On April 2, they had submitted a series of requests to McNamara: increased defense spending, extended tours of duty, limited mobilization of reserves, higher manpower ceilings. The Chiefs were bracing for a bigger war in Vietnam and saw these measures as essential preconditions for fighting it.[37]

Johnson saw them differently—as threats to his domestic agenda. Raising military appropriations meant reducing social expenditures; expanding tours of duty and manpower ceilings entailed heavier draft calls; mobilizing the reserves implied a national emergency—all diverting the country's attention and resources away from his Great Society to Vietnam.

This was something LBJ was determined to avoid. Johnson had acceded to the Pentagon's two-division request, but he refused to let it thwart his domestic political goals. Wheeler and Westmoreland would get their additional troops, but on LBJ's terms: quietly, gradually, and without public disclosure.

The same day Johnson directed McNamara to proceed with the two-division plan, April 5, he ordered McGeorge Bundy to draft a national security directive enumerating this and other recent decisions. Bundy prepared the secret directive, which LBJ signed the following day.

NSAM-328, as the document came to be known, spelled out Johnson's recent military decisions: the two additional Marine battalions to Phubai and Danang; the increase in logistical forces preparatory to larger ground deployments; and the all-important change in troop mission, from base security to active combat. With these decisions, LBJ had carried the United States, unmistakably, across the line from advisory support to war in Vietnam.

Johnson intended to keep that line an invisible one, however. He deliberately limited NSAM-328's distribution to only three officials: Rusk, McNamara, and McCone—the absolute minimum necessary to ensure its implementation. To ensure its secrecy, he warned Rusk, McNamara, and McCone to avoid "premature publicity" about the ground deployments and their change in mission "by all possible precautions." "The actions themselves," the directive read, "should be taken in ways that should minimize any appearance of sudden changes in policy, and official statements on these troop movements will be made only with the direct approval of the Secretary of Defense, in consultation with the Secretary of State." LBJ's desire was explicit: "that these movements and changes should be understood as being gradual and wholly consistent with existing policy." The decisions codified in NSAM-328 represented Johnson's response to accumulated military pressures, framed in the evasive and misleading language of a President fearful of their domestic political consequences.[38]

6

"If I Were Ho Chi Minh,
I Would Never Negotiate"

THROUGHOUT MARCH 1965, President Johnson and his advisers had focused on events in South Vietnam; those events, and the growing pressure for American ground forces to save the situation, had dominated policymakers' attention.

The public's attention, however, had focused increasingly on the bombing of North Vietnam. For ROLLING THUNDER, once under way, had sparked mounting controversy both at home and abroad. By April 1965, that controversy had erupted into open opposition to the bombing, which LBJ's administration could scarcely ignore.

This opposition jolted Washington officials because they had not anticipated it. Most had expected bombing to produce quick and decisive results—stiffening South Vietnamese morale and arresting North Vietnamese infiltration within a matter of months, well before domestic and world opinion mobilized against the air campaign.

Even LBJ, usually skeptical about bombing's effectiveness, had expressed surprising confidence at the outset of ROLLING THUNDER. Less than two weeks into the bombing, on March 14, Johnson had likened North Vietnam's reaction to a "filibuster—enormous resistance at first, then a steady whittling away, then Ho hurrying to get it over with," he had predicted to an aide. The President would bring Hanoi to its knees—and the war to an end—before Vietnam's casualties and costs disrupted domestic support for his Great Society reforms.[1]

Johnson's confidence, like his advisers', stemmed from recent experience. LBJ's administration included many veterans of the Cuban Missile Crisis, who readily assumed that "controlled" escalation would dissuade Ho Chi Minh in 1965 as surely as Nikita Khrushchev had been in 1962. As Cyrus

Vance, a high-ranking official in both Kennedy's and Johnson's Pentagon, later observed,

> We had seen the gradual application of force applied in the Cuban Missile Crisis, and had seen a very successful result. We believed that if this same gradual and restrained application of force were applied in . . . Vietnam, that one could expect the same kind of result; that rational people on the other side would respond to increasing military pressure and would therefore try and seek a political solution.[2]

To Vance and other U.S. policymakers, bombing seemed a limited measure—a mere intimation of the massive force America could unleash against North Vietnam, should it hesitate to yield on Washington's terms. In their minds, Hanoi could not possibly resist this overwhelming pressure.

Such reasoning reflected the tendency of great powers, as the historian Theodore Draper has commented, "to think of 'limited wars' in terms of themselves . . . of the 'limit' as what it would be, in relative terms, if they were taking the punishment or in relation to the total force they are capable of using." "But," Draper has also noted, "neither of these senses may seem very limited to a small power. A great power may use only a very limited portion of its power, but it will be enough to make a small power feel that it must fight an unlimited war or not fight at all."[3]

North Vietnam, apparently, felt just this way. For rather than buckling under to the bombing, as most U.S. planners had expected, Hanoi had reacted by hardening its position. The day after ROLLING THUNDER began, Mai Van Bo, head of North Vietnam's commercial delegation in Paris, had approached the Quai d'Orsay and informed its Indochina chief, Brethes, that "while previously the DRV had been ready to consider negotiation of some sort, US actions had changed the situation." "Negotiations [were] no longer a matter for consideration at this time," Bo had emphasized.[4]

If American policymakers had badly underestimated Hanoi's resistance to bombing, they had also badly overestimated Saigon's ability to capitalize on it. ROLLING THUNDER had not steadied the South Vietnamese regime. It had not increased its effectiveness. Political instability remained as chronic as before.

The pressures generated by Hanoi's unexpected defiance and Saigon's continued weakness had been intensified by growing international opposition to the bombing led by United Nations Secretary-General U Thant. On several occasions beginning in August 1964 and into 1965, Thant had sought to arrange private talks between the United States and North Vietnam in his home capital of Rangoon, Burma. Although Hanoi had expressed an interest in bilateral discussions, according to Thant, Washington had repeatedly spurned these reported overtures. The administration's response, through its U.N. Ambassador Adlai Stevenson, had consistently been: "There may be a time . . . but not now."[5]

Political considerations in both the United States and South Vietnam explained Washington's delay. During the fall of 1964, President Johnson had been absorbed in an election contest against an opponent demanding tougher military action in Vietnam. In this political climate, secret contacts with Hanoi had seemed a dangerous gambit, potentially lambasted by LBJ's conservative rival.

After the election, Washington had continued to shun negotiations, afraid they might undermine the shaky South Vietnamese regime. American policymakers, troubled by Saigon's fragile political equilibrium, had feared leaks about secret U.S.-North Vietnamese contacts might shatter it completely.

Finally, and perhaps most important, the administration had never fancied negotiations which, in its view, would simply ratify the existing military balance in South Vietnam. The communists held that balance by 1964. And with each new Vietcong success, Washington's willingness to negotiate had become all that more remote.

The further Washington had moved from negotiations, however, the more impatient U Thant had grown with the United States. By late January 1965, when Ambassador Stevenson deflected Thant's latest bid for discussions, citing their threat to government morale in Saigon, the Secretary-General had exploded in bitter. frustration. "What government?" he had chided Stevenson, "Minh, Khanh, Suu . . . ?"[6]

Washington's effort to resuscitate that government through air strikes against North Vietnam had deepened Thant's frustration, leading him to press the administration for negotiations once more. At a meeting with Stevenson's U.N. deputy, Charles Yost, on February 12, the Secretary-General had urged Washington to reciprocate Hanoi's "positive" response to bilateral talks. The American government had again demurred.[7]

Thant, therefore, had turned to the American media. In a news statement released later on February 12, the Secretary-General had openly criticized Washington's post-Pleiku air raids, beseeching the administration to shift its efforts "away from the field of battle to the conference table."[8]

Thant's ploy had annoyed Washington but not changed its position, as the Secretary-General had discovered on February 16. Thant had met with Stevenson again that day to reiterate his plea for bilateral discussions. The Secretary-General had probed the North Vietnamese through a Russian intermediary in the U.N. Secretariat, he told Stevenson, and had found them "prepared to meet the United States anytime."[9]

Yet Washington had remained doggedly resistant. Unlike Thant, who had perceived an opening in Hanoi's response, the administration had perceived only empty posturing. Washington's other North Vietnamese contact, Canadian ICSC representative J. Blair Seaborn, had quietly sounded Hanoi in early December, receiving signals which, a high U.S. official later asserted, "had been negative to the point of harshness." This reaction, coupled with Washington's continuing anxiety about its weak bargaining position, had set the administration firmly against Thant's initiative.[10]

But Thant had not relented; he had only intensified his pressure, by openly suggesting that Washington had withheld the full story of his negotiating efforts. On February 24, the Secretary-General had stepped before reporters at U.N. headquarters and publicly declared:

> I am sure the great American people, if only they know the true facts and the background to the developments in South Vietnam, will agree with me that further bloodshed is unnecessary. . . . As you know, in times of war and of hostilities the first casualty is truth.[11]

Thant's remarks had provoked an angry response from Secretary of State Rusk, who had telephoned Thant that night and privately scolded his public comments. Thant had countered by asking whether Rusk knew of his negotiating proposals. Yes, the Secretary had replied, but they were "just procedural"—neglecting substantive issues and promising little hope of agreement.

To Thant, any hope of agreement between Washington and Hanoi first demanded communication. North Vietnam had agreed "right away" to bilateral discussions, the Secretary-General reminded Rusk, yet he had "heard nothing" from the United States. Pressed for a reply, Rusk had rejected talks as "out of the question," because he doubted they would be "fruitful."[12]

"Fruitful," a close associate of Rusk's later explained, "at that time still consisted pretty much of saying to Hanoi, 'Look, let's work out a deal under which you will capitulate.'" And, as Ambassador Stevenson had told Thant on February 27, North Vietnam appeared hardly willing to capitulate. Less than ten days before, according to Stevenson, Hanoi had informed the United States through a "third party"—mainland China's ambassador in Warsaw—that they would not talk with Washington while one American soldier remained in Vietnam; that U.S. air attacks did not frighten them; and that Saigon faced imminent collapse anyway. The gap between Washington and Hanoi seemed unbridgeable.[13]

Yet Thant had tried to close it by deciphering North Vietnam's conflicting signals. Interpreting Hanoi's "no" through Chinese channels as a political gesture toward Peking, the Secretary-General had implored Washington to follow up their "yes" through Russian/U.N. channels.

But Stevenson's response had remained unchanged: no negotiations unless they promised "acceptable results"—an end to North Vietnamese infiltration and the guaranteed independence of South Vietnam. These demands, given Hanoi's objectives, meant no negotiations at all.

Washington seemed resigned to this fact, and had planned accordingly. The administration would achieve "acceptable results" through coercion, if not diplomacy. As Stevenson had explained to Thant at the end of their February 27 meeting, "Hanoi either slows down or we step up."[14]

The ROLLING THUNDER campaign which soon followed had only compounded Washington's international troubles, by provoking new calls for a political settlement from voices far beyond the United Nations. In late March, representatives of seventeen non-aligned countries had met in Belgrade, Yugoslavia, to discuss Vietnam's growing threat to world stability. Afraid that China and Russia might be drawn into the conflict, thus touching off a global war, the neutrals had appealed to Washington for immediate negotiations, "without . . . any preconditions," in Vietnam.[15]

This pressure from non-aligned states for negotiations had coincided with increased pressure from America's own allies. For several years, French President Charles de Gaulle had privately urged Washington to reconvene the Geneva Conference as a step toward neutralization and eventual American disengagement. After Pleiku, however, de Gaulle had begun dispensing his advice publicly. In numerous conversations with journalists and visiting statesmen during February and March 1965, de Gaulle had loudly pressed the United States to pursue a diplomatic solution.[16]

Canadian Prime Minister Lester Pearson had offered similar counsel before an American audience on April 2. Speaking at Temple University in Philadelphia, Pearson had urged an immediate pause in air strikes against North Vietnam in order to break the diplomatic deadlock and thus avert a wider war. Pearson's comment, coming just hours before a scheduled meeting with President Johnson at Camp David, had dramatized the growing friction between Washington and Ottawa over the bombing issue.[17]

The bombing had sparked not just foreign criticism but mounting domestic criticism as well. Within days of the post-Pleiku reprisals, influential commentators had begun challenging Johnson's Vietnam policy, pressing him to reverse America's deepening involvement. "The time has come to call a spade a bloody shovel," James Reston of the *New York Times* had written on February 13. "This country is in an undeclared and unexplained war. . . ." LBJ had plunged the nation further into Vietnam, Reston had complained, even as the negotiating efforts of U Thant and others were being "blithely brushed aside."[18]

Walter Lippmann, another prominent critic of bombing, had also begun urging Johnson toward a settlement. "[W]hile this has . . . been the implied objective of our policy," Lippmann had written of negotiations on February 17, "the time has come when it should be the avowed objective, . . . pursued with all our . . . diplomatic resources." His pointed conclusion: "There is no tolerable alternative [to] a negotiated truce."[19]

Complaints in the media had echoed in the halls of Congress, where protests against the war had widened, especially in the Senate. For more than a year, Ernest Gruening of Alaska and Wayne Morse of Oregon had comprised Johnson's sole opposition in Congress; their's had been the only votes cast against the Tonkin Gulf Resolution in August. But with the bombing had emerged new voices of dissent, denouncing LBJ's recent escalation.

Frank Church of Idaho was a Democrat who had consistently supported Johnson's Vietnam policy in the past. But on the evening of February 17, he had risen in the Senate and delivered a scathing assault on the President's bombing decision. "The systematic and sustained bombing of North Vietnam, unattended by any profferred recourse to the bargaining table, can only lead us into war," Church had warned his colleagues. He had ridiculed the notion that bombing would somehow force the North Vietnamese to abandon their abiding goal of reunification. "[I]f the long, long struggle that these people have engaged upon is any indication of their resolution," Church had cautioned his fellow senators, "then our bombings will not break their spirit or solve our problem."[20]

George McGovern of South Dakota was another Democratic loyalist who had joined the growing ranks of Vietnam critics. The same night as Church, McGovern had taken the Senate floor to denounce the bombing and urge immediate negotiations. "[T]he time for the United States to explore the possibility of a negotiated settlement is now," McGovern had insisted, before America slipped into a massive Asian war.[21]

Church's and McGovern's criticisms had typified Johnson's mounting problems with liberals generally. Though opinion polls had registered broad public support for the President's bombing decision, other indicators had revealed widening liberal disaffection. White House mail, which had run less than two-to-one against the Tonkin Gulf raid in August, had jumped to almost twelve-to-one against the post-Pleiku air strikes in February. Most correspondents had urged negotiations as an alternative to escalation.[22]

This shift reflected not only liberals' growing disenchantment with U.S. involvement in Vietnam but also their growing political assertiveness. Emboldened by Goldwater's defeat in 1964, liberals had moved aggressively to fulfill their reform agenda in 1965. They had returned a President sympathetic to their goals; they had elected a Congress committed to pass their legislation; they had rallied, triumphantly, to Martin Luther King, Jr.'s side in Alabama. Each success had increased liberals' faith in their power to influence events. Now Vietnam seemed the greatest obstacle to domestic reform, and one which they, too, would overcome.

This sense of possibility, of confidence, had suffused the gathering of teachers and students at the University of Michigan on March 24—the first "teach-in" against the Vietnam War. At eight o'clock that evening, over 3,000 people had crowded into Angell Hall to attend an all-night series of rallies, seminars, and speeches denouncing Washington's recent escalation. Speaker after speaker had assailed America's deepening involvement in Vietnam as a threat to America's new age of reform. Determined to conquer historic problems of race and poverty at home, liberals had begun pressing the administration to curb its fledgling war abroad.

A particular vision of the future had stoked liberal opposition to the bombing. But it was a vague uneasiness about the future which had generated anxiety about the bombing among the public generally. Although a majority of Americans had initially supported the bombing, many had grown apprehensive about its consequences. The administration had heightened this apprehension by obscuring its Vietnam policy. Confused about the scope of U.S. involvement in the war, many people had begun demanding talks to end that involvement. By March, a Gallup poll had revealed that while 42 percent of Americans still favored sending "more troops and airplanes" to Vietnam, those favoring "negotiations now" had jumped to 41 percent—a sudden and dramatic rise in peace sentiment.[23]

Johnson's bombing decision had created immense, if unexpected, difficulties for his administration. Instead of bolstering the government in Saigon, it had deepened Hanoi's determination. Instead of strengthening America's international position, it had weakened it substantially. Instead of answering conservative cirticism, it had enflamed liberal sentiment. Instead of reducing the President's political burdens, it had increased them enormously.

Jarred by the unanticipated but rapidly growing opposition to bombing, LBJ set out to blunt the mounting criticism of his Vietnam policy. On March 25, the day after the University of Michigan anti-war "teach-in," the White House released a statement underlining Johnson's commitment to peace in the region. "The United States will never be second in seeking a settlement in Viet-Nam," the bulletin quoted LBJ. "As I have said in every part of the Union," it went on, citing the President, "I am ready to go anywhere at any time, and meet with anyone whenever there is promise of progress toward an honorable peace."[24]

That same afternoon, Johnson instructed McGeorge Bundy and speechwriter Richard Goodwin to draft a major foreign policy address to the nation. In this speech, LBJ would outline his twin objectives in Vietnam: standing firm in the South, while holding open the possibility of negotiations with the North. It was a delicate strategy of toughness and conciliation, but one Johnson hoped would avert the political hazards of either defeat or further escalation.

How would LBJ achieve these seemingly contradictory objectives? The key, Johnson believed, lay in addressing the social and economic problems of both Vietnams. Pitting U.S. resources against poverty, ignorance, and disease in the South would weaken the insurgency's appeal; offering similar resources to the North might coax it into a settlement. American bounty—an exported Great Society—would be the President's trump card in all of Vietnam.

LBJ sketched his ambitious vision to McNamara, Rusk, and McGeorge Bundy at their Tuesday Lunch on April 6. Current drafts of his forthcoming speech to the nation dissatisfied Johnson. They emphasized the military and political aspects of U.S. involvement—ideas like resisting aggression and reaffirming containment of communist expansion.

LBJ wanted something more. He wanted to articulate the "humanitarian" dimension of U.S. involvement as well. Vietnam needed things other than American bullets and bombs, the President believed; it needed "food for stomachs," "drugs for disease," and "schools for children" even more. Instead of commanding troops, Johnson wished that "every general" could be "a surgeon"—"every pilot a nurse"—"every helicopter an ambulance"—that America's capacity for destruction could be transformed into a capacity for healing. It was a deeply personal vision, but also a deeply contradictory one, reflecting LBJ's conflicting objectives.[25]

This tension between Johnson's desire to prevail in Vietnam and his desire to ameliorate its suffering permeated LBJ's nationally televised address at Johns Hopkins University in Baltimore the following night. With university president Milton Eisenhower, his eldest daughter Lynda Bird, Lady Bird, and Vice President Humphrey seated to his left on the stage of Shriver Hall's auditorium, Johnson addressed the audience and the country.

LBJ opened his speech on a note of resolve, stressing Washington's past commitments. "Since 1954 every American President has . . . pledge[d] to help South Viet-Nam defend its independence," Johnson declared, "And I intend to keep that promise."

More than just America's word was at stake, however. So was the fate of Southeast Asia, he asserted. For Johnson, like most of his advisers, harbored an abiding fear of Chinese expansion. He perceived China on the march, menacing not just South Vietnam, but also Burma, Thailand, Laos, Cambodia, Malaysia, and Indonesia. This perception reverberated in Johnson's analysis of the Vietnam conflict:

> Over this war—and all Asia—is another reality: the deepening shadow of Communist China. The rulers in Hanoi are urged on by Peking. This is a regime

which has destroyed freedom in Tibet, which has attacked India, and has been condemned by the United Nations for aggression in Korea. It is a nation which is helping the forces of violence in almost every continent. The contest in Viet-Nam is part of [this] wider pattern of aggressive purposes.

LBJ and his administration clearly viewed China as the primary threat to Asian stability. They aimed, therefore, to limit Chinese expansion, to block what they considered Peking's drive for Asian hegemony. As Johnson's Defense Secretary, Robert McNamara, confided to a prominent journalist some weeks later, the administration's overriding objective in Vietnam was "to contain China in her [present] expansionist phase" as the "Soviet Union was contained" in its earlier "expansionist period."[26]

Washington's fear of Chinese aggression, however misguided, reflected deeply ingrained suspicions. Peking had replaced Moscow in the minds of U.S. policymakers as the wellspring of communist subversion. Mao had replaced Stalin as the fomenter of world revolution. China had replaced Russia, in short, as the focus of America's Cold War suspicions.

These suspicions resonated throughout the President's speech. In stark, almost frightening terms, Johnson depicted China as a hostile and expansive power which would not rest "until all of the nations of Asia are swallowed up." Only American power stood between Peking and a communist Asia, he suggested. To prevent this development, Johnson warned the North Vietnamese—and especially those "who seek to share their conquest"—that the United States would "not be defeated" in South Vietnam, nor "withdraw, either openly or under the cloak of a meaningless agreement."

The President had proclaimed America's determination. He had reaffirmed his toughness. Johnson could now address his other objective: reaching "a peaceful settlement" with North Vietnam. LBJ communicated this goal loudly, seeking to assuage the growing critics of escalation. "We have stated this position over and over again, fifty times and more, to friend and foe alike," Johnson stressed, "[a]nd we remain ready, with this purpose, for unconditional discussions."

But how would LBJ achieve a lasting settlement with Hanoi? By proffering what he believed the North Vietnamese wanted: "food for their hunger; health for their bodies; a chance to learn; progress for their country; and an end to the bondage of material misery." Dangling an enormous carrot, Johnson outlined a billion-dollar development plan for Southeast Asia:

> The vast Mekong River can provide food and water and power on a scale to dwarf even our own TVA. The wonders of modern medicine can be spread through villages where thousands die every year from lack of care. Schools can be established to train people in the skills that are needed to manage the process of development.

"[T]hese objectives, and more," the President hinted, "are within the reach of a cooperative and determined effort." It was a boundless vision of Vietnam's future, as boundless as LBJ's faith in American munificence.

What explained Johnson's almost religious belief in the allure of material bounty? The answer lay in LBJ's early political experiences, in the wonders New Deal economic development had brought to the young congressman's central Texas district some thirty years before. "In the countryside where I was born," Johnson told his audience, "I have seen the night illuminated, and the kitchens warmed, and the homes heated, where once the cheerless night and the ceaseless cold held sway. And all this happened because electricity came to our area along the humming wires of the REA."

The New Deal had transformed the lives of Representative Johnson's impoverished constituents—replacing despair with hope, resignation with confidence. President Johnson believed he could perform similar miracles in war-torn Vietnam. With Hanoi's peaceful cooperation, he would turn the ravaged Mekong delta into a bustling Tennessee Valley.[27]

LBJ's vision reflected an uneasy fusion, as one biographer has noted, of "Vietnamese culture and American values." Projecting his credo of economic and social improvement abroad, Johnson instinctively equated Ho Chi Minh's goals with his own. He failed to perceive reunification as Ho's irreducible objective. In LBJ's mind, Ho Chi Minh really wanted to improve the lives of his people. And LBJ would assist Ho in that effort, in return for abandoning the war.[28]

But would Hanoi abandon the war? On this point, Johnson remained deeply uncertain. On the one hand, LBJ believed he had found Ho Chi Minh's price. He had asked his familiar question, "What do they need from us?," and answered with a seemingly irresistible future for the North Vietnamese. "Old Ho can't turn me down," he confidently asserted to Bill Moyers on his helicopter flight back to Washington that evening.

On the other hand, Johnson knew Hanoi's position was a strong one. Saigon's divided government and demoralized army continued to lose ground to the insurgency. If the communists waited patiently, the prize might simply fall into their lap. LBJ perceived this painfully well. "If I were Ho Chi Minh," he had remarked on another occasion, "I would never negotiate."[29]

Hanoi's reaction to the Baltimore speech confirmed the doubter in Johnson. The day after LBJ's Johns Hopkins address, North Vietnamese Premier Pham Van Dong delivered his government's response to Johnson's proposal. Hanoi's conditions for a settlement were uncompromising: a complete U.S. military withdrawal from South Vietnam; a cessation of all bombing attacks against North Vietnam; and, most important, the governmental reorganization of South Vietnam "in accordance with the program of the

NLFSV"—the political arm of the Vietcong. "[A]ny approach contrary to the above-mentioned stand," Pham Van Dong added, alluding to LBJ's April 7 offer, "is inappropriate."[30]

Hanoi's rejection of negotiations likely stemmed from several motives, including disdain for Johnson's aid-for-peace proposal. It seemed a lopsided exchange to the North Vietnamese. LBJ had asked Hanoi to sever its links to the southern insurgency—to abandon, in effect, its primary goal of reunification—in return for participation in an economic development plan of marginal cost to the United States.

More problematic, perhaps, was North Vietnam's control over the NLF. Hanoi's intransigence toward negotiations may have masked an inability to secure unanimous Vietcong consent to such negotiations. North Vietnam may have avoided the conference table in part because they lacked the means of bringing the NLF bound hand and foot to it.

But the most likely explanation was also the most apparent: the communists held a position of strength in South Vietnam, which improved with each passing day. Military successes afforded them the luxury of diplomatic delay. And as their likelihood of victory increased, so declined their incentive to negotiate.

Without Hanoi's cooperation, however, the elaborate vision which Johnson had charted at Baltimore would remain an elusive and paradoxical one. The bombing would continue. The destruction would persist. America would keep punishing North Vietnam, even as LBJ offered to help it.

As political pressures against the bombing intensified, so did bureaucratic pressures for larger troop deployments. Johnson's secret April 1 decisions—to commit two additional Marine battalions, to change their mission from base security to active combat, and to authorize planning for another two-division deployment—had marked a significant turning point in LBJ's war policy. Johnson's action had shifted leverage decisively toward the military, and the generals quickly moved to exploit it.

Westmoreland, Sharp, and the JCS displayed a new assertiveness, peppering the White House with a flurry of new troop requests. On April 10, the JCS submitted plans for another two-brigade deployment—one to Bienhoa near Saigon, the other to Quinhon along the central South Vietnamese coast. The next day, Westmoreland renewed his bid for an Army division to the central highlands, while seconding the JCS's two-brigade proposal. The two battalions approved by Johnson on April 1 had yet to arrive in South Vietnam, and already the generals wanted thirteen more.

LBJ's reaction to these requests reflected his growing sensitivity to Pentagon demands. By committing the Marines to combat, Johnson had subtly, but profoundly, altered the complexion of the decision-making process. American boys were now at war, and this meant an increased voice for the military in policy councils. It also meant increased political hazards for the President in his relations with the generals and their conservative allies in Congress. By resisting Pentagon calls for more troops, LBJ risked igniting another Truman-MacArthur controversy.

Personal concerns reinforced Johnson's political worries. LBJ had put U.S. soldiers directly at risk and he was uncomfortable not doing all he could to minimize those risks, even if that meant committing additional ground forces. Together, these anxieties diminished Johnson's resistance to the military's quickening troop requests.

During a Tuesday Lunch on April 13, LBJ discussed the Joint Chiefs' two-brigade proposal with McNamara, Rusk, and McGeorge Bundy. At McNamara's urging, the President accepted their request. Two nights later, on April 15, Johnson approved a Defense Department cable to the American mission in South Vietnam announcing the two-brigade deployment.[31]

If LBJ was prepared to move beyond the troop levels established at the April 1 White House meeting, Maxwell Taylor was not. The ambassador had fought hard to limit the JCS requests during his Washington visit, and now the President appeared willing to grant them with minimum delay. This shift confused and dispirited Taylor, who considered it a dangerous path. He did not hesitate, moreover, to express his views to Washington.

On April 17, the ambassador fired an angry cable to the White House, criticizing the latest deployment. "I am greatly troubled" by this decision, Taylor complained. "[I]t shows a far greater willingness to get into the ground war than I had discerned in Washington during my recent trip," he added tartly.

Johnson's action perplexed the ambassador; "having crossed the Rubicon," Taylor later remarked of LBJ's reluctant bombing decision, Johnson now seemed "off for Rome on the double." The ambassador wished to delay the journey, and threatened to by postponing clearance of the two brigades with the South Vietnamese government.[32]

Taylor's stormy cable rocked the White House. By refusing to clear the additional troops with Quat's ministry, he could effectively check this and any future deployments. As ambassador in Saigon, Taylor could thwart the larger troop deployments which he had opposed, unsuccessfully, as an adviser in Washington.

Seeking to calm Taylor's anxieties and restore his necessary cooperation, LBJ suspended his two-brigade decision pending a high-level review of strategy and deployments scheduled for Honolulu on April 20. Taylor, who had not been slated to attend the conference, would join the deliberations.

In this manner, Washington hoped to dispel the ambassador's potentially troublesome reservations. As McGeorge Bundy wrote Johnson, "I am sure we can turn him around if we give him just a little time to come aboard."[33]

On the morning of April 20, Robert McNamara, accompanied by Earle Wheeler, John McNaughton, and William Bundy, strode into the War Room at Pacific Command Headquarters in Honolulu. Seated at a large conference table was Admiral Sharp, together with General Westmoreland and Ambassador Taylor, who had flown in from Saigon the previous afternoon.

Outside, beyond the windows, spread a panoramic view of Pearl Harbor, where America's isolationist illusions had been shattered on an early December morning barely twenty-three years before. The setting seemed an ironically appropriate one, for this day's deliberations would dispel many of contemporary policymakers' illusions about military progress in Vietnam.

The conferees first tackled the bombing issue. They agreed that ROLLING THUNDER would probably not coerce North Vietnam into talks, much less force its capitulation. Hanoi sensed a growing advantage in the South, which steeled its determination to withstand whatever pain American air strikes inflicted on the North. As Ambassador Taylor had written Rusk several days earlier, "No amount of bombardment . . . is going to convince Hanoi to call off its action . . . without real progress in SVN against [the] VC. Hanoi must be convinced that [the] VC cannot win here." The upshot was clear: bombing would not, in McNaughton's words, "do the job alone."[34]

The participants therefore turned their attention to the struggle in the South, which assumed a new, decisive importance. They agreed this arena would likely determine the war. But even here the conferees perceived grave risks ahead. ARVN continued to languish, losing soldiers to desertions and territory to the Vietcong. To forestall Saigon's collapse meant vastly expanding U.S. troop commitments.

But how many troops? How large a commitment? Here, the generals' accumulated requests proved crucial. Wheeler, Sharp, and Westmoreland all favored more deployments—the two divisions which LBJ had resisted on April 1, plus the two brigades he had accepted on April 15. McNamara, McNaughton, and Bundy—sensitive to the JCS pressures on Johnson—were prepared to endorse some of them, at least. Against these forces, Taylor's position seemed weak indeed.

A compromise among the other participants quickly overwhelmed it. McNamara, McNaughton, and Bundy deflected the Joint Chiefs' two-division proposal. But Wheeler, Sharp, and Westmoreland extracted concessions in return: a go-ahead on the two Army brigades; another three Marine battalions to Chulai along the coast south of Danang; and logistical preparation for the two divisions—nearly 50,000 more American soldiers by the middle of June.[35]

The Honolulu recommendations dramatized the generals' rising bureaucratic influence. Wheeler's, Sharp's, and Westmoreland's requests—not Taylor's reservations—had dominated the conference and governed its decisions. McNamara, McNaughton, and Bundy had checked the two-division plan, but at the price of an additional three-battalion deployment. The weight of military demands had thrown civilian policymakers on the defensive, compelling them, however reluctantly, toward ever larger commitments.

With the Honolulu recommendations in hand, and Taylor's compliance secured, McNamara and his party headed back to Washington that night. During the flight, McNamara prepared a memo to the President outlining the agreed-upon deployments. They entailed a marked increase in U.S. ground forces—from 33,000 to nearly 82,000. In his report, McNamara urged LBJ to approve the deployments promptly, in order to "bolster" South Vietnam against an expected communist offensive, while preventing "a spectacular defeat of GVN or US forces."

Although McNamara had resisted even larger deployments at Honolulu, he knew these posed trouble enough for the President. The number of American troops fighting in Vietnam would jump 150 percent. This increase, coupled with the troops' new combat mission, meant inevitably higher casualties and closer public scrutiny of the war.

The political implications seemed obvious and inescapable. McNamara urged Johnson to inform congressional leaders about both the "contemplated deployments" and the recent "change in mission of US forces." To do otherwise, the Secretary suggested, courted serious trouble in the future.[36]

LBJ, together with the other Vietnam Principals, had already gathered in the Cabinet Room when McNamara, McNaughton, and William Bundy arrived at 11:15 the next morning to report on the Honolulu Conference.[37]

McNamara began by recounting the Hawaii deliberations. "We met . . . in a small executive session of six," he told the President, and had a "long and probing" discussion. The upshot, McNamara explained, amounted to this: "We need additional success[es] in [the] South," and that required vastly larger U.S. troops.

George Ball, who had been preoccupied with European affairs throughout March and early April and therefore unaware of the recent debate over force levels as well as Johnson's decision to change the Marines' mission, was stunned by the proposed deployments to 82,000. "This transforms our whole relation to the war," Ball excitedly warned. This means *"a much larger number* of casualties."

Shocked by the rush of events, Ball desperately tried to slow the escalatory momentum. "We ought to take forty-eight hours," he blurted, playing for time—"I have a paper."

The President teased Ball about his February paper. Ball brushed LBJ's needling aside, determined to avert this further plunge into war. The "dangers of this are great[,] if unpredictable," he reminded Johnson, adding prophetically: "to sustain this for two years gives [me] the shudders."

"What's the alternative?" LBJ demanded to know.

"I'll write it today," Ball quickly answered.

Johnson replied with faint hope. "All right, George, I'll give you until tomorrow morning to get me a settlement plan. If you can pull a rabbit out of the hat, I'm all for it!"[38]

John McCone expected no diplomatic miracle—just more military trouble. As he had at the April 2 NSC meeting, McCone challenged further ground deployments without an accompanying step-up in bombing. Warning of a "steady increase of opposition" to combat troops, the CIA director insisted that LBJ "intensify operations against the North." Otherwise, he cautioned, more American forces "will involve us in a situation in which we have no definite result."

"What's the difference?" was Johnson's acid response; he was unconvinced of bombing's effectiveness. And yet, concerned by McCone's point, LBJ now turned to McNamara and said, "Why are they *not* recommending [air] escalation?"

McNamara reiterated the decisive importance of events in the South. What is more, he stressed, further escalation against the North "might bring [the] Chinese in."

"[A]re we pulling away from our theory that bombing would turn 'em off?" the President asked.

"That wasn't our theory," McNamara reminded the President. "We wanted to lift morale" in the South, while "push[ing] [the North] toward negotiations—we've done both," he insisted.

Johnson had doubts: Saigon remained locked in turmoil, Hanoi remained impervious to talks, and world opinion remained hostile to bombing. How long could he sustain this course? "Will they let us go on?" he fretted.

Ball thought not, citing a host of growing domestic and international problems: adverse "intellectual opinion," the troubling "ambiguities" of the Vietnam struggle, the unseemly use of "force by a big country on a little one." "Over a period of time," Ball pointedly concluded, "our position will get badly eroded."[39]

Ball amplified these warnings in the settlement plan he drafted and sent to President Johnson that night. Ball opened his paper by stressing the momentous nature of the Honolulu proposals. "[I]ncreasing our force deployments in South Viet-Nam to over 80,000 requires an important decision of policy," he reminded the President. "This would be a quantum jump of 150 percent. It could not help but have major consequences."

Ball sketched those consequences: large-scale escalation "would multiply our dangers and responsibilities," "transform the character of the war," "substantially increase United States' casualties," and "induce Hanoi . . . to step up the rate of infiltration." LBJ's administration, in Ball's words, hovered "on the threshold of a new military situation."

Before crossing that threshold, Ball cautioned Johnson "to take a hard look at where we are going," to ponder the hazards of further escalation. The generals wanted to continue ROLLING THUNDER, Ball wrote, yet "[t]here is no . . . evidence that our air strikes have . . . halted or slowed down the infiltration efforts of the North Vietnamese." The administration wished to protect its international standing, he noted, but "[w]e cannot continue to bomb the North and use napalm against South Vietnamese villages without a progressive erosion of our world position." The President needed public support for an expanded military effort, Ball added, yet "large and articulate elements in the intellectual community and other segments of United States opinion do not believe in our South Vietnamese policy." LBJ, in short, risked serious military and political dangers by widening the war.

Given these dangers, Ball believed the administration dared not avoid negotiations. He therefore urged Johnson "to test the diplomatic water"—to pursue "a settlement that falls somewhere short of the goals we have publicly stated, but that still meets our basic objectives" of an independent and neutral South Vietnam.

Such a settlement, in Ball's judgment, meant accepting "the continued presence in South Viet-Nam of native-born Viet Cong and . . . their participation in the political processes of the country." This arrangement was inescapable, he stressed, because the United States could not "realistically expect to exterminate the Viet Cong." North Vietnam, in turn, "might be prepared to stop the infiltration and the fighting," convinced, as they were, that "a Viet Cong party in the South" would "ultimately prevail."

Ball knew the notion of Vietcong political participation troubled many in the administration, who feared the VC's potential violence as much as their potential success. Yet he challenged LBJ to test America's commitment to electoral politics:

> Those who know much more about South Viet-Nam than I, advise me that if a free election could be conducted . . . today the non-Communists would win. If that is not the case then clearly our moral position is not what we claim it to

be. Under those circumstances we could not honestly say that we were trying
to help the majority of the South Vietnamese achieve their heart's desire but
merely that we were trying to stop the Communists.

Whether the Vietcong would win a South Vietnamese election was uncertain;
but their participation would affirm Washington's faith in "a democratic
test of strength." And, just as important, Ball concluded, a settlement based
on this principle might avert a massive American intervention "with all the
dangers and responsibilities that entails."[40]

Johnson studied Ball's memo overnight. At eleven o'clock the next morning, he called in Ball and Rusk to discuss its conclusions. Ball soon realized
that he had failed to carry the day. LBJ's three top advisers—McNamara,
Rusk, and McGeorge Bundy—all favored the Honolulu recommendations.
Against them stood only Ball, whose suggested alternative meant Vietcong
participation in South Vietnamese politics, perhaps leading to coalition government with the communists—an eventuality which they abhorred. Ball had
failed, as he later wrote, to produce "a rabbit strong enough to fight off the
hounds of war baying at its heels."[41]

Johnson's reaction was as much a response to bureaucratic pressure as a
rejection of Ball's proposal. Clearly, LBJ disliked the idea of coalition government and the possible communist takeover it entailed. But he also faced
mounting Pentagon pressure. And McNamara's recommendations seemed
the minimum necessary to relieve that pressure. The Honolulu proposals
moderated the larger JCS requests Johnson wished to avoid, while forestalling the South Vietnamese collapse he dreaded.

But they also meant deeper American involvement in the war and deeper
dangers to the Great Society. Less than two weeks before, LBJ had signed
the landmark Elementary and Secondary Education Act into law, providing
$1.3 billion in schooling assistance to the poor. The administration's his-
toric Voting Rights Act approached completion in the Senate. Johnson had
his legislation moving, and he wanted nothing to derail it—in particular,
further escalation in Vietnam sapping political support for his domestic
reforms.

It was an excruciating dilemma that LBJ once again reconciled through
subterfuge. Later on April 22, Johnson approved the Honolulu recommendations. LBJ then ordered Rusk to draft a telegram informing Taylor of the
deployments.

Before transmitting the cable, Rusk sent it to the White House for Johnson's approval. LBJ okayed the telegram, but with a telling amendment. At
the end of the cable, the President inserted this message to Taylor: "it is not
our intention to announce [the] whole program now but rather to announce
individual deployments at appropriate times."[42]

Johnson had authorized a 150 percent increase in American combat forces—nearly 50,000 additional soldiers—yet was determined to obscure the magnitude of this increase. By revealing the "whole program" in piecemeal fashion, LBJ intended to mask the scope of escalation and therefore muffle its domestic political repercussions.

This strategy became apparent during the President's news conference on April 27. Toward the end of the session, a reporter confronted Johnson with whispers about impending escalation. "Mr. President," he asked, referring to the rumored deployments, "could there be circumstances in which large numbers of American troops might be engaged in the fighting of the war rather than in the advising and assistance to the South Vietnamese?"

LBJ, who had approved the Honolulu recommendations just five days earlier, dampened the speculation. "Our purpose in Viet-Nam," he said, "is . . . to advise and to assist those people in resisting aggression." Johnson neglected any mention of the Marines' combat mission, or of the 50,000 additional forces.[43]

7

"What in the World Is Happening?"

As LBJ EDGED DEEPER into Vietnam in late April 1965, he confronted another explosive crisis in the Caribbean, which compounded his political troubles. For the Dominican revolt and the American intervention that followed, despite momentary advantages it afforded LBJ in his dealings with Congress, provoked an angry liberal reaction, which, as two contemporary journalists observed, "sheared away the left wing of Lyndon Johnson's Great Society consensus."[1]

The Dominican Republic in 1965 simmered under decades of authoritarian rule. Governed by Rafael Trujillo since 1930, Dominicans had finally deposed the iron-fisted dictator in May 1961. Trujillo's assassination, in turn, had sparked a chaotic scramble for power among competing factions that the *caudillo* had brutally suppressed for a generation. Between May 1961 and December 1962, an array of politicians and generals had wrangled for control of the Dominican Republic pending democratic elections.

Those elections had vaulted Juan Bosch, a reformer dedicated to eradicating Trujillo's legacy, to power in February 1963. But Bosch's vision had antagonized military officers—some, opponents of Trujillo—who relished their traditional influence and privileges. In September 1963, barely seven months into Bosch's term, a military coup had abruptly ended the Dominican Republic's experiment in popular government. For the next nineteen months, an army-backed civilian regime had ruled uneasily until, on April 24, 1965, the Dominican Republic exploded in political violence.

That day, rebel supporters of deposed president Juan Bosch launched a bloody assault against the government in Santo Domingo. Loyalist military forces, denouncing alleged communist penetration of the Boschist movement, appealed for Washington's intervention. Citing the threat to American lives and, only later, the danger of a communist takeover, President Johnson ordered nearly 22,000 U.S. Marines into the Dominican Republic beginning on April 28.

Johnson's intervention in the Dominican affair, whatever his fluctuating justifications, rested on LBJ's determination to avoid "another Cuba." This fear of a second Castroite regime in the Caribbean conditioned Johnson's perception, however exaggerated, of communist influence within the rebel movement, compelling him to intervene militarily to suppress it.

Conflicting political pressures intensified LBJ's anxieties. Johnson sensed that American intervention courted a firestorm of Latin protest, while the possibility of a communist takeover risked an angry domestic backlash. As LBJ told aides at the time, "I realize I am running the risk of being called a gunboat diplomat, but that is nothing compared to what I'd be called if the Dominican Republic went down the drain."[2]

Popular reaction seemed to confirm Johnson's analysis. Despite loud criticism of LBJ's intervention both at home and abroad, a sizable majority of the American public endorsed the President's action. Some 76 percent of those polled approved Johnson's dispatch of Marines to the Dominican Republic—more than four times the number, 17 percent, who objected.[3]

The Dominican affair had rallied substantial popular support behind President Johnson, while diverting popular attention, suddenly and unexpectedly, from Vietnam. LBJ chose this moment—when fears of another communist regime in the Caribbean gripped the country—to request a major supplemental appropriation from Congress tied, ostensibly, to the Dominican Republic, but, more centrally, to Vietnam. Through skillful political legerdemain, Johnson sought to relieve Vietnam's growing financial pressures and to foreshorten debate over escalation by linking his request to the politically expedient issue of preventing "another Cuba."

LBJ unveiled his stratagem during a meeting with congressional leaders in the White House East Room on the morning of May 4. Speaking to members of the House and Senate Appropriations, Foreign Affairs/Foreign Relations, and Armed Services committees, Johnson stressed the dual nature of his proposed request. "[W]e . . . have unusual and unanticipated needs in both the Viet-Nam theater and the Dominican Republic," LBJ told the legislators, urging them to expedite his $700 million supplemental spending bill. Supporting this request meant supporting the fight against communism in the Caribbean as well as Southeast Asia, the President seemed to suggest.[4]

Johnson shifted his emphasis, subtly but significantly, in a written statement to Congress later that day. In this latter message, LBJ avoided any mention of the Dominican Republic. Instead, Johnson coupled approval of the hastily presented spending bill to blanket endorsement of his entire Vietnam policy. "This is not a routine appropriation," LBJ carefully noted of the request he had submitted just three hours before, asserting that "each member of Congress who supports this request is also voting to persist in our effort to halt communist aggression in South Viet-Nam."

With these words, Johnson had expanded the bill's political importance dramatically, transforming it into a sweeping referendum similar to the Tonkin Gulf Resolution. Yet LBJ pressed Congress to pass the appropriation "at the earliest possible moment." For "[t]o deny and delay this [measure]," Johnson warned, "means to deny and delay . . . support . . . to those brave men who are risking their lives . . . in Viet-Nam." By demanding speedy congressional action, LBJ could ensure minimum congressional debate over a bill which he had tied to the safety of American soldiers already in the field.[5]

Congress swiftly approved the President's supplemental request with only whispers of dissent—408–7 in the House; 88–3 in the Senate. The results surprised no one; as Rhode Island Senator Claiborne Pell had remarked several days earlier, voting against the President on a Vietnam resolution "would be like voting against motherhood." On May 7, LBJ signed the measure into law.[6]

Johnson had used the Dominican crisis to political advantage in his relations with Congress over Vietnam. Not so, however, in his relations with domestic liberals. LBJ's Dominican intervention had only exacerbated tensions between liberals and the President, which spilled over into heightened opposition to his Vietnam policy.

If LBJ perceived his Dominican action as necessary insurance against the possibility of another communist regime on America's doorstep, liberals interpreted it as further disturbing evidence of Johnson's chauvinistic, "shoot from the hip" mentality. In one brief but belligerent moment, LBJ had violated Franklin Roosevelt's Good Neighbor principle of non-intervention in Latin American affairs; betrayed the spirit of John Kennedy's Alliance for Progress; and throttled whatever hopes for genuine democratic revolution had existed in the troubled Dominican Republic. Johnson's Dominican intervention, in short, outraged American liberals.

That outrage almost inevitably provoked louder attacks against LBJ's foreign policy in general and the bombing of North Vietnam in particular. Liberal opposition to ROLLING THUNDER mushroomed dramatically. Vietnam critics on college and university campuses began organizing a massive "teach-in" in Washington, D.C., scheduled for mid-May. President Johnson confronted growing domestic pressure to moderate the war.

LBJ faced mounting international pressure as well. On April 24, Indian president Sarvepalli Radhakrishnan, speaking for many third-world nations, had proposed a comprehensive cease-fire plan, which included a halt in U.S.

air strikes against North Vietnam, a suspension of fighting by both sides in South Vietnam, and the positioning of an Afro-Asian police force along the seventeenth parallel and at points throughout the South to monitor compliance with the agreement.

While Radhakrishnan increased the pressure publicly, U.N. Secretary-General U Thant increased it privately. For weeks, Thant had been urging a bombing pause, leading to negotiations, in confidential talks with U.S. Ambassador Adlai Stevenson. But Washington had repeatedly deflected Thant's appeal, hoping to improve its military position—and therefore its bargaining leverage—through air attacks. By late April, however, Thant had grown impatient, threatening to force the administration's hand by airing his proposal openly.[7]

As Johnson faced rising demands from the left to halt the bombing, he also faced growing demands from the right to pursue a similar tactic, but for decidedly different reasons. Military and especially intelligence officials, doubting ROLLING THUNDER's ability to coerce North Vietnam into a settlement, began prodding LBJ to halt bombing briefly to test Hanoi's interest in negotiations, only to resume even more intense bombing thereafter. Pentagon and CIA officials believed this tactic would expose North Vietnam's opposition to peace talks, and thus blunt domestic and world reaction to a later escalation of U.S. air attacks.

Retired Vice Admiral William Raborn, who had succeeded John McCone as CIA director on April 28, urged this plan in a letter to President Johnson on May 8. It incorporated many points that McCone had made in a parting memo to LBJ on the day of his retirement.[8]

Like his predecessor, Raborn doubted that the present level of ROLLING THUNDER strikes would "exert sufficient pressure on the enemy to cause him to meet our present terms in the foreseeable future." He believed that only expanded bombing, directed against North Vietnam's "principal economic and military targets," would force Hanoi into "meaningful discussions."

Yet Raborn perceived serious risks in stepped-up bombing, which might trigger "extreme world pressures" against Johnson's administration. To diffuse this danger, he recommended intensifying air strikes after a brief pause testing "Communist intentions" toward "serious negotiations." Raborn, who questioned Hanoi's interest in talks as much as he questioned the efficacy of current air strikes, pressed LBJ to adopt a bombing pause as political insurance covering a subsequent expansion of ROLLING THUNDER.[9]

Johnson reacted to these mounting pressures by approving a short bombing halt on May 10. That evening, LBJ cabled Ambassador Taylor about his plan to institute a five- to seven-day bombing pause, code-named MAYFLOWER, beginning at 12:01 a.m., May 13, Vietnam time.

Johnson's MAYFLOWER initiative reflected a response to both public opponents of bombing and private advocates of tougher measures. As LBJ wrote Taylor, he intended to use the bombing halt "to good effect with world opinion" and as "a path toward . . . peace or . . . increased military action, depending upon the reaction of the Communists."

Yet Johnson intended to keep the bombing suspension secret. "My plan," he explained to Taylor, "is not to announce this brief pause but simply to call it privately to the attention of Moscow and Hanoi as soon as possible and tell them that we shall be watching closely to see whether they respond in any way."[10]

Why did LBJ choose to implement MAYFLOWER covertly, thereby diminishing its effect on the rising chorus of liberal critics? Conflicting diplomatic and political factors guided Johnson's decision. The President, and many of his advisers, worried that Hanoi might respond by offering to negotiate, provided the pause continued—thus allowing North Vietnam to maintain, or even increase, its support of the Vietcong under the cover of a bombing suspension.

Administration officials also believed a publicized bombing pause might kindle liberal efforts to prolong it indefinitely. By keeping the bombing halt secret, they hoped to keep critics from mobilizing opposition to any future bombing resumption.[11]

But most important, perhaps, LBJ feared an overt bombing pause risked igniting an angry conservative reaction, thereby intensifying the pressure to hit North Vietnam even harder. As William Bundy, one of Johnson's closest Vietnam aides, later observed:

> [T]he President, his advisors, and almost every experienced Washington observer thought that the most serious pressures of American opinion must come in time from the hard-line right wing. To make a "soft" move and get nothing for it—especially if it could be argued that American military forces paid a price for the move—was, it was deeply believed, likely to open the way to the kind of wide outcry for extreme measures that had characterized the MacArthur crisis . . . during the Korean War.

This fear of a right-wing backlash, William Bundy stressed, "played a very distinct part . . . in the President's attitude toward a bombing halt of any type. Over and over, as I vividly recall, he or others would mention it in council." LBJ was determined to forestall this backlash by concealing the bombing pause.[12]

But for the bombing pause to succeed, in Washington's view, meant securing reciprocal communist concessions. On the evening of May 11, Secretary of State Rusk drafted a message to North Vietnam seeking this objective. In his letter, Rusk announced Washington's bombing halt and explained its purpose. Noting "repeated suggestions . . . by Hanoi . . . that there can be no progress toward peace while there are air attacks on North Viet-Nam," Rusk indicated that U.S. bombing strikes would be suspended "beginning at noon, Washington time, Wednesday, May 12, and running into next week." He warned, however, that if Hanoi "misunderstood" this pause "as an indication of weakness" and failed to respond in kind, "it would be necessary to demonstrate more clearly than ever" American resolve in Southeast Asia. After this veiled threat of future escalation, Rusk ended on a note of conciliation, hoping that "this first pause . . . may meet with . . . equally constructive actions by the other side. . . ."[13]

Rusk cabled his message to Foy Kohler, U.S. Ambassador to the Soviet Union, instructing him to deliver it to the North Vietnamese embassy in Moscow the next morning. Kohler tried to arrange a meeting with Hanoi's ambassador, which his North Vietnamese counterpart rebuffed. Instead, a lower-ranking American diplomat hand-delivered the message to Hanoi's embassy on the evening of May 12. It was returned, without comment, the next morning in a plain envelope marked simply "Embassy of US of A."

Although Washington received no formal response to its proposal in the succeeding days, North Vietnamese radio broadcasts during this period revealed a subtle but intriguing shift in Hanoi's negotiating stance. This shift, buried amid the usual anti-American rhetoric, presented an ambiguous picture, which U.S. intelligence analysts, viewing with customary suspicion, perhaps overlooked or misinterpreted.

Ever since Pham Van Dong's April 8 speech before the North Vietnamese National Assembly, Hanoi had held rigidly to its "Four Points" peace formula, the "third point" of which—and most objectionable to Washington— demanded the governmental reorganization of South Vietnam according to the Vietcong's political program. Premier Dong himself had repeated this condition, almost verbatim, during an interview in Hungary on April 20. "The problem of South Vietnam," he had stated then, "must be solved by the people of South Vietnam themselves *in accordance with the program of the NLFSV"* (emphasis added).[14]

Hanoi's Vietnamese News Agency (VNA) had broadcast similar declarations over the following weeks. On April 29, it had quoted as "the unchangeable stand of the DRV Government" that "the South Vietnamese people settle their own affairs *in accordance with the program of the NFLSV"* (emphasis added). On May 4, the VNA had announced that "the affairs of South Vietnam should be governed by the people of South Vietnam themselves without foreign interference and *in conformity with the program of the NLFSV"* (emphasis added). While on May 6, it had demanded that Washington "let the South Vietnamese people settle themselves their own affairs *in accordance with the program of the National Liberation Front"* (emphasis added). This insistence on a Vietcong-defined government in Saigon remained North Vietnam's "unswerving and unflinching stand," Pham Van Dong had reasserted on May 8—one "that cannot be shaken by any force."[15]

What ROLLING THUNDER had failed to shake, MAYFLOWER seemed to soften. Shortly after the bombing pause began on May 13, Hanoi signaled a change in its negotiating position—away from previous demands for a NLF-determined government in South Vietnam. Two days into the halt, on May 15, the VNA issued a blistering condemnation of Washington's bombing suspension, labeling it "a worn-out trick of deceit and threat." Yet the VNA accompanied this ritual denunciation with a significantly moderated "third point," declaring: "The DRV Government . . . resolutely demands that the U.S. Government . . . let the South Vietnamese people decide their own internal affairs." Noticeably absent was any mention of the NLF, or an insistence on its political program. Although North Vietnam rebroadcast its softened "third point" the next day, American intelligence analysts apparently overlooked this shift, perceiving no appreciable change in Hanoi's position.[16]

Why did CIA officials neglect this shift and, with it, the possibility of a diplomatic opening? The answer, ironically, lay in Vietcong radiocasts during this period, which, holding to the original "third point," persuaded U.S. analysts, convinced of the VC's lockstepped obedience to Hanoi, that nothing had changed. On May 14, the Vietcong's clandestine Liberation Radio broadcast its own version of the "third point," specifically referring to the NLF program that North Vietnam conspicuously dropped the following day. "For our part," the southern Liberation Radio carefully noted, "our stand is extremely clear." "[L]et the Vietnamese people settle their own affairs—*in accordance with the NLFSV platform*" (emphasis added). "This is the only way out," it stressed. The VC, perhaps fearing a repetition of Hanoi's abandonment following the 1954 Geneva Accords, had carefully tied North Vietnam to its political goals, hoping to forestall any Washington-Hanoi discussions at the NLF's expense.[17]

But American intelligence analysts, wedded to notions of North Vietnamese-Vietcong unanimity, disregarded this tantalizing evidence of divergence between them. Intimations of North Vietnamese flexibility therefore went unexplored.

Meanwhile, President Johnson, apparently receiving no positive response from Hanoi, and still fearing right-wing criticism of his bombing pause, moved toward a resumption of ROLLING THUNDER.

In the days since MAYFLOWER had begun, LBJ had listened anxiously for any conservative stirrings against the bombing suspension. What Johnson heard must have reinforced his fears that an unsuccessful pause would only intensify right-wing pressures to expand the bombing.

On May 12, LBJ had sent Lieutenant General Andrew Goodpaster, his liaison with ex-President Eisenhower, to Gettysburg, to solicit Ike's reaction to the upcoming bombing halt. As a former military officer and Republican officeholder, Eisenhower represented those constituencies that had been urging Johnson to take tougher action against North Vietnam.

During their meeting in Ike's Gettysburg farmhouse that afternoon, Goodpaster told Eisenhower about the secret bombing pause. Ike, in turn, expressed general support for Johnson's plan. But he also pressed LBJ, through Goodpaster, to intensify the bombing if Hanoi failed to respond. In that case, Eisenhower urged hitting North Vietnam heavily from the outset, using "everything that can fly."[18]

Johnson confronted more evidence, several days later, which deepened his anxiety over conservative opposition to the bombing suspension. On May 16, the Gallup organization released a poll gauging popular attitudes toward the bombing. The survey revealed widespread support for ROLLING THUNDER: 59 percent of the respondents favored continuing the bombing of North Vietnam—nearly three times the number, 21 percent, who wanted it to stop. And this during the very week of LBJ's bombing halt.[19]

These considerations weighed heavily on Johnson's mind when, on Sunday evening, May 16, he met with several of his top advisers in the Oval Office to discuss resumption of ROLLING THUNDER.[20]

LBJ seemed anxious to renew the bombing quickly. "I thought we were going to pause only five days," he told his aides, referring to the minimum proposed halt. McNamara, however, urged a delay. "To achieve the proper objective," he said, "we should go seven days"—until Wednesday, May 19. Not only would this extend the opportunity for Hanoi to respond, it would also "answer [the *New York*] *Times*" which, McNamara noted, had "wanted us to take a week."

Liberal pressures were the least of Johnson's current concerns. He felt no urgency to answer the *New York Times*, nor his academic critics, whose much-publicized Washington, D.C., "teach-in" was just hours away. "I would do it Monday [May 17]," LBJ repeated.

McNamara, still seeking an extension, proposed a compromise. "We could start again on Tuesday evening [May 18] our time," he suggested, making the pause just over six days.

Johnson still hesitated to postpone resumption. "If there was going to be any interest on the part of Hanoi," he remarked, "we ought to have the reaction by now." "You gave them notice on Tuesday [May 11]," LBJ said, turning to Rusk, therefore "Monday will be six days."

But Johnson finally yielded to McNamara's request. "If you want to start the bombing on Tuesday," he told his Secretary of Defense, "that's okay."

LBJ had no intention, however, of revealing his MAYFLOWER initiative to Congress. "We can tell the Congressional leadership—that we had some 'adjustments' out there," Johnson artfully suggested, determined to keep the pause secret. To divulge an abortive bombing halt only courted a storm of conservative protests in Congress.

LBJ explained this fear with astonishing candor. "To me it's a pure question of what happens in this country," he said. "If we hold off this bombing longer, people are going to say, 'What in the world is happening?' "—Why aren't you hitting North Vietnam harder, Mr. President, rather than giving it a week's respite?! This was precisely what Johnson wished to avert—pressure driving him to escalate the war against Hanoi at the risk of Chinese or Russian intervention.

McNamara, though sympathetic to LBJ's concerns, worried about what to tell the press, which had noticed reduced activity at U.S. airbases in South Vietnam. Johnson dismissed the media issue with his usual guile. "We don't need to disclose every piece of strategy to the press," he snapped.

As for his liberal Senate critics, LBJ seemed willing to inform them, but privately. "I would say to Mansfield, Kennedy, Fulbright that we notified the other people—and for six full days we have held off bombing. Nothing happened. We had no illusions that anything would happen. But we were willing to be surprised." "We are anxious to pursue every diplomatic adventure, to get peace," he went on, "But we can't throw our gun away."

The longer Johnson spoke, the madder he got. LBJ had pursued the pause only reluctantly, at what he considered great political risk, and with no apparent results. "We have laid off them for six days," he noted plaintively, and "[n]o one has even thanked us for the pause."

McNamara shared Johnson's frustration. "Mansfield ought to know Hanoi spit in our face," he added defensively.

But LBJ's anger had subsided. "I'm afraid if we play along with this group," he said, referring to his liberal critics, "we will wind up with no one on our side." "We tried out their notion and got no results."

Johnson repeated his fears of a popular backlash. "My judgment is the public has never wanted us to stop the bombing." "We have stopped in deference to Mansfield and Fulbright," he admitted, "but we don't want to do it too long else we lose our base of support"—the southern conservative leadership in Congress crucial to the administration's legislative success.

Here again lay the nub of LBJ's concern. Pressed by Pentagon and CIA officials to intensify the bombing, Johnson feared provoking powerful congressional conservatives as well by prolonging a seemingly fruitless pause. To antagonize southern Democrats and Republicans, who controlled committees where his domestic reforms would either swim or sink, seemed an intolerable risk to the Great Society. And one the President wished to avoid.

"We will go Tuesday to satisfy you here tonight," LBJ decided, turning toward McNamara. But "I'd go Monday night myself," he carefully added, glancing at CIA Director Raborn. "However, if you have good reasons," Johnson said, shifting his attention back to McNamara, "we'll go when you say."

LBJ then returned to the disclosure issue, reversing his earlier decision not to inform Congress about MAYFLOWER. Johnson now planned to "talk to the leadership and tell them what we did," but in a manner craftily designed to disarm both liberal and conservative critics on the Hill. "I'd call them in and tell them we are starting *Monday* night," the President suggested (emphasis added). "And then you'll be requested to delay again," he predicted to McNamara, "by the *New York Times,* by Mansfield and Fulbright." Thus LBJ, having mollified conservatives by appearing ready to resume the bombing early, could mollify liberals by seemingly extending the pause another day.[21]

But to LBJ's surprise, congressional leaders summoned to the White House the next morning offered no objections to ending the bombing halt that evening. Therefore Johnson, as he had originally intended, ordered ROLLING THUNDER to resume, beginning at 6 a.m., Tuesday, May 18, Vietnam time.[22]

LBJ had renewed the bombing, in large measure, because North Vietnam had apparently ignored the pause. Hanoi seemed unwilling to moderate its position in pursuit of a political settlement. Yet just hours after ROLLING THUNDER resumed, North Vietnam launched a mysterious initiative conceivably aimed at this very purpose.

Early on the morning of May 18, less than twelve hours after U.S. air strikes had resumed, North Vietnam's highest-ranking diplomat in Paris, Mai Van Bo, approached the Quai d'Orsay's Asian Director, Etienne Manac'h, with a message from Hanoi. North Vietnam, probably seeking to avoid the appearance of weakness—responding under the threat of a bombing resumption—had carefully delayed its official reply to MAYFLOWER until after the pause had ended.

Bo, a southern Vietminh veteran whose contact with the French spanned many years, drew Manac'h's attention to Pham Van Dong's "Four Points," a copy of which he pulled from his pocket. Bo softened the declaration by stressing that Hanoi considered the "Four Points" only the "basis" for the "soundest settlement of the Vietnam problem." This meant, Bo emphasized, that Dong's "Four Points" should be viewed not as preconditions but as "working principles" for negotiation.

Manac'h, attempting to clarify Hanoi's stance on the "Four Points," specifically asked Bo: "Is it to say that the positions of your government are the following? First, you formulate the principle of the withdrawal of the American forces, but you admit that the concrete realization will be linked to the conclusions of a negotiation?" "Exactly," answered Bo, stressing that this was his government's view, not just his own. If there were agreement on the "basis," Bo added, the "ways and means" of application of "principles" could be achieved diplomatically. A "way out" for the United States should be found, he said, noting that "our suggestion humiliates no one."[23]

Bo's interpretation of the "Four Points" seemed frustratingly ambiguous. He had denied that they were preconditions for bilateral talks, yet had suggested their adoption as "working principles." He had hinted at Hanoi's bargaining flexibility, yet had alluded to the "Four Points" as the "basis" of any settlement. He had implied North Vietnam's interest in negotiations, but as a prelude to American withdrawal.

Bo's *démarche* may simply have reflected an effort to maintain France's interest in a diplomatic settlement and, thus, France's pressure on the United States to moderate its Vietnam policy. Yet his approach to Manac'h, together with Hanoi's softening of its "third point" through VNA broadcasts, may also have reflected efforts to begin serious negotiations with Washington. But Washington read both Bo's remarks and North Vietnam's radiocasts skeptically, even cynically. "My total impression," William Bundy confided to a friend a short time later, echoing a common feeling among his colleagues, "is that it was a cute diplomatic maneuver designed to muddy the waters." Such thinking discouraged Washington from perceiving, much less pursuing, these tantalizing overtures.[24]

If the United States had overlooked possible North Vietnamese openings, Hanoi soon closed them tightly. Apparently angered by Washington's disregard of its moderated "third point," Hanoi reverted to its original position on May 22. That day, the VNA broadcast an unyielding "third point" similar to Pham Van Dong's initial stance. "The only solution," North Vietnam's news agency now announced, "is that the United States must . . . let the South Vietnamese people themselves settle their own affairs *according to the [National Liberation] [F]ront's political program*" (emphasis added). Washington and Hanoi seemed back to square one.[25]

Whether MAYFLOWER represented an important missed opportunity seems doubtful. Though the United States probably misjudged North Vietnam's reaction to the pause, underestimating its diplomatic flexibility, the gap between their basic positions remained formidable. Washington had sought, through its bombing pause, to secure a reciprocal communist cease-fire—no bombing of North Vietnam in return for no North Vietnamese or Vietcong military operations. Yet under this arrangement, the United States would continue its own military efforts in South Vietnam.

This formula doubtlessly appeared lopsided to Hanoi, even if it could have compelled a complete VC stand-down, which was unlikely. Washington had asked North Vietnam and the Vietcong to cease their activities in the South—to forfeit their strongest bargaining chip—while the United States surrendered only half its chips—the air war against the North. Even American officials recognized the imbalance of this proposal. To expect "the DRV/VC to halt all of their activities in exchange for a cessation of only one-half of the US/GVN activities," John McNaughton wrote McGeorge Bundy before the pause even began, "is asking 'a horse for a rabbit.' "[26]

North Vietnam, for its part, had manifested a curious ambivalence toward negotiations. VNA broadcasts during the bombing halt had implied a softening of Hanoi's position. Yet Bo's subsequent comments to Manac'h suggested a tougher stance—a willingness to talk with Washington, but only about the timing of a U.S. pullout from South Vietnam. In May 1965, North Vietnam remained confident of ultimate victory in the South, and thus willing to discuss little more than a face-saving American withdrawal.

For President Johnson, mid-May 1965 marked a period of deepening pessimism over Vietnam, punctuated by growing anxiety about the political repercussions of the war. The failure of MAYFLOWER, together with accelerating troop requests, had intensified pressures to widen the war. A wider war, in turn, increased the dangers to LBJ's Great Society, by draining congressional attention and popular support from his domestic reforms.

Racked by these conflicting military and political pressures, Johnson turned to an old and trusted friend, Clark Clifford, for advice. Clifford, a savvy Washington insider whose political experience spanned three Democratic administrations over nearly twenty years, understood the capital, the Congress, and the Presidency better than anyone, perhaps, except Lyndon Johnson. And he could understand LBJ's concerns.

Beginning his career as a St. Louis courtroom lawyer defending indigents in criminal cases from a corner table in his firm's law library, Clifford had arrived in Washington in the summer of 1945, as assistant naval aide to fellow Missourian Harry Truman. Within a year, Clifford's remarkable political talents had vaulted him into Truman's closest circle as special presidential counsel. There, Clifford had helped shape many important policies during an exceptionally important era of American history. In the spring of 1947, he had co-authored Truman's message to Congress enunciating the containment doctrine. The following year, he had participated in deliberations leading to U.S. recognition of Israel, as well as charting the election strategy—including the famous "whistle-stop" tour—culminating in Truman's stunning upset of Republican Thomas Dewey.

Retiring to a lucrative corporate law practice during the Eisenhower fifties, Clifford had maintained close ties to the Democratic opposition in Congress, including Senators John F. Kennedy and Lyndon B. Johnson.

After winning the Democratic nomination in 1960, Kennedy had appointed Clifford to his election staff and then head of his transition team. As President, JFK had relied heavily on Clifford's advice—both on private matters, as his personal lawyer, and on political issues, as a member and later chairman of the Foreign Intelligence Advisory Board (FIAB), supervising CIA activities abroad.

Johnson, like Truman and Kennedy before him, respected Clifford's political judgment and trusted his personal discretion. LBJ made Clifford his primary troubleshooter, handling the administration's most sensitive crises, including the post-assassination transition and the scandals surrounding Johnson's Senate secretary Bobby Baker and White House chief of staff Walter Jenkins in 1964. Clifford, meanwhile, continued as chairman of Johnson's FIAB, often serving as a sounding board for the President on foreign policy.

It was in this capacity that LBJ turned to Clark Clifford in mid-May 1965, seeking help on his growing Vietnam predicament. Johnson sent Clifford copies of McCone's and Raborn's memos pressing for heavier air attacks against the North, while warning about the perils of increased U.S. involvement in the South. At the same time, LBJ lamented the war's increasing threat to his Great Society agenda. How should he mediate these conflicting pressures? he asked Clifford. What should he do?

Clifford answered the President in a letter on May 17. "I wish to make one major point," he wrote Johnson. "I believe our ground forces in South Vietnam should be kept to a minimum," he stressed, urging LBJ not to enlarge the commitment beyond present levels. To do so, Clifford warned, would be to signal a political decision "to win the war on the ground."

Clifford considered such a decision dangerously unwise. "This could be a quagmire," he cautioned. "It could turn into an open end commitment on our part that would take more and more ground troops, without a realistic hope of ultimate victory." To avert this disaster, he urged Johnson to continue "probing . . . every avenue leading to a possible settlement. . . ." A negotiated solution "won't be what we want," Clifford told his old friend LBJ, "but we can learn to live with it."[27]

South Vietnam's political situation, meanwhile, began showing renewed signs of trouble among ethnic and religious factions unwilling to live with one another. Ever since Thao's and Phat's abortive February 19 coup, Saigon's militant Catholic minority—which had prominently supported it—had grown increasingly apprehensive about its status in South Vietnamese society, increasingly suspicious of Buddhist influence, and increasingly fearful of government retribution.

Court rulings handed down in early May intensified these anxieties. On

May 7, a military tribunal had passed death sentences against General Phat and Colonel Thao—still on the run—along with stiff prison terms against several of their confederates. South Vietnam's Catholics resented these measures, growing more hostile and rebellious toward the government. Rumors of another Catholic-organized coup mounted, threatening to disrupt Quat's delicately balanced coalition and bringing ARVN's war effort to a standstill. A South Vietnamese commentator summed up the situation well. "In a way," he said, "after all the pent-up years under the French and . . . Diem, we are like children letting off steam. Maybe there will have to be yet another half-dozen coups before we settle down—even though we know we can't afford them."[28]

By early May 1965, Catholic leaders, again in league with the elusive Colonel Thao, began plotting to destabilize Quat's fragile government. They even approached the wily Buddhist leader, Thich Tam Chau, urging a "hands-off" policy toward their planned coup, so that Catholics and Buddhists might unite in "religious understanding" to create a new regime. Chau, not surprisingly, spurned the overture, but he also withheld mentioning it during a subsequent meeting with the Prime Minister.[29]

From his hideout in Saigon, Thao organized the coup. The covert Vietcong agent, together with his eager but unsuspecting Catholic allies, planned to assassinate Premier Quat, kidnap Air Vice-Marshal Ky and General Nguyen Chanh Thi—the powerful Buddhist commander of ARVN's northern I Corps—and proclaim a new government headed by Khanh's old rival, General Duong Van Minh. Saigon police, however, learned of the revolt. On May 20, government forces raided the plotters' headquarters, arresting nearly forty military and civilian officials. The coup had been averted.[30]

But Quat's troubles had not. Within days, discontented Catholics, implacably hostile to Quat, provoked a new political crisis designed to bring down his government. In this effort, they enlisted the help of Chief of State Suu, whose ambition to supplant Quat paralleled the Catholics' desire to oust him.

Phan Khac Suu possessed a reputation for integrity and nonpartisanship seemingly above South Vietnam's swirling factional rivalries. Yet his frail stature and dignified manner masked a cunning political acumen and thirsty personal aspirations. Appointed Chief of State in late October 1964, Suu had maintained his position as first Huong, then Khanh (through Oanh), and now Quat struggled to control affairs as Prime Minister of South Vietnam. As the opposition to each mounted, the Chief of State had remained carefully neutral: avoiding conflict with Khanh, the Young Turks, and the Buddhists as they undermined Huong; with the Young Turks as they, in turn, outmaneuvered Khanh; with Colonel Thao and his compatriots as they plotted against Quat. All the while, Suu had steadily enhanced his own power as Chief of State. And with Quat now weakened, Suu sensed an opportunity to assert his primacy within the government.³¹

The crisis which Suu and his Catholic allies engineered to topple Quat involved cabinet changes aimed, ironically, at answering Catholic charges of underrepresentation in the government. On the morning of May 25, Quat privately approached the Chief of State, revealing plans to dismiss five ineffectual ministers, whose replacements would give his cabinet greater regional and religious balance. Quat wanted Suu's endorsement of the proposed changes before submitting them to the National Legislative Council (NLC)—South Vietnam's interim legislature—for approval. The Chief of State expressed no reservations.³²

Suu expressed very different sentiments to Ambassador Taylor later that day. Suu now challenged the proposed changes, claiming that the provisional charter did not explicitly empower Quat to replace cabinet ministers. Taylor pointed out, rightly, that the charter was vague on this point; that previous premiers had appointed and dismissed officials at their pleasure; and that a constitutional confrontation over this issue needlessly jeopardized South Vietnam's already precarious political stability. Could Quat count on Suu's cooperation? Taylor asked. "Yes," the Chief of State finally remarked.³³

The NLC also tried to diffuse Suu's brewing showdown with the Prime Minister. A delegation of legislative leaders visited the Chief of State that evening. They told Suu that the NLC supported Quat's interpretation of the provisional charter. The Chief of State again seemed accommodating. If the legislators incorporated their views in a formal resolution, Suu pledged to sign it.

The NLC therefore convened that night, prepared a resolution endorsing Quat's position, and approved it unanimously. They presented the resolution to Suu the next morning. The Chief of State refused to sign it.³⁴

Quat, meanwhile, hesitated to confront Suu's growing intransigence. In part, this reflected his natural reticence, which bred an "instinctive fear of confrontations and tests of strength," as Ambassador Taylor had once observed. But it also reflected Quat's political quandry. If he bowed to pressure from Suu and his Catholic allies, Quat risked alienating the Buddhists; if he resisted Suu, the military might intervene to break the deadlock, and stay to run affairs itself.³⁵

For Quat—despite his recent troubles with Suu—had been leery of the general's intentions since the day he became Prime Minister. The Young Turks had never ceased meddling in political affairs, nor renounced their self-proclaimed right to police the government. They remained restlessly ambitious, poised to exploit any divisions among civilian leaders.

To save his government, Quat decided to confront the Chief of State privately. They met at Gia Long Palace on the evening of June 1. Standing beneath the whirring fans and gilded cornices of Suu's office, Quat rebuked the Chief of State for his obstinacy, which, Quat warned, jeopardized the future of civilian rule. Suu appeared contrite and cooperative. His objections were "really not very important," the Chief of State insisted, and could be "readily resolved." If Quat composed a letter requesting the ministers' resignations, Suu promised to sign it.

So Quat, like the NLC a week before, prepared the necessary papers and sent them to Suu the following day. And the Chief of State, like a week before, signed nothing.[36]

Incredibly, Quat tried once more. This time, on June 4, the Prime Minister spoke bluntly. Unless he and Suu resolved their problems—problems which Quat blamed squarely on Suu—he predicted the generals would impose a solution on them. That meant the return of military rule.[37]

Apparently swayed by Quat's warning, Suu agreed to compromise. At a meeting with the Prime Minister and the NLC later that afternoon, the Chief of State promised to withdraw his opposition to Quat's cabinet changes. Quat, in return, promised no further changes pending the NLC's amendment of the provisional charter.[38]

The next day, June 5, Quat prepared a decree summarizing their bargain, which he sent to Gia Long for Suu's signature. The Chief of State reneged yet again. This time, Suu dropped all pretenses. He publicly denounced the Prime Minister, asserting that he had agreed only to leave the matter to the NLC. The Chief of State now told visitors that "Quat must go."[39]

Suu's duplicity and intransigence succeeded. With his government paralyzed and his credibility seriously weakened, Prime Minister Quat resigned on June 11, yielding control to the military.

Phan Huy Quat's departure marked the end of South Vietnam's eight-month-old experiment in civilian government. Quat, whose tenure had outlasted both Huong's and Oanh's, had nevertheless failed, like his predecessors, to contain the generals' ambitions while balancing the country's ethnic, political, and regional rivalries. A man committed to healing South Vietnam's destructive divisions, he had ironically fallen victim to those very divisions. His moderation and restraint, as Ambassador Taylor sadly noted during Quat's final days in office, had proved "an almost fatal posture in the arena of jugular-vein politics in Saigon."[40]

The generals who assumed control of the government proved particularly adept in this arena. Following Quat's resignation, the Young Turks quickly abolished all vestiges of civilian rule. They annulled the provisional charter and disbanded the interim legislature. In place of these institutions, the military created a new "War Cabinet" headed by two powerfully ambitious but mutually distrustful figures: Nguyen Van Thieu and Nguyen Cao Ky.

Nguyen Van Thieu, appointed chairman of the Military Leadership Committee (MLC)—in effect, South Vietnam's new Chief of State—was an intelligent, aspiring, and opportunistic officer with a special flair for political intrigue.

Born into a Buddhist family in the central Vietnamese coastal province of Phamrong in 1923, Thieu had early adopted his French colonizers' Catholicism and social customs. He had studied at French missionary schools both in Hué and abroad, returning to fight alongside Foreign Legionnaires against the Vietminh during the Indochina War. After the Geneva Accords, Thieu had joined Diem's army, where his aggressive leadership and military skills earned him rapid promotions. U.S. military advisers who worked with Thieu during these years had frequently noted his extraordinary professional ability.

They had also noted Thieu's extraordinary political ambitions and appetite for personal advancement, which had increased along with Diem's unpopularity in the late 1950s and early 1960s. In the fall of 1963, Thieu had joined the military cabal which overthrew and assassinated Diem.

Thieu's participation in the coup against Diem had vaulted him into the top echelons of South Vietnam's army, whose dizzying factional rivalries had afforded Thieu a matchless education in political intrigue. Nguyen Khanh, a master at this competition, had enlisted Thieu's support when he launched his own revolt against the post-Diem junta in late January 1964.

Once in power, Khanh had eyed Thieu warily. Here was an equally skillful intriguer, whose political loyalties seemed suspiciously flexible. When rumors of a coup against the general mounted in early September 1964, Khanh had instinctively demanded Thieu's pledge of support. Thieu had given it unequivocally. Nine days later, on September 13, Catholic military officers—whom the CIA linked to Thieu—had moved against Khanh. Thieu, however, had remained carefully aloof; when the rebellion began to sputter, Thieu had broadcast a public denunciation of the uprising, thus saving his position.

In the following months, Khanh's influence had diminished, forcing him into greater reliance on Thieu and the other Young Turks. In January 1965, he had promoted Thieu to major general and designated him liaison with American military forces. The next month, Thieu had been appointed Defense Minister under Quat.

Thieu, meanwhile, had continued his personal maneuvering; the CIA believed he had simultaneously been backing Colonel Thao's plot against Khanh. When Thao launched his revolt on February 19, Thieu had again kept a clever distance. The coup had failed, but it had also triggered Khanh's ouster—thrusting the Young Turks, including Thieu, into control of the military at last.[41]

Thieu's counterpart as the new Prime Minister of South Vietnam, Nguyen

Cao Ky, shared Thieu's affinity for political intrigue, punctuated by a remarkably flamboyant persona.

A native northern Vietnamese Buddhist born in 1930, Ky had also joined France's colonial military as a young man in the early 1950s. He had become a pilot and, after 1954, an officer in the South Vietnamese Air Force (VNAF). Ky's personal daring and outspoken opposition to Diem had attracted considerable support among fellow VNAF pilots. Under his leadership, they had played a crucial role in deposing Diem.

In return, Ky had been awarded command of the VNAF, which he had shrewdly used to support Khanh, while quietly building the power to challenge him. In September 1964, Ky's planes had intervened to thwart the attempted coup against Khanh. In December, he had participated in Khanh's dissolution of the High National Council. In January 1965, he had helped Khanh topple Prime Minister Huong. And then, in February, he had conspired with Thieu and the other Young Turks to supplant Khanh.

Ky, generally deemed the leader of the Young Turks, symbolized the grasping aspirations of these second-echelon commanders. Many Vietnamese and American observers—including Nguyen Khanh—considered him an impetuous, overly aggressive, and irresponsible officer, whose political sophistication ran well behind his military valor. Deputy Ambassador Johnson considered Ky "an unguided missile," while Johnson's superior, Maxwell Taylor, described him as "a gallant, flamboyant airman with a well-developed penchant for speaking out of turn."[42]

Such characterizations stemmed from Ky's personal demanor. In private, Ky drank, gambled, and womanized heavily; while married to his first wife, he had toted an ivory-handled pistol carved with his name and that of his favorite prostitute. In public, Ky sported a zipper-studded black flying-suit, complete with lavender ascot and twin pearl-handled revolvers, which he wore on both bombing missions against the North and private excursions throughout the South aboard his purple turboprop.[43]

Ky's outspokenness matched his ostentation. "People ask me who my heroes are," he told an interviewer in his bright blue-curtained office at Tansonhut airbase shortly before becoming Premier. "I have only one—Hitler." "I admire Hitler because he pulled his country together," Ky said. "But the situation here is so desperate now that one man would not be enough." "We need four or five Hitlers in Vietnam," he remarked.[44]

To intelligent South Vietnamese observers like Quat's chief of staff, Bui Diem, such comments reinforced the image of Thieu and Ky "as trigger happy, intemperate individuals with no discernible concept of government." To the Americans in Saigon, such as Ambassador Taylor, Ky's and Thieu's rise to power seemed an inevitable, if regrettable, expression of the Young Turks' political arrival—one which Taylor hoped might at least bring "stable government as that term may be applied in Vietnamese politics." To officials in Washington, such as Assistant Secretary of State William Bundy, Ky's and Thieu's rise to power appeared quite different. The pair, to him, seemed "the bottom of the barrel, absolutely the bottom of the barrel!"[45]

The collapse of civilian government in Saigon coincided with a new and vigorous Vietcong offensive, which together threw South Vietnam into turmoil, threatening the country's collapse and raising the pressure for more U.S. troops to save it.

In early May, the southwestern monsoons resumed, pelting the Indochina peninsula with heavy, incessant rain from the Gulf of Thailand. In South Vietnam, the poor weather grounded most air operations, including low-flying planes and helicopters, used effectively in mobile counter-insurgency. VC guerrillas seized the opportunity. They launched a wave of new assaults, on a scale unseen before in the war. On May 11, a Vietcong regiment attacked ARVN units at Songbe, fifty miles northwest of Saigon near the Cambodian border, inflicting heavy casualties. Further north, in the central highlands, communist guerrillas forced South Vietnamese troops to abandon several district capitals. The fighting reached a climax on May 30, at Bagia, just west of Quangngai. There, the Vietcong decimated an ARVN battalion in an ambush, and severely mauled a second sent to rescue it. By early June, ARVN losses had reached alarming levels.

The pressure for greater U.S. intervention triggered by ARVN's battlefield failures was intensified by accelerating Pentagon requests. On April 30, the Joint Chiefs, who had won logistical preparation for two divisions at the Honolulu Conference, pressed new demands on the administration. This time, the generals urged deploying the two divisions as soon as possible in "combat operations" alongside the South Vietnamese Army. The recently approved enclave strategy remained largely untested, and still the JCS pushed for wider action.[46]

As did General Westmoreland from MACV headquarters in Saigon. Ever since President Johnson's approval of the Honolulu troop recommendations, Westmoreland had been busy planning their deployment. With the JCS now advocating a broader strategy, Westmoreland climbed aboard. On May 8, the general sent Washington his concept of operations, which would commit American forces far beyond their present mission. First, troops would secure the bases where they landed. Then, they would begin combat patrols beyond the base perimeters. Finally, U.S. troops would conduct long-range "search and destroy" operations along with ARVN forces. Westmoreland saw American soldiers participating directly and extensively in the war.[47]

These calls for expanded action, though unforeseen and unwelcomed by the President, flowed from his earlier troop decisions. By changing the

Marines' mission on April 1, and approving the Honolulu deployments on April 22, Johnson had sparked increasing demands from the military to prosecute the war more vigorously. Marine Corps Commandant Wallace M. Greene's comment to the press in early May dramatized this fact. Returning from a tour of the Danang airbase, General Greene told reporters that the "Marine[s'] mission is to kill Vietcong." "They can't do it sitting on their ditty boxes," he said, "I told them to find the Vietcong and kill 'em. That's the way to carry out their mission."[48]

A growing realization of bombing's ineffectiveness intensified this pressure to expand the ground war. What had been suspected at Honolulu now became apparent: ROLLING THUNDER would not dissuade Hanoi, particularly now that it scented imminent victory in the South. Ambassador Taylor, in a cable to the State Department on June 3, stated this explicitly. Taylor, who six months before had pressed LBJ to go North, now reported:

> we should like to make very clear that we do not believe that any feasible amount of bombing . . . is of itself likely to cause the DRV to cease and desist its actions in the south. Such a change in DRV attitudes can probably be brought about only when . . . there is also a conviction on their part that the tide has turned or soon will turn against them in the south.

It seemed a remote possibility at that moment.[49]

Taylor's deepening pessimism about the bombing discouraged Washington; what he reported two days later about the ground war in South Vietnam jarred it. In a long and forceful telegram on June 5, the Ambassador described an ARVN racing toward defeat. He sketched an under-manned, ill-trained, and poorly led army reeling before the communists' monsoon offensive. In several major skirmishes, Taylor observed, ARVN forces had "broken under pressure and fled from the battlefield." These setbacks, "coupled with the continuing high desertion rate in many units," threatened "a collapse in ARVN's will to continue to fight. . . ." South Vietnam seemed on the verge of disaster.

This sense of crisis forced a dramatic change in Taylor's attitude toward the war. From the arrival of the first Marines in March, he had resisted committing major U.S. forces to combat. Emphasizing the dangers of direct intervention and ARVN's lagging determination, Taylor had warned against America assuming control of the war. The Ambassador now reversed himself. To avert South Vietnam's collapse, Taylor wrote Washington with grim resignation, "it will probably be necessary to commit US ground forces to action."[50]

Maxwell Taylor, one of the administration's most ardent opponents of an Americanized war, had yielded at last. Compelled by the force of events to abandon his reservations, Taylor had endorsed the strategy which he had fought for months. South Vietnam's unraveling situation was rapidly over-whelming the ambassador's calculations and doubts.

A similar process affected those gathered in the Secretary of State's dining room far above Foggy Bottom that Saturday afternoon. Rusk had summoned McNamara, Thompson, the Bundy brothers, and Ball to ponder the implications of Taylor's message.

They brooded together for several minutes when, suddenly and unexpectedly, President Johnson entered the room. "Lady Bird is away, I was all alone, and I heard you fellows were getting together, so I thought I'd come over," LBJ said, pulling a chair up to the table. The others told him about Taylor's cable. Johnson reacted swiftly.

"Who sees our purpose and [the] means of achieving it?" LBJ tensely asked. "How do we ever expect to win? How do you expect to wind this thing up?"

Rusk offered the most hopeful scenario. But his answer, like those of the others, echoed Johnson's own, deep uncertainty. "We're trying . . . to stop infiltration from t[he] North, . . . to demonstrate that [their] current effort will not succeed."

McNamara countered with his usual realism. "We're looking for no more than a stalemate in the South. Can we achieve a stalemate in the South?" The room silent, McNamara laid everyone's doubt on the table: "[The] communists] still think they're winning."

The President listened to this with growing anxiety. "We are trying to do everything we know how to do, aren't we?" he asked, unsettled by South Vietnam's gathering crisis. LBJ seemed troubled and pensive—deeply wary of what lay ahead. "[The] great danger," he concluded darkly, "is we'll pick up a very big problem any day."[51]

8

"Can You Stop It?"

WESTMORELAND'S TELEGRAM began clattering into the Message Room of the Pentagon's National Military Command Center at 3:35 a.m. on June 7. Busily deciphered by the Message Room's whirring teletype machines, his cable would shatter the tranquility of early morning Washington.

Westmoreland's message was clear and disturbing: the communist monsoon offensive, gathering strength for weeks, now threatened "to destroy government forces." Although the Vietcong had committed only two of nine regiments to battle, he warned that ARVN was "already experiencing difficulty in coping with this increased VC capability." Combat losses had been "higher than expected"; desertion rates had reached "inordinately high" levels; South Vietnamese troops had begun showing a "reluctance to assume the offensive"—in some cases, even "their steadfastness under fire is coming into doubt." The Vietcong were grinding ARVN units faster than they could be replaced, and had South Vietnamese forces running.

Westmoreland assessed these conditions bluntly. "[T]he GVN cannot stand up . . . to this kind of pressure without reinforcement," he told Washington. Westmoreland perceived no alternative "except to reinforce . . . SVN with additional U.S. or third country forces as rapidly as is practical during the critical weeks ahead."

The general then outlined his proposed forces. They were sobering. In addition to the thirteen American battalions already committed to South Vietnam, he urged deploying nineteen more, swelling the total to thirty-two battalions. Westmoreland's request meant a nearly 250 percent increase in U.S. combat forces. It also meant a dramatic and open-ended expansion of American military involvement.[1]

That prospect weighed heavily on President Johnson and his advisers as they met the next morning to discuss Westmoreland's cable.[2]

The mood in the Oval Office was bleak, reflecting policymakers' deepening apprehensions. South Vietnam appeared to be crumbling rapidly, with the only antidote a massive injection of U.S. troops. McNamara forcefully summarized the group's anxiety. "We're in a hell of a mess," a mess that he, like the others, was unsure how to solve.

LBJ seemed especially bitter. For weeks, he had been exploring diplomatic channels—first through his Johns Hopkins speech, then through the MAYFLOWER initiative. Yet Hanoi and the Vietcong had only intensified their military efforts. "[T]he more I've done," Johnson snapped, "the less they've responded."

Which seemed all too predictable, given Saigon's quickening decline. The communists, sensing triumph in the South, were pressing their advantage. ARVN, meanwhile, continued to sag under what Taylor described as woefully "bad leadership" and a "poor control of desertion." Without major U.S. intervention, South Vietnam's collapse appeared certain.

McNamara then spelled out Westmoreland's proposed deployments. In all, they "would lead to 170,000 [U.S. troops] in four to six months," he said.

The figure jolted Ball. "*Is this* the French Result?" he worried aloud—the beginning of America's own long and exhausting Indochina war?

LBJ wondered himself, but muttered: "Can you stop it?"

Bundy, too, expressed troubling doubts. "[A]re [we] opening an unlimited account?" he asked—this on behalf of a "straight military" government?

Taylor had no illusions, thanks to Khanh, the Young Turks, and, most recently, Suu. "There will always be a straight military government," he flatly predicted.

Yet Taylor still clung to the enclave strategy. "We can always hold [the] cities and [the] coastal plain," he told the President, thereby preventing South Vietnam's collapse while limiting American deployments.

Bundy agreed. Holding selected areas throughout the South seemed "a real possibility" to him.

"Bus, what do you think?" Johnson said, turning to General Wheeler. The idea of 170,000 U.S. troops fighting on the Asian mainland troubled Wheeler, but so did gainsaying Westmoreland, the commander on the spot. "We don't like it," he confessed, speaking for the Joint Chiefs, "but Westy needs it."

And what did McNamara think? LBJ asked. Whether holding all of South Vietnam or just selected enclaves, the Secretary of Defense believed "we need most of these troops to do any of these things."

Johnson pondered his advisers' suggestions, but decided nothing. Westmoreland's request meant making America the principal combatant defending South Vietnam. LBJ hesitated to make that decision. Instead, he instructed Bundy at the end of the meeting to "[s]ee what alternatives" existed—to see where else America might "make [its] stand" in Southeast Asia.[3]

As the pressure for major deployments mounted on Johnson, so did popular skepticism over his Vietnam pronouncements. Ever since LBJ's secret April 1 decision changing the mission of U.S. forces from base security to active combat, the President had been slowly losing his struggle to conceal this shift in strategy. As more American troops had arrived in South Vietnam throughout April and May, reporters had increasingly questioned Washington's description of their mission. Journalists visiting the airbase at Danang could see that the Marines' widening patrols belied administration explanations of "base security."

They therefore began pressing U.S. officials about the Marines' precise mission. On April 9, reporters had grilled MACV's spokesman about imminent Marine landings at Phubai and Danang. Are these "going to be purely security troops?" they had asked. "Yes," the spokesman had replied.

But the reporters, skeptical, had persisted. On June 5, correspondents at the State Department had sought clarification of the U.S. military mission. The Department's response: "American troops have been sent [to] South Vietnam recently with the mission of protecting key installations there."[4]

The contradictions and denials finally ended on June 8. That day, State Department spokesman Robert McCloskey publicly confirmed the change in mission which President Johnson had secretly approved more than two months before. Under questioning from *New York Times* reporter John Finney, this exchange occurred:

> FINNEY: Let me ask one other question. What you are saying means that the decision has been made in Washington as a matter of policy that if Westmoreland receives a request for U.S. forces in Viet-Nam to give combat support to Vietnamese forces he has the power to make the decision?
>
> McCLOSKEY: That is correct.
>
> FINNEY: Could you give us any understanding . . . as to when Westmoreland got this additional authority?
>
> McCLOSKEY: I couldn't be specific but it is something that has developed over the past several weeks.[5]

The announcement provoked a storm of controversy, which the White House tried to quell with a "clarifying" statement the next day. That morning, presidential spokesman George Reedy told reporters that "[t]here has been no change in the mission of United States ground combat units in Viet Nam in recent days or weeks. The President has issued no order of any kind in this regard to General Westmoreland recently or at any other time. The primary mission of these troops is to secure and safeguard important military installations, like the air base at Da Nang." On the other hand, Reedy added later, "General Westmoreland also has authority within the assigned mission to employ these troops in support of Vietnamese forces faced with aggressive attack . . . when, in his judgment, the general military situation urgently requires it." The White House statement was, as Westmoreland himself later observed, "a masterpiece of obliquity."[6]

This effort to stem the rising controversy through ambiguity failed. Voices in the media and Congress only intensified their criticism of Vietnam policy and Johnson's handling of it. On the day of Reedy's press statement, the *New York Times* editorialized:

> The American people were told by a minor State Department official yesterday that, in effect, they were in a land war on the continent of Asia. This is only one of the extraordinary aspects of the first formal announcement that a decision has been made to commit Amercan ground forces to open combat in South Vietnam: the nation is informed about it not by the President, nor by a Cabinet member, not even by a sub-Cabinet official, but by a public relations officer.[7]

Similar rumblings echoed through Congress, where legislators expressed growing anxiety over the war and LBJ's candor about it. These included New York Republican Senator Jacob Javits, who had supported the Tonkin Gulf Resolution ten months earlier. "We have been moving in the direction of a massive, bogdown land struggle in Asia without any specific consent by Congress or the people," Javits warned the Senate on June 9. He urged the President to seek another resolution specifically authorizing expanded military involvement. To do otherwise, Javits asserted, "would be disastrous," for "[w]ithout a mandate from the Congress and the people, a U.S. land struggle in Asia could engender criticism and division in the country that will make recent protests over our Vietnam policy look like a high school picnic."[8]

Other critics privately satirized the White House's withering credibility. "Do you know when Lyndon Johnson is telling the truth?" people began to ask. "Well, when he goes like this"—rubbing the nose—"he's telling the truth." "When he goes like this"—pulling an ear lobe—"he's telling the truth." "When he goes like this"—stroking the chin—"he's telling the truth." "But, when he starts moving his lips, that's when he's not telling the truth." Or, as Washingtonians quipped, referring to a local landmark: "The old C & O canal which runs north from Georgetown is bounded by the Cumberland Gap at one end and the Credibility Gap at the other."[9]

These remarks epitomized Johnson's deepening dilemma: the escalation that LBJ had resisted yet obscured now threatened to overwhelm his reservations while destroying his credibility. Sensing these dangers, the President turned to his old Senate friend Mike Mansfield once again, seeking help on his Vietnam predicament.

Johnson telephoned Mansfield on the night of June 8. LBJ told the majority leader about Westmoreland's request, which he had discussed with his advisers that morning. What would Mansfield do? Johnson asked. How would he answer the general?

Mansfield, who had prepared a memorandum on Vietnam for LBJ several days before, sent this and another one to Johnson on June 9. In them, Mansfield beseeched the President to avoid further escalation, to resist "pressures for an irreversible extension of the war in Asia." Now was the moment. For "[t]he rate of commitment is accelerating," he warned Johnson, "and a course once set in motion, as you know, often develops its own momentum and rationale whatever the initial intentions."

Mansfield felt that course flowed directly from LBJ's earlier bombing decision—a decision urged on him by Taylor, McNamara, and McGeorge Bundy as a way to bolster Saigon politically. These men and their recommendation, the majority leader contended, should be called to reckoning:

> I think it is about time you got an accounting from those who have pressured you in the past to embark on this course and continue to pressure you to stay on it. . . . What was promised by the initial extension of the war in the air over the North? And what, in fact, has it produced to date?

Mansfield believed that it had led to only greater escalatory pressures, combined with quickening political deterioration in the South. As a result, the President now faced a request for major U.S. forces "at a time when the last semblance of constituted government (the Quat group) . . . is disappearing"—a plea to save South Vietnam when "there is not a government to speak of in Saigon."

Mansfield implored Johnson to confront this reality by confronting difficult and painful questions: "In what direction are we going in Viet Nam? . . . What do we mean when we say we are going to stay in South Viet Nam and for what specific . . . ends are we going to stay there?" Such questions, as recent events ominously attested, would be "asked increasingly at home no less than abroad," the senator warned.

Mansfield's own answer to these questions remained unchanged. "As I see it, . . . there are no significant American interests which dictate [a] . . . massive, unilateral American military effort to control the flow of events in Vie[t] Nam," he wrote. U.S. stakes were limited. And Mansfield urged LBJ to keep them so, by approving "the minimum military effort . . . necessary to hold the situation in the South from falling apart altogether and a maximum initiative on our part to get this whole sorry business to a conference table as soon as possible."

Yet the majority leader specifically counseled Johnson against seeking another congressional resolution sanctioning the commitment of additional ground forces. He feared that such a request, given recent disclosures over the change in troop mission, "could set off a wave of criticism and . . . demands for inquiries" severely damaging the President. LBJ's earlier furtiveness, the senator implied, now paradoxically constrained his political forthrightness.[10]

Mansfield's warnings remained very much on Johnson's mind as he convened another meeting on Westmoreland's request the next morning.[11]

McNamara opened the session by reviewing Westmoreland's proposal. Mindful of LBJ's reluctance to deepen the commitment, he tried to estimate the minimum forces necessary to forestall South Vietnam's collapse. McNamara figured roughly 95,000, or eighteen battalions—slightly more than half the general's requested thirty-two. This "would . . . cut out fourteen battalions," he told the President, but it would also "avoid too large an escalation."

Rusk endorsed this figure, as did Taylor, who urged Johnson to dispatch the forces "rapidly" in order to check further losses during the monsoon season.

Yet LBJ resisted even this reduced number. "Why must we do it?" he demanded.

Taylor, sensing Johnson's hesitation, spoke bluntly. "If we don't," the ambassador warned, "we may lose [more] territory."

Still, LBJ demurred. "Don't you think it will be read as [a] 'land war in Asia'?" he asked, adding insistently, "we have to explain this not that—not a Korean War."

The thought of another Korea weakening the presidency, dividing Congress, and frustrating the country shook Johnson. But so, too, did growing complaints about his Vietnam actions and candor with the public.

"Is there any question about [my] authority powers [as] commander-in-chief?" LBJ asked Rusk.

"None," the Secretary of State responded, citing "SEATO, the Southeast Asia Resolution, the—"

How about Congress, Johnson interrupted, glancing at Senator Russell, "Have we kept 'em informed?"

"Yes we have," Rusk asserted.

Abruptly, LBJ shifted to the situation in South Vietnam. Would larger deployments stoke "anti-Americanism" among the populace, he asked, encouraging a "slackening off" of national resolve?

Taylor agreed that Washington must "watch for [the] 'take over'" effect. But he considered further deployments essential, in order to save the situation and give "Westy a lever" in the field.

Johnson remained wary. "What if we don't do this?" he remarked, doggedly resisting the escalation. "Would we get [more] losses with what we've got?"

Again, Taylor pressed LBJ. To deny Westmoreland's request, he warned, meant "[w]e could lose a province—lose territory—lose towns."

Those prospects concerned Johnson, but the thought of an open-ended commitment made him groan: "Will [these troops] lead to more?" he wondered aloud. "How do we extricate ourselves!"

Taylor tried to assuage LBJ's anxiety. "If we can stalemate [the Vietcong's] monsoon [offensive]," he said, then ARVN could "go back in strong" during the fall, forestalling the need for additional U.S. forces.

Johnson, however, worried about this immediate request and the heavier casualties it entailed. What losses did Westmoreland's figure imply? he wanted to know, "400 [or] 4000?"

McNamara predicted a doubling of current casualties—"another 400 between now and [the first of] October."

Johnson anguished over the figures; he wanted negotiations, not escalation. Speaking to Rusk of the overtures to discussion he had made at Johns Hopkins on April 7, he asked whether "we had any DRV responses."

"No," the Secretary replied, "and we don't expect 'em." Hanoi and the Vietcong sensed their advantage, Rusk told the President, and therefore saw no need to negotiate.

LBJ felt angry and trapped—caught between Westmoreland's demand for more troops and the communists' unwillingness to bargain away their anticipated victory. More than ever, he felt locked on a treacherous course, one which Mansfield had told him flowed from his advisers' earlier bombing recommendation.

The thought nagged Johnson, whose temper suddenly flared. "What is the answer to the argument that the bombing has had no results?" LBJ demanded to know.

"We never thought it would bring them running," Rusk said, following up, however, with the suggestion that bombing had had a "good . . . effect on military and civilian" morale.

"[T]he pause?" Johnson continued.

It had blunted opposition to ROLLING THUNDER, McNamara noted, without silencing public criticism.

Well, "[w]hat do they want now?" the President snorted.

The public wants to know "[w]here you are taking us," McNamara said. "[That] is the question."

"Therefore?" LBJ shot back.

"I'd recommend more explanation," McNamara said, making clear just what the administration intended.

Johnson, irritated, retorted with devastating sarcasm. *"His* reason for going North," LBJ jeered, referring to McNamara, "was to save morale in [the] South."

McNamara said nothing.

At that point, the President grabbed one of Mansfield's memos off the Cabinet table. Clutching the paper, LBJ glared at McNamara, McGeorge Bundy, and Taylor, and had them answer it "line by line."

Johnson's anger at his advisers, however, soon gave way to frustration over the war. And despair at his predicament. The communists "think they're winning—we think they're winning," LBJ observed. He wanted a settlement, yet the North Vietnamese wanted only victory. He favored negotiations, yet faced "pressure on [the] hard right" against them. What could he do and still prove he was "steering carefully?" Johnson lamented.

Above all, Ball told the President, "we need to be careful *not* to regard this decision as defining or pre-deciding what we do after . . . [the] monsoon [season]." Washington must not foreclose its options, he insisted. That meant committing the minimum forces necessary to forestall South Vietnam's collapse during the summer—many less than thirty-two battalions. For to grant Westmoreland's full request, Ball warned LBJ, "puts us all the way in" and "clearly implies more."

Johnson felt in too deep already. "What are we doing this summer then with 95,000!" he said.

McNamara, repeating his earlier arguments, cited the "general need" for additional forces—enough to save the situation without posing "too much" risk of escalation.

"How fast" then? the President asked.

"Aim at 1 August," McNamara suggested, but with "no [firm] commitment."

CIA Director Raborn interjected at this point, expressing his agency's support for a rapid buildup—"the faster the better," he said.

Senator Russell considered the pace of deployments peripherally important. The central question, he told Johnson, was "how to get us out and save face?" Yet this man who had counseled Ike against intervention at Dienbienphu in 1954, and warned LBJ against deeper involvement in 1964, saw no easy way out in 1965. Russell shared the President's trepidation over Vietnam, but could offer no solution to their common worry.

An equally deep worry, in Johnson's mind, remained the issue of disclosure—how Westmoreland's request for major forces should be put to Congress and the people. McNamara's recommendation was clear: explain forthrightly the Vietnamese situation and U.S. commitment. McGeorge Bundy now endorsed that position. Rusk disagreed, stressing the "dangers of a full-fledged debate" over Vietnam. "[T]he commies would use their whole apparatus to stir up trouble," he told the President. This, in turn, might have serious international results," Rusk added.

LBJ's anxieties, however, centered on Vietnam's domestic repercussions. Here, Johnson sensed danger behind every available option. "Fulbright and Stennis" had privately warned that the Tonkin Gulf Resolution and May supplemental appropriation did not sanction large-scale ground action; existing authorizations would therefore stretch it, he feared. Yet the President dreaded renewed congressional debate as well. Opponents would "howl"; partisan divisions would deepen; an impression of American irresolution would emerge; above all, his legislative program would suffer.[12]

These remarks punctuated LBJ's dilemma. He confronted military pressure to escalate the war substantially. Yet the very magnitude of proposed escalation heightened political pressure for another congressional resolution. Johnson feared both. He therefore determined to contain both by obscuring the full dimensions of Westmoreland's request at an NSC meeting the next afternoon.[13]

LBJ opened the meeting on a note of wistful resignation. "We have a treaty obligation," he told the NSC members, "and we intend to keep our commitment. Some say we should get out of Vietnam, while others say we should do more." Johnson, however, intended to follow a middle course: "holding the situation so that we can carry out what we are committed to do."

Ambassador Taylor then reviewed the South Vietnamese situation, summarizing Saigon's latest political chaos. The military picture had also worsened, he reported. The Vietcong had launched a monsoon offensive of greater intensity than in years past. This, combined with mounting ARVN desertions, had produced a "serious" manpower shortage in the South Vietnamese army.

These conditions demanded "the introduction of additional U.S. forces," said Taylor. Without more American troops, South Vietnam would collapse; with them, he hoped, "we will be able to push Hanoi into negotiations."

Whatever Taylor's expectations, Rusk judged current negotiating prospects dismal. "Today we see no possibility of talks," he said. "Although we are alert to all [negotiating] tracks, none appear promising." The reason was obvious. Hanoi and the Vietcong anticipated victory in South Vietnam, and were therefore "awaiting the outcome of the monsoon campaign."

McNamara then broached Westmoreland's plan to check that campaign. At LBJ's direction, he listed proposed deployments well below Westmoreland's actual thirty-two-battalion, 170,000-man request. The general "recommends that the thirteen battalions—70,000 man level now authorized be increased to twenty-three battalions—123,000 men," McNamara asserted.

General Wheeler, privy to Westmoreland's June 7 cable, bridled at this shaved figure. He obliquely challenged McNamara's description, noting that it "calls for deploying fewer troops now than either General Westmoreland or the Joint Chiefs recommend." Carefully avoiding specific numbers, Wheeler pressed Johnson to send the "troops recommended by General Westmoreland."

LBJ carefully deflected Wheeler. "We must delay and deter the North Vietnamese and Viet Cong as much as we can, and as simply as we can, without going all out," he said, for "[w]hen we grant Westmoreland's request, it means we get in deeper and it is harder to get out." Johnson's intention was clear: "We must determine which course gives us the maximum protection at the least cost."[14]

This remark underscored LBJ's struggle to balance conflicting pressures—to commit enough forces to save South Vietnam, but not so many as to spark further escalation or renewed congressional debate. It was a precarious balance, fraught with difficulties and dangers.

Johnson hinted at his dilemma to an interviewer shortly afterward. Henry Graff, a Columbia University historian studying LBJ's decision-making process, arrived at the Oval Office moments after the NSC meeting ended. The President, standing in the doorway scanning a newspaper, greeted Graff and motioned him toward the fireplace sofa, next to his rocker.

Graff opened by querying Johnson about Vietnam. LBJ gestured toward his desk several feet away. On it, he said, lay a request from General Westmoreland for additional forces. The President spoke uncertainly about that request. "What will be enough and not too much?" he mused.

LBJ's sullenness matched his uncertainty. "I know the other side is winning; so they do, too," he said, adding glumly, "No man wants to trade when he's winning." Johnson felt no choice, he told Graff, but "to apply the maximum deterrent till [Ho] sobers up and unloads his pistol."

LBJ had spoken like a frontier sheriff. But his tough words guarded deep anxieties. Just the night before, Johnson said, he had lain awake thinking how he would feel "if my President told me that my children had to go to South Vietnam in a Marine company . . . and possibly die." The thought was anguishing. "And no one knows this better than I do," he said.

But LBJ sensed no escape from his dilemma—trapped, as he felt, between the military pitfalls of escalation and the political pitfalls of withdrawal. Johnson explained his predicament vividly. "When I land troops they call me an interventionist," the President moaned, "and if I do nothing I'll be impeached."

And his Great Society seemed imperiled, too. For LBJ well remembered the fall of China and its devastating impact on the Fair Deal. Yet he also remembered World War I's impact on the New Freedom and World War II's on the New Deal. Reform demanded tranquility, and Johnson wanted this desperately. "God knows peace would be so sweet to us," he told Graff before ending the interview.[15]

Instead, the next few days brought more news of South Vietnam's deterioration and, with it, more pressure to commit additional forces. On June 10, the Vietcong launched a massive attack against Dongxoai, a district capital of Phuoclong province, sixty miles north of Saigon. Striking in unusually large numbers, the VC mauled two local South Vietnamese battalions, and nearly annihilated another three sent to relieve them. By June 14, when Vietcong forces finally withdrew, ARVN had sustained heavy losses—over 900 killed, the highest casualties ever suffered in a single engagement.

These reverses impelled Westmoreland to step up his demands for larger forces. On June 13, the general again cabled Washington, urging prompt approval of his requested deployments. "The VC are destroying [ARVN] battalions faster than they can be reconstituted and faster than they were planned to be organized under the buildup program," Westmoreland warned. "It is MACV's considered opinion," he anxiously added, "that RVNAF cannot stand up to this pressure without substantial US combat support on the ground."[16]

As LBJ wrestled with Westmoreland's latest cable, he sent General Goodpaster to Gettysburg to seek former President Eisenhower's advice on the recommended deployments. Goodpaster met Ike at his Pennsylvania farmhouse on the morning of June 16. He began by describing ARVN's setback at Dongxoai. Two entire South Vietnamese battalions had been annihilated, the general reported. Goodpaster then reviewed Westmoreland's request for major U.S. forces, together with his plan to conduct aggressive "search and destroy" operations. Eisenhower affirmed that the United States had now "appealed to force" in South Vietnam, and therefore "we have got to win." Westmoreland's request should be supported, Ike told Goodpaster to inform the President.[17]

If Eisenhower's comments lessened Johnson's reservations, the confidential polls which LBJ received the next afternoon diminished them further. Several days earlier, Johnson had secretly commissioned a survey testing reaction to larger deployments. The President hungered for signs of their effect on popular opinion.

This poll, like previous studies, revealed an astonishingly hawkish public. Although U.S. involvement in the war had deepened considerably in recent months, Johnson's popularity remained extraordinarily high: 69 percent. So did his handling of Vietnam; respondents supported his overall policy 65 to 35 percent.

The most striking results, however, concerned additional combat forces.

A heavy plurality, 47 percent, favored "sending in more troops because of the monsoon season"—double those "not sure" (23 percent); two and a half times those wishing to "keep [the] present number" (19 percent); and more than quadruple those wanting to "take troops out" (11 percent).

These figures indicated wide support for further action. But they also indicated wide divisions over the war. Sending more troops, though the most popular option, still attracted fewer than half of all Americans. Should those troops prove ineffective, Johnson faced potentially worrisome public opposition.[18]

For the moment, though, rising congressional opposition represented LBJ's greatest worry. This worry echoed throughout Johnson's comments to the press later that afternoon. Huddling around the President's desk, reporters asked LBJ about recent Senate debate surrounding American combat troops in Vietnam and whether he should seek another joint resolution.

Johnson strenuously denied such a need. "The evidence there is very clear for anybody that has read the [Tonkin Gulf] resolution," he insisted. "That language, just as a reminder to you, said the Congress approves and supports the determination of the President as commander in chief to take all—all—all necessary measures to repel any—any—any armed attack against the forces of the United States and to prevent further aggression."[19]

Congressional debate not only troubled LBJ, it rankled him. The clamor of Senate critics seemed out of tune with the polls he had just read. Johnson conveyed his feelings to reporters with an anecdote. "I remember . . . the Louisiana farmer that stayed awake night after night because of the frogs barking in the pond," he said. "Finally he got irritated and angry . . . and he went out and drained the pond and killed both frogs." So LBJ sought to minimize his critics by deprecating them, to diffuse congressional dissent by downplaying it.[20]

As Johnson struggled to limit political pressures for renewed legislative debate over Vietnam, George Ball moved to limit military pressures for escalation. Ball, who had attended the June 8 and 10 White House meetings, recognized the growing momentum for major deployments. Events seemed to be pushing LBJ toward a precipice.

Ball resolved to brake this process. On Friday, June 18, he sent LBJ an impassioned memorandum aimed to stay the President's hand, to dissuade Johnson from irreversible involvement. Knowing that LBJ wished, above all, to preserve his options, Ball opened his memo by quoting Waldo Emerson's famous dictum: "Things are in the saddle, and ride mankind"—his message being that Johnson must "keep control of policy and prevent the momentum of events from taking command." Circumstances demanded it. "For the fact is," Ball wrote, "and we can no longer avoid it, that, in spite of our intentions to the contrary, we are drifting toward a major war—that nobody wants."

Ball described the treacherous currents which had swept Washington to this point:

> Ever since 1961—the beginning of our deep involvement in South Viet-Nam—we have met successive disappointments. We have tended to underestimate the strength and staying-power of the enemy. We have tended to overestimate the effectiveness of our sophisticated weapons under jungle conditions. We have watched the progressive loss of territory to Viet Cong control. We have been unable to bring about the creation of a stable political base in Saigon.

Today, he concluded, the United States found itself tied to a government that "is becoming more and more a fiction"—a country that "has an army but no government."

Ball considered this fact exceedingly dangerous. In the event of major American escalation, it could prove disastrous. "Before we commit an endless flow of forces to South Viet-Nam," he therefore counseled LBJ, "we must have more evidence than we now have that our troops will not bog down in the jungles and rice patties—while we slowly blow the country to pieces."

Ball himself remained profoundly skeptical. France's earlier experience in Vietnam seemed forbidding to him:

> They quoted the same kind of statistics that guide our opinions—statistics as to the number of Viet Minh killed, the number of enemy defectors, the rate of enemy desertions. . . . They fully believed that the Vietnamese people were on their side, and their hopes received intermittent shots of adrenalin from a succession of projects for winning the war. . . .

And yet—despite all their efforts, all their expectations, all their confidence—the French "were finally defeated—after seven years of bloody struggle. . . ."

Ball implored Johnson to avoid a similar fate by avoiding major escalation. Specifically, he urged LBJ to limit additional deployments to "no more" than 100,000, while making clear to "your top advisers . . . that you are *not* committing US forces on an open-ended basis to an all-out land war in South Viet-Nam; that instead you are making a *controlled commitment* for a *trial period* of three months"—until the end of the monsoon season.

Together, these proposals appeared strikingly cautious—not unlike McNamara's "controlled" escalation to 95,000.[21] Ball did differ from McNamara, however, in his sensitivity to ultimate costs, which he beseeched Johnson to ponder carefully. If the trial period provided *"no reasonable assurance"* that the United States could fight in South Vietnam without "vast protracted effort," then Ball advised "limiting the American commitment and finding a political solution at a level below the total achievement of our declared objectives."

He knew such a course hardly attracted LBJ. But fruitless escalation seemed no wiser, Ball thought. "[G]ood statesmanship," he reminded the President, required cutting "losses when the pursuit of particular courses of action threaten . . . to lead to a costly and indeterminant result. . . ." And major escalation threatened just that, while making disengagement infinitely more difficult. For "the more forces we deploy in South Viet-Nam," Ball concluded, "the harder we shall find it to extricate ourselves without unacceptable costs if the war goes badly."[22]

Johnson studied Ball's memorandum carefully over the weekend at Camp David. The Undersecretary's comments moved him deeply, particularly Ball's warning about seeking a diplomatic solution before American forces bogged down in an interminable war. Indeed, on Saturday, June 19, LBJ specifically requested the CIA's most recent estimate of North Vietnam's willingness to negotiate. The President seemed anxious to find a way out before the war escalated sharply.[23]

He also seemed anxious to avoid an open-ended commitment of American combat forces which Westmoreland's request augured. Johnson emphasized this concern to Bill Moyers the following Monday. That day, June 21, LBJ called in Moyers, who had delivered Ball's memo to him on Friday, to discuss it over lunch. "I don't think I should go over 100,000," the President told Moyers, "but I think I should go to that number and explain it." Tell "George to work for the next ninety days—to work up what is going to happen after the monsoon season," he instructed his assistant. "I am not worried about riding off in the wrong direction. I agreed that it might build up bit by bit. I told McNamara that I would not make a decision on this and not to assume that I am willing to go overboard on this. I ain't. If there is no alternative, the fellow who has the best program is the way it will probably go."[24]

Johnson hesitated to commit himself. He wanted more time, more room, more choices—more opportunity to think free from the pressure of decision. The President's handling of another Vietnam conference on June 23 reflected this intention. During the meeting, LBJ remained conspicuously aloof as his advisers heatedly debated what course to follow.[25]

Ball went first. Repeating his arguments to Johnson, the Undersecretary urged capping deployments at 100,000, while preparing plans to shift U.S. efforts to Thailand.

Rusk vigorously objected. Voicing what one witness later described as "an extreme statement" of the domino theory, the Secretary of State predicted dire consequences flowing from an American withdrawal from South Vietnam. Thailand, even India, would surely fall to communist China, Rusk asserted.

McNamara also challenged Ball's proposal, despite its parallels to his own

June 10 recommendation. Jarred by ARVN's recent spectacular losses, the Secretary of Defense abandoned his earlier reluctance. He now urged meeting Westmoreland's full request. McNamara had decisively shifted his position and, with it, the balance of opinion among LBJ's advisers.

Johnson seemed determined, however, to restore that balance and thus preserve his options. Interjecting for the first time in the discussion, the President ordered McNamara and Ball to prepare memos arguing their positions in greater detail. He wanted them in a week, he said, giving no promise that a decision would follow soon.[26]

McNamara and Ball immediately set to work on their competing proposals. As part of his preparation, McNamara had cabled Saigon the day before seeking General Westmoreland's reaction to a thirty-four-battalion deployment—two more than the general's June 7 request. Would this persuade the North Vietnamese and Vietcong to desist, the Secretary of Defense wanted to know?[27]

Westmoreland, replying in a telegram on June 24, doubted the communists would "back off" regardless of how many forces Washington committed in the coming months. He believed thirty-four battalions would, however, prevent South Vietnam's defeat, while re-establishing a "military balance" by the end of 1965. At the same time, Westmoreland hinted at the need for substantially more forces in 1966. The general now expected a long and costly war, involving increasing numbers of American troops.[28]

Westmoreland's cable jolted McNamara, compelling him toward even tougher recommendations. He therefore drafted a memo, circulated to the other principals on June 26, outlining drastically expanded U.S. military action in Vietnam.[29]

McNamara's draft startled McGeorge Bundy, crystallizing his recent apprehensions about the war. Although Bundy had pushed bombing in February, urged deploying the first Marines in March, and opposed negotiations throughout April and May, he now sensed the gathering force of events, the pressure for major escalation which those earlier recommendations had unleashed.

Bundy conveyed his apprehensions vividly to McNamara in a note on June 30. Your "draft recommendation . . . seems to me to have grave limitations," he wrote. "It proposes a doubling of our presently planned strength in South Vietnam, a tripling of air effort in the north, and a new and very important program of naval quarantine. It proposes this new land commitment at a time when our troops are entirely untested in the kind of warfare projected. It proposes greatly extended air action when the value of the air action we have taken is sharply disputed. It proposes naval quarantine by mining at a time when nearly everyone agrees the real question is not in

Hanoi, but in South Vietnam. My first reaction is that this program is rash to the point of folly."

Bundy considered McNamara's inattention to "the upper limit of US liability" particularly reckless. "If we need 200 thousand men now for these quite limited missions," he wrote, "may we not need 400 thousand later?" "Is this a rational course of action?" Bundy judged McNamara's proposals "a slippery slope toward total US responsibility and corresponding feckless-ness on the Vietnamese side."

These comments reflected Bundy's slim faith in the Saigon regime. He doubted that major deployments would improve that regime. Instead, they might pull America deeper into a war fought alongside an increasingly in-effective and unpopular government.

This danger prompted Bundy to raise surprising questions about ultimate objectives in Vietnam. Given Saigon's political debilities and the military risks of escalation, he wrote McNamara in conclusion, "do we want to invest 200 thousand men to cover an eventual retreat? Can we not do that just as well where we are?"[30]

Bundy's comments sounded astonishingly similar to Ball's. He seemed to be converging on Ball's position of resisting further deployments, while seek-ing a negotiated exit. This convergence proved short-lived, however. For just as Bundy embraced Ball's "hold the line" position, the Undersecretary moved well beyond it, to advocate "cutting losses" through prompt Ameri-can withdrawal.

Ball's shift came on the morning of June 28. Up to that time, Ball had argued a cautious policy: limiting, not opposing, further deployments; ex-ploring, not urging, disengagement. But no more. "In an intense meet-ing . . . with his State Department helpers," remembered William Bundy, who attended the session, Ball repeated "what he had put in his June 18th memorandum for the President. . . . This time, however, his ending was not to hold the line, but to find a way to 'cut our losses' just as soon as pos-sible." Ball had concluded America must now extricate itself from Viet-nam.[31]

William Bundy concluded differently. Accepting Ball's warnings about the dangers of escalation, Bundy refused to accept the idea of withdrawal. He therefore broke with Ball. Joining the Undersecretary in his office after the meeting, Bundy announced his plan to draft a third recommendation, out-lining a middle course between McNamara and Ball.[32]

By week's end, Johnson's advisers had forged three alternatives in Vietnam: Robert McNamara urging substantial escalation; George Ball urging cutting losses; and William Bundy urging holding the line. These options went to LBJ on the night of July 1.

McNamara, in the opening paragraph of his memorandum, urged the President to "expand substantially" American military pressures in Vietnam. He believed these increased pressures, together with a "vigorous" negotiating effort, would, in time, "create conditions for a favorable settlement." McNamara then outlined his proposed actions: raising U.S. forces to 175,000 within three months, with a call-up of reserves and extended tours of duty; intensifying air strikes against Vietcong base areas in South Vietnam; imposing a naval quarantine on North Vietnam, including the mining of Haiphong harbor; destroying rail and bridge lines between Hanoi and China; and substantially expanding ROLLING THUNDER—from 1800 to 5000 sorties a month.

McNamara advised coupling these increased military pressures with increased political approaches to Moscow, Hanoi, and Peking. Specifically, he urged sending a high-level U.S. representative to the Soviet Union to seek Moscow's help in reconvening a Geneva Conference; initiating contacts with the Vietcong and North Vietnamese about terms of a potential settlement; and pressing China to moderate its support of Hanoi.

Whatever his long-term hopes for these efforts, McNamara admitted they would do little more than "demonstrate US good faith" in the near future. He felt a "pay off" would come "only after the tide begins to turn" in South Vietnam. And on this crucial issue, McNamara expressed troublesome doubts, despite his boldly hawkish advice. Noting that "troops once committed as a practical matter cannot be removed," he predicted ever-increasing casualties straining domestic support for the war. Advising increased pressure against the Vietcong, he feared the VC might still "find ways of continuing almost indefinitely their present intensive military, guerrilla and terror activities, particularly if reinforced with some regular PAVN units." Urging intensified bombing of North Vietnam, he nevertheless wondered "whether [its] POL [petroleum, oil, lubricants], ammunition, and cadres can be cut off and if they are cut off whether this really renders the Viet Cong impotent." McNamara appeared deeply divided over the efficacy of his own recommendations.[33]

Ball's memo expressed no such ambivalence. Sensing this might be his last chance to sway the President, Ball argued passionately and bluntly against escalation. He spelled out his case to Johnson:

> The decision you face now . . . is crucial. Once large numbers of US troops are committed to direct combat they will begin to take heavy casualties in a war they are ill-equipped to fight in a non-cooperative if not downright hostile countryside.
>
> Once we suffer large casualties we will have started on a well-nigh irreversible process. Our involvement will be so great that we cannot—without national humiliation—stop short of achieving our complete objectives. *Of the two possi-*

bilities I think humiliation would be more likely than the achievement of our objectives—even after we had paid terrible costs.

Ball beseeched LBJ to avert this debacle. The President must, he pleaded, "seek a compromise settlement which achieves less than our stated objectives and thus cut our losses while we still have the freedom of maneuver to do so. . . ."

Ball knew such a decision would be most difficult for Johnson, given the dangers to his domestic standing and therefore his legislative program, as well as America's international position. But weighed against the perils of escalation, Ball considered withdrawal far less damaging to the President and the country. And its costs greatly exaggerated. Analyzing the impact of U.S. disengagement throughout the East Asia, Ball rebutted the domino theory. He cited America's most important ally in the region, Japan, as an example. Far from fearing withdrawal, Ball told LBJ, Japan "would prefer wisdom to valor in an area remote from its interests where escalation could involve its Chinese or Russian neighbors, or both. . . ." Its citizens, moreover, viewed U.S. involvement in South Vietnam not as a struggle to preserve a beleaguered democracy but as an effort "to prop up a tottering government that lacks adequate indigenous support." This perception extended far beyond Japan, to include many other U.S. allies and neutrals. Whatever our expectations, he wrote, "we cannot ignore the fact that the war is vastly unpopular and that our role in it is perceptibly eroding the respect and confidence with which other nations regard us." Ball feared further involvement would only exacerbate this trend, further undermining "the effectiveness of our world leadership."

Escalation, then, posed a double threat—to America's power and to America's reputation. Ball evoked this double threat when he concluded, "[I]f we act before we commit substantial US forces to combat in South Viet-Nam we can, by accepting some short-term costs, avoid what may well be a long-term catastrophe."[34]

The third alternative, William Bundy's, argued a "middle way" between McNamara and Ball—capping U.S. deployments at approximately 85,000, and waiting through the summer to see how this worked.

Bundy's plan, while eschewing withdrawal, still reflected grave misgivings about escalation: increasing American combat involvement, he wrote, risked causing "the Vietnamese government and especially the army to let up," while fostering "adverse popular reactions to our whole presence"; imposing an air and naval quarantine threatened "to throw North Vietnam into the arms of Communist China"; expanding ROLLING THUNDER to urban industrial areas "would not *now* lead Hanoi to give in but might on the contrary toughen it." Given these dangers, Bundy urged LBJ to *"hold on for the next two months"*—*"to test* the military effectiveness of US combat forces and the reaction of the Vietnamese army and people to the increasing US role."[35]

Bundy's proposal completed the options for Johnson's consideration. But not the contest for Johnson's mind. For LBJ received another note that night which, while not endorsing a specific recommendation, greatly influenced his thinking.

Dean Rusk seldom wrote Johnson. He limited that practice to important moments, like the bombing decision in February. Rusk knew a similar moment beckoned. LBJ stood on the threshold of another crucial Vietnam decision, involving a major escalation of the war.

Rusk's basic advice remained unchanged. "The central objective of the United States in South Viet-Nam," he told the President, "must be to insure that North Viet-Nam not succeed in taking over or determining the future of South Viet-Nam by force." This admonition crisply summarized Rusk's understanding of the war. A man wedded to the principle of collective security and the perception of a monolithic world communism, Rusk necessarily viewed Vietnam in stark and apocalyptic terms:

> The integrity of the U.S. commitment is the principal pillar of peace throughout the world. If that commitment becomes unreliable, the communist world would draw conclusions that would lead to our ruin and almost certainly to a catastrophic war. So long as the South Vietnamese are prepared to fight for themselves, we cannot abandon them without disaster to peace and to our interests throughout the world.

Beneath Rusk's fear of quitting the South Vietnamese regime, however, lurked deep doubts about that regime's political viability and commitment to the war. Rusk poured out those doubts to Johnson:

> We must insist that the South Vietnamese leaders declare a moratorium on their bickering and knuckle down to the increased effort needed to defeat the Viet Cong. They must be told bluntly that they cannot take us for granted but must earn our help by their own performance.

Sure that the United States must save South Vietnam, Rusk remained unsure about South Vietnam's determination to save itself.[36]

LBJ had now heard from all of his senior advisers except McGeorge Bundy. The national security assistant's turn came in a covering note he sent to the President transmitting the other papers. Bundy's advice to Johnson differed markedly from his comments to McNamara the previous day. Addressing the President, Bundy suppressed his thoughts about eventual disengagement and many of his concerns about escalation. "My hunch," he in fact wrote, "is that you will want to listen hard to George Ball and then reject his proposal. Discussion could then move to the narrower choice between my brother's course and McNamara's."

What explained Bundy's shift in attitude? Like his brother, McGeorge Bundy refused to accept Ball's solution. However much he feared the consequences of escalation, Bundy refused to countenance withdrawal. He therefore muted his anxieties about the war's ultimate costs, and encouraged Johnson toward the remaining options.[37]

The President's national security assistant, the Secretary of Defense, the Secretary of State—all had stressed the importance of maintaining a noncommunist South Vietnam, regardless of the costs. Against them stood only the Undersecretary of State. The imbalance was formidable, and increased the pressure on Johnson to commit additional forces.

Yet LBJ continued to resist this pressure, ever reluctant to escalate the war. The depth of his reluctance emerged vividly during a telephone conversation with former President Eisenhower the next morning.

Eisenhower, whom Johnson had phoned to discuss his Vietnam options, returned the President's call shortly after 11 a.m. LBJ began by asking Ike about major troop deployments. Eisenhower, as he had during the February bombing deliberations, offered pointedly hawkish advice. "When you once appeal to force in an international situation involving military help for a nation," he told Johnson, "you have to go all out! This is war, and as long as the enemy are putting men down there, my advice is do what you have to do!"

LBJ expressed nagging skepticism about escalation's effectiveness. "Do you really think we can beat the Viet Cong?" he asked plaintively. Ike responded coolly. "We are not," he said, "going to be run out of a free country that we helped to establish."

Johnson, struggling with the legacy of Eisenhower's earlier commitment, remained deeply apprehensive of a larger war. He faced growing criticism from Congress and the allies, LBJ said. If he escalated further, the President told Ike, "we will lose the British and Canadians and will be alone in the world." "We would still have the Australians and the Koreans—and our own convictions," Eisenhower curtly replied. With that, the two men ended their conversation, and Johnson headed to the Cabinet Room to discuss the previous evening's papers.[38]

During this meeting with McNamara, Rusk, and the Bundy brothers, LBJ offered few clues about his ultimate intentions. Instead, Johnson remained deliberately vague and noncommittal, seizing on recommendations from competing memos. He ordered McNamara to Saigon to scrutinize Westmoreland's troop needs. Averell Harriman, meanwhile, would visit Moscow to explore reconvening the Geneva Conference. At the same time, LBJ instructed Ball to develop his option further, particularly the idea of opening direct contact with North Vietnam's representative in Paris.[39]

The President sought, through these actions, to keep his options open—to delay the day of decision. Still uncertain which path to follow, Johnson wanted more time to ponder his choices.

And more time to shepherd key domestic measures through Congress. For the President, by the beginning of July, faced a crossroads in his legislative calendar. The Voting Rights Act neared its last hurdle on the House floor. Medicare/Medicaid approached a final Senate vote. Conclusive action also loomed on the housing, urban renewal, and antipoverty initiatives. Securing these bills' passage represented a powerful incentive to defer controversial Vietnam decisions and the all-consuming debate they threatened.

Yet heated resistance to Ball's negotiating gambit—particularly from Taylor—slowly narrowed LBJ's room for maneuver. On July 3, the State Department cabled Saigon about Ball's proposed contact with Hanoi and the Vietcong. Taylor wasted little time in denouncing the plan. On July 5, he telegrammed the President, loudly condemning such "premature" and "highly dangerous" talks. Taylor's unusually sharp dissent, which even McGeorge Bundy found "surprising," further limited Johnson's range of options.[40]

LBJ sensed this tightening pressure. However much he wished to postpone agonizing choices, he knew events would not long let him. Realizing the day of decision neared, Johnson summoned a group of elder statesmen to Washington on July 8 to discuss the Vietnam War.

This group, created as a bipartisan advisory committee during LBJ's fall campaign against Goldwater, comprised men who had played leading roles in American government during the postwar years—men who embodied the knowledge, experience, and prestige of America's foreign policy establishment—men, in short, who had fixed and perpetuated the policy of global containment now reaching its fullest expression in Vietnam.

They included Dean Acheson, a major architect of U.S. Cold War policies. His diplomatic career had paralleled America's rise to global preeminence. Joining the State Department on the eve of U.S. entry into World War II, Acheson had helped administer Lend-Lease aid to Britain; participated in planning the United Nations; secured congressional funding for the Truman Doctrine; and guided the nation's foreign policy as Secretary of State from 1949 to 1953.

Omar Bradley, another panel member, radiated the quiet, cool professionalism of America's military establishment. An infantry commander during World War II, his troops had spearheaded the drive against Axis forces from North Africa to the heart of Germany. After the war, Bradley had served as Army Chief of Staff and, later, first Chairman of the Joint Chiefs of Staff during Korea.

John Cowles, liberal Republican publisher of the *Minneapolis Star and*

Tribune and *Look* magazine, exemplified the internationalism of America's leading newspapers and journals—an outlook deepened by Cowles' involvement in the Lend-Lease program during World War II. Like his friend and colleague Henry Luce, Cowles preached a commitment to U.S. activism in this, the "American Century."

Attorney and diplomat Arthur Dean shared Cowles' liberal Republicanism and dedication to bipartisan internationalism. A law partner of Eisenhower's Secretary of State, John Foster Dulles, Dean had served as Ike's negotiator during the Korean armistice talks in 1953, and, subsequently, as Kennedy's ambassador to the Geneva Disarmament Conference during 1961–1962.

Another Kennedy veteran, Roswell Gilpatric, symbolized the continuities between JFK's and LBJ's stewardship of national security affairs. Second-in-command at the Pentagon from 1961 to 1964, Gilpatric had shared McNamara's analytical, technocratic approach to military issues. And like his boss, Gilpatric had enthusiastically embraced the "flexible response" and counter-insurgency doctrines applied in the laboratory of Vietnam.

Millionaire industrialist Paul Hoffman typified American business know-how harnessed in the service of American foreign policy. Transforming the troubled Studebaker Corporation from receivership to prosperity during the 1930s, Hoffman had focused similar energy and talent on devastated Europe as head administrator of the Marshall Plan from 1948 to 1950.

George Kistiakowsky, a distinguished Harvard chemist, personified the interrelationship of science and politics in the nuclear era. A native Cossack who had fought against the Bolsheviks during the Russian Revolution, Kistiakowsky later emigrated to America, where he had worked on the Manhattan Project, aided development of the intercontinental ballistic missile, and counseled Eisenhower as special scientific advisor.

Duke University law professor Arthur Larson signified the alliance between academia and government forged during the Second World War. The Oxford-trained educator and author had served every recent President except Truman—as a member of Roosevelt's Foreign Economic Administration; Undersecretary of Labor and later U.S.I.A. Director under Eisenhower; counselor to Kennedy's and Johnson's State Department.

Robert Lovett epitomized America's foreign policy elite. Protégé of the legendary soldier-statesman George Marshall, Lovett's career had echoed that of his illustrious mentor. During World War II, he had directed the rise of American air power under Marshall. After the war, Lovett had joined Marshall at the State Department, helping the Secretary shape his European recovery program and NATO alliance. Then, in 1950, he had returned with Marshall to the Pentagon, as the defense chief's deputy and eventual successor from 1951 to 1953.

Lovett's World War II colleague, John McCloy, completed LBJ's roster of senior statesmen. Like his peers, McCloy had held key posts in several administrations: Assistant Secretary of War under Roosevelt; president of the World Bank and American proconsul in occupied Germany under Truman; disarmament adviser to both Eisenhower and Kennedy. And like his peers, McCloy projected the determination, confidence, and assurance of a generation steeped in the successes of World War II and the early Cold War.

Five of these men—Bradley, Gilpatric, Kistiakowsky, Larson, and Mc-Cloy—comprised a smaller subpanel which met with Rusk, McNamara, Thompson, and William Bundy at the State Department on the morning of Thursday, July 8.

Discussion first focused on U.S. stakes in Vietnam. The subpanel considered them "very high indeed." They felt a communist victory in Vietnam endangered not just Southeast Asia—as the administration believed—but Japan, India, and even Europe as well, while jeopardizing the credibility of America's global commitments. Only Larson dissented, doubting that Saigon would ever become a viable government—even if Hanoi stopped supporting the Vietcong—and that what Washington might achieve as a military "success" would be any better than what it might achieve now, through negotiations.

On military issues, the subpanel offered staunchly hawkish advice, urging administration officials to commit "whatever" forces needed to South Vietnam. Several members, in fact, criticized the President's previous actions as "too restrained."

Similar views emerged during a meeting of the full group later that afternoon. During this session, only Hoffman joined Larson in calling for negotiations rather than escalation in Vietnam. And their stance encountered heated resistance. All the others—especially Acheson and Dean—vehemently resisted the idea. This is no time to "turn over our Far East policy to the UN" or any other body, insisted Dean.

McCloy expressed the group's overwhelming consensus. America faced rough going, he said. Even if U.S. forces checked the monsoon offensive, McCloy predicted that Hanoi and the Vietcong would persevere, inflicting heavier U.S. casualties while stubbornly resisting talks. Pausing for emphasis, McCloy added, "we are about to get our noses bloodied." And yet he insisted to Rusk and McNamara: "You've got to do it. You've got to go in."

These elders also urged the administration to explain the military situation and need for further troops to the public. Cowles and Lovett stressed this point, faulting the President for painting "too rosy a picture" of the war to date. Johnson must do nothing less, they insisted, with America's global containment policy—their legacy—at risk.

Several of these men journeyed to the White House that evening. Gathered like a board of directors around the Cabinet table, Acheson, Bradley, Cowles, Dean, Lovett, and McCloy greeted LBJ when he arrived shortly after 6:30. Acheson, the group's informal leader, described what followed in a letter two days later to former President Truman.

Almost immediately, reported Acheson, Johnson launched into

> a long complaint about how mean everything and everybody was to him—Fate, the Press, the Congress, the Intellectuals & so on. For a long time he fought the problem of Vietnam (every course of action was wrong; he had no support from anyone at home or abroad; it interfered with all his programs, etc. etc.).
>
> Finally, I blew my top & told him . . . that he had no choice except to press on. . . .
>
> With this lead my colleagues came thundering in like the charge of the Scots Greys at Waterloo . . . [O]ld Bob Lovett, usually cautious, was all out, &, of course, Brad[ley] left no doubt that he was with me all the way. I think . . . we scored.[41]

George Ball, who sat in that night along with Rusk, McNamara, and McGeorge Bundy, was appalled by what he considered the elders' hasty and imprudent counsel. When the meeting ended, Ball walked over to Acheson and Dean. "You goddamned old bastards," he reproached them, "[y]ou remind me of nothing so much as a bunch of buzzards sitting on a fence and letting the young men die. You don't know a goddamned thing about what you're talking about. . . . You just sit there and say these irresponsible things!" Then, looking directly at Acheson, Ball asked, "Would you have ever put up with this if you had been secretary of state?" His words did not go entirely unregistered. Acheson "said afterwards that I shook the hell out of him," Ball later recalled.[42]

The wise men's advice, on the other hand, certainly shook the hell out of Johnson. As William Bundy has written, "the President [had] probably expected that *most* of the Panel would be *generally* in favor of a firm policy. What he found was that *almost all* were *solidly* of this view. . . ." For an unsure diplomatist like LBJ, these men represented the established wisdom, the beguiling stature, the unassailable authority of a successful foreign policy tradition. Now, the fathers of that tradition had admonished Johnson to carry on in Vietnam.[43]

The panel's profound effect on Johnson's thinking became clear during an impromptu news conference in the Oval Office the next afternoon. Summoning reporters around his desk, the President appeared somber and resigned. He spoke quietly, almost inaudibly, of the dark road ahead. "We expect that it will get worse before it gets better," LBJ said in response to questions about Vietnam. Citing the recent buildup of U.S. forces—something Johnson had always avoided in the past—he warned that "others . . . will be required," adding, "Whatever is required I am sure will be supplied."[44]

LBJ spoke even more unambiguously on July 13. Addressing a formal press gathering in the White House East Room, Johnson prepared the country for "new and serious decisions . . . in the near future." He left little doubt what those decisions entailed. "It will be necessary . . . to have substantially larger increments of troops" committed to South Vietnam, LBJ said.[45]

But the clearest, most unmistakable clue to Johnson's intentions came during a Rose Garden speech to the National Rural Electric Cooperative Association (NRECA) the next evening. The summer sun, streaking low across the undulating South Lawn, provided a fitting setting as LBJ reminisced with old colleagues about the accomplishments of the NRECA. Johnson seemed at home and relaxed, speaking frankly with kindred spirits. Gradually, his thoughts drifted to Vietnam:

> Now there are going to be some long debates, there are going to be some eloquent speeches, there are going to be some differences of opinion, and there is going to be some criticism of your President. But three Presidents—President Eisenhower, President Kennedy, and your present President—have made a commitment in the name of the people of the United States, and our national honor is at stake in southeast Asia. And we are going to protect it, and you just might as well be prepared for it. . . .[46]

Having privately debated and personally struggled over Vietnam for weeks, LBJ appeared resigned to a larger war.

But if Johnson had resigned himself to this eventuality, he did so with grudging resentment. The moment seemed particularly cruel to him. Just five days before, on July 9, the House of Representatives had narrowly passed the Voting Rights Act, while the Senate had finally approved Medicare. Both bills would soon enter conference. LBJ's legislative dreams seemed within reach at last.

And now Vietnam threatened to unravel it all. Already, congressional conservatives, scenting major decisions ahead, had begun pressing Johnson to confront the consequences of a larger war. In the House, Republicans Gerald Ford and Melvin Laird had demanded the administration increase defense spending $1 to $2 billion and mobilize at least 200,000 reserves. In the Senate, Mississippi Democrat John Stennis, chairman of the Armed Services Preparedness Subcommittee, had criticized Johnson for financing Vietnam "out of a peacetime budget," while Minority Leader Everett Dirksen, on July 13, had urged the President to seek "additional authority and more money—a good deal of money." Said another congressman: "It is time to get ready for a big war."[47]

Johnson understood, only too well, what these comments augured for the Great Society. Having labored to keep congressional attention and financial resources focused on his domestic reforms, LBJ now seemed in danger of losing both to Vietnam. The prospect stung Johnson, intensifying his desperation to finish the legislative race before the storm.

This sense of urgency filled LBJ's thoughts as he strolled from the Rose Garden, through the Oval Office, to his small study adjoining it for an interview with *Newsweek* editor James Cannon and correspondent Charles Roberts. The journalists, seated on a beige velvet couch, greeted the President as he sat down in a butterfly chair beneath autographed photographs of FDR and Truman.

During the interview, Cannon and Roberts queried Johnson about his overriding goal as President. "[T]o make life better and more enjoyable and more significant" for the people, LBJ answered without hesitation. The newsmen, recalling Johnson's conservative Senate career, asked LBJ to explain his conversion. The President responded honestly and simply. "I'm more aware of the problems of more people than before," he confessed. "I am more sensitive to the injustices we have put on the Negro, for instance, because I see and talk to him more now. I'm a little less selfish, a little more selfless." "In this place," Johnson said, sweeping his arm around the room, "you can't go any higher and the only thing you want to do is what's right."

Yet LBJ sensed dwindling opportunities to achieve that vision. "We've got to do it now," he told his visitors, insisting that the "Presidential mandate runs out." "I expect to be down to forty-five percent, too," he ruefully added.[48]

Johnson had confided a similar lament to McNamara and Rusk a short time before, noting the disturbing parallels between his own circumstances and those of earlier Democratic reformers such as Wilson and Roosevelt: "[E]very time we have gotten near the culmination of our dreams, the war bells have rung." Those bells were no more welcome to him than to his predecessors: "If we have to fight, I'll do that. But I don't want . . . to be known as a War President."[49]

About the time Johnson concluded his *Newsweek* interview, a military transport jet carrying Secretary of Defense McNamara and his party lifted off from Andrews Air Force Base in nearby Maryland bound for Saigon.[50]

McNamara's mission, planned since July 2, had assumed particular importance in recent days. Now that the President had largely reconciled himself to additional deployments, he counted on McNamara to identify the precise number of forces needed.

McNamara's party landed at Tansonhut airport on the morning of July 16. From there, they motored under heavy security to downtown Saigon, for a meeting at MACV headquarters. During this conference, McNamara questioned Westmoreland about his troop requirements. Westmoreland cited thirty-four U.S. battalions (175,000) by the end of 1965. More ominous, he now predicted another twenty-four battalions (100,000) during 1966.[51]

Westmoreland's estimate doubtless shook McNamara. So too did an encounter that night at Deputy Ambassador Johnson's residence. Johnson had arranged an informal dinner for McNamara with South Vietnam's newest rulers, Thieu and Ky. The Americans arrived first, followed by General Thieu in a conservative business suit. Several minutes later, Ky made a splashing entrance. As Chester Cooper, one of those present, later recalled, Ky "walked in breezily, wearing a tight, white dinner jacket, tapered, formal trousers, pointed, patent leather shoes, and brilliant red socks. A Hollywood central casting bureau would have grabbed him for a role as a sax player in a second-rate Manila night club." McNamara was speechless. "At least no one could confuse him with Uncle Ho!" someone nearby managed to mutter.[52]

The following day, McNamara met again with Ky and Thieu at the Prime Minister's office on Thong Nhut Street. A South Vietnamese official present later described McNamara's demeanor: "Precise but affable, scribbling notes on a yellow pad as he went, he fired his questions about numbers, organization, management, and logistics as if he were bent on assembling all the factors and components for the solution of some grand mathematical equation."[53]

McNamara first quizzed Ky and Thieu about U.S. troop levels. How many American forces did Saigon need? he asked. Thieu said thirty-four battalions, plus another infantry division.

McNamara, noting this would bring U.S. forces to nearly 200,000, asked if the South Vietnamese people would tolerate an American presence of this magnitude.

Ky saw no problems. Thieu, however, thought the increase required an extensive "propaganda program" to explain the heightened U.S. presence.

If Washington sent 200,000 troops, could it count on stable government in Saigon? McNamara inquired.

Thieu insisted his government could demonstrate its ability to govern, once American forces relieved ARVN.

What if the communists responded by increasing infiltration and attacks? McNamara continued. What then?

Thieu dismissed these fears, claiming the Vietcong were already finding it harder to increase their numbers.

At this point, Ky jumped back into the discussion, reiterating his desire for more U.S. forces. Saigon wanted American troops not because it lacked the will to fight, he asserted, but because they could clear and hold territory while his government "reorganized the rear."[54]

Back in Washington, meanwhile, the administration began organizing the process for committing additional combat forces, as well as related measures such as mobilizing reserves, raising draft calls, and increasing defense expenditures. On July 15, President Johnson ordered a CIA study estimating reactions to a substantial U.S. buildup in South Vietnam, assuming a call-up of reserves, extended tours of duty, heavier conscription, and a $2 to $3 billion defense appropriation. Then, the following day, LBJ stepped back, instructing Deputy Defense Secretary Vance to prepare a much smaller supplementary request. Johnson explained his shift to Vance in telling terms. As Vance secretly cabled McNamara on July 17, the President felt it "was impossible for him to submit [a] supplementary budget request of more than $300–400 million to the Congress before next January" because "[i]f a larger request is made . . . , he believes it will kill [his] domestic legislative program."[55]

Here, in stark language, lay LBJ's deepest fear—that revealing the war's full costs spelled doom for his Great Society. Johnson had sensed this danger all along, but acutely now, in mid-summer. As he brooded anxiously to those around him that week, "I can get the Great Society through right now—this is a golden time. We've got a good Congress and I'm the right President and I can do it. But if I talk about the cost of war, the Great Society won't go through." Oh no, he said, "Old Wilbur Mills will sit down there and he'll thank me kindly and send me back my Great Society, and then he'll tell me that they'll be glad to spend whatever we need for the war."[56]

LBJ mulled gloomily, irascibly over his predicament. The tension between Vietnam and the Great Society seemed excruciating—almost unmentionable, as the President's comment to McGeorge Bundy on July 19 suggested. That day, Johnson asked his national security assistant to draft a memo outlining reasons for avoiding a billion-dollar Vietnam appropriation. Bundy prepared a list, which he sent the President that night:

1. It would be a belligerent challenge to the Soviets at a time when it is important to do only the things which we have to do (like calling reserves).

2. It would stir talk about controls over the economy and inflation—at a time when controls are not needed and inflation is not that kind of problem.

3. It would create the false impression that we have to have guns, not butter—and would help the enemies of the President's domestic legislative program.

4. It would play into the hands of the Soviets at Geneva, because they could argue that it was a flagrant breach of the policy of "mutual example" on defense budgets.

5. It is not needed—because there are other ways of financing our full effort in Vietnam for the rest of the calendar year, at least.

LBJ returned the memo, scrawling this message across the bottom: "Rewrite eliminating 3.—L."[57]

For Johnson, Bundy's remark represented a painful reminder of his dilemma, a disturbing sign of Vietnam's domestic implications. Disturbing signs of Vietnam's international implications reached LBJ the following evening, in a CIA estimate of world reactions to escalation, which he had commissioned five days earlier.

Johnson's gloom surely deepened as he studied the report late into the night on July 20. Intelligence authorities, anticipating Vietcong and North Vietnamese reaction to an American military buildup, wrote:

> We do not believe that inauguration of the US policy here assumed would basically alter the[i]r expectations. The Viet Cong . . . and the DRV probably have come to expect increased US commitments, and they probably believe that the VC, with increased North Vietnamese assistance, can find ways to offset the effect of larger US forces. Nor do we think that the exten[s]ion of air attacks to selected military targets in the Hanoi and Haiphong areas . . . would significantly injure the VC ability to persevere in the South or persuade the Hanoi government . . . that the price of persisting was unacceptably high.

More troops and heavier bombing would not foreshorten the war, nor dissuade the communists. Instead, the CIA predicted,

> the Communists would almost certainly undertake measures to increase their own strength in South Vietnam for a higher level of struggle. They are already augmenting VC units and dispatching additional PAVN forces to South Vietnam; the assumed US actions would probably result in a speeding up of this process.

Escalation threatened counter-escalation, triggering an even larger and bloodier conflict.

This conflict, moreover, would be likely fought on communist, not American, terms. For intelligence officials doubted the Vietcong and North Vietnamese would accommodate U.S. strategy by concentrating their forces in large fixed battles, vulnerable to American mobility and firepower. Rather, the CIA surmised, they would continue "harassments intended to bleed and humiliate US forces, trapping and destroying isolated units where possible."

Diplomatic factors intensified these military dangers. Intelligence experts believed Peking, fearing Moscow's participation in any negotiations, would press Hanoi to resist talks. Russia, in turn, would be driven by countervailing pressures to expand its military aid to North Vietnam, thus risking a direct confrontation with Washington. The result: a Vietnamese foe masterfully exploiting the Sino-Soviet rivalry, combined with heightened Cold War tensions.[58]

As LBJ brooded over the CIA study, McNamara and his party sped eastward over the Pacific, headed back to Washington. Their jet landed at Andrews Air Force Base shortly after dawn on July 21. Within hours, McNamara's crucial report had reached Johnson.

McNamara opened his pivotal memorandum to the President with a disturbing but candid assessment of the war.

> The situation in South Vietnam is worse than a year ago (when it was worse than a year before that). After a few months of stalemate, the tempo of the war has quickened. A hard VC push is now on to dismember the nation and to maul the army. The VC main and local forces, reinforced by militia and guerrillas, have the initiative and, with large attacks (some in regimental strength), are hurting ARVN forces badly.

Other troubles abounded. Economic conditions had deteriorated; political divisions had deepened; pacification had stalled; army desertions had skyrocketed. The Vietcong, meanwhile, continued to widen their control over population and territory, aided by North Vietnamese infiltration which bombing had barely throttled. South Vietnam teetered "near collapse," with the communists anticipating "a complete take-over."

McNamara then reviewed the three, by now familiar, options.

> (a) Cut our losses and withdraw under the best conditions that can be arranged—almost certainly conditions humiliating the United States and very damaging to our future effectiveness on the world scene.

> (b) Continue at about the present level, with the US forces limited to say 75,000, holding on and playing for the breaks—a course of action which, because our position would grow weaker, almost certainly would confront us later with a choice between withdrawal and an emergency expansion of forces, perhaps too late to do any good.

> (c) Expand promptly and substantially the US military pressure against the Viet Cong in the South and maintain the military pressure against the North Vietnamese in the North while launching a vigorous effort on the political side to lay the groundwork for a favorable outcome by clarifying our objectives and establishing channels of communication. This alternative would stave off defeat in the short run and offer a good chance of producing a favorable settlement in the longer run; at the same time it would imply a commitment to see a fighting war clear through at considerable cost in casualties and materiel and would make any later decision to withdraw even more difficult and even more costly than would be the case today.

None sounded inviting. But given McNamara's assumptions about the consequences of (a) and (b), (c) seemed the only choice. There could, in fact, be no other, since he considered additional deployments "prerequisite to the achievement of *any* acceptable settlement."

All this LBJ had largely accepted, as his comments to the press the previous week attested. But the number of additional forces, how to raise them, at what cost—these remained crucial and open questions.

Here, McNamara urged substantial and forthright escalation: increasing U.S. troops to 175,000 promptly, with perhaps another 100,000 in 1966; intensifying ROLLING THUNDER strikes against the North; mobilizing 235,000 Reserves and National Guardsmen; enlarging the regular armed forces by 375,000 through heavier conscription and extended tours of duty; and sizably expanding the defense budget. These proposals meant a major American war; its costs frankly acknowledged to Congress and the country.[59]

Reading McNamara's report, Johnson must have shuddered at his dilemma. He faced a commitment of up to 275,000 combat troops, involving the mobilization of over 600,000 additional soldiers, costing billions of extra dollars—this at a time when his most cherished domestic programs awaited congressional completion. The tensions between Vietnam and the Great Society, between guns and butter, had never seemed more immediate or more intense.

LBJ's moment of decision had come. Beginning later that morning, and for seven critical days thereafter, Johnson would struggle with the deeply conflicting pressures of war and reform. From that struggle would emerge the most fateful decision of his presidency.

9

"Better'n Owl"

THE SAME MORNING Johnson received McNamara's report, he received a telephone call from his congressional liaison, Lawrence O'Brien. O'Brien delivered heartening news to the President. He told LBJ to expect conference approval of the Medicare bill that day, with final congressional action within a week. O'Brien also expected the Voting Rights Act, which had recently entered conference, to be reported shortly. This news, together with Senate passage of the Housing bill on July 15 and tomorrow's House vote on an expanded anti-poverty measure, bolstered Johnson's hope that this would prove the greatest week of legislative achievement since the opening days of FDR's New Deal.

The sense of imminent triumph, and Vietnam's overshadowing threat to that triumph, preoccupied Johnson as he headed for the Oval Office shortly after 10:30. At that same moment, top officials gathered in the Cabinet Room to discuss McNamara's recommendations with the President.[1]

McNamara, awaiting LBJ's arrival, passed copies of his secret report around the Cabinet table. Rusk quizzed him about Saigon's military efforts. "What is the capability of GVN to mobilize their own forces?" Rusk asked.

"They are trying to increase by 10,000 per month," McNamara answered, noting MACV's optimism about this target. The Defense Secretary himself, however, doubted South Vietnam's "non-government" could ever muster sufficient forces to counter the Vietcong.

Wheeler agreed, while faulting military rather than civilian leaders. The "weakness in [South] Vietnam's forces [is the] lack of [an] adequate officer corps—in their training and attitude," he said.

"What is the timing on how we should proceed?" Rusk continued.

184

"There ought to be a statement to the American people no later than a week," McNamara said.

Candor, not timing, concerned Ball. "It is one thing to ready the country for this decision," he reminded his colleagues, "and another to face the realities of the decision. We can't allow the country to wake up one morning and find heavy casualties." Ball added: "We need to be damn serious with the American public."

McNamara nodded. He felt the administration must make it clear that U.S. troops had already entered combat in South Vietnam.

Just as McNamara finished, President Johnson entered the room. He looked somber and drawn, wearing a gray suit which matched his mood that day. Nodding to the group, LBJ pulled his high-backed chair up to the Cabinet table. Johnson's eyes darted around the room, taking the measure of each adviser. Speaking in an unusually low voice, the President warned them against any leaks to the press about the discussions at hand. Johnson then turned to McNamara. "[P]lease begin, Bob," he said.

McNamara summarized his recommendations. "To support an additional 200,000 troops in Vietnam by the first of the year, the reserves in the United States should be reconstituted by [a] like amount. I recommend calling up 235,000 a year from now, replac[ing] the reserves with regulars." By "mid-1966 we would have approximately 600,000 additional men."

LBJ leaned back slowly in his chair. "What has happened in [the] recent past that requires this decision on my part? What are the alternatives? Also, I want more discussion [about] what we expect to flow from this decision. Discuss in detail."

Before McNamara could answer, Johnson fired another barrage of questions: "Have we wrung every single soldier out of every country we can? Who else can help? Are we the sole defenders of freedom in the world? Have we done all we can in this direction? [What are] the reasons for the call-up? [What are] the results we can expect? What are the alternatives?"

LBJ seemed irritable and uncomfortable about the decision at hand. "We must make no snap judgments," he warned those seated around him. "We must carefully consider all our options."

They included, only faintly now, the possibility of cutting losses, of withdrawal. Johnson quickly retraced this step. "We know we can tell South Vietnam 'we're coming home,'" he said. "Is that the option we should take? What flows from that?"

But LBJ already had his answer to that question. "The negotiations, the pause, . . . the other approaches—have all been explored," he said. "It makes us look weak—with cup in hand." We have tried—and failed, Johnson concluded wearily.

Gathering himself once more, Johnson spoke: "Let's look at all our

options so that every man at this table understands fully the total picture."
As he recapitulated the themes, Johnson gazed at both McNamara and Ball,
whose conflicting advice weighed so heavily upon him.

After LBJ finished, McNamara lifted a map showing ARVN and Vietcong positions throughout South Vietnam. Pointing to communist-controlled
areas, he told the President that "[o]ur mission would be to seek out the
VC in large scale units." Wheeler backed him up: "By continuing to
probe, we think we can make headway." Together, they had summarized
Westmoreland's "search and destroy" strategy.

CIA Director Raborn doubted the Vietcong would oblige General Westmoreland. His analysts feared the VC might avoid conventional engage-
ments altogether, bleeding U.S. forces instead through hit-and-run ambushes.

Wheeler dismissed the danger. The Vietcong will have to "come out and
fight" at some point, he insisted.

Ball had doubts. "Isn't it possible that the VC will do what they did
against the French—stay away from confrontation and not accommodate
us?"

"Yes, but by constantly harassing them, they will have to fight somewhere," Wheeler contended.

Even "[i]f [the] VC doesn't fight in large units," McNamara added. "it
will give ARVN a chance to re-secure hostile areas." Yet, despite the upbeat
assessment he had just given the President, McNamara harbored some uncertainty. "We don't know what VC tactics will be when [it] is confronted
by 175,000 Americans," he frankly admitted.

Johnson, following silently, now spoke up. "Is anyone of the opinion we
should not do what [McNamara's] memo says—If so, I'd like to hear from
them."

The invitation to Ball seemed unmistakable. He seized it immediately.
"I . . . foresee a perilous voyage—very dangerous," Ball said, "[I have]
great apprehensions that we can win under these conditions."

Whatever his fears, however, Ball sensed the direction of LBJ's thinking
and responded accordingly. "[L]et me be clear," he said, "if the decision
is to go ahead, I'm committed."

Johnson knew that; he wanted to know if there was "another course
in the national interest that is better than the McNamara course?" "We
know it's dangerous and perilous," the President observed. "But can it be
avoided?"

"There is no course that will allow us to cut our losses" easily, Ball
admitted, but "[i]f we get bogged down, our cost might be substantially
greater. The pressures to create a larger war would [then] be irresistible."

"What other road can I go?" LBJ asked with some emotion.

"Take what precautions we can—take losses—let their government fall apart—negotiate—[with a] probable takeover by [the] Communists. This is disagreeable, I know."

"Can we make a case for this?" the President said, seeking to draw Ball out. "[D]iscuss it fully."

"We have discussed it," Ball impatiently remarked, "I have had my day in court."

"I don't think we have made a full commitment," Johnson hastened to note. He wanted to hear Ball out again, if only to soften the pressure from McNamara. LBJ therefore encouraged Ball to restate his case, to present "an alternative course." After all, "[w]e haven't always been right," he said. "We have no mortgage on victory."

Then, just as abruptly, Johnson reversed himself. "I feel we have very little alternative to what we are doing," he brooded. Although LBJ intended to "look at all other courses carefully," deep down he felt "it would be more dangerous for us to lose this now, than endanger a greater number of troops."

Rusk traced Johnson's present quandary to accumulated decisions of the past. "What we have done since 1954–1961 has not been good enough," the Secretary reflected, speculating that "[w]e should have probably committed ourselves heavier in 1961."

Rusk could not rewrite the past, however, nor the troubled legacy of South Vietnamese politics. Outgoing USIA Director Rowan emphasized this point, stressing the dangerous "weakness of the Ky government." "Unless we put the screws on the Ky government," Rowan warned, compelling it to behave responsibly, then "175,000 men will do us no good."

Lodge agreed. "There is no tradition of a national government in Saigon," he said, putting his finger on South Vietnam's fundamental problem. "There are no roots in the country. Not until there is tranquility can you have any stability. I don't think we ought to take this government seriously," he flatly stated. "There is no one who can do anything."

Despite his misgivings, Lodge pressed LBJ to act, doing what "[w]e have to do . . . regardless of what the Saigon government does." Washington, to this Brahmin, had a "right"—indeed a "duty"—"to do certain things with or without [Saigon's] approval."

Johnson remained less certain himself. Turning from Lodge to Ball, he asked: "George, do you think we have another course?"

"I would not recommend that you follow McNamara's course."

LBJ urged Ball to explain why, and "offer another course of action." "I think it is desirable to hear you out and determine if your suggestions are sound and ready to be followed," he said. Johnson seemed to be challenging Ball to persuade the group and, by implication, a President sensitive to consensus judgment.

"I think I can present to you the least bad of two courses," Ball responded. "What I would present is a course that is costly, but [one that] can be limited to short term costs."

"Then, let's meet . . . this afternoon to discuss Ball's proposals." "Now," LBJ said, turning to McNamara, "let Bob tell us why we need to risk those 600,000 lives."

McNamara outlined the reasons for more troops. He told Johnson the current level of forces—75,000—offered no hope; "it will let us lose slowly instead of rapidly," he said. More Americans, on the other hand, would stabilize the situation," giving ARVN "breathing room" while posing "no major risk of catastrophe."

"But you will lose a greater number of men," the President said, impatiently flicking his tie-clasp.

"The more men we have the greater the likelihood of smaller losses," Wheeler interjected.

"What makes you think if we put in 100,000 men, Ho Chi Minh won't put in another 100,000?" LBJ asked.

"This means greater bodies of men," Wheeler smiled, "which will allow us to cream them."

"What are the chances of more North Vietnamese . . . coming [in]?" Johnson repeated, unmoved by Wheeler's assurance.

"Fifty-fifty chance," the general predicted. "H[o] would be foolhardy to put one-quarter of his forces in[to] South Vietnam" because "[i]t would expose him too greatly in North Vietnam."

At that point, the meeting ended. Before leaving, the President asked everyone to reassemble at 2:30. He then stood up and walked from the room.

When 2:30 arrived, the same group of advisers filed back into the Cabinet Room. Several minutes later, LBJ appeared, and the meeting resumed.[2]

"All right, George," Johnson said, gesturing for Ball to begin.

Voices hushed around the table. As one participant later put it, "It was George Ball's last stand."[3]

Ball carefully arranged his notes. He cleared his throat and began. "We can't win," he flatly stated, warning that the "most we can hope for is [a] messy conclusion" to a "long [and] protracted" war.

Such prospects alarmed Ball, reminding him of the "galling" experience of Korea. Ball sketched those parallels, using a chart correlating U.S. casualties with public support for that earlier war.

The statistics told a sobering story. As American casualties in Korea had mounted, domestic support had slipped dramatically. Ball feared a similar trend in Vietnam. If Washington escalated U.S. involvement, casualties would mount steadily. "As casualties increase," he warned, the President would confront growing demands "to strike at [the very] jugular" of North Vietnam, thus risking an even wider and more dangerous war.

This spelled not just domestic but international trouble as well, argued Ball. "If we could win in a year's time—win decisively," he said, then "world opinion would be all right." But in a "long and protracted war"—the very war Ball expected would develop—America would suffer the impression that "a great power cannot beat guerrillas."

LBJ sat with his chin cupped in hand, following Ball closely. "Every great captain in history [was] not afraid to make a tactical withdrawal if conditions [were] unfavorable to him," Ball told him. And the conditions confronting Johnson in Vietnam were miserable. "The enemy cannot even be seen; he is indigenous to the country, and he always has access to much better intelligence. He knows what we're going to do but we haven't the vaguest clue as to his intentions. I have serious doubt[s] if an army of westerners can fight orientals in [an] Asian jungle and succeed."

LBJ seemed impressed. "This is important," he said, distilling Ball's argument, "[C]an westerners, in [the] absence of intelligence, successfully fight orientals in jungle rice-paddies? I want McNamara and Wheeler to seriously ponder this question."

"I think we have all underestimated the seriousness of this situation," Ball resumed, likening America's efforts in South Vietnam to a doctor "giving cobalt treatment to a terminal cancer case." Escalation would not bring remission. Instead, he believed "a long protracted war" would only "disclose our weakness," exposing Saigon's utter dependence on Washington.

Ball considered this sheer folly. Wiser, he thought, "to cut losses in South Vietnam" by putting reform proposals to the government "that they can't accept." "[T]hen," he predicted, "it would move into a neutralist position" and ask the United States to leave. "I have no illusions that after we were asked to leave, SVN would be under Hanoi['s] control," Ball conceded. "That's implicit in our predicament."

Anticipating criticism on this last score, Ball surveyed the consequences of a unified communist Vietnam. "If we wanted to make a stand in Thailand," he said, "we might be able to make it." In South Korea, "[w]e have two [combat] divisions"—ample deterrent to communist aggression. America's closest and most important Asian ally, Japan, "thinks we are propping up a lifeless government. . . ." "Between a long war and cutting our losses," Ball said, "the Japanese would go for the latter."

Johnson appeared skeptical. "Wouldn't all these countries say Uncle Sam is a paper tiger—wouldn't we lose credibility breaking the word of three presidents? . . ." "It would seem to be an irreparable blow," he grumbled.

"The wors[e] blow would be that the mightiest power in the world is unable to defeat a handful of guerrillas," Ball answered.

"Then you are not . . . troubled by what the world would say about pulling out?"

Yes, Ball said, "[i]f we were . . . helping a country with a stable, viable government"—that "would be a vastly different story."

"But I believe that these people are trying to fight," LBJ shot back, illustrating his feelings with a typically Johnsonesque metaphor: "They're like Republicans who try to stay in power, but don't stay there long."

Ball considered the Ky-Thieu clique nothing like America's Republican party. "Thieu spoke the other day and said the Communists would win the election," he said.

"I don't believe that," LBJ snapped. "Does anyone believe that?"

Ball found no supporters, though McNamara did confess misgivings about Saigon's current junta. "Ky will fall soon," he predicted. "He is weak. We can't have elections until there is physical security, and even then there will be no elections because as Cabot said, there is no democratic tradition."

McNamara's comments seemed to rekindle the President's own anxieties about escalation. Leaning forward, Johnson shared those anxieties with the men around him. "There are two basic troublings within me," he said. "1. That westerners can ever win in Asia. 2. [I] don't see how you can fight a war under [the] direction of other people whose government changes every month. Now go ahead, George, and make your other points," LBJ said, slumping back in his chair.

Ball summarized the alternatives. "On one hand," he said, "[w]e can continue a dragged out, bitterly costly, and increasingly dangerous war, with the North Vietnamese digging in for a long term since that's their life and driving force." Or, "we can face the short-term losses of pulling out." "It's distasteful either way," Ball admitted, but then "life's full of hard choices."

McGeorge Bundy, who had been following without comment, now interrupted to say that while Ball had raised "important questions," his course represented a "radical switch" from present policy. "It goes in the face of all we have said and done," Bundy argued, while failing to address "losses suffered by the other side."

Bundy felt Ball had seriously underestimated the war's costs to North Vietnam, but not its costs to the United States. Like Ball, he considered it imperative that Johnson "make clear this is a somber matter—that it will not be quick—no single action will bring quick victory." "We are asking Americans to bet more to achieve less," Bundy noted, and the administration must acknowledge it forthrightly.

On the basic issue, however, Bundy remained adamant. America must stay the course in Vietnam. After all, he predicted, there would be ample time to get out after Washington had given it a good try.

"We won't get out," Ball desperately said, "we'll double our bet and get lost in the rice paddies."

Bundy, his irritation rising, branded Ball's course "disastrous," urging LBJ to "waffle through" rather than withdraw.

Rusk entered the fray. Speaking slowly and carefully, his quiet manner diffused the growing tension between Ball and Bundy. It also magnified the weight of his counsel. As he had countless times before, Rusk stressed the indivisibility of America's global commitments. "If the Communist world finds out we will not pursue our commitment to the end," he gravely intoned, "I don't know where they will stay their hand. On the other hand," Rusk said, "I am more optimistic than some of my colleagues" about the risks of deeper involvement. So far, Washington had increased bombing and ground forces without provoking counter-escalation by Hanoi. He therefore doubted the need to accompany further troop increases with dramatic public gestures.

McNamara also weighed in. Like Bundy, he criticized Ball for underestimating the costs of withdrawal, while exaggerating the costs of escalation. Given enough time—at least two years—and enough forces—perhaps another 100,000—McNamara believed the war winnable.

Wheeler qualified this assertion. He doubted a "win" within a year, no matter how many troops the President committed. That would take longer, perhaps three years. Still, Wheeler insisted that America could ultimately prevail in the jungles of Southeast Asia.

Johnson asked Wheeler why, given past military failures, he now expected success. Wheeler again cited the advantage of more troops.

Lodge intervened. He expressed the sentiments of many in the room—a generation schooled in the crucible of the 1930s. Fearing "a greater threat [of] World War III if we don't go in," he pleaded: "Can't we see the similarity of our own indolence at Munich?" Besides, Lodge added with his generation's equally typical confidence, "I can't be as pessimistic as Ball. We have great seaports in Vietnam. We don't need to fight on roads. We have the sea. Visualize our meeting [the] VC on our own terms. We don't have to spend all our time in the jungles."

Discussion then shifted to press coverage of Vietnam, particularly McNamara's recent mission to Saigon. "How can we get everybody to compete with McNamara in the press?" LBJ demanded to know. "We are trying to do so many other things with our economic and health projects," Johnson observed. "Can't we . . . remind the people that we are doing something besides bombing?" Perhaps—but for now, LBJ's burden of military decision remained.[4]

Johnson continued to wrestle with Vietnam that evening. Shortly after

8 p.m., he received a memo from McGeorge Bundy concerning McNamara. Aware of LBJ's desire to limit Vietnam spending increases, McNamara had begun drafting the $300 to $400 million supplemental appropriation requested by Johnson, through Vance, on July 16. This troubled McNamara, who considered it far below what was necessary to meet the contemplated deployments. As Bundy explained, McNamara was "afraid we simply cannot get away with the idea that a call-up of the planned magnitude can be paid for by anything so small as another few hundred million." "Cy Vance," Bundy matter of factly added, "told me . . . the overall cost is likely to be on the order of $8 billion. . . ."[5]

Eight billion dollars. The figure rattled Johnson, who well imagined its effect on his domestic program. Angry at this prospect, LBJ mimicked McNamara bitterly before aides that evening. One was Horace Busby, an old Johnson confidant and speechwriter who had attended the day's meetings on Vietnam. "What does this man want?" LBJ said, imitating McNamara's flat, matter-of-fact voice. "Does he want to listen to his Secretary of Defense, or does he want to grab people off the street and count heads?"[6]

Johnson resented his predicament. Events seemed to be conspiring against him, pushing him toward a decision he sensed spelled political disaster. LBJ hinted as much in a telephone call to McGeorge Bundy the next morning. Get "ready for some real deep trouble" on Vietnam, he told Bundy. Johnson then offered a clue to his current thinking: "a position that doesn't go beyond [the] first 100,000—then we're going to have peace." LBJ seemed to be groping toward a solution he hoped would avert defeat in Vietnam, while minimizing domestic disruption.[7]

The President seemed near a decision. Before committing himself, however, LBJ called a meeting with the Joint Chiefs that afternoon, July 22. This meeting served two purposes for Johnson. He wanted their military advice about the precise number of forces needed and, just as important, their political support for whatever decision he reached. Making them part of the process, LBJ believed, promised him protection against what had befallen Truman, with MacArthur, in Korea.[8]

Johnson's meeting with the military leadership began promptly at noon. Nearly every top Pentagon official attended: Secretary McNamara, Deputy Secretary Vance, JCS Chairman Wheeler, Army Chief of Staff Harold Johnson, Chief of Naval Operations David McDonald, Air Force Chief of Staff John McConnell, Marine Corps Commandant Wallace Greene, Army Secretary Stanley Resor, Navy Secretary Paul Nitze, Air Force Secretary Harold Brown and his assistant, Eugene Zuckert, and, at the President's request, McGeorge Bundy, Jack Valenti, and Clark Clifford.

Johnson opened the meeting with a few comments. "I asked McNamara to invite you here to counsel with [me] on these problems and the ways to meet them," he said, seeking their advice on the Vietnam situation "from a military point of view."

LBJ then framed these options: "1. Leave the country, with as little loss as possible—the 'bugging out' approach; 2. Maintain present force[s] and lose slowly; 3. Add 100,000 men—recognizing that may not be enough and adding more next year." The disadvantages Johnson perceived in the first and second options showed through in the language he used to describe them; the disadvantages of number 3, he said, included the "risk of escalation," the prospect of "high" casualties, and the danger of "a long war without victory." Having thus recited his dilemma, LBJ asked the military chiefs "where we can go."

Admiral McDonald spoke first. "I agree with McNamara that we are committed to [the] extent that we can't move out. If we continue the way we are it will be a slow, sure victory for the other side. By putting more men in it will turn the tide and let us know what further we need to do. I wish we had done this long before."

"But you don't know if 100,000 will be enough," the President interrupted. "What makes you conclude that if you don't know where we are going—and what will happen—we shouldn't pause and find . . . out?"

Because "[s]ooner or later we'll force them to the conference table," McDonald insisted.

But "[i]f we put in 100,000 won't they put in an equal number?" LBJ shot back.

"No," the admiral replied, "if we step up our bombing—"

"Is this a chance we want to take?" the President carefully asked.

"Yes, when I view the alternatives. Get out now or pour in more men."

"Is that all?"

"I think our allies will lose faith in us if we withdraw."

"We have few allies really helping up now," Johnson pouted.

"[Take] Thailand, for example," McDonald continued. "If we walk out of Vietnam, the whole world will question our word. We don't have much choice."

LBJ turned to Navy Secretary Nitze, a veteran of Truman's ordeal in Korea. "Paul, what is your view?"

Nitze counseled persistence. "[T]o acknowledge that we couldn't beat the VC" would be ominous, he argued; "the shape of the world will change."

But "[w]hat are our chances of success?" Johnson wanted to know.

"If we want to turn the tide, by putting in more men, it would be about sixty-forty."

"Would you send in more forces than Westmoreland requests?"

"Yes. [It] depends on how quickly they—"

"How many?" the President interrupted. "200 instead of 100?"

"[We] need another 100 in January."

"Can you do that?" the President asked.

"Yes," Nitze answered.

McNamara interjected: "The current plan is to introduce 100,000—with [the] possibility of a second 100,000 by the first of the year."

"What reaction is this going to produce?" LBJ asked, looking at Wheeler.

"Since we are not proposing an invasion of North Vietnam, the Soviets will [probably] step up [only] material and propaganda—same with Chicoms."

"Why wouldn't North Vietnam pour in more men?" Johnson said, and "call on volunteers from China and Russia?"

"[T]hey . . . can't win by putting in forces they can't afford. At most," Wheeler insisted, they "would put in two more divisions. Beyond that they strip their country and invite a countermove on our part." As for volunteers, the general said, "the one thing all North Vietnamese fear is Chinese. For them to invite Chinese volunteers is to invite China's take[over of] North Vietnam." The "weight of military judgment," Wheeler concluded, "is that North Vietnam may reinforce their forces, [but] they can't match us on a buildup. From a military view, we can handle, if we are determined to do so, [both] China and North Vietnam."

LBJ swung back to McDonald, asking him to "summarize what you think we ought to do."

McDonald ticked off several steps. "1. Supply [the] forces Westmoreland has asked for. 2. Prepare to furnish more in 1966. 3. Commence build[up] in air and naval forces, step up air attacks on North Vietnam. 4. Bring in needed reserves and draft calls."

"Any idea on cost of what this would be?" the President asked.

"Yes," McNamara said. "$12 billion [in] 1966."

LBJ stared at McNamara. "Any idea what effect this will have on our economy?"

"It would not require wage and price controls," McNamara answered, "the price index ought not go up more than one point or two."

Air Force Chief McConnell interrupted. "If you put in these requested forces and increase the air and sea effort, we can at least turn the tide [to] where we are not losing anymore. We need to be sure we get the best we can out of South Vietnam—[and we] need to bomb all military targets available to us in North Vietnam." "[W]hether we can come to a satisfactory solution with these forces," he added, pausing a moment, "I don't know." "[But] with these forces properly employed, and cutting off their supplies, we can do better than we're doing."

Johnson let McConnell finish. "Have . . . [our] bombing actions been as fruitful and productive as we anticipated?" he asked.

"No sir, they haven't been. [They have been] productive in South Vietnam, but not as productive in North Vietnam because we are not striking the targets that hurt them."

LBJ understood McConnell's concerns; he wanted McConnell to understand his. "Are you seriously concerned [that] when we change targets we escalate the war?" the President demanded. "[Can you] be certain it won't escalate their efforts on the ground? Won't it hurt our chances at a conference if we started killing civilians?"

"We need to minimize civilian killings," McConnell admitted.

"Would you go beyond Westmoreland's recommendations?" the President asked him.

"No sir," the general answered.

Assistant Air Force Secretary Zuckert ventured his own opinion, declaring, "It's worth taking a major step to avoid [the] long-run consequences of walking away from it."

A major step indeed, thought Johnson. "Doesn't it mean if we follow Westmoreland's requests we are in a new war? [Isn't] this going off the diving board?"

"This is a major change in US policy," McNamara stressed. "We have relied on South Vietnam to carry the brunt. Now we would be responsible for [a] satisfactory military outcome."

The import of McNamara's words unsettled LBJ, who asked, quite unexpectedly, "Are we in agreement we would rather be out of there and make our stand somewhere else?"

The "least desirable alternative is getting out," Army Chief of Staff Johnson declared. "[The] second least is doing what we are doing. [The] best is to get in and get the job done."

"But I don't know how we are going to get that job done," LBJ fretted. "There are millions of Chinese. I think they are going to put their stack in. Is this the best place to do this? We don't have the allies we had in Korea."

"It seems that all of our alternatives are dark," Air Force Secretary Brown said, voicing everyone's feelings. Still, Brown found himself "in agreement with the others"—that Washington must hold the line in South Vietnam.

Johnson resisted Brown's assertion. "Is there anything to the argument [that Saigon's] government is likely to fail, and we will be asked to leave?" he wondered aloud. "If we try to match the enemy, [won't] we be bogged down in [a] protracted war and have the government ask us to leave? . . . Are we starting something that in two to three years we can't finish?"

"It is costly to us to strangle slowly," Brown answered, "but [our] chances of losing are less if we move in" with more troops.

"Suppose we told Ky of [the political] requirements we need," Johnson suggested, "he turns them down—and we have to get out and make our stand in Thailand." What then?

"The Thais will go with the winner," Brown replied.

"If we didn't stop in Thailand, where would we stop?" LBJ continued.

McNamara offered a gloomy answer. "Laos, Cambodia, Thailand, Burma surely affect Malaysia," he said, invoking an extreme version of the domino theory. "In two to three years Communist domination would stop there, but [the] ripple effect would be great—[in] Japan [and] India . . . Ayub [Khan of Pakistan] would move closer to China. Greece and Turkey would move to [a] neutralist position. Communist agitation would increase in Africa."

Marine Corps Commandant Greene followed with an analysis of the military picture. "Here are the stakes as I see them," the general said: "1. The national security stake; it is a matter of time before we go in someplace else. 2. There is the pledge we have made. 3. There is our prestige before the rest of the world. If you accept these stakes," Greene told the President, "there are two courses of action. 1. Get out. 2. Stay in and win."

"How to win in the South and in the North?" Greene went on. "The enclave concept will work. I would like to introduce enough Marines to do this. Two Marine divisions and one air wing. We have 28,000 out there now. We need an additional 72,000."

"Greene suggests these men over and above the Westmoreland request," McNamara explained.

"Then you will need 80,000 more to carry this out?" Johnson asked.

"Yes," Greene answered. "I am convinced we are making progress with the South Vietnamese—in food and construction. We are getting evidence of intelligence from South Vietnam. In the North, we haven't been hitting the right targets. We should hit POL storage, which is essential to their transportation. Also, we must hit their airfields, MIGs, and IL28s."

"What would they do" in response? LBJ asked.

"Nothing," Greene contended. "We can test it by attacking [their] POL storage. Then we should attack [the] industrial complex in North Vietnam, mine [their ports], blockade Cambodia, and stop supplies from coming down. How long would it take? Five years—plus 500,000 Americans. Will [the] U.S. people back us? Yes, they will—they need to know the stakes."

"How would you tell the American people what the stakes are?" Johnson wondered.

"The place where they will stick by you is the national security stake," Greene replied.

Army Chief of Staff Johnson interjected. "We are in a face-down [situation], the general said, and "[t]he solution, unfortunately, is long-term. Once the military problem is solved," he added, "the problem of [a] political solution will be more difficult."

"If we come in with hundreds of thousands of men and billions of dollars, won't this cause [Russia and China] to come in?" the President frowned.

"No," the general answered, "I don't think they will."

"MacArthur didn't think they would come in either," LBJ groused.

"Yes, but this is not comparable to Korea—"

"But China has plenty of divisions to move in, don't they?" the President said.

"Yes, they do."

"Then what would we do?"

A long silence followed. "If so," General Johnson said, "we have another ballgame."

"I have to take into account they will," LBJ stressed.

"I would increase the buildup near North Vietnam," General Johnson went on.

"If they move in thirty-one divisions, what does it take on our part?" LBJ persisted.

"[A]ssuming [the] Thais contributed forces," McNamara said, "it would take 300,000 plus what we needed to combat [the] VC."

The President seemed increasingly agitated. "[R]emember[,] they're going to write stories about this like they did the Bay of Pigs. Stories about me and my advisors. That's why I want you to think very carefully about alternatives and plans." Again, he pressed, "Are you concerned about Chinese forces moving into North Vietnam?"

"There is no evidence of [Chinese] forces," General Johnson answered. "It could be they are investigating areas which they could control later."

"What is your reaction to Ho's statement he is ready to fight for twenty years?" LBJ asked.

"I believe it."

"What are Ho's problems?"

"His biggest problem is doubt about what our next move will be. He's walking a tightrope between the [Soviets] and the Chicoms. Also, he's worrying about the loss of caches of arms in the South."

LBJ switched to the issue of civilian casualties. "Are we killing civilians along with VC?" he asked.

"Certain civilians accompanying the VC are being killed," General Wheeler responded. "It can't be helped."

Johnson grabbed a paper in front of him and started reading. "The VC dead is running at a rate of 25,000 a year. At least 15,000 have been killed by air—half of these are not a part of what we call VC. Since 1961 a total of 89,000 have been killed. South Vietnamese are being killed at a rate of 12,000 a year." He tossed the paper back on the table and sat quietly.

Army Secretary Resor broke the silence. "Of the three courses the one we should follow is the McNamara plan," Resor said. "We can't go back on our commitment. Our allies are watching carefully."

"Do all of you think the Congress and the people will go along with 600,000 people and billions of dollars 10,000 miles away?" LBJ asked.

Resor nodded. The "Gallup poll shows people are basically behind our commitment."

'But if you make a commitment to jump off a building," the President frowned, "and you find out how high it is, you may withdraw the commitment . . ."

No response. "I judge though that the big problem is one of national security, is that right?"

Nods around the table.

"What about our intelligence," Johnson said, changing the subject. "How do they know what we are doing before we do it? What about the B-52 raid—weren't they gone before we got there?"

"They get it from infiltration in [the] South Vietnamese forces," McNamara said.

"Are we getting good intelligence out of North Vietnam?"

"Only reconnaissance and technical soundings," McNamara answered. "None from combat intelligence."

LBJ then motioned to McGeorge Bundy. Before the meeting, he had instructed Bundy to prepare a memo addressing the complaints of Vietnam critics. Why Johnson followed this course is curious; Ball had spoken at length just the previous day. Still, LBJ chose to raise these concerns once more, perhaps to probe—for a final time—his advisers' reaction to the possibility of withdrawal—a politically risky course Johnson hesitated to follow without their support.

LBJ spoke. "Some Congressmen and Senators think we are going to be the most discredited people in the world. What Bundy will tell you is not his opinion or mine—I haven't taken a position yet—but what we hear."

"[This is the] argument we will face," Bundy said, reading from the paper before him:

> For ten years, every step we have taken has been based on a previous failure. All we have done has failed and caused us to take another step which failed. As we get further into the bag, we get deeply bruised. Also, we have made excessive claims we haven't been able to realize.
>
> . . . [A]fter twenty years of warnings about war in Asia, we are now doing what MacArthur and others have warned against. We are about to fight a war we can't fight and win, as the country we are trying to help is quitting.

[There is] [t]he failure on our own to fully realize what guerrilla war is like. We are sending conventional troops to do an unconventional job.

How long—how much? Can we take casualties over five years? Aren't we talking about a military solution when the solution is political? Why can't we interdict better? Why are our bombings so fruitless? Why can't we blockade the coast? Why can't we improve our intelligence? Why can't we find the VC?

If Johnson expected this exercise to provoke re-examination, it did not occur. Everyone sat quiet.

Several moments passed. Then Clark Clifford, who had remained conspicuously silent throughout the meeting, addressed one question to General Wheeler. "If the military plan is carried out," Clifford carefully asked, "what is the ultimate result if it is 'successful'?"

Wheeler thought a minute. The "political objective is to maintain South Vietnam as free and independent," he said. "If we follow the [proposed] course of action, we can carry out this objective. Probably after success, we would withdraw most of our forces; [though some,] international and otherwise, would have to stay on. If we can secure the military situation," Wheeler concluded with less certainty, "it seems likely that we can get some kind of stable government."[9]

An hour later, LBJ convened a second and smaller meeting attended by his closest political advisers, together with two eminent Republicans outside the administration. Johnson clearly wished to lay the groundwork for broad bipartisan support for whatever decision he reached, while also speaking more openly and candidly about his continuing Vietnam troubles in this more intimate setting.[10]

LBJ's problems included, prominently, the issue of public disclosure. Having urged a substantial escalation of U.S. involvement, McNamara wanted Johnson to drive home the reality of this escalation through important political and symbolic gestures such as mobilizing reserves, increasing conscription, and raising defense spending. McNamara knew his proposals meant carrying the United States into war, and he wanted LBJ to convey this fact clearly to the American people.[11]

Few of McNamara's recommendations, however, distressed Johnson more. They meant acknowledging the full scope and costs of the war—something LBJ had steadfastly refused to do in the past. He refused to do so this time as well. "I don't think that calling up the reserves in itself is a change of policy," Johnson told his small group of advisers, though he conceded some "question" "that we are going into a new kind of activity in Vietnam." "[The] basic objective is to preserve the independence and freedom of Vietnam," LBJ insisted. "This is not necessarily tied in with calling up reserves."

Rusk agreed that the "essence of [our] policy is why we are there and what our war aims are." Still, he cautioned Johnson, "Moving from 75,000 to 185,000 men is a change of policy." Nevertheless, Rusk contended there was "much . . . to be said for playing this low-key."

"That . . . needs to be stressed with [the] Congressional leadership," LBJ interrupted, while in the same breath asserting his desire "to explain with candor what we are doing to the American people." "But when we do," he quickly added, "we help the North Vietnamese get their requests fulfilled by China and Russia."

This last comment illustrated Johnson's other motive for downplaying any escalation: his fear that dramatic gestures might trigger counter-escalation, "set[ting] off," as he often put it, "those secret treaties" between Hanoi and Peking—thereby bolstering North Vietnam's military strength and resistance to negotiations.[12]

Whatever their motive, LBJ's equivocations irritated McNamara. "We can stay away from 'change of policy,'" he told the President, "but it is a change in risk and commitment. We need to explain why it is in our interest to do it." Seeking to move Johnson in this direction, McNamara promised that he could "cut . . . down" the military's $12 billion supplemental budget request "by half or more."

The President's new press secretary, Bill Moyers, offered his own advice about disclosure. "I don't think the press thinks we are going to change basic policy, but . . . the requirements to meet that policy."

"That's right and we ought to say it," LBJ broke in, impressed with Moyers' clever distinction.

"I hope we can avoid a debate on whether it is a 'change,'" Ball observed with exasperation. "We always lose on this. We are becoming co-defendants with South Vietnam."

McCloy considered all the talk about a change in policy beside the point. "The country is looking to getting on with the war," McCloy said, and he urged Johnson to do it.

McCloy had forced discussion back to the basic issue, which LBJ addressed once more. "There are three alternatives," he said, again summarizing his options: "1. Sit and lose slowly; 2. Get out; 3. Put in what needs to go in."

Rusk clearly favored the latter—but in the way of more troops to the South, not more bombing of the North. As he explained, "What we do in South Vietnam is not of great concern to China. But a progressive step-up in bombing increases [the] risk of China['s] intrusion."

"But the chiefs say what we are doing in the North is not enough," the President interrupted—"only pin-pricking them, just goosing them."

"But it is contradictory to do this when we can't find anybody in the

South," countered Rusk. He cited another reason, too. "Both China and the Soviets have pressure on them . . . to preserve another 'socialist state,' " Rusk said. "This is a distinction we must bear in mind" if Washington wished to avoid pulling Peking and Moscow into the war.

McCloy wondered whether Washington could ever win the war without destroying Hanoi—whether the North Vietnamese would "let go" as long as they had "sanctuary."

"Their only sanctuary is one-fifth of the country," Rusk noted, citing the civilian population centers around Hanoi and Haiphong.

"What do you do if the war drags on with mounting casualties?" Dean interrupted, "Where do we go? The people say if we are not doing what is necessary to end it, [then] why don't we do what is necessary?"

"We are begging the questions," McNamara insisted. "If we bomb Haiphong, would this end the war? and the answer is NO."

Dean listened, unpersuaded. "If this carries on for some years," the old negotiator grumbled, "we'll get in the same fix we were in [in] Korea and the Yalu."

Rusk disagreed. "We were under no pressures to make it a larger war until the war was practically over," he contended, suggesting the same held true in South Vietnam today. "We've got to 80,000 and we have *not* had reminiscences of Korea."

Now that Washington had reached 80,000 troops, McCloy observed, "What are our objectives? What do we have to negotiate?"

Rusk listed several items: "1. Infiltration from the North must stop. 2. We have no interests in a permanent military base there. 3. 1954–1962 [Geneva] agreements ought to be solved by peaceful means and not—"

"When do the troops get withdrawn?" McCloy interrupted.

"When [there is] proof infiltration [is] stopping," said Rusk.

What about the thornier political issues, McCloy continued, like the "kind of government" Washington would accept and the Vietcong's participation in it?

Bundy fielded the question. His brief answer spoke volumes about America's problem in Vietnam. "If we really were the ones for free elections," Bundy said, "it would be good. [But] it is difficult for Saigon to sign on."

"Would we be willing to take a Tito[ist] government or a VC victory?" McCloy asked.

"That's where our plan begins to unravel," Bundy flushed.

"We're going to announce plenty of bombs," the President broke in, "but we've got to use both hands." "It's like a prizefight," he explained, raising both arms. "Our right is our military power, but our left must be our peace proposals. Every time you move troops forward, you move diplomats forward. I want this done. The generals want more and more—and [to] go farther and farther. But State has to supply me with some, too."

Rusk raised the timing of a presidential announcement, suggesting that Johnson "meet with the leadership on Tuesday [July 27] and make a statement on Wednesday [July 28]."

"We can't delay this from the public," McNamara frowned.

"We ought to decide what our decision is," LBJ said, then "write it, brief Ambassadors, and . . . tell the people." "Is the message a personal talk to the Congress or a normal message?" he wondered aloud. "Possibly a normal message"—one signaling no departure and therefore threatening no domestic disruption.[13]

As the meeting broke up and people started to leave the room, Ball quickly approached Clifford. "Come into the Fish Room with me," the Undersecretary motioned to his old law friend, "I want to talk to you." Clifford's question of the previous afternoon had impressed Ball, who sensed a potential ally in his lonely effort to forestall escalation.

Together, they crossed the hall to the Fish Room. "Look," Ball explained, referring to Clifford's comment the day before, "You . . . said the only sensible thing I have heard said by anybody in that group for a very, very long time. I can tell you that you and I are in total agreement. I have been looking for support for a long time. I think your influence with the President is tremendously important." Ball then bid his case. "I want to put into your hands a series of memoranda which I have sent to the President. Can you handle them? They are highly classified."

"Yes," Clifford answered, "I am a member of the Intelligence Advisory Board and I have a secure safe at my house. Have the memos hand-delivered to me, and I will see that they are properly taken care of." Ball promised to have his personal aide deliver them to Clifford's office that afternoon.[14]

As Clifford started to leave, a White House guard approached and said the President wished to see him. LBJ had noticed Clifford's silence during the day's meetings, and wanted to hear his old friend's reaction to the deliberations.

The guard escorted Clifford to the small anteroom adjoining the Oval Office, where Johnson awaited him. What Clifford told LBJ confirmed Ball's hunch. The generals' assurances of success troubled Clifford, who told the President that he "didn't like [the] military['s] attitude." "The way the JCS acted today reminded me of the way the military dealt with President Truman during the Korean War," he cautioned. "Some of what General Wheeler said today was ridiculous—'the more men we have, the greater the likelihood of smaller losses.' And if they infiltrate more men into the South, it will allow us to 'cream them.' These are disturbing statements. I don't believe they are being straight with us."

"I am bearish about the whole exercise," Clifford continued. "I know what pressure you're under from McNamara and the military. If you handle it carefully, you don't have to commit yourself and the nation. If you overplay the decisions now under consideration, the nation will be committed to win a ground war in Asia."

"I asked myself two questions today as I listened to McNamara and the Chiefs," Clifford finally said, eyeing Johnson directly: "First, can a military victory be won? And second, what do we have if we do win? Based on what we have heard, I do not know the answers to these questions."[15]

With Clifford's doubts ringing in his mind, LBJ called together several advisers the following afternoon. The circle had narrowed to Rusk, McNamara, Ball, Wheeler, Busby, Moyers, and McGeorge Bundy—a sure sign Johnson neared his final decision.

LBJ's comments at this meeting reflected the deep impact of Clifford's thinking. Although Johnson announced no definitive steps, he appeared determined to minimize reaction to whatever action he took. As Ball recalled his comments to State Department subordinates that evening, LBJ appeared "anxious to present the decisions which might be made in the next few days in a low-key manner . . . ."[16]

Ball refused to abandon hope of dissuading the President, however. His last and best chance, Ball thought, lay in alliance with Clifford, whose voice Johnson particularly respected and trusted.

Ball found a sympathetic ally. After reading Ball's papers and jotting notes late into the night of July 22, Clifford called him the following day from his office high above Connecticut Avenue overlooking Lafayette Square and the White House. As Ball remembered, "Clifford told me that he had spent the previous evening until two in the morning carefully studying my memoranda. They were, he said, 'impressive and persuasive.' "

Ball was elated. Although headed for another meeting at the White House, he promised to contact Clifford once he returned to the State Department.

A few hours later, Ball called Clifford back. He said his meeting earlier that afternoon with LBJ had convinced him that Clifford's advice had had a "salutary effect" on the President. Clifford seemed less hopeful. He confided that "another source," Bill Moyers, had told him reversing the President's course required a herculean effort—changing not just Johnson's mind but also Rusk's, McNamara's, and McGeorge Bundy's. Clifford doubted the prospect. As he explained to Ball, "individuals sometimes become so bound up in a certain course it is difficult to know where objectivity stops and personal involvement begins." Clifford nevertheless promised to have "a very hard and long talk" with the President.

Ball, anxious to make that talk convincing, alerted Clifford that he must address LBJ's gravest concern: fear of a right-wing backlash in the event of failure. Ball emphasized the point by repeating to Clifford a comment Johnson had made to him: "George, don't pay any attention to what those little shits on the campuses do. The great beast is the reactionary elements in this country. Those are the people that we have to fear."[17]

Shortly before nightfall, LBJ boarded a helicopter bound for Camp David. There, at the presidential retreat in Maryland's Catoctin Mountains, Johnson planned to spend Saturday and Sunday making his final Vietnam decision.

Before leaving the White House, LBJ invited Clifford and McNamara to join him over the weekend. Each had Johnson's highest confidence. Each viewed Vietnam in fundamentally different terms. Each symbolized LBJ's deeply conflicting emotions toward the most difficult choice of his Presidency.

Clifford and McNamara arrived at Camp David the following afternoon, July 24. They and others spent the evening resting and relaxing with Johnson, who quietly searched his mind in anticipation of tomorrow's momentous verdict.

Before retiring for the night, LBJ organized steps for implementing his approaching decision. He telephoned speechwriter Richard Goodwin to begin drafting a presidential address to the nation. He readied plans to brief congressional leaders early in the week. Johnson prepared, at last, to act.

Sunday, July 25, 1965, dawned sunny and warm at Camp David. After a late morning breakfast, LBJ left his cabin, Aspen Lodge, for a solitary walk around the grounds. At noon, he went to Hickory Lodge for services conducted by the Reverend Bill Baxter of Washington Episcopal Church. Afterwards, he returned to Aspen Lodge for more quiet reflection.

Finally, at five o'clock, the President summoned Clifford and McNamara for an informal but crucial conference. Three others joined this meeting. Adlai Stevenson's successor at the United Nations, Arthur Goldberg, had been brought up to discuss U.N. contacts following a presidential announcement. Horace Busby and Jack Valenti sat in as Johnson's personal aides. Clifford and McNamara, however, held center stage, competing actors in the great drama for LBJ's mind.

The participants gathered at a small dining table in a corner of the room looking out to the forested hills beyond. Johnson, seated at the head of the table, put McNamara to his left, Clifford to his right, directly facing one another. Clifford spoke first. He knew the President confronted a fateful decision. Clifford's instincts, together with Ball's dark predictions, had convinced him that LBJ faced only one acceptable course: to get out, before Vietnam sundered his presidency and the country.

"I believe that we are talking too much, too loudly, too publicly, about Vietnam," Clifford began. "We must not create an impression that we have decided to replace the South Vietnamese and win a ground war in Vietnam. If the decisions about to be made are interpreted as the beginning of a permanent and long-range policy, it will severely limit the flexibility which the President must have."

Clifford sought to persuade Johnson, not to place blame. "What happened in Vietnam is no one person's fault," he said. "The bombing might have worked, but it hasn't. A commitment like the one that we have made in Vietnam can change as conditions change. A failure to engage in an all-out war will not lower our international prestige. This is not the last inning in the struggle against communism. We must pick those spots where the stakes are highest for us and we have the greatest ability to prevail."

Clifford neared his conclusion. "I do not believe that we can win in South Vietnam," he told the President. "I hate this war. If we send in 100,000 more men, the North Vietnamese will match us. If the North Vietnamese run out of men, the Chinese will send in 'volunteers.' Russia and China don't intend for us to win the war. If we 'won,' we would face a long occupation with constant trouble." His stentorian voice hushed for a moment, Clifford slammed both fists on the table. "[I]f we don't win after a big buildup, it will be a huge catastrophe. We could lose more than 50,000 men in Vietnam. It will ruin us. Five years, 50,000 men killed, hundreds of billions of dollars—it is just not for us."

Clifford closed with this advice: "For the time being, Mr. President, let us hold to our present course, without dramatic escalation. You will probably need to send some additional men now for this strategy, but not many. At the end of the year, after the monsoon season, let us probe, let us quietly search with other countries for an honorable way out. Let us moderate our position in order to do so, and lower our sights—lower the sights of the American people—right away. Let the best minds in your Administra-_tion look for a way out, not ways to win this unwinnable war." Otherwise, he darkly predicted, "I can't see anything but catastrophe for my country."

LBJ sat silently for a moment. Then, he grabbed a private letter from Harvard University economist John Kenneth Galbraith off the table. It was headed, tellingly, "How to Take Ninety Percent of the Political Heat out of Vietnam." Johnson paraphrased aloud from Galbraith's letter, as if to convince himself and the others:

Vietnam is not of intrinsic value—if there is no high principle involved. . . . [The] basic issue is not to get thrown out under fire. . . . Political questions are what we make them. . . . Instruct officials to stop saying all humankind is at stake. . . . Stop saying we are going to pacify the country. [Use] patience—pressure—quietly marking areas we can hold. Hold these for years if need be. Make a safe haven. Vietcong cannot attack these areas frontally. . . . Gradually stop bombings north and south. Maximum attention to it . . . is wrong. . . . Keep offer of negotiations open.

After finishing the letter, LBJ asked for McNamara's advice. The Secretary of Defense methodically but forcefully restated his position: without more U.S. troops, South Vietnam would fall to the communists, and this posed an intolerable risk to American security and credibility. Johnson listened quietly, then dismissed the group.[18]

Leaving Aspen Lodge again, LBJ drove alone around Camp David for nearly an hour. He returned at dusk, then set out for another private stroll.

As he walked along the wooded footpaths late that summer evening, Johnson searched his mind and his heart for answers. The events of recent months—both anguished Vietnam decisions and joyous Great Society triumphs—filled his memory. The two seemed cruelly intertwined to him, inseparable yet irreconcilable. The President felt trapped in a terrible vice, with no way to relieve the pressure. At that moment, he later said,

> [I] could see and almost touch [my] youthful dream of improving life for more people and in more ways than any other political leader, including FDR. . . . I was determined to keep the war from shattering that dream, which meant I simply had no choice but to keep my foreign policy in the wings. I knew the Congress as well as I know Lady Bird, and I knew that the day it exploded into a major debate on the war, that day would be the beginning of the end of the Great Society.[19]

Thus Johnson decided. He would not allow a ruinous debate about "who lost Vietnam" to destroy his domestic dreams. The troops would be sent— but quietly, with minimum public disclosure. LBJ would have both guns and butter, and this, to quote William Bundy, would be "his way of trying to get the best of both."[20]

That night, the State Department flashed a secret cable, drafted earlier that evening and awaiting presidential approval, to key American embassies around the world. Quoting the President, it read, in part:

> I have been reviewing [Vietnam] situation during the last few days in the light of up-to-date reports from my trusted associates. While final decisions have not been made here, I can tell you that it now appears certain that it will be necessary to increase United States armed forces in South Vietnam by a number which may equal or exceed the 80,000 already there.[21]

With the real choice behind him, Johnson now focused on how to announce it publicly. He addressed this issue at an NSC meeting the next afternoon, July 26.[22]

During this meeting, LBJ revealed his intention to send additional troops, but without the accompanying steps McNamara recommended. He refused to mobilize the reserves. He refused to seek a declaration of war from Congress. He refused to explain his decision as a major departure from existing policy. "My thinking," the President instead told his advisers, "would be . . . [to] play all our decisions low-key."

Several present, including Clifford, supported this tactical decision. "[W]e are in a paradox," Clifford said. "On one hand, we are ready to meet commitments, but we are really ready to get out." Therefore, "[t]alking at this time publicly will not accomplish anything."

Others, however, such as Lodge, thought candor essential. "How do you send young men there in great numbers without telling why?" he asked.

"We have already explained why we are there," Clifford insisted, echoing his comments at Camp David. "We cannot win the war in South Vietnam. China and Russia don't intend for us to win the war. They will match us in manpower. No matter how many men we send, they will match us. The great danger," he said, "is that additional troops are not a notice to the world that we intend to make it a land war"—one Clifford considered unwinnable. "We should get through the monsoon season and quietly see if we can work out an adjustment. I don't believe we will suffer [a loss of] prestige if we can't sustain."

Ball, impressed by the force of Clifford's argument but sensing the struggle was indeed lost, penciled Clifford a brief, wistful note: "Clark—I'm glad to have such an eloquent and persuasive comrade bleeding on the same barricade. I thought your statement was great."[23]

LBJ finalized his decision at two meetings the following evening. Johnson used the first—another NSC session—to announce his decision to subordinates and enlist their support for it.

LBJ opened by asking McNamara to summarize the military situation. The Secretary vividly described South Vietnam's sinking fortunes—the increase in communist forces; spreading Vietcong control of the countryside; declining ARVN morale and skyrocketing desertions.

McNamara then addressed planned U.S. deployments. The numbers he cited differed noticeably—and tellingly—from his written figures to the President. "An additional 13 battalions and 50,000 men must be announced," McNamara said as Johnson followed carefully. That means "we'll have 125,000 men there," McNamara finished—without mentioning the 50,000 more due to arrive by year's end.

LBJ then took the floor. "We have these choices," he said. "1. We can bring the enemy to his knees by using our Strategic Air Command and other air forces—blowing him out of the water tonight. I don't think our citizens would want us to do it—though some do.

"2. Another group thinks we ought to pack up and go home," but "[I] don't think too many of our people want us to do this" either. Besides, "Ike, Kennedy and I have given [our] commitment.

"3. [We] could stay there as we are . . . continue to lose territory and casualties. You wouldn't want your boy to be out there . . . crying for help and not get it.

"4. [We can] go to Congress and ask for great sums of money; call up the reserves and increase [the] draft; [go] on [a] war footing; declare a state of emergency." Johnson conceded there was "a good deal of feeling that that ought to be done." But he rejected this course on international grounds; the Great Society remained an unmentionable factor in the decision. "If we make [a] land war," he said, "then North Vietnam would go to its friends—China and Russia—and ask them to give help. They would be forced into increasing aid. For that reason," the President asserted, "I don't want to be dramatic and cause tension. I think we can get our people to support us without having to be provocative.

"5.," LBJ finally said, "[we can] give . . . commanders the men they say they need out of forces in this country—get[ting] such money as we need and must have [by] us[ing] [our] transfer authority . . . until January.

"I had concluded that the last course was the right one," Johnson later wrote, "and everyone there knew it. Thus, as the President went around the table asking whether anyone opposed this course, he got the expected answer. Each nodded his approval or said "yes." LBJ had his consensus.[24]

Johnson next marshaled congressional support. When the NSC meeting ended, House and Senate leaders filed into the Cabinet Room. LBJ had summoned a bipartisan delegation: Democratic Senators Mike Mansfield of Montana, Russell Long of Louisiana, and George Smathers of Florida; Republican Senators Everett Dirksen of Illinois, Bourke Hickenlooper of Iowa, and Thomas Kuchel of California; Democratic Representatives Carl Albert of Oklahoma, Hale Boggs of Louisiana, and John McCormack of Massachusetts, Speaker; and Republican Congressmen Leslie Arends of Illinois and Gerald Ford of Michigan.[25]

At first glance, this group seemed typical of larger congressional sentiment. All had publicly endorsed American involvement in Vietnam except Mansfield, who had confined his doubts to private exchanges with Johnson. The small core of Senate critics—first only Frank Church, Ernest Gruening, George McGovern, and Wayne Morse, but now growing to include George Aiken, John Sherman Cooper, William Fulbright, Richard Russell, and John Sparkman—remained conspicuously absent. That fact suggested LBJ's desire for ratification, not debate, of his decision.[26]

Johnson began by describing the same five courses outlined earlier to the NSC. The real choice, LBJ said, lay between the latter two—"to go the full congressional route now" or "to give the congressional leadership the story now and the bill later."

Johnson then called on Ambassador Lodge, who knocked down courses 1, 2, and 3. No one objected. That left only 4 and 5.

Senator Smathers asked if either involved a change in policy. "There is no change in policy," LBJ calmly insisted, explaining that as "aid to the VC increases," so "our need to increase . . . forces goes up."

One guest asked why Congress had not been consulted earlier. Johnson stammered a moment, then answered, "I couldn't call you down until I had all the information."

Senator Long felt he had enough information. He believed the choice narrowed to this: "put in more men or take a whipping." "We'd better go in," Long said.

"I don't think we have any alternatives," Speaker McCormack agreed. "Our military men tell us we need more and we should give it to them. The lesson of Hitler and Mussolini is clear. I can see five years from now a chain of events far more dangerous to our country if we don't." McGeorge Bundy, scrawling notes of the meeting, noted at this point: "The Leadership seems might hawky so far."

One of the most vocal hawks, Representative Ford, said he understood "why we can't do 1, 2, or 3," but asked LBJ for "an explanation of 4 and 5."

"We will ask Congress for money" in either case, Johnson said, telling Ford he could "guess" a larger appropriation or "ask for a reasonable request now and see what happens." LBJ hesitated to mobilize reserves, he added, because if called up now, they "really won't be ready."

On the other hand, Johnson said, he would have things "better worked out" by January 1966—after his domestic agenda had moved through Congress. In the meantime, LBJ planned to "ask for no [war] legislation, call up no reserves, . . . and send troops in as we need them"—perhaps in three installments of 30,000.

"[I'm] not entirely clear," Ford interjected. "Under 4 you would—"

"Would call up reserves now and make out [spending] estimates in [a] new bill," answered the President impatiently.

"How much is the difference" between 4 and 5? Ford pressed.

"In both cases Westmoreland gets what he wants," interrupted House Majority Leader Albert.

"How many men?" Republican Arends inquired.

"We don't know," McNamara answered, evidently uncomfortable. "[W]e will meet requirements," which "right now" meant "50,000 additional" troops.

LBJ moved to block Ford's and Arend's troublesome queries. "I've asked you to come here not as Democrats or Republicans but as Americans. I don't want any of you to talk about what is going on. The press is going to be all over you. Let me appeal to you as Americans to show your patriotism by not talking to the press."

"I agree," Senator Dirksen said, seated directly across from Johnson. He explained his feelings with an anecdote. "I remember World War I when Teddy Roosevelt wanted to raise a brigade and go to Europe to fight. President Woodrow Wilson stopped that with one sentence: 'The business at hand is undramatic.'"

LBJ smiled approvingly. "That's exactly the way I feel about it, Everett," Johnson croaked, "the fewer theatrics the better."

But Dirksen hadn't finished. You must "tell the country we are engaged in very serious business," he admonished the President. "[W]e don't need to withhold information."

"We won't withhold," Johnson answered defensively. "We want to announce as soon as troops arrive. In the morning I will consult Ike and tell him what we hope to do and get his views. I will see the chairman of Foreign Relations, Appropriations, and Armed Forces, then announce [my] decision in press conference."

"Five months is a long time," Dirksen interrupted. "I don't think you can wait. If you need the money, you ought to ask for it."

LBJ anxiously insisted otherwise. "We have the money. . . . When you come back in January," he told Dirksen, "you'll have a bill of several billion dollars."

Johnson glanced around the room. "Is there any other comment?"

"I would not be true to myself if I didn't speak," Senator Mansfield announced. Faces turned in astonishment as Mansfield pulled a paper from his pocket and began reading a sharp warning against LBJ's action. "This position has [a] certain inevitability," the majority leader said. "Whatever pledge we had was to *assist* South Vietnam in its own defense."

Ambassador Lodge, seated just feet away, gazed ahead blankly as Mansfield recounted the political chaos since Diem's assassination. "Since then there has been no government of legitimacy. . . . We owe this [present] government nothing—no pledge of any kind."

He paused. "We are going deeper into war. Even total victory would be vastly costly. [Our] best hope for salvation is a quick stalemate and negotiations. We cannot expect our people to support a war for 3–5 years. [W]e are about [to embark on] an anti-Communist crusade." Remember, he ended, "Escalation begets escalation."

"Well, Mike," Johnson grumbled, fists clenched in front of him, "what would *you* do?"

Mansfield said nothing, but stared into LBJ's face.[27]

* * *

Minutes after 12:30 the next day, July 28, 1965, President Johnson walked into the East Room accompanied by Lady Bird and several White House aides. Beneath the room's large, ornate chandeliers waited some 200 newspaper and television reporters.

LBJ slowly approached the podium. In front of it perched a large television camera with a protruding, beak-like teleprompter. Johnson looked into the camera, squinting under the bright klieg lights above him.

LBJ had purposely chosen this moment to announce his decision to the nation, knowing the midday television audience to be much smaller than in the evening. The circumstances, moreover—a news conference rather than a personal appearance before a joint session of Congress—belied the President's intent to underplay his Vietnam decision.

To that end, LBJ delivered a low-key and undramatic message. Speaking in a subdued, matter-of-fact voice, he announced: "I have asked the Commanding General, General Westmoreland, what more he needs to meet this mounting aggression. He has told me. We will meet his needs."

Although Johnson had authorized a vast increase in American combat forces—from 75,000 to 175,000 by year's end, with the prospect of another 100,000 in 1966—he deliberately obscured the magnitude of this escalation. LBJ simply said, "I have today ordered to Viet-Nam . . . certain . . . forces which will raise our fighting strength from 75,000 to 125,000 men. . . . Additional forces will be needed later," he remarked, "and they will be sent as requested."

Johnson also concealed the new and much greater U.S. combat involvement. When a reporter later asked him, "Does the fact that you are sending additional forces to Viet-Nam imply any change in the existing policy?" the President answered: "It does not imply any change in policy whatever."

LBJ had equivocated about Vietnam to the American public—not for sinister but for real and palpable reasons. Johnson alluded to those reasons in language of personal pain. "There is something else, too," he told the nation after discussing Vietnam:

When I was young, poverty was so common that we didn't know it had a name. An education was something that you had to fight for, and water was really life itself. I have now been in public life 35 years, . . . and in each of those 35 years I have seen good men, and wise leaders, struggle to bring the blessings of this land to all of our people.

And now I am the President. It is now my opportunity to help every child get an education, to help every Negro and every American citizen have an equal opportunity, to have every family get a decent home, and to help bring healing to the sick and dignity to the old.

> As I have said before, that is what I have lived for, that is what I have
> wanted all my life since I was a little boy, and I do not want to see all those
> hopes and all those dreams of so many people for so many years now drowned
> in the wasteful ravages of cruel wars.

LBJ's words conveyed deep emotion and conviction. They expressed the
heartfelt desires of a domestic reformer struggling against the onslaught of
a far-away and threatening war. They evoked, then, a poignant and tragic
irony which came to haunt Lyndon Johnson and the country he loved
long after this day had ended.[28]

President Johnson's July 1965 decisions climaxed a series of steps, reaching
back to the summer of 1964, which locked the United States on a path
toward massive military intervention in Vietnam. That path eventually
destroyed LBJ's presidency and polarized American society.

How had LBJ reached this critical juncture in America's Vietnam odyssey?
The road to 1964–1965 had been charted years before, at the dawn of the
Cold War, when U.S. leaders fixed a course of global containment that,
over the decades, assumed the status of political writ—unassailable, unchangeable, unquestionable.

The compass of global containment, in turn, had eventually pointed to
South Vietnam. It proved a fateful destination for the United States. Riven
by chronic political factionalism, profound social antagonisms, and a nationalist movement tragically usurped by the communists, South Vietnam
remained a quicksand of instability—treacherous ground on which to build
a growing American effort.

That fact escaped few U.S. leaders, who felt Washington's strategic interests mortgaged to a succession of corrupt, inept, and repressive Saigon regimes well aware, as one early 1965 Buddhist leaflet put it, that "[w]e can
insult the Americans as much as we please and they must still do our bid-
ding and grant us aid." Dean Rusk, in a moment of private despair, dubbed
this "the tyranny of the weak." William Bundy called it the "black cloud
hanging over everything" America did. But Lyndon Johnson, characteris-
tically, put it best: "I didn't like the smell of it. I didn't like anything about
it," he later said, "but I think the situation in South Vietnam bothered me
most. They never seemed able to get themselves together down there. Always
fighting with one another. Bad. Bad."[29]

And as South Vietnam's deterioration quickened in 1964–1965, the pressures to escalate intensified sharply. All through this critical period, President Johnson navigated reluctantly and furtively, continually pushed forward by events in Vietnam and growing bureaucratic momentum, while
struggling to limit and conceal the war's domestic repercussions.

It was a difficult and ambiguous course befitting LBJ's difficult and ambiguous problem. Complex, intractable, and full of danger, the war aroused Johnson's bitterness, resentment, and anger. He confronted Vietnam as an unsure and troubled leader grappling with an unwanted and ominous burden. For a domestic reformer who, in the words of one acquaintance, "would chop off the rest of the world if he could," the war represented a loathsome threat to his dreams.[30]

LBJ perceived his dilemma acutely. On the one hand, he recognized the dangers a larger war posed to the Great Society. On the other hand, he judged a lost war ruinous to his political standing and legislative effectiveness. Johnson later described his predicament vividly: "If I left the woman I really loved—the Great Society—in order to get involved with that bitch of a war on the other side of the world, then I would lose everything at home. All my programs. All my hopes to feed the hungry and shelter the homeless. All my dreams to provide education and medical care to the browns and the blacks and the lame and the poor. But if I left that war and let the Communists take over South Vietnam, . . . there would follow in this country an endless national debate—a mean and destructive debate— that would shatter my Presidency, kill my administration, and damage our democracy." LBJ felt trapped, in Walter Lippmann's apt phrase, "between the devil of unlimited war and the deep blue sea of defeat."[31]

As a result, Johnson moved cautiously and warily, constantly shifting and hesitating in the face of momentous decisions like the beginning of bombing in February and the deployment of major combat forces in July. At each turning point, LBJ acted with marked reluctance, saying nothing more than absolutely necessary, and oftentimes considerably less. That is why Johnson appeared, to many of those around him, "always reacting, always responding" to successive Vietnam crises.[32]

But the ultimate crisis, in LBJ's mind, involved the "loss" of South Vietnam, which he feared would trigger a right-wing reaction devastating to his presidency and the Great Society. This prospect terrified Johnson. He resolved to prevent it by preserving South Vietnam at increasing military and political risk. LBJ dreaded these increasing risks, but he dreaded defeat even more. Johnson summed up his feelings with a bittersweet parable. "That reminds me of two Indians," he said at one point during the July deliberations. "The first invited the second home to dinner. 'What are you having?' asked the second. 'Crow,' said the first. 'Crow—that's not fit to eat, is it?' complained the second. 'Better'n owl,' replied the first."[33]

Haunted by his plight, LBJ tried to hide it from the country. To him, Vietnam seemed an ugly and insoluble problem best kept from public scrutiny. "If you have a mother-in-law with only one eye and she has it in the center of her forehead," he grimly joked during this period, "you don't keep her in the living room."[34]

Instead, Johnson kept Vietnam in the back closet. To some, like Mc-George Bundy, LBJ's action seemed "an extreme case of guarding one's hand." To others, like journalist Hugh Sidey, it seemed indicative of Johnson's compulsive secretiveness—his lifelong habit of thinking "the shortest distance between two points was through a tunnel." But the most fateful legacy of LBJ's furtiveness, as William Bundy observed, was that it "sowed dragon's teeth in terms of [the] credibility gap charge."[35]

Johnson sowed those dragon's teeth when he realized Vietnam's escalating costs themselves jeopardized the Great Society. This stinging realization compelled LBJ to mask the scope and price of a war he shuddered to lose. But Johnson's behavior, in time, alienated the American public profoundly. The resulting decline in LBJ's credibility, together with Vietnam's spiraling costs, ultimately undid both his Presidency and the Great Society. In his struggle to avert the disastrous "loss" of Vietnam, Johnson slid into a major war which proved equally disastrous. Here lay the most tragic irony of LBJ's Vietnam ordeal.

Conclusion

THE LEGACY OF VIETNAM, like the war itself, remains a difficult and painful subject for Americans. As passions subside and time bestows greater perspective, Americans still struggle to understand Vietnam's meaning and lessons for the country. They still wonder how the United States found itself ensnared in an ambiguous, costly, and divisive war, and how it can avoid repeating such an ordeal in the future.

The experience of Lyndon Johnson and his advisers during the decisive years 1964–1965 offers much insight into those questions. For their decisions, which fundamentally transformed U.S. participation in the war, both reflected and defined much of the larger history of America's Vietnam involvement.

Their decisions may also, one hopes, yield kernels of wisdom for the future; the past, after all, can teach us lessons. But history's lessons, as Vietnam showed, are themselves dependent on each generation's knowledge and understanding of the past. So it proved for 1960s policymakers, whose ignorance and misperception of Southeast Asian history, culture, and politics pulled America progressively deeper into the war. LBJ, Rusk, McNamara, Bundy, Taylor—most of their generation, in fact—mistakenly viewed Vietnam through the simplistic ideological prism of the Cold War. They perceived a deeply complex and ambiguous regional struggle as a grave challenge to world order and stability, fomented by communist China acting through its local surrogate, North Vietnam.

This perception, given their mixture of memories—the West's capitulation to Hitler at Munich, Stalin's postwar truculence, Mao's belligerent rhetoric—appears altogether understandable in retrospect. But it also proved deeply flawed and oblivious to abiding historical realities. Constrained by their

215

memories and ideology, American policymakers neglected the subtle but enduring force of nationalism in Southeast Asia. Powerful and decisive currents—the deep and historic tension between Vietnam and China; regional friction among the Indochinese states of Vietnam, Laos, and Cambodia; and, above all, Hanoi's fanatical will to unification—went unnoticed or unweighed because they failed to fit Washington's worldview. Although it is true, as Secretary of State Rusk once said, that "one cannot escape one's experience," Rusk and his fellow policymakers seriously erred by falling uncritical prisoners of their experience.[1]

Another shared experience plagued 1960s policymakers like a ghost: the ominous specter of McCarthyism. This frightful political memory haunted LBJ and his Democratic colleagues like a barely suppressed demon in the national psyche. Barely ten years removed from the traumatic "loss" of China and its devastating domestic repercussions, Johnson and his advisers remembered its consequences vividly and shuddered at a similar fate in Vietnam. They talked about this only privately, but then with genuine and palpable fear. Defense Secretary McNamara, in a guarded moment, confided to a newsman in the spring of 1965 that U.S. disengagement from South Vietnam threatened "a disastrous political fight that could . . . freeze American political debate and even affect political freedom."[2]

Such fears resonated deeply in policymakers' minds. Nothing, it seemed, could be worse than the "loss" of Vietnam—not even an intensifying stalemate secured at increasing military and political risk. For a President determined to fulfill liberalism's postwar agenda, Truman's ordeal in China seemed a powerfully forbidding lesson. It hung over LBJ in Vietnam like a dark shadow he could not shake, an agony he would not repeat.

McCarthyism's long shadow into the mid-1960s underscores a persistent and troubling phenomenon of postwar American politics: the peculiar vulnerability besetting liberal Presidents thrust into the maelstrom of world politics. In America's postwar political climate—dominated by the culture of anti-communism—Democratic leaders from Truman to Kennedy to Johnson remained acutely sensitive to the domestic repercussions of foreign policy failure. This fear of right-wing reaction sharply inhibited liberals like LBJ, narrowing what they considered their range of politically acceptable options, while diminishing their willingness to disengage from untenable foreign commitments. Thus, when Johnson did confront the bitter choice between defeat in Vietnam and fighting a major, inconclusive war, he reluctantly chose the second because he could not tolerate the domestic consequences of the first. Committed to fulfilling the Great Society, fearful of resurgent McCarthyism, and afraid that disengagement meant sacrificing the former to the latter, LBJ perceived least political danger in holding on.

But if Johnson resigned never to "lose" South Vietnam, he also resigned never to sacrifice his cherished Great Society in the process. LBJ's determination, however understandable, nonetheless led him deliberately and seriously to obscure the nature and cost of America's deepening involvement in the war during 1964–1965. This decision bought Johnson the short-term political maneuverability he wanted, but at a costly long-term political price. As LBJ's credibility on the war subsequently eroded, public confidence in his leadership slowly but irretrievably evaporated. And this, more than any other factor, is what finally drove Johnson from the White House.

It also tarnished the presidency and damaged popular faith in American government for more than a decade. Trapped between deeply conflicting pressures, LBJ never shared his dilemma with the public. Johnson would not, or felt he dare not, trust his problems with the American people. LBJ's decision, however human, tragically undermined the reciprocal faith between President and public indispensable to effective governance in a democracy. Just as tragically, it fostered a pattern of presidential behavior which led his successor, Richard Nixon, to eventual ruin amid even greater popular political alienation.

Time slowly healed most of these wounds to the American political process, while reconfirming the fundamental importance of presidential credibility in a democracy. Johnson's Vietnam travail underscored the necessity of public trust and support to presidential success. Without them, as LBJ painfully discovered, Presidents are doomed to disaster.

Johnson, in retrospect, might have handled his domestic dilemma more forthrightly. An equally serious dilemma, however, remained always beyond his—or Washington's—power to mend: the root problem of political disarray in South Vietnam. The perennial absence of stable and responsive government in Saigon troubled Washington policymakers profoundly; they understood, only too well, its pivotal importance to the war effort and to the social and economic reforms essential to the country's survival. Over and over again, American officials stressed the necessity of political cooperation to their embattled South Vietnamese allies. But to no avail. As one top American in Saigon later lamented, "[Y]ou could tell them all, 'you've got to get together [and stop] this haggling and fighting among yourselves,' but how do you make them do it?" he said. "How do you make them do it?"[3]

Washington, alas, could not. As Ambassador Taylor conceded early in the war, "[You] cannot order good government. You can't get it by fiat." This stubborn but telling truth eventually came to haunt Taylor and others. South Vietnam never marshaled the political will necessary to create an effective and enduring government; it never produced leaders addressing the aspirations and thus attracting the allegiance of the South Vietnamese people. Increasing levels of U.S. troops and firepower, moreover, never offset this fundamental debility. America, as a consequence, built its massive military effort on a foundation of political quicksand.[4]

The causes of this elemental flaw lay deeply imbedded in the social and political history of the region. Neither before nor after 1954 was South Vietnam ever really a nation in spirit. Divided by profound ethnic and religious cleavages dating back centuries and perpetuated under French colonial rule, the people of South Vietnam never developed a common political identity. Instead, political factionalism and rivalry always held sway. The result: a chronic and fatal political disorder.

Saigon's fundamental weakness bore anguished witness to the limits of U.S. power. South Vietnam's shortcomings taught a proud and mighty nation that it could not save a people in spite of themselves—that American power, in the last analysis, offered no viable substitute for indigenous political resolve. Without this basic ingredient, as Saigon's turbulent history demonstrated, Washington's most dedicated and strenuous efforts will prove extremely vulnerable, if not futile.

This is not a happy or popular lesson. But it is a wise and prudent one, attuned to the imperfect realities of an imperfect world. One of America's sagest diplomats, George Kennan, understood and articulated this lesson well when he observed: "When it comes to helping people to resist Communist pressures, . . . no assistance . . . can be effective unless the people themselves have a very high degree of determination and a willingness to help themselves. The moment they begin to place the bulk of the burden on us," Kennan warned, "the whole situation is lost." This, tragically, is precisely what befell America in South Vietnam during 1964–1965. Hereafter, as perhaps always before—*external* U.S. economic, military, and political support provided the vital elements of stability and strength in South Vietnam. Without that *external* support, as events following America's long-delayed withdrawal in 1973 showed, South Vietnam's government quickly failed.[5]

Washington's effort to forge political order through military power spawned another tragedy as well. It ignited unexpected pressures which quickly overwhelmed U.S. policymakers, and pulled them ever deeper into the war. LBJ and his advisers began bombing North Vietnam in early 1965 in a desperate attempt to spur political resolve in South Vietnam. But their effort boomeranged wildly. Rather than stabilizing the situation, it instead unleashed forces that soon put Johnson at the mercy of circumstances, a hostage to the war's accelerating momentum. LBJ, as a result, began steering with an ever looser hand. By the summer of 1965, President Johnson found himself not the controller of events but largely controlled by them. He had lost the political leader's "continual struggle," in the words of Henry

Kissinger, "to rescue an element of choice from the pressure of circumstance."[6]

LBJ's experience speaks powerfully across the years. With each Vietnam decision, Johnson's vulnerability to military pressure and bureaucratic momentum intensified sharply. Each step generated demands for another, even bigger step—which LBJ found increasingly difficult to resist. His predicament confirmed George Ball's admonition that war is a fiercely unpredictable force, often generating its own inexorable momentum.

Johnson sensed this danger almost intuitively. He quickly grasped the dilemma and difficulties confronting him in Vietnam. But LBJ lacked the inner strength—the security and self-confidence—to overrule the counsel of his inherited advisers.

Most of those advisers, on the other hand—especially McGeorge Bundy and Robert McNamara—failed to anticipate such perils. Imbued with an overweening faith in their ability to "manage" crises and "control" escalation, Bundy and McNamara, along with Maxwell Taylor, first pushed military action against the North as a lever to force political improvement in the South. But bombing did not rectify Saigon's political problems; it only exacerbated them, while igniting turbulent military pressures that rapidly overwhelmed these advisers' confident calculations.

These advisers' preoccupation with technique, with the application of power, characterized much of America's approach to the Vietnam War. Bundy and McNamara epitomized a postwar generation confident in the exercise and efficacy of U.S. power. Despite the dark and troubled history of European intervention in Indochina, these men stubbornly refused to equate America's situation in the mid-1960s to France's earlier ordeal. To them, the United States possessed limitless ability, wisdom, and virtue; it would therefore prevail where other western powers had failed.

This arrogance born of power led policymakers to ignore manifest dangers, to persist in the face of ever darkening circumstances. Like figures in Greek tragedy, pride compelled these supremely confident men further into disaster. They succumbed to the affliction common to great powers throughout the ages—the dangerous "self-esteem engendered by power," as the political philosopher Hans Morgenthau once wrote, "which equates power and virtue, [and] in the process loses all sense of moral and political proportion."[7]

Tradition, as well as personality, nurtured such thinking. For in many ways, America's military intervention in Vietnam represented the logical fulfillment of a policy and outlook axiomatically accepted by U.S. policymakers for nearly two decades—the doctrine of global containment. Fashioned at the outset of the Cold War, global containment extended American interests and obligations across vast new areas of the world in defense against perceived monolithic communist expansion. It remained the lodestar of America foreign policy, moreover, even as the constellation of international forces shifted dramatically amid diffused authority and power among communist states and nationalist upheaval in the post-colonial world.

Vietnam exposed the limitations and contradictions of this static doctrine in a world of flux. It also revealed the dangers and flaws of an undiscriminating, universalist policy which perceptive critics of global containment, such as the eminent journalist Walter Lippmann, had anticipated from the beginning. As Lippmann warned about global containment in 1947:

> Satellite states and puppet governments are not good material out of which to construct unassailable barriers [for American defense]. A diplomatic war conducted as this policy demands, that is to say conducted indirectly, means that we must stake our own security and the peace of the world upon satellites, puppets, clients, agents about whom we can know very little. Frequently they will act for their own reasons, and on their own judgments, presenting us with accomplished facts that we did not intend, and with crises for which we are unready. The "unassailable barriers" will present us with an unending series of insoluble dilemmas. We shall have either to disown our puppets, which would be tantamount to appeasement and defeat and loss of face, or must support them at an incalculable cost. . . .[8]

Here lay the heart of America's Vietnam troubles. Driven by unquestioning allegiance to an ossified and extravagant doctrine, Washington officials plunged deeply into a struggle which itself dramatized the changed realities and complexities of the postwar world. Their action teaches both the importance of re-examining premises as circumstances change and the costly consequences of failing to recognize and adapt to them.

Vietnam represented a failure not just of American foreign policy but also of American statesmanship. For once drawn into the war, LBJ and his advisers quickly sensed Vietnam's immense difficulties and dangers—Saigon's congenital political problems, the war's spiraling military costs, the remote likelihood of victory—and plunged in deeper nonetheless. In their determination to preserve America's international credibilty and protect their domestic political standing, they continued down an ever costlier path.

That path proved a distressing, multifaceted paradox. Fearing injury to the perception of American power, diminished faith in U.S. resolve, and a conservative political firestorm, policymakers rigidly pursued a course which ultimately injured the substance of American power by consuming exorbitant lives and resources, shook allied confidence in U.S. strategic judgment, and shattered liberalism's political unity and vigor by polarizing and paralyzing American society.

Herein lies Vietnam's most painful but pressing lesson. Statesmanship requires judgment, sensibility, and, above all, wisdom in foreign affairs—

the wisdom to calculate national interests prudently and to balance commitments with effective power. It requires that most difficult task of political leaders: "to distinguish between what is desireable and what is possible, . . . between what is desireable and what is essential."[9]

This is important in peace; it is indispensable in war. As the great tutor of statesmen, Carl von Clausewitz, wrote, "Since war is not an act of senseless passion but is controlled by its political object, the value of this object must determine the sacrifices to be made for it in *magnitude* and also in *duration*. Once the expenditure of effort exceeds the value of the political object," Clausewitz admonished, "the object must be renounced. . . ." His maxim, in hindsight, seems painfully relevant to a war which, as even America's military commander in Vietnam, General William Westmoreland, concluded, "the vital security of the United States was not and possibly could not be clearly demonstrated and understood. . . ."[10]

LBJ and his advisers failed to heed this fundamental principle of statesmanship. They failed to weigh American costs in Vietnam against Vietnam's relative importance to American national interests and its effect on overall American power. Compelled by events in Vietnam and, especially, coercive political pressures at home, they deepened an unsound, peripheral commitment and pursued manifestly unpromising and immensely costly objectives. Their failure of statesmanship, then, proved a failure of judgment and, above all, of proportion.

Bibliographical Note

Manuscripts

Serious study of LBJ and the Vietnam War properly centers on the vast holdings of the Lyndon Baines Johnson Library in Austin, Texas. Teeming with over half a million Vietnam documents expertly managed by a superb archival staff, the LBJ Library offers unparalleled riches to enquiring and diligent scholars.

Fortunately, nearly all of the Library's Vietnam holdings through July 1965 have been opened for research. Students of Johnson's escalation decisions, therefore, have much material to explore.

A sensible starting point is the National Security File (NSF), a massive assemblage of cables, memoranda, and notes. Within the NSF, the Vietnam Country File—containing each outgoing State Department and incoming Saigon embassy cable during this period—promises heavy but rewarding labor to investigators. McGeorge Bundy's Memos to the President and personal Files, though less extensive, are equally important for tracing both Bundy's thinking and the White House decision-making process.

Four other collections within the NSF merit special attention as well: the NSC Meetings File, for notes of sessions where LBJ frequently disclosed decisions to the larger government; the International Meetings and Travel File, particularly useful on McGeorge Bundy's February 1965 mission to South Vietnam and Saigon political figures; Speech File materials on LBJ's April 1965 Johns Hopkins address; and the NSC History on Deployment of Major U.S. Forces to Vietnam, July 1965—a compilation of many, though not all, key documents on this issue culled from the wider NSF.

Much important material bearing on Johnson's escalation decisions also lies outside the NSF. Among the most significant are handwritten notes of high-level White House Vietnam deliberations, including "Tuesday Lunches," in the Papers of McGeorge Bundy; minutes of Cabinet Room and Camp David sessions in the Meeting Notes File; and confidential polling data, together with Senate Majority Leader Mike Mansfield's private letters to LBJ, in White House Central File, Confidential File.

Beyond the Johnson Library, archival collections relevant to Vietnam decision-making, 1964–1965, are scattered and spotty. Senate Foreign Relations Committee Chairman J. William Fulbright's papers, housed at the University of Arkansas' Mullins Library, contain surprisingly few exchanges between Fulbright and LBJ on Vietnam. The same, regrettably, is true of Senate Armed Services Committee Chairman Richard B. Russell's papers, at the University of Georgia's Russell Memorial Library.

Manuscripts in the Library of Congress are more rewarding, especially those of journalist Joseph Alsop. Alsop, a veteran observer of many Washington policy wars, maintained close contact with several high Johnson administration officials throughout this period, particularly the Bundy brothers; his correspondence with both offer fascinating clues to contemporary political concerns. The papers of another journalist, *St. Louis Post-Dispatch* diplomatic correspondent Richard Dudman, include penetrating interviews and notes gathered during Dudman's travel through South Vietnam in early 1965.

Perhaps the richest journalistic collection, however, may be Arthur Krock's papers at Princeton University's Seeley G. Mudd Manuscript Library. Krock, the *New York Times'* long-serving Washington bureau chief and capital insider, gathered a valuable cache of background notes by himself and *New York Times* colleagues Turner Catledge, Max Frankel, and Charles Mohr. U.N. Ambassador Adlai Stevenson's papers, also at Princeton's Mudd Manuscript Library, give clues to Stevenson's general thinking, but contain few revealing details.

Oral Histories and Interviews

Reminiscences of participants and observers give added texture to the written record. The Johnson Library's prodigious Oral History Collection stands out here. Among its multitude of Vietnam-related interviews, those with George Ball, William Bundy, Clark Clifford, Alexis Johnson, Lyndon Johnson, Dean Rusk, Maxwell Taylor, Cyrus Vance, and Earle Wheeler are particularly enlightening. Two important oral histories—McGeorge Bundy's and Robert McNamara's—remain closed at this time, however.

Published interviews augment the LBJ Library's voluminous holdings. Two important works in this vein are Michael Charlton & Anthony Moncrieff, *Many Reasons Why: The American Involvement in Vietnam* (New

York: Hill and Wang, 1978), based on BBC radio interviews broadcast in 1977; and Merle Miller, *Lyndon: An Oral Biography* (New York: G. P. Putnam's Sons, 1980), covering a much broader range of topics than its title suggests.

Personal interviews with George Ball, Horace Busby, Clark Clifford, Alexis Johnson, Dean Rusk, and Jack Valenti have supplemented existing collections. Each generously shared his time and thoughts on Washington's escalation decisions.

Government Publications

The most celebrated—and controversial—body of government documents on Vietnam, the *Pentagon Papers,* present special challenges to historians. Originally a secret Defense Department study commissioned by Robert McNamara in June 1967 and leaked to the press by Daniel Ellsberg in 1971, the *Pentagon Papers* are available in three published versions: the twelve-volume "Hébert edition," *United States–Vietnam Relations, 1945– 1967* (Washington: U.S. Government Printing Office, 1971); the five-volume "Gravel edition," *The Pentagon Papers: The Defense Department History of United States Decisionmaking on Vietnam* (Boston: Beacon, 1971); and the one-volume *"New York Times* edition," *The Pentagon Papers as Published by the New York Times* (New York: Bantam, 1971).

Each version has its limitations. The "Hébert edition," although generally the most comprehensive, omits much material for 1964–1965 included in the other two, and is marred by numerous deletions of official documents. The *"New York Times* edition" provides better coverage for 1964– 1965, but lacks valuable background material for 1945–1963 found elsewhere. The "Gravel edition" balances the others' deficiencies—approaching Hébert's range without its deletions, while successfully matching, and occasionally exceeding, the *New York Times'* on the 1964–1965 period. Overall, Gravel is the best.

Whichever version, the *Pentagon Papers* must be used cautiously. Compilers of the study, though privy to most Defense Department and some CIA records, lacked access to top-level State Department and all White House files. The study, consequently, emphasizes military factors at the expense of all-important political considerations, while inadvertently inflating the role of working-level officials in the decision-making process.

Equally problematic, the Gravel, Hébert, and *New York Times* editions also lack the original study's sections on United States–North Vietnamese diplomatic contacts (although Gravel does include material on MAYFLOWER, the initial, May 1965 bombing pause). An essential corrective to this omission, published several years later, is George C. Herring, ed.,

The Secret Diplomacy of the Vietnam War: The Negotiating Volumes of the Pentagon Papers (Austin: Univ. of Texas Press, 1983), clearly organized and knowledgeably annotated.

Public Papers of the Presidents of the United States: Lyndon B. Johnson (Washington: U.S. Government Printing Office, 1964–1965), collects LBJ's major speeches, statements, and press conferences in easy-to-use, chronologically arranged volumes.

Because the State Department's ongoing publication of selected documents from its files, *Foreign Relations of the United States: Diplomatic Papers,* has yet to reach the years 1964–1965, scholars must rely on contemporary releases for official department thinking. Two notable works in this regard are *Viet-Nam: The Struggle for Freedom,* published at the time of the Tonkin Gulf Resolution, which stresses the limited, advisory nature of America's military commitment to South Vietnam; and *Aggression from the North: The Record of North Viet-Nam's Campaign to Conquer South Viet-Nam,* a white paper released in conjunction with the start of ROLL-ING THUNDER, which journalist I. F. Stone carefully rebutted in his "Reply to the White Paper," *I. F. Stone's Weekly,* v. 13, n. 9, March 8, 1965, pp. 1–4. Press statements and speeches by high State officials are gathered in the department's regular *Bulletin.*

Senate and House debates on Vietnam may be followed in the *Congressional Record.* Although frequently rambling and wordy, these debates dramatically capture the Eighty-ninth Congress' growing preoccupation with, and division over, the war. *Congressional Quarterly Almanac: 89th Congress, 1st Session . . . 1965* (Washington: Congressional Quarterly Service, 1966), conveniently summarizes the historic Great Society legislation dominating Johnson's concern during this period.

A useful compendium of official statements from various sources—the White House, the State Department, Congress, the United Nations, even Hanoi and the NLF—is Marcus G. Raskin and Bernard B. Fall, eds., *The Viet-Nam Reader: Articles and Documents on American Foreign Policy and the Viet-Nam Crisis* (New York: Random House, 1965).

Newspapers and Periodicals

For comprehensive coverage of daily events in Vietnam and Washington, researchers should consult the *New York Times,* staffed by experienced, sophisticated reporters with good access to the Saigon embassy and the White House. Its editorial page, moreover, nicely reflects the shift in liberal opinion from support to increasing criticism of LBJ's Vietnam policy in 1965.

Two other newspapers worth examining are the *New York Herald-Tribune,* particularly dispatches from its well-informed Saigon correspondent, Beverly Deepe; and the *Washington Post,* a sensitive barometer of administration thinking and the mood on Capitol Hill. The *Post* also carries the influential columns of Joseph Alsop and Walter Lippmann, prominent Washington voices with contrasting views on Vietnam.

Three major national newsweeklies of the mid-1960s—*Time, Newsweek,* and *U.S. News & World Report*—devote considerable attention to the growing war, with varying emphasis and effectiveness. *Time* highlights strategic factors and domestic politics; *U.S. News,* the war's economic impact; *Newsweek,* Saigon's chronic instability. Although *Time* editorializes in its news columns more frequently and heavily than the other two, all three magazines project a mildly hawkish tone characteristic of much of the press during this period.

Other periodicals occasionally running important articles and interviews concerning Vietnam include *Foreign Affairs, Life,* the *New Republic,* and, especially, the *New York Times Magazine.*

Memoirs and Autobiographies

Several principals have published accounts of their role in the Vietnam escalation decisions. President Johnson stresses devotion to containment and the domino theory, together with defense of prior commitments and national prestige, in his memoir, *The Vantage Point: Perspectives of the Presidency, 1963–1969* (New York: Holt, Rinehart and Winston, 1971). Throughout his discussion of Vietnam, LBJ defensively emphasizes the continuity of his diplomacy with previous administrations, as well as the ostensibly unanimous agreement of his advisers during the critical 1964–1965 debates.

An important voice in those debates, Secretary of State Dean Rusk, shares straightforward and unusually reflective reminiscences with his son, Richard Rusk, in *As I Saw It,* ed. Daniel S. Papp (New York: W. W. Norton, 1990). While defending America's basic commitment to South Vietnam, Rusk nonetheless reveals his doubts about escalation in early 1965 and bombing's effectiveness throughout the war.

An early and enthusiastic bombing advocate, Maxwell Taylor, vividly recounts the tumultuous factionalism he witnessed as U.S. Ambassador to South Vietnam; his support for air strikes against North Vietnam; and his initial wariness toward U.S. combat troop deployments in *Swords and Ploughshares* (New York: W. W. Norton, 1972).

George Ball, another figure close to Johnson who raised early and persistent warnings about escalation, first addressed the issue of Vietnam in his *Discipline of Power: Essentials of a Modern World Structure* (Boston: Atlantic/Little, Brown, 1968), and, more fully and revealingly, in his later, literate *Past Has Another Pattern: Memoirs* (New York: W. W. Norton, 1982).

LBJ's Vice President, Hubert Humphrey, attended many White House conferences on Vietnam during this period, contrary to popular perception. The reservations Humphrey voiced about ROLLING THUNDER and its domestic repercussions are discussed in his *Education of a Public Man: My Life and Politics,* ed. Norman Sherman (Garden City: Doubleday, 1976), a frank and often bitter portrait of Johnson's frostiness toward inner-circle dissent.

Perhaps the most thorough and detached memoir by a senior official—Assistant Secretary of State for Far Eastern Affairs William P. Bundy's study of Vietnam decision-making, 1961–1965—presently remains unpublished, although it is available in manuscript form at the LBJ Library. Written close to the events in question, Bundy's work effectively recreates the contemporary atmosphere in which officials acted.

Accounts by White House assistants provide additional insight into contemporary thinking. *A Very Human President* (New York: W. W. Norton, 1975), by LBJ's appointments secretary, Jack Valenti, whose position bestowed access to many key Vietnam deliberations, emphasizes the weight of previous commitments and Saigon's rapid deterioration as factors in the President's 1964–1965 decisions. Johnson's press secretary at the time, George Reedy, stresses the peril of unquestioned assumptions in his more analytical and critical *Twilight of the Presidency* (New York: New American Library, 1970).

Less central figures in the Vietnam drama have also treated this issue in detail. Chester Cooper, an Asian affairs specialist on McGeorge Bundy's NSC staff, analyzes events knowledgeably and dispassionately in his *Lost Crusade: America in Vietnam* (New York: Dodd, Mead, 1970), concluding that the February 1965 bombing decision made further military steps inevitable. The State Department's Policy Planning chief in 1964–1965, W. W. Rostow, offers a different view. In *The Diffusion of Power: An Essay in Recent History* (New York: Macmillan, 1972), Rostow argues that Washington consciously embraced major escalation in order to preserve America's strategic interest in a non-communist South Vietnam.

U.S. military commanders have also discussed the 1964–1965 decisions. The most comprehensive and important military memoir, COMUSMACV William Westmoreland's *A Soldier Reports* (New York: Doubleday, 1976), highlights the political chaos weakening Saigon and compelling Washington forward, while faulting Pentagon civilians for imposing what Westmoreland judged debilitating restrictions on the war effort. Westmoreland's Navy counterpart, CINCPAC U.S. Grant Sharp, delivers a similar, though cruder, indictment in his *Strategy for Defeat: Vietnam in Retrospect* (San Rafael:

Presidio, 1978). A more sophisticated and subtle treatment is Army General Bruce Palmer, Jr.'s *The 25-Year War: America's Military Role in Vietnam* (Lexington: Univ. Press of Kentucky, 1984), which carefully explores the tensions arising from LBJ's vaguely defined war objectives.

American diplomats have perceptively described political developments across Southeast Asia during this period. Among the most useful are U. Alexis Johnson with Jef Olivarius McAlister, *Right Hand of Power* (Englewood Cliffs, N.J.: Prentice-Hall, 1984), a penetrating, vivid account of South Vietnam's turmoil by Washington's experienced Deputy Ambassador to Saigon from 1964–1965; and William H. Sullivan, *Obbligato, 1939–1979: Notes on a Foreign Service Career* (New York: W. W. Norton, 1984), an important source of information on the secret war between CIA-backed Hmong tribesmen and Vietcong infiltrators along the Ho Chi Minh Trail in Laos by America's long-serving Ambassador to Vientiane.

A few South Vietnamese officials have also given their view of events. Saigon's Air Force commander and later premier, Nguyen Cao Ky, heavily downplays his and other Young Turks' political interference during 1964–1965 in his *Twenty Years and Twenty Days* (New York: Stein and Day, 1976), while offering revealing insights into South Vietnam's military establishment. A more balanced and candid portrait of Saigon's troubles may be found in Bui Diem with David Chanoff, *In the Jaws of History* (Boston: Houghton Mifflin, 1987), by the chief of staff and U.S. embassy liaison for South Vietnam's last civilian Prime Minister, the hapless Phan Huy Quat.

Accounts in English by Vietcong veterans are regrettably scarce. One notable exception, however, is *A Vietcong Memoir* (San Diego: Harcourt Brace Jovanovich, 1985), by Truong Nhu Tang with David Chanoff and Doan Van Toai. A high NLF official who later defected to the West, Tang recounts the popular antipathy bred by ARVN corruption and incompetence, which bolstered VC fortunes and invited ready manipulation by covert communist agents such as Pham Ngoc Thao.

Public Opinion

Surveys of popular sentiment toward the escalating war are abundant, yet ambiguous. Rarely unanimous, U.S. public opinion proved particularly fractured on Vietnam. The fullest collection of relevant opinion data, *The Gallup Poll: Public Opinion, 1935–1971* (New York: Random House, 1972), amply documents these complexities, as does Louis Harris' confidential White House surveys, which often subsequently appeared in the *Washington Post*.

Rolland H. Bushner, ed., *American Dilemma in Viet-Nam: A Report on the Views of Leading Citizens in Thirty-three Cities* (New York: Council on Foreign Relations, 1965), reveals similar divisions among urban elites across the country.

Scholarly analyses of popular attitudes toward Vietnam in 1964–1965 include Philip E. Converse and Howard Schuman, " 'Silent Majorities' and the Vietnam War," *Scientific American,* v. 222, n. 6, June 1970, pp. 17–25, which argues the theme of early, "inattentive tolerance"; John E. Muller, "Trends in Popular Support for the Wars in Korea and Vietnam," *American Political Science Review,* v. 65, n. 2, June 1971, pp. 358–375, a comparative treatment stressing the "rally-round-the-flag" phenomenon, more fully developed in his *War, Presidents and Public Opinion* (New York: John Wiley & Sons, 1973); William L. Lunch and Peter W. Sperlich, "American Public Opinion and the War in Vietnam," *Western Political Quarterly,* v. 32, n. 1, March 1979, pp. 21–44, authoritatively synthesizing the Converse-Schuman and Mueller theses; and Mark Lorell, Charles Kelley, Jr., and Deborah Hensler, *Casualties, Public Opinion, and Presidential Policy During the Vietnam War* (Santa Monica: Rand Corporation, 1985).

Two recent studies focusing on the anti-war movement—largely inchoate in 1965—are Melvin Small, *Johnson, Nixon, and the Doves* (New Brunswick, N.J.: Rutgers Univ. Press, 1988); and Charles DeBenedetti and Charles Chatfield, *An American Ordeal: The Antiwar Movement of the Vietnam Era* (Syracuse: Syracuse Univ. Press, 1990), which should be compared with Sidney Verba and Richard A. Brody, "Participation, Policy Preferences, and the War in Vietnam," *Public Opinion Quarterly,* v. 34, n. 3, Fall 1970, pp. 325–332, highlighting the hawkishness of most activists during this period.

Contemporary Books on the Vietnam Escalation

Written in an increasingly heated political atmosphere, studies of Vietnam in the mid-1960s exhibited a strong polemicism indicative of growing domestic debate. This applied to both early defenses of administration policy and later indictments of it.

Most works published in 1965–1966 supported Washington's commitment to South Vietnam. One such book is Marguerite Higgins' *Our Vietnam Nightmare* (New York: Harper & Row, 1965), by the *New York Herald-Tribune's* vocally conservative diplomatic correspondent, who faulted Johnson for hesitating on military imperatives to save an imperiled regime. More temperate accounts criticizing methods while defending basic objectives included *New York Times* Saigon reporter David Halberstam's *Making of a Quagmire* (New York: Random House, 1965); White House speechwriter Richard N. Goodwin's *Triumph or Tragedy: Reflections on Vietnam* (New York: Random House, 1966); *New Yorker* East Asian correspondent Robert Shaplen's *Lost Revolution: The U.S. in Vietnam, 1946–1966* (New York:

Harper & Row, 1966); and the knowledgeable French-born Indochina scholar Bernard Fall's *Viet-Nam Witness: 1953–66* (New York: Frederick A. Praeger, 1966).

Critics of U.S. intervention—relatively lonely voices in 1965—mushroomed in 1966–1967 as American involvement and casualties intensified. An unusually perceptive harbinger of things to come, Hans J. Morgenthau's *Vietnam and the United States* (Washington: Public Affairs Press, 1965), emphasized the limited nature of U.S. interests in Southeast Asia and the limited effectiveness of U.S. military power in the region.

Later critiques, usually with a sharper message, included Senate Foreign Relations Committee Chairman J. William Fulbright's *Arrogance of Power* (New York: Random House, 1966), which scorned postwar America's transformation of major responsibilities into a universal mission beyond the reach of available power; French journalist Jean Lacouture's *Vietnam: Between Two Truces,* trans. Konrad Kellen and Joel Carmichael (New York: Random House, 1966), which underlined Saigon's muddled political divisions; historian Arthur M. Schlesinger, Jr.'s *Bitter Heritage: Vietnam and American Democracy, 1941–1966* (Boston: Houghton Mifflin, 1966), which faulted the "inadvertence" of Indochina decision-making from Eisenhower through Johnson; and scholarly commentator Theodore Draper's *Abuse of Power* (New York: Viking, 1967), severely critical of LBJ's political legerdemain during the months of escalation.

Secondary Accounts

Vietnam, quite understandably, has kindled an immensely rich, varied, and contentious literature. It continues to grip historians' attention much as it did the nation's consciousness in the 1960s. That fact, together with the increasing perspective of time, has yielded a massive—and maturing—body of scholarship.

Rather than attempt an exhaustive review of this huge literature, the following guide discusses those works particularly useful in preparing this study. Readers will find additional items in the footnotes, the bibliographies of cited works, and two indispensable reference aids: Richard Dean Burns and Milton Leitenberg, eds., *The Wars in Vietnam, Cambodia, and Laos, 1945–1982: A Bibliographic Guide* (Santa Barbara: ABC-Clio, 1983), and Richard Dean Burns, ed., *Guide to American Foreign Relations Since 1700* (Santa Barbara: ABC-Clio, 1983).

Surprisingly few books have focused on America's contact with Southeast Asia over the centuries. Two journalistic studies specifically devoted to this purpose are Marvin Kalb and Elie Abel, *Roots of Involvement: The U.S. in Asia* (New York: W. W. Norton, 1971), and Stanley Karnow's *Vietnam:*

A History (New York: Viking, 1983), a much fuller and more authoritative treatment.

General appraisals of American involvement in Vietnam have often proved argumentative but stimulating. Early, critical accounts include George McTurnan Kahin and John W. Lewis, *The United States in Vietnam* (New York: Dial, 1967), emphasizing political misjudgments; Gabriel Kolko, *Roots of American Foreign Policy: An Analysis of Power and Purpose* (Boston: Beacon, 1969), a radical analysis stressing imperialist motivations, somewhat softened in Kolko's later *Anatomy of a War: Vietnam, the United States, and the Modern Historical Experience* (New York: Random House, Pantheon, 1985); Richard J. Barnet, *Roots of War: The Men and Institutions Behind U.S. Foreign Policy* (New York: Atheneum, 1972), faulting the arrogance of Washington's national security elite; and Frances Fitz-Gerald, *Fire in the Lake: The Vietnamese and the Americans in Vietnam* (Boston: Atlantic/Little, Brown, 1972), underscoring cultural misperceptions.

Such critiques inevitably invited reaction, especially in the conservative climate of the 1980s. Guenter Lewy's *America in Vietnam* (New York: Oxford Univ. Press, 1978), opened the revisionist campaign with provocative vigor, defending the conduct of U.S. military operations, while blaming America's failure on domestic sources. Harry G. Summers, Jr., *On Strategy: A Critical Analysis of the Vietnam War* (Novato: Presidio, 1982), and Norman Podhoretz, *Why We Were in Vietnam* (New York: Simon and Schuster, 1983), elaborated similar themes, criticizing political leaders—particularly President Johnson—for denying the military an achievable victory by failing to mobilize the nation behind the war effort.

Other works have sought a middle ground, emphasizing explanation over accusation. They include Leslie H. Gelb with Richard K. Betts, *The Irony of Vietnam: The System Worked* (Washington: Brookings Institution, 1979), highlighting political pressures against failure; George C. Herring, *America's Longest War: The United States in Vietnam, 1950–1975* (New York: John Wiley & Sons, 1979), a short, balanced survey underscoring the legacy of containment; and George McT. Kahin, *Intervention: How America Became Involved in Vietnam* (New York: Alfred A. Knopf), an impressively detailed study sharper in its judgments of U.S. policies.

The subject of Washington decision-making, 1964–1965, has sparked considerable interest and disagreement. Most books on Vietnam address this important topic at least briefly; interpretations, therefore, are many and varied. Two early accounts defending the administration's position are Henry Brandon, *Anatomy of Error: The Inside Story of the Asian War on the Potomac, 1954–1969* (Boston: Gambit, 1969), and Henry F. Graff, *The Tuesday Cabinet: Deliberation and Decision on Peace and War under*

Lyndon B. Johnson (Englewood Cliffs, N.J.: Prentice-Hall, 1970). Early studies more critical of LBJ's diplomatic inexperience and reliance on hawkish advisers are Edward Weintal and Charles Bartlett, *Facing the Brink: An Intimate Study of Crisis Diplomacy* (New York: Charles Scribner's Sons, 1967), and Townsend Hoopes, *Limits of Intervention: An Inside Account of How the Johnson Policy of Escalation in Vietnam Was Reversed* (New York: David McKay, 1969).

Much attention has centered on the bureaucratic antecedents and pressures influencing Vietnam policy in 1964–1965. A pioneering analysis stressing the post-McCarthy dearth of State Department Asian expertise and the dangers of group conformity is James C. Thomson, Jr., "How Could Vietnam Happen?: An Autopsy," *Atlantic*, v. 221, no. 4, April 1968, pp. 47–53. Similar themes emerge in David Halberstam's sprawling and compelling *The Best and the Brightest* (New York: Random House, 1972); and Irving L. Janis' briefer *Victims of Groupthink: A Psychological Study of Foreign-Policy Decisions and Fiascoes* (Boston: Houghton Mifflin, 1972).

Perhaps the most subtle but significant influence on Vietnam decision-making during this period—domestic politics—has received far too little attention. Fortunately, those few studies addressing this underexplored topic are unusually perceptive and penetrating; they include Daniel Ellsberg, *Papers on the War* (New York: Simon & Schuster, 1972); Leslie H. Gelb, "The Essential Domino: American Politics and Vietnam," *Foreign Affairs*, v. 50, n. 3, April 1972, pp. 459–475; and Larry Berman, *Planning a Tragedy: The Americanization of the War in Vietnam* (New York: W. W. Norton, 1982). Ellsberg and Gelb, veterans of the Vietnam-era Pentagon, stress the traumatic lessons of China; Berman, the conflicting pressures of the Great Society. Understanding the interaction of both holds the key to even greater insight.

Biographies of Vietnam decision-makers add a necessary human touch to this often abstract story. Predictably and appropriately, Lyndon Johnson has attracted the most attention. Two early and astute portraits emphasizing LBJ's domestic prowess and diplomatic limitations are Rowland Evans and Robert Novak, *Lyndon B. Johnson: The Exercise of Power* (New York: New American Library, 1966), and Philip Geyelin, *Lyndon B. Johnson and the World* (New York: Frederick A. Praeger, 1966). Hugh Sidey, *A Very Personal Presidency: Lyndon Johnson in the White House* (New York: Atheneum, 1968), and Tom Wicker, *JFK and LBJ: The Influence of Personality upon Politics* (New York: William Morrow, 1968), are more sympathetic to the President's predicament.

Critics of LBJ have invariably focused on his political cunning and personal insecurities. Three books highlighting these qualities to varying degrees are Alfred Steinberg, *Sam Johnson's Boy: A Close-up of the President from Texas* (New York: Macmillan, 1968), roundly faulting LBJ's simplicity and swagger; Eric F. Goldman, *The Tragedy of Lyndon Johnson* (New York: Alfred A. Knopf, 1969), a more sensitive critique lamenting LBJ's slowness to rapidly changing circumstances; and, most important, Doris Kearns, *Lyndon Johnson and the American Dream* (New York: Harper & Row, 1976), a penetrating study of a quintessentially American politician's struggle with the larger world, based on candid conversations with LBJ.

More recent assessments include George Reedy, *Lyndon B. Johnson: A Memoir* (New York: Andrews and McMeel, 1982), depicting a skeptical but stoic war leader; Vaughn Davis Bornet, *The Presidency of Lyndon B. Johnson* (Lawrence: Univ. Press of Kansas, 1983), a moderately conservative appraisal defending LBJ's Vietnam commitment while faulting his limited-war strategy; and Paul K. Conkin, *Big Daddy from the Pedernales: Lyndon Baines Johnson* (Boston: Twayne, 1986), a breezy portrait nicely capturing LBJ's complexities and contradictions.

Unlike those of Johnson, there are relatively few biographies of his influential Vietnam advisers. A central and enigmatic figure, Defense Secretary Robert McNamara, has been assessed in David Halberstam, "The Programming of Robert McNamara," *Harper's*, v. 242, n. 1449, Feb. 1971, pp. 37–71, highly critical of his technocratic approach to political issues; Henry L. Trewhitt, *McNamara* (New York: Harper & Row, 1971), a more sympathetic profile drawing similar conclusions; and, more recently, Paul Hendrickson, "A Man Divided Against Himself," *Washington Post Magazine*, June 12, 1988, pp. 20–31; 50–53, an unforgiving portrait of McNamara's inner turmoil over Vietnam.

Another major architect of the 1964–1965 escalation decisions, national security adviser McGeorge Bundy, has received little attention as well. Brief, unflattering evaluations appear in David Halberstam, "The Very Expensive Education of McGeorge Bundy," *Harper's*, v. 239, n. 1430, July 1969, pp. 21–41, and Milton Viorst's sketch in *Hustlers and Heroes: An American Political Panorama* (New York: Simon & Schuster, 1971).

Kennedy's and Johnson's Secretary of State, Dean Rusk, has been treated in more detail. Revealing studies of this taciturn man include Joseph Kraft, "The Enigma of Dean Rusk," *Harper's*, July 1965, pp. 100–103, stressing his conventional outlook; Warren I. Cohen, *Dean Rusk* (Totowa: Cooper Square, 1980), emphasizing his personal loyalty and private misgivings; and Thomas J. Schoenbaum's semi-official biography, *Waging Peace and War: Dean Rusk in the Truman, Kennedy, and Johnson Years* (New York: Simon and Schuster, 1988), a sensitive, balanced treatment of a remote figure.

LBJ's Washington included many other interesting and important people—Cabinet officers, White House aides, "kitchen" advisers. Useful sketches may be found Charles Roberts, *LBJ's Inner Circle* (New York: Delacorte,

1965), focusing on Johnson's immediate staff; Joseph Kraft, *Profiles in Power: A Washington Insight* (New York: New American Library, 1966), particularly good on the "defense intellectuals"; and, more generally, David Halberstam's *The Best and the Brightest,* cited earlier. One of LBJ's closest confidants, Abe Fortas, is thoroughly dissected in Bruce Allen Murphy, *Fortas: The Rise and Ruin of a Supreme Court Justice* (New York: William Morrow, 1988).

Few studies exist on military figures. A contemporary biography, Ernest B. Furgurson, *Westmoreland: The Inevitable General* (Boston: Little, Brown, 1968), is good on his early military career, but quite brief on Vietnam. Westmoreland's diplomatic counterpart and fellow West Pointer, Maxwell Taylor, receives a sympathetic hearing from his son, John M. Taylor, in *General Maxwell Taylor: The Sword and the Pen* (New York: Doubleday, 1989). There is no full-length portrait of JCS Chairman Earle Wheeler, although Mark Perry, *Four Stars* (Boston: Houghton Mifflin, 1989), traces Wheeler's and the Joint Chiefs' views in detail. Douglas Kinnard, *The War Managers* (Hanover, N.H.: Univ. Press of New England, 1977), surveys the experiences of several U.S. field commanders.

Congressional leaders, who played a much smaller role early in the war than later, have been the subject of several biographies. Senate Foreign Relations Committee Chairman William Fulbright's gradual estrangement from LBJ on Vietnam during 1964–1965 is plotted in Haynes Johnson and Bernard M. Gwertzman, *Fulbright: The Dissenter* (Garden City: Doubleday, 1968), a sympathetic study based on interviews with the senator; and William C. Berman, *William Fulbright and the Vietnam War: The Dissent of a Political Realist* (Kent, Ohio: Kent State Univ. Press, 1988), which makes greater use of Fulbright's papers. Senate Minority Leader Everett Dirksen's close friendship and staunch support for Johnson's Vietnam policy is traced in Neil MacNeil, *Dirksen: Portrait of a Public Man* (New York: World Publishing, 1970). Majority Leader Mike Mansfield and his prescient warnings to LBJ await serious study. A longtime colleague of Fulbright, Dirksen, and Mansfield—Vice President Humphrey—is fully and perceptively treated in Carl Solberg, *Hubert Humphrey: A Biography* (New York: W. W. Norton, 1984).

A broader and more detailed survey of congressional reaction to Johnson's escalation decisions may be found in William Conrad Gibbons, *The U.S. Government and the Vietnam War: Executive and Legislative Roles and Relationships, Part III, January-July 1965* (Washington: U.S. Government Printing Office, 1988).

To understand the 1964–1965 escalation decisions, one must understand political conditions in South Vietnam. Several writers have analyzed this complex subject quite adeptly. Joseph Buttinger's *Vietnam: A Political His-*

tory (New York: Frederick A. Praeger, 1968)—an abridgment of his two earlier works, *The Smaller Dragon: A Political History of Vietnam* (1958), and *Vietnam: A Dragon Embattled* (1967)—cogently and persuasively explores the centrifugal forces paralyzing Saigon and drawing Washington in deeper. A more impassioned study, Frances FitzGerald's *Fire in the Lake,* cited earlier, includes many penetrating observations on the local political effect of U.S. military intervention. Two books by Robert Shaplen—*The Lost Revolution,* mentioned before, and *A Turning Wheel: Three Decades of the Asian Revolution as Witnessed by a Correspondent for the New Yorker* (New York: Random House, 1979), contain shrewd reflections on South Vietnam's political divisions and their consequences for American policy.

The nature and aims of Vietnamese communists—northern and southern—have been extensively studied by western scholars. An early and thorough treatment of the latter, Douglas Pike's *Viet Cong: The Organization and Techniques of the National Liberation Front of South Vietnam* (Cambridge: MIT Press, 1966), stresses its political connections to Hanoi, a conclusion echoed with greater attention to conditions in South Vietnam in Carlyle A. Thayer, "Southern Vietnamese Revolutionary Organizations and the Vietnam Workers' Party: Continuity and Change, 1954–1974," in Joseph J. Zasloff and MacAlister Brown, eds., *Communism in Indochina* (Lexington, Mass.: D. C. Heath, 1975), 27–55.

Hanoi's relationship with the Vietcong and its skillful exploitation of the Sino-Soviet split has been treated in several books. Douglas Pike, *History of Vietnamese Communism, 1925–1976* (Stanford: Hoover Institution Press, 1978), and William J. Duiker, *Communist Road to Power in Vietnam* (Boulder: Westview, 1981), focus on Vietminh organization and political-military strategy against the South. Donald S. Zagoria, *Vietnam Triangle: Moscow, Peking, Hanoi* (New York: Western Publishing, 1967), and W. R. Smyser, *Independent Vietnamese: Vietnamese Communism Between Russia and China, 1956–1969* (Athens: Ohio Univ. Center for International Studies, 1980), place Hanoi's efforts in the wider context of communist-bloc politics, describing North Vietnam's shrewd manipulation of Sino-Soviet friction to win military assistance with minimal dependence on its rival allies.

U.S.–North Vietnamese diplomatic contacts in late 1964 and early 1965 have drawn continuing attention over the years—especially the much-publicized Stevenson–U Thant exchanges. A contemporary analysis, Mario Rossi, "U Thant and Vietnam: The Untold Story," *New York Review of Books,* Nov. 17, 1966, pp. 8–13, contains much speculation redressed in Walter Johnson, "The U Thant–Stevenson Peace Initiatives in Vietnam, 1964–1965," *Diplomatic History,* v. 1, n. 3, Summer 1977, pp. 285–295, which nonetheless overstates Stevenson's—and therefore Washington's—desire for early, substantive talks.

General surveys of U.S.–North Vietnamese contacts offer a more convincing picture of American reluctance due to weak South Vietnamese morale and a military balance favoring the communists. An early, generally accurate journalistic account stressing these themes is David Kraslow and Stuart H. Loory, *The Secret Search for Peace in Vietnam* (New York: Random House, 1968). Later studies emphasizing North Vietnamese obstinacy for similar reasons include Allan E. Goodman, *The Lost Peace: America's Search for a Negotiated Settlement of the Vietnam War* (Stanford: Hoover Institution Press, 1978), drawing on interviews with U.S. diplomats; and Wallace J. Thies, *When Governments Collide: Coercion and Diplomacy in the Vietnam Conflict, 1964–1968* (Berkeley: Univ. of California Press, 1980).

Few works have explored the strategic thinking behind American involvement in Southeast Asia. Two which have in searching and critical ways are Bernard Brodie, *War and Politics* (New York: Macmillan, 1973), faulting Washington's misunderstanding of the fundamentally political nature of the war; and John Lewis Gaddis, *Strategies of Containment: A Critical Appraisal of Postwar American National Security Policy* (New York: Oxford Univ. Press, 1982), highlighting contradictions in the Kennedy/Johnson doctrine of "flexible response"—a limited-threat, limited-means strategy which came to assume massive and costly proportions.

LBJ's troubles with the media over Vietnam have received increasing attention in recent years. Thorough, balanced appraisals of this tense and tempestuous relationship may be found in Kathleen J. Turner, *Lyndon Johnson's Dual War: Vietnam and the Press* (Chicago: Univ. of Chicago Press, 1985), which accents LBJ's sensitivity to criticism and lack of candor; and Daniel C. Hallin, *The "Uncensored War": The Media and Vietnam* (New York: Oxford Univ. Press, 1986), focusing on newspapers' and television's reflection of prevailing public sentiment.

Finally, and most important, reflections on Vietnam's meaning and lessons offer guideposts for the future. Early and penetrating observations on the war are gathered in *The Vietnam Hearings* (New York: Random House, Vintage, 1966), particularly the conflicting judgments of Dean Rusk and George Kennan; and Richard M. Pfeffer, ed., *No More Vietnams?: The War and the Future of American Foreign Policy* (New York: Harper & Row, Harper Colophon, 1968), a lively and challenging exchange among government officials, journalists, and scholars.

Debate over Vietnam's legacy continued into the 1970s, as U.S. involvement ran its course. Discerning studies from this period include Ernest R. May, *"Lessons" of the Past: The Use and Misuse of History in American Foreign Policy* (New York: Oxford Univ. Press, 1973), underscoring policymakers' uncritical reliance on the Munich analogy; Anthony Lake, ed., *The Vietnam Legacy: The War, American Society, and the Future of American*

Foreign Policy (New York: New York Univ. Press, Council on Foreign Relations, 1976), valuable for musings of several key participants; and W. Scott Thompson and Donaldson D. Frizzell, eds., *The Lessons of Vietnam* (New York: Crane, Russak, 1977), more narrowly focused on military issues, but also comprising a broad range of viewpoints.

Reflections on the Vietnam War accelerated and deepened in the 1980s with the growth of perspective and the decline of polemics. Four collections capturing this maturing outlook are Peter Braestrup, ed., *Vietnam as History: Ten Years After the Paris Peace Accords* (Washington, D.C.: Univ. Press of America, 1984); Harrison E. Salisbury, ed., *Vietnam Reconsidered: Lessons from a War* (New York: Harper & Row, 1984); Richard E. Neustadt and Ernest R. May, *Thinking in Time: The Uses of History for Decision-makers* (New York: Free Press, 1986); and John Schlight, ed., *The Second Indochina War* (Washington: U.S. Army Center of Military History, 1986).

Notes

Preface

1. Lyndon Baines Johnson, *The Vantage Point: Perspectives of the Presidency, 1963–1969* (New York: Holt, Rinehart and Winston, 1971; rep. ed., New York: Popular Library, 1971), ix–x.

2. Adlai Stevenson, quoted in Philip Geyelin, *Lyndon B. Johnson and the World* (New York: Frederick A. Praeger, 1966), 232.

3. Carl von Clausewitz, *On War,* ed. and trans. by Michael Howard and Peter Paret (Princeton: Princeton Univ. Press, 1976), 165.

4. Richard Hofstadter, "History and the Social Sciences," in Fritz Stern, ed., *The Varieties of History: From Voltaire to the Present* (Cleveland: World Publishing, 1956; rep. ed., New York: Random House, Vintage, 1973), 364–365.

Introduction

1. Harold D. Lasswell, quoted by Richard J. Barnet, in Richard M. Pfeffer, ed., *No More Vietnams?: The War and the Future of American Foreign Policy* (New York: Harper & Row, Harper Colophon, 1968), 67.

1. To the Crossroads in Vietnam

1. The dimensions of Johnson's triumph proved staggering. LBJ garnered the largest popular vote margin in U.S. electoral history—61 percent of a record 70 million votes. He carried every part of the country except Goldwater's home state of Arizona and the conservative Deep South—Alabama, Georgia, Louisiana, Mississippi, and South Carolina. For specific results, see Theodore H. White, *The Making of the President—1964* (New York: Atheneum, 1965; rep. ed., New York: New American Library, Signet, 1966), 480–481.

2. See Presidential Message to Congress, March 12, 1947, reprinted in the *Department of State Bulletin* (hereafter cited as *DSB*), v. 16, n. 403, March 23, 1947, pp. 534–537.

3. See Report to the National Security Council by the Executive Secretary on

United States Objectives and Programs for National Security, April 14, 1950, re-printed in *Naval War College Review,* v. 27, n. 6, May/June 1975, pp. 51–108.

4. President's News Conference, April 7, 1954, *Public Papers of the Presidents of the United States* (hereafter cited as *Public Papers*): *Dwight D. Eisenhower, 1954* (Washington: U.S. Government Printing Office, 1960), 383.

5. See Agreement on the Cessation of Hostilities in Vietnam, July 20, 1954; and Final Declaration of the Geneva Conference, July 21, 1954, in *Further Documents Relating to the Discussion of Indochina at the Geneva Conference* (London: Great Britain Parliamentary Sessional Papers), v. 31 (1953/54), pp. 27–38 and 9–11, re-spectively. Britain served with Russia as co-chairmen of the Geneva Conference. For Washington's position, see Closing Remarks of the Geneva Conference, July 21, 1954, ibid., pp. 5–9.

6. See U.S. Senate, Eighty-third Congress, Second Session, *Southeast Asia Col-lective Defense Treaty* (Washington: U.S. Government Printing Office, 1954).

7. Dwight D. Eisenhower, *Mandate for Change, 1953–1956* (Garden City: Double-day, 1963), 372.

8. The insurgents became known as Vietcong—a pejorative contraction of Viet-namese communists; its political arm, established under Hanoi's ultimate direction in December 1960, assumed the title of National Front for the Liberation of South Vietnam (NLF).

9. Debate still surrounds the number of Vietminh which remained in southern Vietnam after Geneva. Bernard Fall estimated 5000 to 6000; Douglas Pike, another Vietnamese scholar, calculated 15,000. See Bernard Fall, "How the French Got Out of Vietnam," *New York Times Magazine,* May 2, 1965, pp. 115–116; and Douglas Pike, *History of Vietnamese Communism, 1925–1976* (Stanford: Hoover Institution Press, 1978), 122.

10. See excerpts of Taylor/Rostow Report, reprinted in Senator Gravel Edition, *The Pentagon Papers: The Defense Department History of United States Decision-making on Vietnam* (hereafter cited as *Pentagon Papers*) (Boston: Beacon, 1971), v. 2, pp. 87–98, 652–654.

11. Transcript, Dean Rusk Oral History Interview (hereafter cited as OHI), Sept. 26, 1969, by Paige E. Mulhollan, tape 1, p. 2, Lyndon B. Johnson Library (hereafter cited as LBJL).

12. Quoted in *U.S. News & World Report* (hereafter cited as *USN&WR*), March 15, 1965, p. 29.

13. Quoted in Doris Kearns, *Lyndon Johnson and the American Dream* (New York: Harper & Row, 1976), 252.

14. Johnson before the House of Representatives, May 7, 1947, in *Congressional Record* (hereafter cited as *CR*), v. 93, pt. 4, pp. 4695–4696.

15. LBJ quote is in Kearns, *Lyndon Johnson and the American Dream,* 143.

16. Johnson to Kennedy, May 23, 1961, "Southeast Asia," Aides File, McGeorge Bundy (hereafter cited as ADF, MB), Box 18/19, National Security File (hereafter cited as NSF), LBJL.

17. Quoted in Kearns, *Lyndon Johnson and the American Dream,* 174.

18. Johnson to Max Frankel, July 8, 1965, Notebook 3, Box 1, Arthur Krock Papers, Seely G. Mudd Manuscript Library, Princeton University (hereafter cited as SGMML, PU).

19. Quoted in Henry F. Graff, *The Tuesday Cabinet: Deliberation and Decision*

on Peace and War under Lyndon B. Johnson (Englewood Cliffs, N.J.: Prentice-Hall, 1970), 42–43.

20. Johnson quotes are in David Halberstam, *The Best and the Brightest* (New York: Random House, 1972), 41; and Kearns, *Lyndon Johnson and the American Dream*, 177. See also transcript, Lyndon B. Johnson OHI, Aug. 12, 1969, by William J. Jorden, p. 10, LBJL.

21. Quoted in *Time,* June 25, 1965, p. 29.

22. McGeorge Bundy's father, Harvey, had worked for Stimson both as Assistant Secretary of State in the Hoover administration and as special assistant in the War Department under Franklin D. Roosevelt. Stimson had recognized the young Bundy's promise and commissioned him to prepare his autobiography for publication. See Henry L. Stimson and McGeorge Bundy, *On Active Service in Peace and War* (New York: Harper & Brothers, 1948).

23. Harriet Bundy Belin, quoted in Milton Viorst, *Hustlers and Heroes: An American Political Panorama* (New York: Simon & Schuster, 1971), 273.

24. Quoted in *Time,* June 25, 1965, p. 28.

25. Quote is in Graff, *Tuesday Cabinet,* 56.

26. See Taylor briefing for Washington, Nov. 27, 1964, *Pentagon Papers,* v. 3, p. 668.

27. Embassy telegram (hereafter cited as Embtel) 2052 (Saigon), Taylor to Rusk, Jan. 6, 1965, "Deployment of Major U.S. Forces to Vietnam, July 1965" (hereafter cited as "Deployment"), Vol. 1, Tabs 1–10, National Security Council History (hereafter cited as NSCH), Box 40, NSF, LBJL.

28. Quotes are in CIA, Office of Central Reference, Biographic Register, "Nguyen Khanh," Jan. 1965, "Trip, McGeorge Bundy—Saigon, Vol. 4, 2/4/65," International Meetings and Travel File (hereafter cited as IMATF), Box 28/29, NSF, LBJL; U. Alexis Johnson with Jef Olivarius McAllister, *Right Hand of Power* (Englewood Cliffs, N.J.: Prentice-Hall, 1984), 414; Maxwell D. Taylor, *Swords and Ploughshares* (New York: W. W. Norton, 1972), 329; and Bui Diem with David Chanoff, *In the Jaws of History* (Boston: Houghton Mifflin, 1987), 109.

29. See Joint Resolution on Southeast Asia, Aug. 7, 1964, reprinted in *DSB,* v. 51, n. 1313, Aug. 24, 1964, p. 268.

30. Remarks in New York City before the American Bar Association, Aug. 12, 1964, *Public Papers: Lyndon B. Johnson, 1963–64* (Washington: U.S. Government Printing Office, 1965), Book II, pp. 952–955.

31. Remarks at a Barbecue in Stonewall, Texas, Aug. 29, 1964, ibid., 1019–1024.

32. Remarks in Oklahoma at the Dedication of the Eufala Dam, Sept. 25, 1964, ibid., 1122–1128.

33. Remarks in Manchester to Members of the New Hampshire Weekly Newspaper Editors Association, Sept. 28, 1964, ibid., 1160–1169.

34. Remarks in Memorial Hall, Univ. of Akron, Oct. 21, 1964, ibid., 1387–1393.

35. Transcript, Michael V. Forrestal OHI, Nov. 3, 1969, by Paige E. Mulhollan, p. 21, LBJL.

36. Khanh quotes are in Jean Lacouture, *Vietnam: Between Two Truces,* trans. Konrad Kellen and Joel Carmichael (New York: Random House, Vintage, 1966), 135.

37. Quotes are in Robert Shaplen, *Lost Revolution: The U.S. in Vietnam, 1946–1966,* rev. ed. (New York: Harper & Row, Harper Colophon, 1966), 291; and Embtel

1292 (Saigon), Taylor to Johnson, Oct. 28, 1964, "President/Taylor NODIS CLORES & Code Word Messages to and from Taylor" (hereafter cited as "President/Taylor NODIS"), Country File, Vietnam (hereafter cited as CNF, VN), Box 195, NSF, LBJL.

38. See Taylor to State Department, Nov. 3, 1964, *Pentagon Papers,* v. 3, p. 591; and above.

2. "The Day of Reckoning Is Coming"

1. William Bundy manuscript on Vietnam (hereafter cited as WB, MS-VN), ch. 18, p. 1.

2. Radio and Television Report to the American People on Recent Events in Russia, China, and Great Britain, October 18, 1964, *Public Papers: Lyndon B. Johnson, 1963–64,* Book II, pp. 1377–1380.

3. See *Time,* Feb. 26, 1965, p. 25; and A.I.P.O. Survey #701-K, released Nov. 25, 1964, in George H. Gallup, ed., *The Gallup Poll: Public Opinion, 1935–1971* (hereafter cited as *Gallup Poll*) (New York: Random House, 1972), v. 3, *1959–1971,* pp. 1908–1909. Some 59 percent judged China the gravest danger to peace; 20 percent identified Russia.

4. Quoted in Kearns, *Lyndon Johnson and the American Dream,* 252–253.

5. Quoted in Tom Wicker, *JFK and LBJ: The Influence of Personality upon Politics* (New York: Penguin, 1968), 205.

6. See Bundy's report, "US Objectives and Stakes in South Vietnam and Southeast Asia," excerpted in *Pentagon Papers,* v. 3, pp. 216–217, 622–628.

7. Mustin to Working Group, Nov. 10, 1964, reprinted in ibid., 619–621.

8. McNaughton to Working Group, Nov. 6, 7, 1964, reprinted in ibid., 598–601, 601–604.

9. Bundy to Working Group, Nov. 10, 1964, reprinted in ibid., 610–619.

10. State Department telegram (hereafter cited as Deptel) 1034, Rusk to Taylor, Nov. 8, 1964, "President/Taylor NODIS," CNF, VN, Box 195, NSF, LBJL.

11. Quoted in Halberstam, *Best,* 424–425.

12. Johnson to Turner Catledge, Dec. 5, 1964, Notebook 3, Box 1, Arthur Krock Papers, SGMML, PU.

13. Quote is in Rowland Evans and Robert Novak, *Lyndon B. Johnson: The Exercise of Power* (New York: New American Library, 1966), 490.

14. These comments are curious. All three men—McGeorge Bundy, Rusk, and William Bundy—actually knew otherwise. Ball had completed a long memorandum challenging prevailing assumptions about Vietnam and pleading the case against escalation on October 5. He had given copies of his memo to Rusk, McNamara, and McGeorge Bundy, which they had discussed together on November 7, just twelve days before this meeting with the President. William Bundy, if not privy to Ball's paper, had received a lengthy analysis advocating a negotiated exit from Robert Johnson of the State Department's Policy Planning Council only the day before. Ball, for his part, chose not to pass his memo on to LBJ for another three and a half months. See George W. Ball, *The Past Has Another Pattern: Memoirs* (New York: W. W. Norton, 1982), 380, 383, 392; and Robert Johnson to William Bundy, Nov. 18, 1964, "Meeting of the Principals Book," CNF, VN, Box 202, NSF, LBJL.

15. For an account of this November 19 White House meeting, see Memorandum

for the Record (by James C. Thomson, Jr.), drafted Nov. 24, 1964, "Miscellaneous Meetings," ADF, MB, Box 18/19, NSF, LBJL.

16. The participants at this session included Rusk and Ball from the State Department, McNamara and JCS Chairman General Earle Wheeler from the Pentagon, CIA Director John McCone, and McGeorge Bundy.

17. See McGeorge Bundy's notes of this meeting, scrawled in the margin of his copy of William Bundy to Rusk et al., Nov. 24, 1964, "Courses of Action in Southeast Asia 11/64," CNF, VN, Box 45/46, NSF, LBJL.

18. Quoted in *New York Times* (hereafter cited as *NYT*), Nov. 27, 1964, p. 17.

19. President's News Conference at the LBJ Ranch, Nov. 28, 1964, *Public Papers: Lyndon B. Johnson, 1963–64,* Book II, pp. 1611–1620.

20. William Bundy and John McNaughton, "Courses of Action in Southeast Asia," Nov. 26, 1964, reprinted in *Pentagon Papers,* v. 3, pp. 656–666.

21. WB, MS-VN, ch. 19, p. 2.

22. Maxwell Taylor, "The Current Situation in South Vietnam—November 1964," reprinted in *Pentagon Papers,* v. 3, pp. 666–673. Taylor had been promoting the idea of escalation, despite Saigon's political weakness, for weeks. As he had cabled Rusk on November 10, "If the government falters and gives good reason to believe that it will never attain the desired level of performance, I would favor going against the North anyway." "The purpose of such an attack," he added, "would be to give pulmotor treatment [to] a government in extremis and to make sure that the DRV does not get off unscathed in any final settlement." Embtel 1445 (Saigon), Taylor to Rusk, Nov. 10, 1964, "President/Taylor NODIS," CNF, VN, Box 195, NSF, LBJL. See also Embtel 1440 (Saigon), Taylor to Rusk, Nov. 9, 1964, "Vol. 21," CNF, VN, Box 10, ibid.

23. Before Taylor had left Saigon, Westmoreland had advised him the South Vietnamese government should be "on a reasonably firm political, military, and psychological base before we risk the great strains that may be incurred" by bombing North Vietnam. Westmoreland explained his reluctance in his memoirs. "[S]uch tangential benefits as a bombing program might produce were to my mind too minor to justify risking a North Vietnamese reaction [i.e. increased infiltration] that might overwhelm the existing unstable government." General William C. Westmoreland, *A Soldier Reports* (New York: Doubleday, 1976; rep. ed., New York: Dell Publishing, 1980), 142, 143.

24. See "Memorandum of Meeting on Southeast Asia" (by William Bundy), Nov. 27, 1964, reprinted in *Pentagon Papers,* v. 3, pp. 674–676.

25. William Bundy, "Draft Position Paper on Southeast Asia," Nov. 29, 1964, reprinted in ibid., 678–679.

26. Those present included Rusk and William Bundy from State; McNamara, Wheeler, and McNaughton from Defense; Ambassador Taylor; CIA Director McCone; McGeorge Bundy; and Vice President-elect Hubert Humphrey.

27. See John McNaughton's and McGeorge Bundy's handwritten notes of this meeting, in Box 1, Meeting Notes File (hereafter cited as MNF), LBJL; and Papers of McGeorge Bundy (hereafter cited as MB-MSS), ibid., respectively.

3. "Stable Government or No Stable Government"

1. Johnson to Rusk, McNamara, and McCone, Dec. 7, 1964, "Vol. 23, Memos, 12/1–18/64," CNF, VN, Box 11, NSF, LBJL.

2. Mansfield to Johnson, Dec. 9, 1964, "CO 312 VIETNAM (1964–1965)," Confidential File (hereafter cited as CFF), Box 12, White House Central File (hereafter cited as WHCF), LBJL.

3. McGeorge Bundy to Johnson, Dec. 16, 1964, "Memos to the President, Vol. 7, 10/1–12/31/64," ADF, MB, Box 2, NSF, LBJL.

4. Johnson to Taylor, Dec. 3, 1964, ibid.

5. See Taylor's report to South Vietnamese leaders, excerpted in *Pentagon Papers*, v. 2, pp. 343–345; v. 3, pp. 90–92. Khanh quote is in CIA Weekly Report on South Vietnam, Dec. 9, 1964, *CIA Research Reports: Vietnam and Southeast Asia, 1946–1976* (hereafter cited as *CIARR*) (Frederick, Md.: Univ. Publications of America, 1982), reel 4, frame 472.

6. See "Tam Chau," CIA, Office of Central Reference, Biographic Register, Jan. 29, 1965, "Trip, McGeorge Bundy—Saigon, Vol. 4, 2/4/65," IMATF, Box 28/29, NSF, LBJL. Quote is in *Time*, Dec. 4, 1964, p. 38.

7. Quoted in *Time*, Dec. 11, 1964, p. 39.

8. See "Thich Tri Quang," CIA, Office of Central Reference, Biographic Register, Jan. 29, 1965, "Trip, McGeorge Bundy—Saigon, Vol. 4, 2/4/65," IMATF, Box 28/29, NSF, LBJL.

9. Ibid. Khanh had made a similar advance to ARVN's I Corps Commander, General Nguyen Chanh Thi, in late November. See CIA Intelligence Information Cable, Dec. 3, 1964, *CIARR*, reel 4, frame 398.

10. See "Summary of Conversation, Sunday, December 20" (by Robert H. Miller), transmitted to Washington as Embassy Airgram (hereafter cited as Embair) A-493, "Vol. 25, Memos, 12/26/64–1/9/65," CNF, VN, Box 12, NSF, LBJL; and Ky's remarks in Michael Charlton & Anthony Moncrieff, *Many Reasons Why: The American Involvement in Vietnam* (New York: Hill and Wang, 1978), 218.

11. Quote is in Embtel 1877 (Saigon), Taylor to Rusk et al., Dec. 20, 1964, "President/Taylor NODIS," CNF, VN, Box 195, NSF, LBJL.

12. See Embtel 1881 (Saigon), Taylor to Rusk, Dec. 21, 1964, "Vol. 24, Cables, 12/19–25/64," CNF, VN, Box 11, NSF, LBJL.

13. Quotes are in *New York Herald Tribune* (hereafter cited as *NYHT*), Dec. 23, 1964, p. 4; and *NYT*, Dec. 23, 1964, p. 4.

14. Quoted in Ronald Steel, *Walter Lippmann and the American Century* (Boston: Atlantic/Little, Brown, 1980; rep. ed., New York: Random House, Vintage, 1981), 556.

15. See Nov. 1964, Survey Research Center poll, cited in John E. Mueller, "Trends in Popular Support for the Wars in Korea and Vietnam," *American Political Science Review*, v. 65, n. 2, June 1971, p. 363; and Nov. 29 and Dec. 3, 1964, Gallup releases, in Department of State, "American Opinion Survey," Dec. 3, 1964, "Meeting of the Principals Book," CNF, VN, Box 201/202, NSF, LBJL.

16. See Annual Budget Message to the Congress, Fiscal Year 1966, submitted Jan. 25, 1965, *Public Papers: Lyndon B. Johnson, 1965* (Washington: U.S. Government Printing Office, 1966), Book I, pp. 82–99.

17. Quoted in Halberstam, *Best*, 507.

18. JPS 663, Taylor to William and McGeorge Bundy, Dec. 18, 1964, "President/Taylor NODIS," CNF, VN, Box 195, NSF, LBJL.

19. Joseph Alsop, "Accepting Defeat," *Washington Post* (hereafter cited as *WP*), Dec. 23, 1964, p. A21.

20. Joseph Alsop, "Johnson's Cuba II," *WP*, Dec. 30, 1964, p. A19.

21. Hoyt to Johnson, with Hosokawa enclosure, Dec. 19, 1964, "Vol. 25, Memos, 12/26/64–1/9/65," CNF, VN, Box 12, NSF, LBJL.

22. Johnson to McGeorge Bundy, Dec. 29, 1964, ibid.

23. Embtel 1988 (Saigon), Taylor to Johnson, Dec. 30, 1964, "President/Taylor NODIS," CNF, VN, Box 195, NSF, LBJL.

24. CAP-64375, Johnson to Taylor, Dec. 31, 1964, "Vol. 1 (B), NODIS-LOR 1/65–3/65," CNF, VN, Box 45, NSF, LBJL. McGeorge Bundy, who drafted this message for the President, had originally included stronger language in the cable: "Any recommendation that you or General Westmoreland make . . . will have very favorable consideration . . ."; "I myself am ready to double the number of Americans in Vietnam. . . ." LBJ's approved telegram, though similar in spirit, reflected much greater ambiguity and caution. See CAP-64374, McGeorge Bundy to Johnson, Dec. 30, 1964, "President/Taylor NODIS," CNF, VN, Box 195, NSF, LBJL.

25. Embtel 2058 (Saigon), Taylor to Rusk, Jan. 6, 1965, "Deployment," Vol. 1, Tabs 1–10, NSCH, Box 40, NSF, LBJL.

26. Quote is in Embtel 2059 (Saigon), Taylor to Johnson, Jan. 6, 1965, "NODIS-LOR, 1/65–2/65," CNF, VN, Box 45, NSF, LBJL.

27. Embtel 2052 (Saigon), Taylor to Rusk, Jan. 6, 1965, "Deployment," Vol. 1, Tabs 1–10, NSCH, Box 40, NSF, LBJL.

28. For a record of this January 6 meeting, see MB-MSS, LBJL.

29. Deptel 1419, Johnson to Taylor, Jan. 7, 1965, "NODIS-LOR 1/65–2/65," CNF, VN, Box 45/46, NSF, LBJL.

30. When LBJ edited Bundy's draft presidential message, he struck out the Special Assistant's call for a "[j]oint announcement in Saigon of [the] US/GVN decision." See Draft 2 of Johnson to Taylor, Jan. 7, 1965, "Vol. 1 (B), NODIS-LOR 1/65–3/65," ibid.

31. See Annual Message to the Congress on the State of the Union, Jan. 4, 1965, *Public Papers: Lyndon B. Johnson, 1965,* Book I, pp. 1–9.

32. The President's Inaugural Address, Jan. 20, 1965, ibid., 71–74.

33. WB, MS-VN, ch. 20, p. 2.

34. Those present included Senators Aiken, Dirksen, Kuchel, Long, Mansfield, Saltonstall, and Smathers; Representatives Albert, Arends, Boggs, Ford, Laird, and McCormack; Vice President Humphrey; Secretary of State Rusk; Defense Secretary McNamara; CIA Director McCone; and McGeorge Bundy, Horace Busby, Douglass Cater, Bill Moyers, Lawrence O'Brien, George Reedy, and Jack Valenti of the White House staff.

35. See "President's Meeting with Congressional Leaders" (by Bromley Smith), Jan. 22, 1965, "Miscellaneous Meetings, Vol. 1," ADF, MB, Box 18, NSF, LBJL.

36. Quotes are in *Newsweek,* Jan. 18, 1965, p. 32; and *NYHT,* Dec. 21, 1964, p. 6.

37. See Chester Cooper and McGeorge Bundy to Johnson, "Political Developments in South Vietnam," Jan. 8, 1965, "Vol. 25, Memos, 12/26/64–1/9/65," CNF, VN, Box 12, NSF, LBJL; and CIA Intelligence Information Cable, Jan. 21, 1965, *CIARR,* reel 4, frames 622–628.

38. For Alexis Johnson's report of this encounter, see Embtel 2102 (Saigon), Taylor to Rusk, Jan. 9, 1965, "Vol. 25, Cables, 12/26/64–1/9/65," CNF, VN, Box 11, NSF, LBJL.

39. Tri Quang had assured an American embassy officer, during a private interview on January 16, that the Buddhists planned no more demonstrations through Tet (Jan. 31–Feb. 6). Quang had no intention, he claimed, of disturbing the faith-

fuls' enjoyment of the New Year holidays. See Memorandum of Conversation (by James D. Rosenthal), transmitted to Washington as Embair A-563, "Vol. 26, Memos, 1/10–31/65," CNF, VN, Box 12, NSF, LBJL.

40. Quoted in Shaplen, *Lost Revolution*, 301.

41. Ibid.

42. See McNaughton's summary of this meeting, reprinted in *Pentagon Papers*, v. 3, pp. 686–687.

43. McGeorge Bundy to Johnson, Jan. 27, 1965, "Memos to the President, Vol. 8, 1/1–2/28/65," ADF, MB, Box 2, NSF, LBJL.

44. Transcript, George Ball OHI, July 8, 1971, by Paige E. Mulhollan, tape 1, p. 27, LBJL.

45. See McGeorge Bundy's notes of this Jan. 27 meeting, in MB-MSS, LBJL.

46. Deptel 1570, McGeorge Bundy to Taylor, Jan. 30, 1965, "Trip, McGeorge Bundy–Saigon, Vol. 2, 2/4/65," IMATF, Box 28/29, NSF, LBJL.

47. Quoted in Halberstam, *Best*, 530.

4. "A Bear by the Tail"

1. See Bundy's comments in Bromley Smith to Johnson, Feb. 4, 1965, "Trip, McGeorge Bundy–Saigon, Vol. 1, 2/4/65," IMATF, Box 28/29, NSF, LBJL.

2. Ibid.

3. See Embtel 2420 (Saigon), McNaughton to McNamara and Vance, Feb. 7, 1965, ibid.

4. Quotes are in Halberstam, *Best*, 533.

5. Those present included McNamara, Vance, and Wheeler from the Pentagon; Ball, William Bundy, and Ambassador Llewellyn Thompson from the State Department–Rusk being ill and in Florida until February 15; Treasury Secretary Douglas Dillon; USIA Director Carl Rowan; Marshall Carter and William Colby of the CIA; Senator Mike Mansfield and Speaker John McCormack from Capitol Hill; and Bill Moyers of the White House staff.

6. Ball explained his irresolution in his memoirs. "Faced with a unanimous view," he wrote, "I saw no option but to go along. . . ." Ball, *Past*, 390. The recommendation for reprisal was not unanimous; one participant–Mike Mansfield–dissented vigorously.

7. See "Summary Notes of 545th NSC Meeting" (by Bromley Smith), Feb. 6, 1965, Box 1, MNF, LBJL; and Johnson, *Vantage Point*, 124–125.

8. The participants at this meeting included McNamara, Vance, Wheeler, Ball, William Bundy, Thompson, Dillon, Rowen, Carter, Colby, Mansfield, McCormack, House Minority Leader Gerald Ford, Moyers, and Jack Valenti.

9. See "Summary Notes of 546th NSC Meeting" (by Bromley Smith), Feb. 7, 1965, "Vol. 3, Tab 28, 2/7/65, Vietnam Reprisals," NSC Meetings File (hereafter cited as NSCMF), Box 1, NSF, LBJL; and transcript, William Bundy OHI, May 29, 1969, by Paige E. Mulhollan, tape 2, p. 12, ibid.

10. McGeorge Bundy to Johnson, Feb. 7, 1965, "Vol. 3, Tab 29, 2/8/65, Situation in Vietnam, Tab B," ibid.; and Annex A, "A Policy of Sustained Reprisal" (drafted by McNaughton for Bundy), "McGeorge Bundy–Memos to the President, Vol. 8, 1/1–2/28/65," ADF, MB, Box 2, NSF, LBJL.

11. Quote is in Johnson, *Vantage Point*, 128.

12. Those attending included Ball, Thompson, William Bundy, and Leonard

Unger from State; McNamara, Vance, McNaughton, Wheeler, and Andrew Good-paster from Defense; CIA Director McCone; Treasury Secretary Dillon; David Bell and William Gaud from the Agency for International Development (AID); USIA Director Rowan; Speaker McCormack and Minority Leader Ford from the House; Senators Mansfield and Everett Dirksen; and McGeorge Bundy, Moyers, Valenti, Chester Cooper, and Lawrence O'Brien of the President's staff.

13. See "Summary Notes of 547th NSC Meeting," Feb. 8, 1965, "Vol. 3, Tab 29, 2/8/65, Situation in Vietnam," NSCMF, Box 1, NSF, LBJL.

14. Deptel 1653, Johnson to Taylor, Feb. 8, 1965, "NODIS-LOR, Vol. 1 (A), 1/65–3/65," CNF, VN, Box 45/46, NSF, LBJL.

15. The participants at this meeting included most of the administration officials present two days before, in addition to Vice President Humphrey, who had returned from a political trip to Minnesota, and Admiral David McDonald, Chief of Naval Operations, sitting in for JCS Chairman Wheeler.

16. See "Summary Record of National Security Council Meeting No. 548," Feb. 10, 1965, "Vol. 3, Tab 30, 2/10/65, Vietnam," NSCMF, Box 1, NSF, LBJL.

17. See White House Statement, Feb. 7, 1965, reprinted in *NYT*, Feb. 8, 1965, p. 14; and White House Statement, Feb. 11, 1965, reprinted in *NYT*, Feb. 12, 1965, p. 13.

18. Quoted in Geyelin, *Lyndon B. Johnson and the World*, 219.

19. Transcript, William Bundy OHI, May 29, 1969, by Paige E. Mulhollan, tape 2, p. 14, LBJL.

20. Ball to Johnson, Feb. 13, 1965, "Deployment," Vol. 1, Tabs 42–60, NSCH, Box 40, NSF, LBJL.

21. Deptel 1718, Ball to Taylor, Feb. 13, 1965, "NODIS-LOR, Vol. 1 (B), 1/65–3/65," CNF, VN, Box 45, NSF, LBJL.

22. Humphrey to Johnson, Feb. 15, 1965, reprinted in Hubert H. Humphrey, *The Education of a Public Man: My Life and Politics,* ed. Norman Sherman (Garden City: Doubleday, 1976), 320–324.

23. Quotes are in Eric F. Goldman, *The Tragedy of Lyndon Johnson* (New York: Alfred A. Knopf, 1969), 484; and Mark Lorell, Charles Kelley, Jr., and Deborah Hensler, *Casualties, Public Opinion, and Presidential Policy During the Vietnam War* (Santa Monica: Rand Corporation, 1985), 45.

24. That need rested, primarily, with Defense Secretary McNamara, who had told Bundy the previous afternoon that "we should have a military action soon" in order "to get off [this] tit-for-tat kick." See Feb. 15 notes, in MB-MSS, LBJL.

25. McGeorge Bundy to Johnson, Feb. 16, 1965, "Deployment," Vol. 1, Tabs 42–60, NSCH, Box 40, NSF, LBJL.

26. For notes of this February 16 conference, see MB-MSS, LBJL. State Department representatives Rusk, Ball, Thompson, and William Bundy also attended this midday session.

27. See confidential Louis Harris polls in Moyers to Johnson, Feb. 16, 1965, "ND 19/CO 312 VIETNAM (Situation in 1964–1965)," CFF, Box 71, WHCF, LBJL. Much of this material later appeared in the *WP,* Feb. 23, 1965, p. A9.

28. Quote is in Charles Roberts, *LBJ's Inner Circle* (New York: Delacorte, 1965), 25.

29. Quotes are in Hugh Sidey, *A Very Personal Presidency: Lyndon Johnson in the White House* (New York: Atheneum, 1968), 207; and Johnson, *Vantage Point,* 130.

30. See "Memorandum of Meeting with the President, 17 February 1965" (by General Andrew Goodpaster, liaison between Eisenhower and Johnson), "February 17, 1965—10:00 A.M. Meeting with General Eisenhower and Others," Box 1, MNF, LBJL.

31. See MB-MSS, LBJL; Memorandum for the Record (by McGeorge Bundy), dated Feb. 20, 1965, "Memos for the Record, 1964 [sic]," ADF, MB, Box 18, NSF, LBJL; and Deptel 1268, Rusk to Martin (America's Ambassador to Thailand), Feb. 18, 1965, reprinted in *Pentagon Papers*, v. 3, p. 324.

32. Quoted in *Time*, Jan. 8, 1965, p. 20.

33. Diem, *In the Jaws of History*, 124.

34. See "Phan Huy Quat," CIA, Office of Central Reference, Biographic Register, Jan. 29, 1965, "Trip, McGeorge Bundy—Saigon, Vol. 4, 2/4/65," IMATF, Box 28/29, NSF, LBJL.

35. Quoted in Shaplen, *Lost Revolution*, 307.

36. For information about Pham Ngoc Thao's role as a secret communist agent, see Truong Nhu Tang with David Chanoff and Doan Van Toai, *A Vietcong Memoir* (San Diego: Harcourt Brace Jovanovich, 1985), 42–62; and Stanley Karnow, *Vietnam: A History* (New York: Viking, 1983), 38.

37. The Thao-Ky exchange is quoted in Tang, *Vietcong Memoir*, 60. Tang, who was in the phone booth with Thao, overheard the conversation.

38. Quoted in Karnow, *Vietnam*, 384. According to one source, General Thieu's brother, the Young Turks had been plotting to depose Khanh from at least November 1964. Ky, for his part, had informed American officials on February 3 that Khanh was "almost finished." He had lost the AFC's support, Ky said, and was now "une carte brulee." See CIA Weekly Report on Situation in South Vietnam, Dec. 9, 1964, *CIARR*, reel 4, frame 471; and CIA Report, Feb. 3, 1965, "Trip, McGeorge Bundy—Saigon, Vol. 1, 2/4/65," IMATF, Box 28/29, NSF, LBJL.

39. Huynh Tan Phat to Nguyen Khanh, Jan. 28, 1965, reprinted in George McT. Kahin, *Intervention: How America Became Involved in Vietnam* (New York: Alfred A. Knopf, 1986), 295–296.

40. For the Young Turks' soundings of alarm to Taylor, which the ambassador repeated to Washington, see Embtel 2386 (Saigon), Taylor to Rusk, Feb. 2, 1965; Embtel 2382 (Saigon), Taylor to Rusk, Feb. 3, 1965; and Embtel 2389 (Saigon), Taylor to Rusk, Feb. 3, 1965, "Trip, McGeorge Bundy—Saigon, Vol. 1, 2/4/65," IMATF, Box 28/29, NSF, LBJL.

41. Quoted in John M. Taylor, *General Maxwell Taylor: The Sword and the Pen* (New York: Doubleday, 1989), 307.

42. See Deptel 1757, Rusk to Taylor, Feb. 19, 1965, "Vol. 1 (B), NODIS-LOR 1/65–3/65," CNF, VN, Box 45, NSF, LBJL.

43. See Deptel 1783, Rusk to Taylor, Feb. 20, 1965, ibid.

44. Quoted in Evans and Novak, *Lyndon B. Johnson*, 536.

45. Rusk to Johnson, Feb. 23, 1965, "Deployment," Vol. 2, Tabs 61–87, NSCH, Box 40, NSF, LBJL.

46. See Deptel 1815, Rusk to Taylor, Feb. 24, 1965, "Vol. 1 (B), NODIS-LOR 1/65–3/65," CNF, VN, Box 45, NSF, LBJL, reporting the President's bombing decision.

47. Transcript, George Ball OHI, July 8, 1971, by Paige E. Mulhollan, tape 1, pp. 15–17, LBJL.

48. Ball, *Past*, 384.

49. Quote is in ibid., 377–378.

50. George W. Ball, "How Valid Are the Assumptions Underlying Our Viet-Nam Policies?," Oct. 5, 1964, reprinted as "Top Secret: The Prophecy the President Rejected," *Atlantic*, v. 230, n. 1, July 1972, pp. 35–49.

51. Quoted in Ball, *Past*, 392.

52. See Halberstam, *Best*, 516.

53. Transcript, George Ball OHI, July 8, 1971, by Paige E. Mulhollan, tape 1, p. 29, LBJL.

54. During this interval, on February 27, the State Department released a lengthy "white paper" detailing Hanoi's infiltration of men and supplies into the South. See Department of State, *Aggression from the North: The Record of North Viet-Nam's Campaign to Conquer South Viet-Nam* (Washington: Government Printing Office, Feb. 1965). This report had originally been timed for publication in conjunction with the bombing.

5. "Where Are We Going?"

1. Quotes are in transcript, Maxwell D. Taylor OHI, June 1, 1981, by Ted Gittinger, p. 40, LBJL; and Marvin Kalb and Elie Abel, *Roots of Involvement: The U.S. in Asia* (New York: W. W. Norton, 1971), 184.

2. Embtel 2699 (Saigon), Taylor to Rusk and the JCS, Feb. 22, 1965, "Deployment," Vol. 2, Tabs 61–87, NSCH, Box 40, NSF, LBJL.

3. Deptel 1840, Rusk to Taylor, Feb. 26, 1965, "Vol. 29, Cables, 2/20–28/65," CNF, VN, Box 14, NSF, LBJL.

4. Westmoreland, *Soldier*, 159.

5. Quoted in Halberstam, *Best*, 564; and Westmoreland, *Soldier*, 161.

6. McGeorge Bundy to Johnson, March 6, 1965, "Memos to the President, v. 9, Mar.–Apr. 14, 1965," ADF, MB, Box 3, NSF, LBJL.

7. Quoted in Lady Bird Johnson, *A White House Diary* (New York: Holt, Rinehart and Winston, 1970; rep. ed., New York: Dell, 1971), 269.

8. See McGeorge Bundy's notes of this March 9 "Tuesday Lunch," in MB-MSS, LBJL.

9. See President's News Conference, March 13, 1965, *Public Papers: Lyndon B. Johnson, 1965*, Book I, pp. 274–281. For Johnson's strong advocacy of voting rights legislation, see his Special Message to Congress, "The American Promise," delivered in person on March 15, 1965, ibid., 281–287; and the accompanying legislative analysis contained in Special Message to the Congress on the Right to Vote, March 15, 1965, ibid., 287–291. In this latter message, LBJ revealed the particular importance he attached to the voting rights bill among his other Great Society initiatives: "While I have proposed to you other measures," he wrote Congress, "I regard action on . . . this Message to be first in priority."

10. See General Harold K. Johnson's "Report on Survey of the Military Situation in Vietnam," March 14, 1965, CNF, VN, Box 191, NSF, LBJL.

11. McGeorge Bundy, "Memorandum for Discussion, Tuesday, March 16, 1:00 PM," "Deployment," Vol. 2, Tabs 88–119, NSCH, Box 40, NSF, LBJL. This memo served as the focus of discussion at that day's "Tuesday Lunch."

12. Embtel 3003 (Saigon), Taylor to Rusk, March 17, 1965, ibid.

13. Mansfield to Johnson, March 18, 1965, "Memos to the President, v. 9, Mar.–Apr. 14, 1965," ADF, MB, Box 3, NSF, LBJL.

14. President's News Conference, March 20, 1965, *Public Papers: Lyndon B. Johnson, 1965,* Book I, pp. 299–307.

15. McGeorge Bundy notes on Vietnam, March 21, 1965, "Vietnam Speeches," ADF, MB, Box 17, NSF, LBJL.

16. See McGeorge Bundy's notes of this meeting, scrawled in the margins of his copy of the luncheon agenda: "Meeting with the President—Luncheon, Tuesday, March 23, [1965]," "Luncheons with the President, Vol. 1 (Part 1)," ADF, MB, Box 18/19, NSF, LBJL.

17. See CINCPAC 192207Z and JCS Memorandum 204–65, cited in *Pentagon Papers,* v. 3, p. 406.

18. John McNaughton, "Proposed Course of Action Re Vietnam," March 24, 1965, "Deployment," Vol. 2, Tabs 120–140, NSCH, Box 40, NSF, LBJL.

19. Mansfield to Johnson, March 24, 1965, "Memos to the President, v. 9, Mar.–Apr. 14, 1965," ADF, MB, Box 3, NSF, LBJL.

20. The participants at this March 26 meeting included Vice President Humphrey; Rusk, Ball, William Bundy, and Thompson from State; McNamara, Vance, McNaughton, and Wheeler representing Defense; CIA Director McCone and Deputy Director for Operations Richard Helms; Treasury Secretary Dillon; USIA Director Rowan; and McGeorge Bundy, Moyers, Valenti, and Reedy of the White House staff.

21. See Bromley Smith's "Summary Notes of 550th NSC Meeting," March 26, 1965, "Vol. 3, Tab 32, 3/26/65, Vietnam," NSCMF, Box 1, NSF, LBJL.

22. See report of Taylor's arrival in *NYT,* March 29, 1965, p. 1.

23. See Taylor's summary of this meeting in Deptel 2131, Taylor to Deputy Ambassador Johnson and General Westmoreland, March 30, 1965, "Vol. 31, Cables, 3/12–31/65," CNF, VN, Box 15, NSF, LBJL.

24. This figure coincided, interestingly, with McNaughton's March 24 recommendation, as well as Westmoreland's supplemental request for one Army division, which his assistant, General William DePuy, had brought from Saigon. On the latter, see William Bundy to Rusk, McNamara, and McGeorge Bundy, March 28, 1965, "Vol. 31, Memos (A), 3/12–31/65," CNF, VN, Box 15, NSF, LBJL. Westmoreland apparently remained more cautious about increasing American ground forces than his Pentagon superiors, even after learning of their two-division proposal.

25. See McGeorge Bundy's handwritten notes of this meeting, in the margins of his copy of "Agenda for Luncheon, March 30, 1965," "Luncheons with the President, Vol. 1 (Part 1)," ADF, MB, Box 18/19, NSF, LBJL.

26. President's News Conference, April 1, 1965, *Public Papers: Lyndon B. Johnson, 1965,* Book I, pp. 364–372.

27. Those present at this "off-the-record" meeting included only McNamara, Rusk, McGeorge Bundy, Taylor, McCone, Wheeler, Vance, McNaughton, and William Bundy—a smaller, more discreet group than usually attended NSC deliberations.

28. Quoted in Kearns, *Lyndon Johnson and the American Dream,* 270.

29. Johnson and Ball quotes are in Lorell et al., *Casualties, Public Opinion, and Presidential Policy During the Vietnam War,* 45.

30. Rusk's private admission contrasted sharply with his later public assertion that the Vietcong's struggle against Saigon "could end literally in twenty-four hours . . . if [the] people in Hanoi should come to the conclusion that they are not going to try to seize Vietnam . . . by force." Rusk testimony before the Senate Foreign Relations Committee, Jan. 28, 1966, reprinted in *Vietnam Hearings* (New York: Random House, Vintage, 1966), 16.

31. See McGeorge Bundy's notes of this April 1 meeting in MB-MSS, LBJL.

32. The attendants at this April 2 NSC session included Rusk, Taylor, McGeorge and William Bundy, Vance, McNaughton, Wheeler, McCone, Moyers, Valenti, Cooper, Gaud, Rowan, newly appointed Treasury Secretary Henry Fowler, and House Naval Affairs Committee Chairman Carl Vinson.

33. Although McCone did not specifically reveal the Marines' new combat mission to the NSC group, he made clear his reservations about the changed strategy in a memo to Rusk, McNamara, McGeorge Bundy, and Taylor that same day. Without a substantial increase in air attacks, McCone wrote, Hanoi would continue to "build up the Viet Cong capabilities . . . and thus bring an ever-increasing pressure on our forces." "In effect," he said, "we will find ourselves mired down in [a] combat . . . effort that we cannot win, and from which we will have extreme difficulty in extracting ourselves." "Therefore it is my judgment that if we are to change the mission of the ground forces, we must also change the ground rules of the strikes against North Vietnam." McCone to Rusk et al., April 2, 1965, "Deployment," Vol. 2, Tabs 120–140, NSCH, Box 40, NSF, LBJL.

34. See "Summary of NSC Meeting on April 2, 1965," drafted by Chester Cooper on April 5, "Vol. 3, Tab 33, 4/2/65, Situation in South Vietnam," NSCMF, Box 1, NSF, LBJL.

35. Deptel 2184, Rusk to Deputy Ambassador Johnson, April 3, 1965, "Vol. 32, Cables, 4/1–20/65," CNF, VN, Box 16, NSF, LBJL.

36. See McNamara to Wheeler, April 5, 1965, cited in *Pentagon Papers*, v. 3, p. 408.

37. See JCS Memorandum 238–65, cited in ibid., 407.

38. Draft National Security Action Memorandum (NSAM) 328, by McGeorge Bundy, April 5, 1965, "Deployment," Vol. 1, Tabs 1–10, NSCH, Box 40, NSF, LBJL. The final, slightly edited version, dated April 6, is reprinted in *Pentagon Papers*, v. 3, pp. 702–703.

6. "If I Were Ho Chi Minh, I Would Never Negotiate"

1. Quote is in Goldman, *Tragedy*, 404.

2. Transcript, Cyrus Vance OHI, March 9, 1970, by Paige E. Mulhollan, Interview 3, p. 11, LBJL.

3. Theodore Draper, in Pfeffer, ed., *No More Vietnams?*, 28.

4. Quoted in George C. Herring, ed., *The Secret Diplomacy of the Vietnam War: The Negotiating Volumes of the Pentagon Papers* (Austin: Univ. of Texas Press, 1983), 9.

5. See State Department Chronology of Thant Initiative, [December 1965?], "United Nations—Vol. 1, 1965," Agency File (hereafter cited as AGF), Box 71, NSF, LBJL.

6. Quoted in David Kraslow and Stuart H. Loory, *The Secret Search for Peace in Vietnam* (New York: Random House, 1968), 101.

7. See Adlai Stevenson, Memorandum of Conversation with U Thant, Feb. 16, 1965, "United Nations—Vol. 1, 1965," AGF, Box 71, NSF, LBJL.

8. Thant Statement on Vietnam, Feb. 12, 1965, reprinted in *NYT*, Feb. 13, 1965, p. 6.

9. See note 7 above.

10. Comment is William Bundy's, in WB, MS-VN, ch. 22, p. 20. His assertion

cannot be corroborated, however; Seaborn's report of his December 1964 Hanoi mission has been deleted from the relevant volume of the *Pentagon Papers*. See Herring, ed., *Secret Diplomacy*, 38.

11. U Thant Press Conference on Southeast Asia, Feb. 24, 1965, rep:inted in Marcus G. Raskin and Bernard B. Fall, eds., *The Viet-Nam Reader: Articles and Documents on American Foreign Policy and the Viet-Nam Crisis* (New York: Random House, Vintage, 1965), 263–268.

12. Memorandum of Telephone Conversation between Dean Rusk and U Thant, Feb. 24, 1965, "United Nations—Representative of the United States to the United Nations (Stevenson), 11/63–4/65," AGF, Box 71, NSF, LBJL.

13. See transcript, George Ball OHI, July 8, 1971, by Paige E. Mulhollan, tape 1, p. 39, LBJL.

14. See summary of Stevenson-Thant conversation in Mission telegram (hereafter cited as Mistel) 3426 (New York), Stevenson to Rusk, Feb. 27, 1965, "United Nations—Representative of the United States to the United Nations (Stevenson), 11/63–4/65," AGF, Box 71, NSF, LBJL.

15. Appeal of Non-aligned Nations, reprinted in *NYT*, April 2, 1965, p. 2. The following countries signed the Belgrade communique: Afghanistan, Algeria, Ceylon, Cyprus, Egypt, Ethiopia, Ghana, Guinea, India, Iraq, Kenya, Nepal, Syria, Tunisia, Uganda, Yugoslavia, and Zambia.

16. See, for example, de Gaulle's comments as reported in *NYT*, Feb. 11, 1965, p. 1.

17. Pearson quote is in *NYT*, April 3, 1965, p. 3.

18. James Reston, "Washington: The Undeclared and Unexplained War," *NYT*, Feb. 14, 1965, p. 8E.

19. Walter Lippmann, "The VietNam Debate," *WP*, Feb. 18, 1965, p. A21.

20. Frank Church before the Senate, Feb. 17, 1965, in *CR*, v. 111, pt. 3, pp. 2872, 2886.

21. George McGovern before the Senate, Feb. 17, 1965, ibid., 2880.

22. See McGeorge Bundy to Johnson, Feb. 9, 1965, "Deployment," Vol. 1, Tabs 11–41, NSCH, Box 40, NSF, LBJL.

23. See A.I.P.O. Survey #707-KA-5, released April 7, 1965, in *Gallup Poll*, v. 3, *1959–1971*, pp. 1932–1933.

24. Statement by the President on Viet-Nam, March 25, 1965, *Public Papers: Lyndon B. Johnson, 1965*, Book I, p. 319.

25. Quotes are from McGeorge Bundy's notes of this meeting, scribbled in the margins of his copy of "Agenda for Luncheon Meeting, April 6, [1965]," "Luncheons with the President, Vol. 1 (Part 1)," ADF, MB, Box 18/19, NSF, LBJL.

26. Memorandum of Background Session with Robert McNamara, April 22, 1965, Notebook 3, Box 1, Arthur Krock Papers, SGMML, PU.

27. Address at Johns Hopkins University: "Peace Without Conquest," April 7, 1965, *Public Papers: Lyndon B. Johnson, 1965*, Book I, pp. 394–399.

28. Quote is from Kearns, *Lyndon Johnson and the American Dream*, 268.

29. Quotes are in Geyelin, *Lyndon B. Johnson and the World*, 155; and Karnow, *Vietnam*, 419.

30. North Vietnam's "Four-Points" Peace Formula is reprinted in *NYT*, April 14, 1965, p. 13.

31. See Defense telegram (hereafter cited as Deftel) 9164, McNaughton to Taylor and Westmoreland, April 15, 1965, quoted in *Pentagon Papers*, v. 3, pp. 451, 455.

32. Embtel 3421 (Saigon), Taylor to McGeorge Bundy, April 17, 1965, "NODIS-LOR, Vol. 2, 3/65–9/65," CNF, VN, Box 46, NSF, LBJL; and Taylor, *Swords*, 341.

33. See CAP 65120, McGeorge Bundy to Taylor, April 17, 1965, "NODIS-LOR, Vol. 2, 3/65–9/65," CNF, VN, Box 46, NSF, LBJL; and McGeorge Bundy to Johnson, April 14, 1965, "Memos to the President, v. 9, Mar.–Apr. 14, 1965," ADF, MB, Box 3, ibid.

34. See Embtel 3248 (Saigon), Taylor to Rusk, April 7, 1965, "Vol. 32," CNF, VN, Box 16, NSF, LBJL.

35. To supplement these U.S. deployments, the conferees also recommended three South Korean battalions to Quangngai and an Australian battalion to Vungtau. See John McNaughton, "Minutes of April 20, 1965, Honolulu Meeting," in "McNaughton XV—Miscellaneous, 1964–1966," John McNaughton Files, Papers of Paul Warnke (hereafter cited as JMF, PPW), Box 7, LBJL.

36. McNamara to Johnson, April 21, 1965, "Vietnam 2EE, 1965–67," CNF, VN, Box 74/75, NSF, LBJL. This memo, curiously absent McNamara's advice regarding congressional consultation, is reprinted in *Pentagon Papers*, v. 3, pp. 705–706.

37. Others present that morning included Rusk and Ball from State; Vance from the Pentagon; retiring CIA Director McCone and his designated successor, Vice Admiral William F. Raborn; and McGeorge Bundy.

38. Johnson quote is in Ball, *Past*, 393. In his memoirs, Ball incorrectly dates this meeting on April 20.

39. For notes of this April 21 meeting, see MB-MSS, LBJL.

40. Ball to Johnson, April 21, 1965, "Political Track Papers, 4/65," CNF, VN, Box 213, NSF, LBJL.

41. Ball, *Past*, 394.

42. See draft of Rusk to Taylor, April 22, 1965, "Vol. 32," CNF, VN, Box 16, NSF, LBJL; and the final, amended version, Deptel 2397, Rusk to Taylor, April 22, 1965, "NODIS-LOR, Vol. 2 (B)," CNF, VN, Box 45/46, NSF, LBJL.

43. President's News Conference, April 27, 1965, *Public Papers: Lyndon B. Johnson, 1965*, Book I, pp. 448–456.

7. "What in the World Is Happening?"

1. Evans and Novak, *Lyndon B. Johnson*, 511.

2. Quoted in *Time*, May 14, 1965, p. 23.

3. See A.I.P.O. Survey #711-K, conducted May 13 to May 18, 1965, in *Gallup Poll*, 1942.

4. See Remarks to Committee Members on the Need for Additional Appropriations for Military Purposes in Viet-Nam and the Dominican Republic, May 4, 1965, *Public Papers: Lyndon B. Johnson, 1965*, Book I, pp. 484–492.

5. See Special Message to the Congress Requesting Additional Appropriations for Military Needs in Viet-Nam, May 4, 1965, ibid., 494–498.

6. Pell quote is in Paul Kesaris, ed., *Top Secret Hearings by the U.S. Senate Committee on Foreign Relations: First Installment, 1959–1966* (Frederick, Md.: Univ. Publications of America, 1981), April 30, 1965, pp. 33–34.

7. On Thant's growing restiveness, see Stevenson to Johnson, April 28, 1965, "United Nations—Representative of the United States to the United Nations (Stevenson), 11/63–4/65," AGF, Box 71, NSF, LBJL.

8. See McCone to Johnson, April 28, 1965, "Deployment," Vol. 4, Tabs 221–241, NSCH, Box 41, NSF, LBJL.

9. Raborn to Johnson, May 8, 1965, ibid.

10. Deptel 2553, Johnson to Taylor, May 10, 1965, "NODIS–MAYFLOWER," CNF, VN, Box 190, NSF, LBJL.

11. These, and other, considerations are addressed in John McNaughton's memo to McGeorge Bundy, "Risks in 'Possible Pause Scenario,'" April 25, 1965, "Deployment," Vol. 3, Tabs 200–220, NSCH, Box 41, NSF, LBJL.

12. See WB, MS-VN, ch. 24, pp. 14–15.

13. The text of Washington's peace feeler is reprinted in Herring, ed., *Secret Diplomacy*, 57–58.

14. Pham Van Dong, April 20, 1965, quoted in CIA memorandum, "Selected North Vietnamese References to Negotiations in the South," June 16, 1965, "Southeast Asia, Special Intelligence Material, Vol. 6 (A), 4/65–6/65," CNF, VN, Box 49, NSF, LBJL.

15. VNA International Service in English, April 29, May 4 and 6, 1965; Pham Van Dong, May 8, 1965, excerpted in ibid.

16. See VNA International Service in English, May 15, 1965, quoted in Herring, ed., *Secret Diplomacy*, 65; and CIA memorandum, "Selected North Vietnamese References," June 16, 1965, "Southeast Asia, Special Intelligence Material, Vol. 6 (A), 4/65–6/65," CNF, VN, Box 49, NSF, LBJL.

17. See Liberation Radio, May 14, 1965, excerpted in CIA memorandum, "Selected References by the South Vietnamese National Liberation Front on Negotiations in the South," ibid.

18. See Andrew Goodpaster, Memorandum of Meeting with General Eisenhower, May 12, 1965, drafted May 13, 1965, "President Eisenhower," Name File (hereafter cited as NF), Box 3, NSF, LBJL.

19. See A.I.P.O. Survey #710-KB, conducted April 23 to April 28, 1965, in *Gallup Poll*, 1940.

20. Those present included Rusk, McNamara, Ball, Raborn, Valenti, and former Secretary of State Dean Acheson, who had recently prepared, along with Ball, a South Vietnamese reconstruction plan for LBJ's consideration. McGeorge Bundy had flown to Santo Domingo the previous day to mediate the continuing Dominican crisis.

21. See Jack Valenti's notes of this meeting in "Meeting Notes 4/30–5/15/65 [sic]," Box 13, Office Files of the President (hereafter cited as OFP), LBJL.

22. For Washington's execute message, see JCS 2230, cited in Deptel 2600, Rusk to Taylor, May 17, 1965, "NODIS–MAYFLOWER," CNF, VN, Box 190, NSF, LBJL.

23. Bo quotes are in CIA memorandum, "An Assessment of Mai Van Bo's 18 May Approach to the French Government," May 27, 1965, "Vol. 34, Memos (A), 5/65," CNF, VN, Box 17, NSF, LBJL; and Embtel 6612 (Paris), May 20, 1965, reprinted in Herring, ed., *Secret Diplomacy*, 89. French translations courtesy Department of French, University of California, Los Angeles.

24. William Bundy to Charles E. Bohlen, June 9, 1965, cited in William Conrad Gibbons, *The U.S. Government and the Vietnam War: Executive and Legislative Roles and Relationships, Part III, January–July 1965* (Washington: U.S. Government Printing Office, 1988), 258–259. Bo, interestingly, revisited Manac'h on June 14, to inquire whether the American government had any reply to their May 18

conversation. He also asked Manac'h to reveal the name of the U.S. diplomat the Quai had notified. Manac'h did not. See Embtel 7071 (Paris), June 14, 1965, excerpted in Herring, ed., *Secret Diplomacy*, 90.

25. See VNA International Service in English, May 22, 1965, quoted in CIA memorandum, "Selected North Vietnamese References," June 16, 1965, "Southeast Asia, Special Intelligence Material, Vol. 6 (A), 4/65–6/65," CNF, VN, Box 49, NSF, LBJL.

26. See John McNaughton, "Criticism of the Initiative by 'the Unsympathetic,'" April 25, 1965, "Deployment," Vol. 3, Tabs 200–220, NSCH, Box 41, NSF, LBJL.

27. Clifford to Johnson, May 17, 1965, "Vietnam 2E, 5/65–7/65, 1965 Troop Decision," CNF, VN, Box 74/75, NSF, LBJL.

28. Quoted in Shaplen, *Lost Revolution*, 321.

29. See CIA Intelligence Information Cable, May 6, 1965, "Vol. 34, Cables, 5/65," CNF, VN, Box 17, NSF, LBJL.

30. For information on the attempted *putsch*, see Embtel 3838 (Saigon), Taylor to Rusk, May 21, 1965, ibid. Colonel Thao, who again eluded capture, remained at large until collared by security forces near Bienhoa on July 16. Wounded during arrest, Thao was taken to a Saigon hospital, where rivals in the South Vietnamese military murdered him. After the communists seized power in 1975, they transferred Thao's remains to a "patriots' cemetery" near Ho Chi Minh City—formerly Saigon. See Shaplen, *Lost Revolution*, 344; and Karnow, *Vietnam*, 38.

31. In addition to his political ambitions, Suu apparently harbored a desire for personal enrichment as well. According to several South Vietnamese sources, Suu and his wife directed an extensive smuggling operation, involving military planes and trucks, through the Chief of State's office. See Embtel 3627 (Saigon), Taylor to Rusk, May 3, 1965, "Vol. 34, Cables, 5/65," CNF, VN, Box 17, NSF, LBJL.

32. See Embtel 3884 (Saigon), Taylor to Rusk, May 25, 1965, ibid.

33. See Embtel 3875 (Saigon), Taylor to Rusk, May 25, 1965, ibid.

34. Suu later justified his about-face by asserting that Economic Minister Vinh—one of the five officials Quat sought to replace—had come to him late on the night of May 25, threatening demonstrations by supporters if the Chief of State countersigned his dismissal. Suu thus stalled, he claimed, in order to avert civil unrest. In fact, Suu pressured Vinh—who had initially agreed to resign—to defy Quat. See Embtel 3902 (Saigon), Taylor to Rusk, May 26, 1965; and Embtel 3931 (Saigon), Taylor to Rusk, May 28, 1965, ibid.

35. Taylor quote is in Embtel 3645 (Saigon), Taylor to Rusk, May 4, 1965, "Deployment," Vol. 3, Tabs 200–220, NSCH, Box 41, NSF, LBJL. For an analysis of Quat's political dilemma, see State Department Bureau of Intelligence and Research, "The Cabinet Crisis in South Vietnam," May 28, 1965, "Vol. 34, Memos (A), 5/65," CNF, VN, Box 17, NSF, LBJL.

36. See Embtel 4003 (Saigon), Taylor to Rusk, June 2, 1965, "Vol. 35, Cables (A), 6/1–21/65," CNF, VN, Box 18, NSF, LBJL.

37. See Embtel 4049 (Saigon), Taylor to Rusk, June 4, 1965, ibid.

38. See Embtel 4056 (Saigon), Taylor to Rusk, June 4, 1965, "Memos to the President, v. 11, June 1965," ADF, MB, Box 3, NSF, LBJL.

39. Suu quote is in CIA Situation Report for June 3–9, 1965, "Vol. 35, Memos (B), 6/1–15/65," CNF, VN, Box 18, NSF, LBJL.

40. Taylor quote is in Embtel 4074 (Saigon), Taylor to Rusk, June 5, 1965, "Deployment," Vol. 4, Tabs 258–280, NSCH, Box 41, NSF, LBJL.

41. See "Nguyen Van Thieu," CIA, Office of Central Reference, Biographic Register, Jan. 29, 1965, "Trip, McGeorge Bundy–Saigon, Vol. 4, 2/4/65," IMATF, Box 28/29, NSF, LBJL; and "Nguyen Van Thieu," CIA, Office of Central Reference, Biographic Register, June 24, 1965, "Biographical," ADF, MB, Box 17, NSF, LBJL.

42. Johnson, *Right Hand,* 437; Taylor, *Swords,* 345.

43. See "Nguyen Cao Ky," CIA, Office of Central Reference, Biographic Register, Jan. 29, 1965, "Trip, McGeorge Bundy–Saigon, Vol. 4, 2/4/65," IMATF, Box 28/29, NSF, LBJL.

44. Ky interview with Brian Moynahan, published in [*London*] *Sunday Mirror,* July 4, 1965, p. 9.

45. Diem, *In the Jaws of History,* 149; Taylor, *Swords,* 345; and transcript, William Bundy OHI, May 29, 1969, by Paige E. Mulhollan, tape 2, p. 30, LBJL.

46. See JCSM 321–65, April 30, 1965, quoted in *Pentagon Papers,* v. 3, p. 458.

47. See MACV 15182, May 8, 1965, cited in ibid., pp. 411–12; 459–460.

48. Quoted in *Newsweek,* May 10, 1965, p. 49.

49. See Embtel 4035 (Saigon), Taylor to Rusk, June 3, 1965, "Vol. 2 (A), 3/65–9/65," CNF, VN, Box 45/46, NSF, LBJL.

50. Embtel 4074 (Saigon), Taylor to Rusk, June 5, 1965, "Deployment," Vol. 4, Tabs 258–280, NSCH, Box 41, NSF, LBJL.

51. For notes of this June 5 meeting, see, primarily, MB-MSS, LBJL, and WB, MS-VN, ch. 26, pp. 3–6.

8. "Can You Stop It?"

1. MACV 19118, Westmoreland to Sharp and Wheeler, June 7, 1965, "Deployment," Vol. 4, Tabs 258–280, NSCH, Box 41, NSF, LBJL. In addition to his recommended U.S. deployments, Westmoreland also urged committing ten South Korean battalions to Vietnam. Together, this would bring Allied forces to forty-two battalions.

2. The participants at this session included McNamara, Wheeler, and Vance from the Pentagon; Rusk and Ball from State; Ambassador Taylor, just in from Saigon; and McGeorge Bundy.

3. For a record of this June 8 meeting, see MB-MSS, LBJL.

4. MACV statement, April 9, 1965, in Joseph A. Califano, Jr., to McGeorge Bundy, June 9, 1965, "Deployment," Vol. 4, Tabs 258–280, NSCH, Box 41, NSF, LBJL; State Department announcement, June 5, 1965, quoted in Deptel 2810, Rusk to Taylor, June 5, 1965, ibid. In a confidential cable to Saigon later that day, Rusk had nevertheless reiterated that "COMUSMACV has the authority to authorize [the] commitment [of] US ground forces to action in combat support on the basis of operational coordination and cooperation with RVNAF." See Deptel 2812, Rusk to Taylor, June 5, 1965, ibid.

5. Excerpted in Halberstam, *Best,* 586.

6. White House statement, June 9, 1965, "Deployment," Vol. 4, Tabs 258–280, NSCH, Box 41, NSF, LBJL; and Westmoreland, *Soldier,* 174.

7. "Ground War in Asia," *NYT,* June 9, 1965, p. 46.

8. Jacob Javits before the Senate, June 9, 1965, in *CR,* v. 111, pt. 10, p. 12983.

9. Quoted in Goldman, *Tragedy,* 410; and James Deakin, *Lyndon Johnson's Credibility Gap* (Washington: Public Affairs Press, 1968), 60.

10. Mansfield to Johnson, June 5 and 9, 1965, "Deployment," Vol. 6, Tabs 341–356, NSCH, Box 43, NSF, LBJL.

11. Those attending included McNamara and Vance from Defense; Rusk, Ball, and William Bundy from State; Ambassador Taylor; CIA Director Raborn; McGeorge Bundy, Bill Moyers, and George Reedy of the White House staff; and Senate Armed Services Committee Chairman Richard Russell, who joined the gathering late.

12. For notes of this June 10 meeting, see especially MB-MSS, LBJL, and WB, MS-VN, ch. 26, pp. 7–15.

13. Those present included McNamara, McNaughton, and Wheeler from the Pentagon; Rusk, Ball, and William Bundy from State; Ambassadors Taylor and Stevenson; CIA Director Raborn; Treasury Secretary Henry Fowler; Acting Attorney General Nicholas Katzenbach; AID Administrator Bell; USIA Director Rowan; Office of Emergency Planning (OEP) Director Buford Ellington; and McGeorge Bundy, Horace Busby, Douglass Cater, George Reedy, Bromley Smith, and Marvin Watson of the White House staff.

14. See Bromley Smith's "Summary Notes of 552nd NSC Meeting," June 11, 1965, "Vol. 3, Tab 34, 6/11/65, Vietnam," NSCMF, Box 1, NSF, LBJL.

15. Quotes are in Henry F. Graff, "How Johnson Makes Foreign Policy," *New York Times Magazine,* July 4, 1965, pp. 18–20; and Graff, *Tuesday Cabinet,* 53–55.

16. MACV 20055, Westmoreland to Sharp and Wheeler, June 13, 1965, reprinted in *Pentagon Papers,* v. 4, pp. 606–609.

17. See A. J. Goodpaster's Memorandum of Meeting with General Eisenhower, June 16, 1965, "President Eisenhower," NF, Box 3, NSF, LBJL. Johnson read Goodpaster's report that evening.

18. See confidential Louis Harris surveys in Hayes Redmon to Johnson, June 17, 1965, "ND 19/CO 312 VIETNAM (Situation in 1964–1965)," CFF, Box 71, WHCF, LBJL; and "PR 16 Public Opinion Polls (April 1964–June 1965)," CFF, Box 80, ibid.

19. Johnson's assertion contrasted vividly with an NSC analysis of the Tonkin Gulf Resolution which he had read the week before. It had noted, in part, that the Tonkin Gulf Resolution "was passed on the understanding that there would be consultation with the Congress 'in case a major change in present policy becomes necessary.'" See James C. Thomson, Jr., and McGeorge Bundy to Johnson, June 11, 1965, "Vol. 4," CNF, VN, Box 54, NSF, LBJL.

20. President's News Conference, June 17, 1965, *Public Papers: Lyndon B. Johnson, 1965,* Book II, pp. 669–685.

21. Ball suggests a much greater contrast between McNamara's June 10 recommendation and these June 18 proposals in his memoirs. "Secretary McNamara," he writes, had "proposed a total deployment of 395,000 personnel in South Vietnam by the end of the year," adding "I sought vainly to forestall this escalation." Rather, Ball had counseled only limiting the escalation at this point. See Ball, *Past,* 395.

22. Ball to Johnson, June 18, 1965, "Deployment," Vol. 5, Tabs 314–325, NSCH, Box 42, NSF, LBJL. Only Rusk received a copy of this memo.

23. See CIA Deputy Director for Intelligence Ray Cline to Jack Valenti, June 21, 1965, answering LBJ's June 19 request, in *CIARR,* reel 2, frames 467–468.

24. Quoted in Ball, *Past,* 396. Moyers relayed LBJ's comments to Ball that night.

25. The attendants at this session included Rusk, Ball, William Bundy, and Thompson from State; McNamara, Vance, and McNaughton from the Pentagon;

CIA Director Raborn and Deputy Director for Operations Richard Helms; and White House staffers Busby, Cater, and McGeorge Bundy.

26. For an account of this June 23 meeting, see WB, MS-VN, ch. 26, pp. 22–23.

27. See JCS 2400, Wheeler to Westmoreland, June 22, 1965, cited in *Pentagon Papers,* v. 3, pp. 414, 471. McNamara's proposal also included one Australian and nine South Korean battalions, for a combined total of forty-four.

28. MACV 3320, Westmoreland to Sharp and Wheeler, June 24, 1965, cited in ibid., pp. 415, 471, and 481.

29. See McNamara draft memorandum, June 26, 1965 (revised July 1, 1965), "Vol. 3, Tab 35, 7/27/65, Deployment of Additional U.S. Troops in Vietnam," NSCMF, Box 1, NSF, LBJL.

30. McGeorge Bundy to McNamara, June 30, 1965, "Deployment," Vol. 6, Tabs 341–356, NSCH, Box 43, NSF, LBJL. Bundy had expressed similar, though far more restrained, reservations to LBJ three days earlier. See McGeorge Bundy to Johnson, June 27, 1965, "Memos to the President, v. 11, June 1965," ADF, MB, Box 3, NSF, LBJL.

31. See WB, MS-VN, ch. 26, p. 25. Ball elaborated his case in two memorandums to Rusk et al., June 28 and 29, 1965, "Deployment," Vol. 6, Tabs 341–356, NSCH, Box 43, NSF, LBJL.

32. See WB, MS-VN, ch. 26, p. 26; and William Bundy to Rusk et al., June 30, 1965, "Vol. 35, Memos (C), 6/16–30/65," CNF, VN, Box 18, NSF, LBJL.

33. McNamara to Johnson, July 1, 1965, "Vol. 3, Tab 35, 7/27/65, Deployment of Additional U.S. Troops in Vietnam," NSCMF, Box 1, NSF, LBJL.

34. Ball to Johnson, July 1, 1965, "Vol. 37, Memos (C), 7/65," CNF, VN, Box 20, NSF, LBJL. A partial copy of this memo, missing its first two pages and incorrectly dated June 23, 1965, is in "Deployment," Vol. 5, Tabs 314–325, NSCH, Box 42, NSF, LBJL.

35. William Bundy, "A 'Middle Way' Course of Action in South Vietnam," July 1, 1965, "Deployment," Vol. 5, Tabs 314–325, NSCH, Box 42, NSF, LBJL.

36. Rusk to Johnson, July 1, 1965, "Deployment," Vol. 6, Tabs 357–383, NSCH, Box 43, NSF, LBJL.

37. McGeorge Bundy to Johnson, July 1, 1965, ibid.

38. See "Memorandum of Telephone Conversation: 10:55 A.M., July 2, 1965" (by Lillian H. Brown, Eisenhower's confidential secretary), Eisenhower Post-Presidential Papers: Augusta Series, Box 10, Dwight D. Eisenhower Library.

39. For an account of this July 2 meeting, see WB, MS-VN, ch. 27, p. 13.

40. Embtel 41 (Saigon), Taylor to Rusk, July 5, 1965, "Memos to the President, v. 12, July 1965," ADF, MB, Box 4, NSF, LBJL; and McGeorge Bundy to Johnson, July 7, 1965, ibid.

41. Acheson to Truman, July 10, 1965, "Acheson Correspondence (1964–1971)," Post Presidential Name File, Harry S Truman Library.

42. Transcript, George Ball OHI, July 9, 1971, by Paige E. Mulhollan, tape 2, p. 8, LBJL.

43. For details of these July 8 deliberations, see William Bundy, "Vietnam Panel" (drafted July 10, 1965), "Deployment," Vol. 7, Tabs 401–420, NSCH, Box 43, NSF, LBJL; WB, MS-VN, ch. 27, pp. 15–21; and Walter Isaacson and Evan Thomas, *The Wise Men: Six Men and the World They Made* (New York: Simon & Schuster, 1986), 650–652.

44. President's News Conference, July 9, 1965, *Public Papers: Lyndon B. Johnson, 1965,* Book II, pp. 725–730.

45. President's Press Conference, July 13, 1965, ibid., 735–744.

46. Remarks to the National Rural Electric Cooperative Association, July 14, 1965, ibid., 749–752.

47. Quotes are in *USN&WR,* July 26, 1965, p. 45.

48. James Cannon and Charles Roberts interview with Johnson, July 14, 1965, reprinted in *Newsweek,* Aug. 2, 1965, pp. 20–21.

49. Quoted in Sidey, *Very Personal Presidency,* 234.

50. Those accompanying McNamara included Henry Cabot Lodge, recently designated successor to Ambassador Taylor; Generals Wheeler and Goodpaster; Assistant Defense Secretaries John McNaughton and Arthur Sylvester of Public Affairs; Deputy Assistant Secretary of State Leonard Unger; and NSC staffer Chester Cooper.

51. See *Pentagon Papers,* v. 3, p. 482; and Westmoreland, *Soldier,* 183.

52. Account and quote is in Chester Cooper, *The Lost Crusade: America in Vietnam* (New York: Dodd, Mead, 1970), 281.

53. Diem, *In the Jaws of History,* 152.

54. For record of this July 17 meeting, see Memorandum of Conversation (by Melvin L. Manfull), transmitted to Washington on July 27 as Embair A-66, "Deployment," Vol. 7, Tabs 421–438, NSCH, Box 43, NSF, LBJL. Manfull incorrectly dates the conversation on July 16.

55. See Rusk to Raborn, July 15, 1965, "Vol. 37, Cables, 7/65," CNF, VN, Box 19, NSF, LBJL; and Deftel 172042Z, Vance to McNamara, July 17, 1965, Mandatory Declassification Review Case 87–224, Office of the Secretary of Defense.

56. Quoted in William Manchester, *The Glory and the Dream: A Narrative History of America, 1932–1972* (Boston: Little, Brown, 1974; rep. ed., New York: Bantam, 1975), 1053.

57. McGeorge Bundy to Johnson, July 19, 1965, "Deployment," Vol. 6, Tabs 384–400, NSCH, Box 43, NSF, LBJL. *

58. Special National Intelligence Estimate (SNIE) 10-9-65: Communist and Free World Reactions to a Possible US Course of Action, July 20, 1965, ibid.

59. McNamara to Johnson, July 20, 1965 (submitted July 21), "Vietnam 2EE, 1965–67," CNF, VN, Box 74/75, NSF, LBJL.

9. "Better'n Owl"

1. The participants at this July 21 morning session included McNamara, Vance, McNaughton, and Wheeler from the Pentagon; Rusk, Ball, William Bundy, and Unger from State; Raborn and Helms from the CIA; Ambassador-designate Lodge; outgoing USIA Director Rowan and his successor, Leonard Marks; and McGeorge Bundy, Cooper, Moyers, and Valenti of the White House staff.

2. One other person joined this afternoon session—the President's old friend and counselor, Clark Clifford.

3. Quote is in WB, MS-VN, ch. 27, p. 31.

4. See Valenti notes, "July 21–27, 1965, Meetings on Vietnam," MNF, Box 1, LBJL; Memorandum for the Record (by Chester Cooper), dated July 22, 1965, "Deployment," Vol. 7, Tabs 401–420, NSCH, Box 43, NSF, ibid.; Jack Valenti,

A Very Human President (New York: W. W. Norton, 1975), 321–340; and Ball, *Past*, 399–402.

5. McGeorge Bundy to Johnson, July 21, 1965, "Deployment," Vol. 7, Tabs 401–420, NSCH, Box 43, NSF, LBJL.

6. Personal interview with Horace Busby, Washington, D.C., May 20, 1987.

7. See MB-MSS, LBJL.

8. Johnson and his advisers remained keenly sensitive to the Truman-MacArthur controversy and its political lessons. Several months earlier, Jack Valenti had counseled the President that "before you make final decisions on the problems in Viet Nam, you 'sign on' the Joint Chiefs in that decision. . . . That way, they will have been heard, they will have been part of the consensus, and our flank will have been covered in the event of some kind of flap or investigation later." Valenti to Johnson, Nov. 14, 1964, "ND 19/CO 312 Vietnam (Situation in 1964–1965)," CFF, Box 71, WHCF, LBJL.

9. See Valenti notes, "July 21–27, 1965, Meetings on Vietnam," MNF, Box 1, LBJL; MB-MSS, ibid.; and Valenti, *Very Human President*, 340–352.

10. Those attending included McNamara, Vance, and Wheeler from the Pentagon; Rusk and Ball from State; White House assistants Bundy, Busby, Cater, Moyers, and Valenti; Presidential counsel Clifford; and Republicans Dean and McCloy.

11. General Wheeler shared McNamara's belief in the political importance of a reserve call-up. The JCS wanted to mobilize reserves, he later recalled, "in order to make sure that the people of the United States knew that we were in a war and not engaged [in] some two-penny military adventure." Transcript, Earle Wheeler OHI, Aug. 21, 1969, by Dorothy Pierce McSweeney, tape 1, p. 19, LBJL.

12. Quote is in Kearns, *Lyndon Johnson and the American Dream*, 270.

13. See Valenti notes, "July 21–27, 1965, Meetings on Vietnam," MNF, Box 1, LBJL; and MB-MSS, ibid.

14. Transcript, George Ball OHI, July 9, 1971, by Paige E. Mulhollan, tape 2, pp. 10–11, LBJL; and manuscript, Clark M. Clifford memoirs (New York: Random House, forthcoming). See also Ball, *Past*, 402–403.

15. MB-MSS, LBJL; and manuscript, Clark M. Clifford memoirs.

16. See Ball's account of this meeting to State Department assistant secretaries, in Benjamin Read Memorandum, July 23, 1965, "Vol. 37," CNF, VN, Box 20, NSF, LBJL.

17. Quotes are in Ball, *Past*, 403; transcript, George Ball OHI, July 9, 1971, by Paige E. Mulhollan, tape 2, p. 11, LBJL; and manuscript, Clark M. Clifford memoirs.

18. Valenti notes, "July 21–27, 1965, Meetings on Vietnam," MNF, Box 1, LBJL; and manuscript, Clark M. Clifford memoirs. For the full text of Galbraith's letter, see Galbraith to Johnson, July 22, 1965, "Vietnam (Situation in) 1964–65," CFF, Box 71, WHCF, LBJL.

19. Quoted in Kearns, *Lyndon Johnson and the American Dream*, 282–283.

20. Transcript, William Bundy OHI, May 29, 1969, by Paige E. Mulhollan, tape 2, p. 44, LBJL.

21. State Department Circular 128, July 25, 1965, "Deployment," Vol. 7, Tabs 401–420, NSCH, Box 43, NSF, LBJL.

22. Participants at this session included Vice President Humphrey; McNamara and Wheeler from the Pentagon; Rusk, Ball, Lodge, and Goldberg from State; Raborn and Helms representing the CIA; White House staffers McGeorge Bundy, Busby, Moyers, and Valenti; and Clark Clifford.

23. Valenti notes, "July 21–27, 1965, Meetings on Vietnam," MNF, Box 1, LBJL; and manuscript, Clark M. Clifford memoirs.

24. See Valenti notes, "July 21–27, 1965, Meetings on Vietnam," MNF, Box 1, LBJL; McGeorge Bundy memorandum, prepared Nov. 1968, ibid.; and Lyndon Johnson, *Vantage Point,* 149.

25. Several administration officials also joined this session: Rusk, McNamara, Wheeler, Lodge, and Raborn, together with White House staffers Bundy, Busby, Califano, Cater, Goodwin, Moyers, O'Brien, and Valenti.

26. A letter from Mansfield to the President earlier on July 27 supports this conclusion. After meeting with Aiken, Cooper, Fulbright, Russell, and Sparkman at 3:30 that afternoon, Mansfield had informed Johnson "there was full agreement that insofar as Viet Nam is concerned we are deeply enmeshed in a place where we ought not to be; that the situation is rapidly going out of control; and that every effort should be made to extricate ourselves." Mansfield to Johnson, July 27, 1965, "Deployment," Vol. 1, Tabs 42–60, NSCH, Box 40, NSF, LBJL.

27. See Valenti notes, "July 21–27, 1965, Meetings on Vietnam," MNF, Box 1, LBJL; McGeorge Bundy memorandum, prepared Dec. 1968, ibid.; Lyndon Johnson, *Vantage Point,* 150–151; *Time,* Aug. 6, 1965, pp. 19–20; Evans and Novak, *Lyndon B. Johnson,* 551; and Alfred Steinberg, *Sam Johnson's Boy: A Close-up of the President from Texas* (New York: Macmillan, 1968), 780.

28. President's News Conference, July 28, 1965, *Public Papers: Lyndon B. Johnson,* Book II, pp. 794–803.

29. Quotes are in *Newsweek,* Feb. 8, 1965, p. 37; U. Alexis Johnson, *Right Hand,* 420; transcript, William Bundy OHI, May 29, 1969, by Paige E. Mulhollan, tape 2, p. 1, LBJL; and Kearns, *Lyndon Johnson and the American Dream,* 252.

30. Quote is in Edward Weintal and Charles Bartlett, *Facing the Brink: An Intimate Study of Crisis Diplomacy* (New York: Charles Scribner's Sons, 1967), 137.

31. Quotes are in Kearns, *Lyndon Johnson and the American Dream,* 251–252; and Lippmann, "Today and Tomorrow," *WP,* July 8, 1965, p. A21.

32. Adlai Stevenson, March 14, 1965, quoted in Geyelin, *Lyndon B. Johnson and the World,* 232.

33. Quoted in Sidey, *Very Personal,* 223.

34. Quoted in Halberstam, *Best,* 424.

35. Quotes are in Kalb and Abel, *Roots of Involvement,* 180; transcript, Hugh Sidey OHI, July 22, 1971, by Paige Mulhollan, tape 1, p. 12, LBJL; and transcript, William Bundy OHI, May 29, 1969, by Paige Mulhollan, tape 2, p. 31, ibid.

Conclusion

1. Rusk, quoted in Graff, *Tuesday Cabinet,* 40.

2. See Memorandum of Background Session with Robert McNamara, April 22, 1965, Notebook 3, Box 1, Arthur Krock Papers, SGMML, PU.

3. Transcript, U. Alexis Johnson OHI, June 14, 1969, by Paige E. Mulhollan, p. 27, LBJL.

4. For Taylor quote, see "Alert in Vietnam," *Life,* Nov. 27, 1964, p. 46.

5. See George Kennan testimony before Senate Foreign Relations Committee, Feb. 10, 1966, reprinted in *Vietnam Hearings,* 163.

6. Henry Kissinger, *White House Years* (Boston: Little, Brown, 1979), 54.

7. Hans J. Morgenthau, "The Pathology of Power," *American Perspective*, v. 4, n. 1, Winter 1950, pp. 8–9.

8. Walter Lippmann, *The Cold War: A Study in U.S. Foreign Policy* (New York: Harper & Brothers, 1947), 23.

9. Hans J. Morgenthau, *In Defense of the National Interest: A Critical Examination of American Foreign Policy* (New York: Alfred A. Knopf, 1951; rep. ed., Washington, D.C.: Univ. Press of America, 1982), 117.

10. See Clausewitz, *On War*, 92; and Westmoreland, *Soldier*, 541.

Index

Acheson, Dean, 25, 173, 175–76
Africa, 7, 196
Aiken, George, 208, 208 *n.* 26
Albert, Carl, 208–9
Alsop, Joseph, 47–48
Anti-war protests, 120, 134, 139
Arends, Leslie, 208–9
Armed Forces Council (AFC), 45–46, 57, 79–82
Army of the Republic of Vietnam (ARVN), 6–7; declining performance, 126, 151, 153–54, 163; weaknesses, 22, 51, 93, 184
Asia, 7, 121, 157–58, 198, 203
Austin, Texas, 3
Australia, 109, 172

Bagia, 150
Ball, George: argues against escalation, 53, 85–90, 164–66; background and experience, 85; on Bundy and McNamara, 59; challenges Honolulu proposals, 127–30; consults Clifford, 202–4; emphasizes dangers of bombing, 71–72; and July 1965 troop debate, 185–91, 200, 207; October 1964 dissenting memo, 31 *n.* 14, 85–90; reproaches Acheson, 176; urges disengagement, 168–70, 189; on Westmoreland thirty-two–battalion plan, 160
Bao Dai, 6, 79
BARREL ROLL, 42
Bay of Pigs, 7, 110, 197
Bienhoa, 25–26, 63–64, 81, 124
Bo, Mai Van, 115, 141–43
Boggs, Hale, 208
Bombing: mounting opposition to, 114–20, 134–35; and policymakers' fear of triggering wider war, 72, 107–8, 140; as tool to

spur stability in South Vietnam, 218–19; in World War II, 82. *See also* ROLLING THUNDER
Bradley, Omar, 13, 173, 175–76
Brezhnev, Leonid, 23
Brink Hotel, 50, 63–64
Brown, Harold, 192, 195–96
Buddhists: anti-Diem protests, 8; subvert Huong, 43–44, 56–57. *See also* Chau, Thich Tam; Quang, Thich Tri
Bundy, McGeorge: abandons concept of stability before escalation, 58–59; advises candor to LBJ, 67; and July 1965 troop debate, 190–92, 198–99, 201, 203, 209; ponders premises and goals of Vietnam policy, 100–102; questions proposed McNamara buildup, 167–68; rebuts Mansfield, 41–42; relationship with LBJ, 12–14; reports on Saigon trip, 65–67; suppresses concerns about escalation, 168 *n.* 30, 171–72; trip to South Vietnam, 61–63; urges ground deployments, 97–98; urges sustained bombing, 65–67, 75–76, 219
Bundy, William P.: chairs Working Group, 26–27, 29, 31, 33; at Honolulu Conference, 126–27; on LBJ's "guns v. butter" dilemma, 206; on meeting of "Wise Men," 176; on South Vietnam's instability, 212; urges holding the line, 168, 170–71; on Young Turks' rise to power, 150
Burma, 115, 121, 196
Busby, Horace, 192, 203–4

Cambodia: China's perceived threat to, 121; communist infiltration through, 62; danger of extending war to, 41; and domino theory, 196; friction with Vietnam, 216;

263